Beyond Fitting In: Rethinking First-Generation Writing and Literacy Education

Beyond Fitting In: Rethinking First-Generation Writing and Literacy Education

Edited by

Kelly Ritter

The Modern Language Association of America
New York 2023

85 Broad Street, New York, New York 10004
www.mla.org

To order MLA publications, visit mla.org/books. For wholesale and international orders, see mla.org/bookstore-orders.

The MLA office is located on the island known as Mannahatta (Manhattan) in Lenapehoking, the homeland of the Lenape people. The MLA pays respect to the original stewards of this land and to the diverse and vibrant Native communities that continue to thrive in New York City.

Library of Congress Cataloging-in-Publication Data

Name: Ritter, Kelly, editor.
Title: Beyond fitting in : rethinking first-generation writing and literacy education / edited by Kelly Ritter.
Description: New York : Modern Language Association of America, 2023. | Includes bibliographical references. |
Identifiers: LCCN 2022029869 (print) | LCCN 2022029870 (ebook) | ISBN 9781603296021 (hardcover) | ISBN 9781603296038 (paperback) | ISBN 9781603296045 (EPUB)
Subjects: LCSH: English language—Rhetoric—Study and teaching (Higher)—United States. | Literacy—Study and teaching—United States. | First-generation college students—United States. | College teachers—Training of. | BISAC: LANGUAGE ARTS & DISCIPLINES / Study & Teaching | LANGUAGE ARTS & DISCIPLINES / Literacy
Classification: LCC PE1405.U6 B49 2023 (print) | LCC PE1405.U6 (ebook) | DDC 808/.0420711—dc23/eng/20220921
LC record available at https://lccn.loc.gov/2022029869
LC ebook record available at https://lccn.loc.gov/2022029870

Contents

Acknowledgments

This project would not have been possible without the scores of faculty members nationwide in rhetoric and composition, including the contributors to this book, who have devoted their careers to teaching, mentoring, and generally caring for first-gen students in their classrooms and on their campuses. I thank each of them for their service and for their research and teaching that have improved first-gen students' lived experiences at institutions of higher education. I also want to thank all the informal mentors that helped me personally as a first-generation college student. Chief among those are my former managers at the Coralville, Iowa, Kmart store where I worked from 1986 to 1991, especially Claudia Portman, my "work mom." Thank you for always looking out for me as a student and as an employee and for making sure that I always put college first.

Turning to the production of this book, I thank Allison Kranek, who was my research assistant, copyeditor, and sounding board. I learned so much from her input and insight and thank her profusely for help in assembling the book that you are reading now. I also thank James Hatch at the Modern Language Association for asking me to lead this project and for his trust in my expertise and interest in highlighting the experience of first-gen students in my field. Finally, I thank my husband, Josh Rosenberg, and my daughter, Sarah Rosenberg. Both have been unwavering in their support of my various scholarly projects and my own ongoing identity as a first-gen faculty member, with all the cognitive dissonance that identity brings.

Foreword

Anne Ruggles Gere

A box of tissues sits prominently in my office because I have learned that when students come to talk, they may share burdens that move one or both of us to tears. Among the many sad stories I've heard, there are themes. One of these is *I wish I had* (as in "I wish I had started my paper sooner," "studied for the test," or "done the assignment"). Another is *I should tell you* (as in "I should tell you that I need to have surgery," "that my dad died," or "that I was raped"). The one that makes me especially sad is the theme *I wish I had known* (as in "I wish I had known that I could ask a professor questions during office hours," "how to join a study group," or "how to use the course management system for my class"). The stories with this third theme are usually about the ways my university has failed students. I'm sad because the students who tell these *I wish I had known* stories usually blame themselves for not knowing, and nearly always they are first-gen students. I've also heard *I wish I had known* stories tinged with shame: "I wish I had known how badly prepared I was for college writing. I always got A's in high school English, and my teachers told me I was a good writer, but I'm not"; "I wish I'd known that most kids at this school are really rich and don't have to take time from their studies to work so they can pay for college expenses"; or "I wish I'd known how to come here as a first-year student instead of waiting to transfer in my junior year." In all these and many other cases I see how my university could have done better by these students.

This book offers instructors and administrators a valuable alternative to listening and wiping tears away. First of all, it shows that first-gen students are a real group. I still encounter students who don't know about the concept of being first-gen; they simply assume that they are responsible for not being prepared for college life. The authors in this collection remind us that first-gen students can experience higher education differently than their peers and often face special challenges. It highlights the importance of mitigating these challenges, and it offers strategies for doing so. It is not enough to offer sympathy; we need to take up transformative initiatives to lessen the work of adjusting to college life for first-gen students and to assure that they can thrive in our colleges and universities.

Instead of expecting first-gen students to adapt themselves to existing structures and practices, this collection considers how our colleges and universities can be more receptive to first-gen students. Enabling these students to move beyond fitting in requires that institutions make adjustments. This is especially true because a significant percentage of first-gen students come from minoritized or low-income groups. At the same time that they are trying to figure out how to use a course website, they may be dealing with feelings of isolation or may be worrying about how to pay for their books.

This collection rightly focuses on literacy education. As Kelly Ritter observes in the introduction, literacy skills mark individuals, and this marking can cleave groups into those who feel competent and included and those who do not. To be academically successful, students must be able to decode specialized texts and unpack complex topics with little assistance from the professor, and for first-gen students whose backgrounds didn't include training in these skills, this literacy expectation can engender feelings of alienation. Similarly, college writing assignments typically require the use of discourses that can differ significantly from the discourses familiar to first-gen students, leading them to feel that they don't belong in college, as Christina Saidy observes in this volume. Language usage (a concept often conflated with grammar) is another sensitive literacy subject for first-gen students: students who speak a dialect different from that of their peers may question their own place in the academy. What would happen if the teaching conventions of language were shifted to emphasize the interesting variations of language?

Dialectal differences also reflect the intersectionality of first-gen students because students whose home dialects differ from the Standard English prized in the academy often come from minoritized racial or ethnic populations, from working-class families, or from both. As Shurli Makmillen notes in this volume, unless students develop critical language awareness through writing and literacy education and come to understand and value variations in the English language, they will be left to think that their ways of speaking and writing—even their ways of being—are wrong. What would happen if students were encouraged to see their home dialects as valuable resources rather than as things to be eliminated?

Similarly, the constructs of writing that first-gen students bring to college may not, depending on where they attended high school, conform to prevailing ideas about college writing, where processes of invention, peer review, and revision are common. First-gen students are more likely to have attended under-resourced high schools where writing is commonly evaluated in timed tests. In these contexts students learn that writing is something one does alone, and neither peer review nor revision is part of the scene. Since first-gen students are more likely to hold jobs while taking classes than their peers are, we have something to learn from Aubrey Schiavone's finding, discussed in this volume, that first-gen students can often deepen their understanding of writing by looking closely at the writing they do at work. What would happen if first-year writing courses were restructured to begin with students' work-related writing?

The COVID-19 pandemic, decreasing numbers of college-aged youths in the United States, and economic uncertainty will cause seismic shifts in higher education during the next decade and will demand that we give serious attention to the ways we can change our classrooms and our programs to meet the needs of first-gen students. We cannot afford to expect first-gen students to be the only ones who adapt. We may not be able to change institution-wide processes like orientation programs that fail to consider the needs of first-gen students, websites that assume readers have prior knowledge about higher education, or financial aid offices that fail to alert first-gen students to all the resources available to them, but we in writing and literacy studies have an opportunity to initiate these students into practices that will enable them to be successful academically. That is much better than reaching for another tissue.

Introduction: On the Precipice

Kelly Ritter

Beyond Fitting In interrogates how the cultural capital and lived experiences that first-gen students possess or lack make a difference in how we as scholar-teachers and administrators frame literacy studies and the writing-centered classroom. The contributors to this book examine how scholar-teachers in the field of rhetoric and composition create and replicate best practices for teaching first-gen students and for facilitating their learning in writing classrooms, writing centers, and writing programs and across other occasions for writing at two- and four-year, public and private, and open-access and elite colleges and universities. I am both personally and professionally invested in the problems and strategies presented in this book, because I was a first-gen student. Though nearly thirty-five years have passed since I entered college, the stories we tell about our first-gen lives, and literacies, are evergreen. Yet as we have learned through decades of observation, consternation, and aggravation, stories alone will get us nowhere.

If your origin story is anything like mine, then you are a statistical anomaly. I was a child of divorced, working-class parents and successfully found my way not just through college but also through graduate school without family or other structural supports or knowledge of higher education's processes or norms. I was the classic first-gen student who, in Collier and Morgan's term, was unable to be a "role expert" regarding university procedures and faculty interaction (430). I could not benefit from my parents' college experiences, "a valuable source of cultural capital that helps students navigate college (e.g., understanding the significance of the syllabus, what 'office hours' means, or how to cite sources in written assignments)," the absence of which "negatively affects even those first-generation students who are academically well prepared for college" (Chen and Carroll 2). Also like many first-gen students, for financial reasons I did not live in on-campus housing and was therefore isolated from many activities and socialization processes that help inculcate students into college life and that also increase academic success.[1]

If you are like me, you have transcended your birth class and your socioeconomic conditions inside and outside of school to become a graduate student, faculty member, administrator, or independent researcher in academia and are part of the cultural elite. You are lucky and rare. Maybe you feel guilty because you got out while others did not. As someone who went to college constantly being reminded that college wasn't where you belonged, your life has been, in sociological terms, a life on the precipice, and you've had a constant fear of falling back to where you started. Your college degree has been regarded, as the education journalist Paul Tough puts it, as "simply an insurance policy against moving *down*" (257).

Questions abound: Where did you get a break? Where did you learn the "hidden curriculum," as Buffy Smith terms it, or the "norms, values, and expectations" of how students, faculty members, and administrators interact on a college campus? These norms, values, and expectations correspond to white middle-class values and are engendered in many students from an early age, both in their schooling and outside of it, so that they possess the "institutional cultural capital and social capital" rewarded in higher education (xiv). As an adult, you live and work and maybe raise your own children within an educational system that is not and was never made for you. Even though students like you were once treated as one in a million, one-third of the student body today is made up of first-gen students (Cataldi et al.). And if you are not like me—if you became a graduate student, faculty member, or other academic community member through a path that we might categorize as more traditional in nature, because your parents and grandparents went to college (or even were professors themselves)—then you can still benefit from hearing and understanding the origin stories of first-gen students, and this book is therefore especially for you.

Collections such as Bill Thelin and Genesea Carter's *Class in the Composition Classroom: Pedagogy and the Working Class* or, more historically speaking, John McMillan, Alan Shepard, and Gary Tate's *Coming to Class: Pedagogy and the Social Class of Teachers* have thus far filled this important role of sharing first-gen stories and educating those in the English studies community about the importance of social class and writing instruction.[2] Indeed, my own story is just a different version of that of Thelin and Carter's example student Travis, who, as described in their introduction, has parents without college degrees who expect Travis to "get a bachelor's degree and find a job that would pay him more" than his current wage at the 3M factory (3). But the stories that we as scholar-teachers and administrators tell must also be accompanied by concrete, collective action moving forward, including pedagogical and administrative strategies that build on research. This book therefore goes beyond stories—which may put us in an infinite loop that educates without explicitly moving us forward—and proceeds to concrete strategies that can be shared and implemented.

As we progress to solutions and actions that will better the literacy experiences of first-gen students, we must use these solutions and actions not only to augment our stories but also to clarify what *first-generation student* means on our campuses, including definitions that are local in nature. Even as Thelin and Carter note the diversity of the term *working class* and the typical markers of this class (e.g., median or below-median income, employment in certain job types, and lack of agency over career choices), they also note that being a first-generation student is a part of the experience of that class, according to Boiarsky, Hagemann, and Burdan's definition (7). While true in many cases, such an equation leads to a collapsing of socioeconomic status and first-generation status that I wish to complicate and unpack. Many of our students—particularly international and immigrant students and students whose first language isn't English (L2 students) or who speak two or more languages fluently (generation 1.5 students)—may reside above or below the working-class designation but still may be classified as first-generation students. In broadening this definition, I am also purposefully separating out the sometimes stereotypical definition of a first-generation student as one who is white, working class, and further, as developmental or remedial in terms of reading and writing (and math) skills.[3] Simply put, the term *literacy* in this book is not synonymous with basic writing or basic literacy functions any more than basic writers are exclusively part of the lower social classes. The rich trove of scholarship on basic writing students, curricula, and theory may intersect in focus with some first-gen students, but not all—and therefore is not the way in which literacy skills are primarily addressed or defined in this book.[4]

Certainly, *Beyond Fitting In* is concerned with social class, because there is no way to discuss higher education—especially in the twenty-first century neoliberal economy that includes for-profit education institutions and mass credentialing—without talking about socioeconomic conditions that affect us all. But this collection's primary focus is how first-gen students of any class background or demographic interact with and affect literacy instruction in our institutions. This collection also asks how we can better those interactions and refocus our conceptions of college life to be more inclusive of students who increasingly do not reflect the educational experiences of most instructors and administrators or the expectations and designs of our institutions—particularly elite institutions that are accustomed to serving white, upper-class students with generational college legacies and advantages. As such, there is attention throughout this book on BIPOC students in our institutions and on how their particular experiences and perspectives significantly shape how we view first-gen identities today. As Bernice Olivas's important 2016 dissertation articulates, land-grant universities were originally designed to educate first-gen students and thus to become a broad national basis for wider access to higher education outside the private coastal elite schools. Yet the ensuing systems and structures of these universities have not always allowed BIPOC students to gain equal access to them. While this collection makes a concerted effort to focus on the experiences of BIPOC students as central to first-gen student research and pedagogy, especially as such students were and will continue to be disproportionately affected by the COVID-19 pandemic, additional attention is needed in our field's literature to these ongoing intersections between first-gen and BIPOC experiences and identities. In particular, there is a need for additional study of Native American students who are also first-gen students, both at tribal colleges and at other public and private universities nationwide.[5]

Who Are First-Generation Students?

In order to best help first-gen students in their classrooms and programs, even the most informed and dedicated faculty may need answers to some critical questions that inform such work, namely, what does college represent to a first-gen student? How do the broadly defined literacy needs of first-gen students differ from what we are trained to teach and even who some faculty members want to teach? And finally, as this collection's contributors more specifically address, how are we even defining *literacy* in the first place, and do our definitions help or hinder first-gen students?

According to a 2018 report from the Center for First Generation Student Success, first-gen students are relatively easy to classify in terms of who they are not—children of parents with a college degree—but less easy to classify in terms of who they are (Whitley et al.). The 2017 survey the report cites indicates that first-gen students categorically do not have a parent or guardian who completed a college degree, though the value of that indicator can be further complicated, in an experiential sense, by whether a parent received a degree outside the United States, completed a two-year as opposed to a four-year degree (or took a degree from an online, for-profit institution rather than from a traditional college or university), or completed some college but did not receive a degree of any kind (17). But as Lee Ward, Michael Siegel, and Zebulun Davenport argue, the most broadly inclusive description of a first-gen student is one rooted in cultural capital more broadly—and does not just consider whether a parent or parents have a college degree. In this case, cultural capital is the experience gained through the acquisition of that degree, for both parent and student:

> Cultural capital relevant to college attendance is not obtained only when a parent graduates from college; it is obtained when a parent acquires significant and meaningful college experiences—going through the admissions process, experiencing freshman orientation, interacting with faculty, doing college-level work, being self-directed, learning the language and customs of higher education, living with other students, taking finals, navigating the library, making decisions about majors and career pathways, developing help-seeking skills. . . . The institution does not grant cultural capital to its students on the same day it grants a degree. (8)

Ward and colleagues also note that the questions first-gen students ask themselves deeply inform how they experience college. Such questions include "[W]hat can I potentially achieve that will make my parents happy?" and "What will the entrance into the world of the educated require me to sacrifice with respect to family, friends, and identity?" (13). As Ward and colleagues further observe, first-gen students experience a paradox in higher education. On the one hand, they are more invested because "they shoulder the burden of achievement" to a greater extent than their non-first-gen peers (39). On the other hand, they may be less ashamed of leaving college without earning a degree precisely because even completing some college means they have gone beyond what their family members have achieved (39–40). What these deeper attributes of first-gen students indicate is that a definition based on parental college achievement may, in fact, be too limited when thinking about the greater educational needs of first-gen students once they arrive on our campuses.

It should be said, however, that the concept of cultural capital so prevalent in the literature of first-gen studies puts an unfair spotlight on lack and on those who appear to not have the skills they need to succeed—thereby minimizing the innate strengths that students bring to the table from outside dominant academic and other cultures. The concept of cultural capital unfairly privileges a particular kind of knowledge within alternative structures of knowing and being and discounts the many ways students grow and learn—and bring their diverse experiences to a college campus, enriching the experiences of others around them. As Tara Yosso's 2006 article "Whose Culture Has Capital?" contends, critical race theory (informed by the categories of aspirational, familial, social, navigational, linguistic, and resistant capital) can reveal other kinds of "community cultural wealth" that BIPOC students bring to campus through familial and community experiences and that counter the primacy of Pierre Bourdieu's model as applicable to deficit models of higher education (78). As Yosso explains, critical race theory "shifts the research lens away from a deficit view of Communities of Color as places full of cultural poverty or disadvantages, and instead focuses on and learns from these communities' cultural assets and wealth" (82). Following Yasso's lead, we must ultimately resist framing first-gen students, including BIPOC students, as lacking skills that only the academy can provide—a point that many authors in this collection will also argue, chief among them Todd Ruecker in his study of rural first-gen Latinx students (see also Ruecker). We must also recognize how a diversity of experience puts some attributes and forms of knowledge more or less in focus, strengthens these students' preparation in nondominant cultural ways, and complicates the idea of being ready for college alongside the various definitions of first-gen students.

In addition to those students whose parents might have gone to college but not gained the status expected from a college degree, and other students who resist the notion of capital gained or lost as an all-or-nothing calculation, some students are first-gen students by definition because their parents have had educational experiences that occurred outside the United States, were incomplete, or were outside the standard definition. Perhaps this variety is why only sixty-three percent of the institutions surveyed by the Center for First-Generation Student Success had a consistent definition of first-gen students that they used across all programs and services (Whitley et al. 19). As the center's report also notes, the original definition came from the Council for Educational Opportunity circa 1980 and included those who were "underserved students, like those from low-income, racial minority, or rural backgrounds, who did not have the benefit of cultural capital and college-going knowledge because their parents did not complete a four-year college degree," but the definition did not explicitly include students of all races or ethnicities (20). Given the diversification of the student body over the four decades since the term *first-gen student* was coined, its definition must now also be expanded to explicitly include students who are not American-born or who have different citizenship status, and whose parents do not have a four-year degree (Cataldi et al. 2). Many of these are L2 students, though not all L2 students are first-gen. Several contributors to this book discuss L2 students and their absence in some studies of first-gen students, which, as noted above, is often understood to include only poor, white, working-class students and, more recently, African American students from urban areas. In particular, William DeGenaro and Michael T. MacDonald echo the point in this volume, in their study of support websites for first-gen students, that *first-gen students* is not and cannot be a stand-in term for white working-class or monolingual students.

Ultimately, however, socioeconomic status drives the most current definitions of first-gen students, since such students are rarely, if ever, defined completely independently of social class, a condition uniformly magnified in the United States since 1980 by the importance placed on postsecondary education as leading to financial stability and success. Whereas in previous generations a first-gen student without a college degree might make a so-called decent living in a service industry, a trade, or even a small family business, that window of vocational opportunity is perceived to now be closed. Such a perception was led by President Barack Obama's America's College Promise initiative, unveiled in January 2015, which called for all US citizens to earn at least a two-year college degree, and lauded those states (e.g., Tennessee) that were already offering free two-year college tuition to all (Hudson).

Obama's call was not immediately taken up at the federal level, arguably because of the result of the 2016 presidential election, but it has been reanimated under President Joe Biden's administration.[6] This national call has also been followed by many local responses at the state level. New York's Excelsior Scholarship was one of the most visible of such responses, launched in 2017 and guaranteeing free tuition for all students at the City University of New York and at the State University of New York whose family income is less than $125,000 a year ("Tuition-Free Degree Program"). Shortly thereafter, University of Michigan's Go Blue program was announced, which guarantees free tuition for students with family incomes of less than $65,000 (goblueguarantee.umich.edu). The University of Illinois, Urbana-Champaign, in 2018 launched the Illinois Commitment program, which guarantees free tuition for all students whose family income is at or below $67,100, the median income in the state. As of fall 2020, over one-third of Illinois's incoming students qualified for this program ("Illinois Commitment").[7] Tuition programs such as these, which benefit lower-income, in-state students admitted to public institutions, provide a measure of economic relief to many first-generation students but are not specifically targeting that population in their mission or their specifications. New York's scholarship program, for example, has income requirements that fall well within middle-class incomes, as the Pew Research Center's range for middle-class income was $42,500 to $135,600 in 2016, depending on location (Bennet).

In addition, these programs do little to erase the inequities that many first-gen students faced in their secondary education, including isolation from college counseling and information, nor do they erase the lack of socialization and integration of first-gen students once they arrive on campus. As Anthony Abraham Jack has argued in *The Privileged Poor*, attention to social class on elite college campuses, especially in the recruitment and support of BIPOC students, is often lacking. Distinguishing between the "Privileged Poor" (lower-class students who attended elite private high schools) and the "Doubly Disadvantaged" (lower-class students who attended poorly funded public high schools; 11), Jack argues that while privileged poor students learned the social norms and structures of elite campuses by virtue of their high school experiences, and doubly disadvantaged students did not, both groups are equally adrift in terms of the cultural assumptions they encounter on campus regarding their ongoing financial resources and advantages.[8]

Only when campuses are intentional about supporting first-gen and other marginalized students can these students succeed, as has been detailed by Tough in his 2019 book *The Years That Matter Most*, in which he follows the experiences of several first-generation students from across the country and also highlights groundbreaking initiatives for first-gen students at the University of Texas, Austin. Tough argues that higher education, as a system that already privileges the wealthy, can be "an instrument that reinforces a rigid social hierarchy and prevents [students] from moving beyond the circumstances of their birth" (25). To mitigate this effect, institutions must not only admit a more diverse student body in terms of race and class, among other factors, but must also intentionally help those students to be a part of the campus fabric throughout their time there. Elaine Maimon's afterword in this collection forcefully extends this point to call for comprehensive training of graduate students and faculty members to understand noncognitive, trauma-related factors in literacy acquisition and to recognize the "new student majority" that first-gen students represent. Similarly, Sarah Elizabeth Snyder and Eric Lee's essay in this volume on concurrent enrollment at a Hispanic-serving institution explains the value of program partnerships for first-gen students that account for their transitional needs both in and out of the classroom.

One of Tough's points that resonates on my campus, as well as on many others, is how first-gen students from underserved rural and urban areas often lack access to an economic and curricular advantage taken en masse by other entering college freshmen, namely, precollege credit programs such as Advanced Placement (AP) and International Baccalaureate, and also dual enrollment or dual credit programs. Even before students set foot on our campuses in fall 2020—the first full semester of remote and socially distanced learning under pandemic conditions—the pandemic had created an increasingly complex landscape for those preparing for college, such as in the adjustments that were made to test-based credit examinations, which only magnified how these tests privileged certain socioeconomic groups in our country.[9] Yet as fraught as AP and other test-based credits may be as tools for judging students' college readiness, the economic reality for many lower-income families is that paying for college is difficult, and precollege test-based course credits may cushion that blow. Beyond the money saved on credits earned, however—which for lower-income students often means a shortened time to degree and which for upper-income students means the ability to take a second major or minor, further segregating students by social class within curricular pathways—AP and International Baccalaureate in particular may expose students to a more rigorous college preparatory curriculum that will help them understand and complete their college-level work. Yet as the College Board notes, the gap between rural and suburban students in terms of AP course availability and AP course completion is notable, and the success rate for students of color on AP exams is still markedly below those of white students (see Mann et al.). Faculty members need to take these disparities in precollege credit opportunities into account when working with first-gen students—a point highlighted in Casie Moreland's essay in this book on the history and present mission of dual enrollment programs.

Ultimately, various income-based initiatives to provide college for all undergirded Obama's initiative, and certain beliefs about higher education also lay behind it—namely, the belief that students who do not receive a college education will be adrift in society, in an economy where a degree is increasingly important. This fear-based belief was written into the former Chicago mayor Rahm Emanuel's April 2017 announcement that "in order to graduate, high school students must show an acceptance letter to a four-year university, a community college, a trade school or apprenticeship, an internship, or a branch of the armed services," even if all other graduation criteria had been met ("Mayor"), with Emanuel's administration even enlisting help from counselors at the City Colleges of Chicago to help students meet this requirement (Perez).

Such fear of falling behind in society, both economically and socially, has also led to the rise of for-profit institutions and, concomitantly, the rise in student indebtedness to such institutions—including students who leave before completing their degree. As Tressie McMillan Cottom famously wrote in her 2017 book *Lower Ed*, such institutions prey upon the fears of first-gen students—often working adults, another invisible group on many college campuses—by promising financial security through open admission into a very expensive pseudo-college that offers "flexible" (typically online) curricula attractive to nontraditional, financially at-risk students, but which requires thousands of dollars in loans, and whose credits are often worthless for transfer into another institution (170). Given the misleading and fear-based rhetoric regarding higher education at work in state and national politics, and the advent of online technologies that are designed to take advantage of various student populations and that are difficult to distinguish from the legitimate online curricula now proliferating at accredited institutions following the COVID-19 pandemic, the division between first-gen and other students stands to be wider than ever.

Of course, it is true that a college degree increases a person's so-called earning power, and having parents who completed college puts students at an advantage once they arrive on campus. But we know also that simply getting to college is no guarantee of success at or after college, and therein lies the problem.

Students who require remediation in English and mathematics may add as much as one full year to their degree paths, and students—first-generation or otherwise—who in general are underprepared for college risk dropping out with substantial debt and nothing to show for their efforts. Within the last decade, a wave of book-length studies have been published on social class and college life that illustrate these and other issues facing first-gen students: some of them broadly address class and academic success (Stich; Mettler; Lee; Stuber; Rivera), while others focus on women's experiences (Armstrong and Hamilton; Hamilton; Mullen) or on the experiences of other groups (Cottom) or of individuals (Westover).

Reading these studies as a group produces a foreboding sense of sameness, as even though the case studies are diverse, similar conclusions are reached: students from privileged backgrounds achieve at higher rates academically and socially than those from lower classes. Students with college-educated parents have knowledge of and access to internships and jobs that are invisible to first-generation students. Students who are not first-gen are more likely to participate in extracurricular activities and take advantage of campus resources for academic and social advancement. Those with college-educated parents are better able to navigate entrance exams and to field admission offers, settle into dormitory and particularly fraternity or sorority living, and have greater access to curricula that yields the best academic results with the least amount of effort—even as they have more time to spend on their studies than do their first-gen counterparts, who often hold part-time jobs while in school and may be more strongly tied to their home communities through family or other relationships, some of which pull hard enough on the students so as to overtake their college experiences entirely.[10] Though the concept has now become cliché, tinged with a sharp stigma that divides concepts like *work* from *education* in characterizations of academia, many first-gen students treat school like a job alongside their actual one. As Anthony Carnevale and colleagues assert, on today's campus "70 percent to 80 percent of college students are both active in the labor market and formally enrolled in some form of postsecondary education or training." Forty percent of undergraduates work thirty or more hours a week, but unlike some past students who worked, they cannot count on those wages being enough to cover their tuition and fees (*Learning* 9–10).

Finally, students with college-educated parents are more likely to finish their degrees, and when they do, they are minimally or significantly less likely to be in debt than are first-gen students. And for each of the above challenges or negative outcomes, students from underrepresented racial backgrounds always fare even worse. For students from any background who do finish college, the earnings forecasts are anywhere from thirty-three percent greater than the earnings of students with only a high school diploma, depending on the source of the estimation (Carnevale et al., *College Payoff*), to sixty-six percent greater (Ma et al.), even as, according to a 2014 Bureau of Labor Statistics report, the highest percentage of jobs (thirty-nine percent) only require a high school diploma (though these are not necessarily the highest paid jobs) .

So if we consider whether college "matters" in a multigenerational, socioeconomic sense, it absolutely does. Going to college will only increase one's chances of moving up the economic ladder. The question is whether first-gen students are yet poised, as a whole, to benefit equally from the opportunities that higher education can provide. Because at present, our system of higher education is deeply bifurcated and at best serves as an opportunity rather than as a guarantee of social mobility. And there is no greater factor in determining social mobility than literacy.

What Are First-Generation Literacies?

Rhetoric and composition scholars have long been invested in researching the literacy practices of groups (students and nonstudents alike) whose profiles reside outside the mainstream; as noted earlier, research on social class and literacy is of special concern. As the field responsible for developing, sustaining, and theorizing first-year writing in postsecondary institutions, rhetoric and composition has at its foundation a pedagogical imperative unique among the humanities, including literary studies. Much of the work of first-year writing has been concerned with the sheer diversity of experience in first-year writing classrooms, so the need for this collection, and the rhetoric and composition field more generally, to focus on social class and literacy is clear. First-year writing is the one course that is often still universally required across the vast majority of US colleges and universities in some form and that thus enrolls the greatest variety of students in terms of background, interests, and experiences. However, as precollege credits proliferate in the direction of non-first-gen students, the first-year writing classroom is statistically more likely to include students who lack prior college credits, regardless of their actual reading, writing, and critical thinking abilities. As such, first-year writing stands to be perceived as a de facto remedial course simply through the exclusion of more privileged students who no longer must take the requirement, especially at more elite institutions where exemptions can abound.[11] This trend is one way attention in general education offerings is becoming more attuned to first-gen students, even as this attention ghettoizes those students as lacking skills, despite the fact that general education courses are not remedial in nature. While writing across the curriculum or writing in the disciplines courses on many campuses seek to join students from both exempt and nonexempt first-year-course backgrounds and to advance their writing skills and competencies—and in the best cases, to address the need for multiple literacy strategies across fields, disciplines, and rhetorical occasions—the overall stigma connected to literacy skill levels is firmly entrenched at the first-year level, where the work of improving literacy is deemed a repetition of high school coursework. In Aubrey Schiavone's essay in this book, as well as in the work of other basic writing theorists in rhetoric and composition studies, we can see ample evidence that first-gen students bring to campus strong (and often incorrect) assumptions about literacy requirements for certain professional fields of study and bring to their writing work sometimes limiting compliance-focused work habits.

In another dimension of the literacy studies curriculum—specifically, the English major courses that require critical reading, writing, and analysis—we also see shifting demographics, but in the other direction, as first-generation students nationwide are becoming less likely to major in humanities fields. As detailed in Joe Pinsker's July 2015 *Atlantic Monthly* piece provocatively titled "Rich Kids Study English," it is the case that "kids from lower-income families tend toward 'useful' majors, such as computer science, math, and physics. Those whose parents make more money flock to history, English, and performing arts," largely because—as Kim Weedon from Cornell University proposes, according to Pinsker—the type of institutions selected by students from lower- and higher-income families offer different majors that skew toward the profile of the typical graduates from those respective schools, and this difference in turn is a by-product of the influences these children felt at home (i.e., in lower-class families, humanities and the arts may have been deemphasized). Noting the sociologist Dalton Conley's assertion that parents' education and parents' wealth are the two most critical factors in what a student chooses as a college major,[12] Pinsker's article closes by observing that "from this angle, college majors and occupations start to look more and more like easily-interpreted, if slightly crude, badges doled out to people based on the wealth and educational levels of the parents they were born to." Such aversion to humanistic fields of study can be especially damaging for first-gen transfer students moving into research universities, the topic of two essays in this book: Caitlin Larracey's essay on branch campus transfer students and Christie Toth and Clint Gardner's essay, cowritten by six transfer students when they were entering the writing major at the University of Utah.

These broad observations about students' choice of major are borne out in longitudinal studies. Sam Trejo's 2016 analysis of first-gen students profiled in the National Longitudinal Study of Youth's 1997 cohort concludes that "first-generation status has a statistically and economically significant effect on college major selection . . . independent of the compositional differences of first-generation students, including sex, AFQT score, family income, and race" (47). In Trejo's analysis, "first-generation students, compared to otherwise identical students, are more likely to select major groups with strong labor market rewards and a clear career path" (52). Similarly, Xianglei Chen and C. Dennis Carroll's 2005 longitudinal study of 7,400 students for the National Center for Education Statistics revealed that careers perceived to be either more stable and secure or more financially rewarding were the top choices for first-gen students. Business was the most popular (chosen by fourteen percent of students), followed by health science and services and social sciences (chosen by eight percent and seven percent of students, respectively); these fields were also the most frequently selected by non-first-generation students (chosen by ten percent and fourteen percent of them, respectively), but first-generation students were almost twice as likely to choose a vocational or technical field as their non-first-generation peers, who were more likely to choose majors in science, mathematics, engineering, architecture, humanities, arts, social sciences, and journalism or communication (14).[13] In other words, the students most likely to take first-year composition (or literature, or both) are the students least likely to major in the humanities, a set of fields that emphasize writing and require sustained engagement with the literacy skills taught in first-year courses.

Looking at these data, one might conclude that English departments should therefore be less, not more, focused on the literacy concerns of first-gen students. After all, outside their required general education courses in writing or literature, these students are flocking to majors, by and large, outside of the humanities. The response to this conclusion is simple: we do first-gen students no favors by widening the gap between their interests and experiences and our degree programs and by making the postgraduate career options or areas of intellectual interest supported by our field less attractive to these students. Further, we do our field a disservice by positioning it as one embodied only by the educational elite—especially when scholars and teachers in our field find significant overlap between social justice initiatives and the work of English studies writ large. Rather, the economic realities of major selection for first-generation college students is a strong impetus for collections such as this one, which aims to restructure and refocus our efforts in literacy instruction—a category of work that crosses the often hard boundary between rhetoric and composition and literary studies, both inside and outside English departments—toward a stronger and more diverse student and faculty community, one cognizant of the collapsing differences between students in writing programs and in writing- and reading-focused courses across institutional types and of the growing chasms between the educational haves and have-nots. Such strengthening of English studies as a site for students of all backgrounds—including those in majors that speak to growing career fields, such as technical writing—is especially critical given the mark that literacy skills, or lack thereof, leave on a student. Numerous authors in our field have noted the ways in which individuals are socially sorted based on their literacies; rarely do we see such social sorting, in contrast, based on a student's mathematical or scientific acumen.

Literacy—which, in its most basic definition, refers to how well we read, write, speak, understand, evaluate, and analyze texts—is the chief marker of social class. First-year composition is one sorting mechanism, as Sharon Crowley has argued; in addition, writing centers are arguably construed on many campuses as sites of cleanliness and maintenance, as Harry Denny has argued. And everywhere in between, students are judged for the way they communicate, especially when that communication falls outside the mainstream—for example, African American Vernacular English, Spanglish, and code-switching (or code-meshing) utterances that are practiced in marginalized communities. So yes, the literacy practices—and successes and struggles—of first-generation students are worth studying because to date they have not been the primary or singular focus of a collection of work and because, as an area of study, they are defining to these students in ways that no other academic subject has ever been.

About This Book

In order to tell the story of first-gen literacy experiences through as many angles and perspectives as possible, *Beyond Fitting In* is divided into three parts, each focusing on different aspects and sites of first-gen literacy. These parts focus on defining first-gen students in our writing classrooms and other writing spaces; analyzing first-year, first-gen writers; and considering cross-disciplinary contexts for first-gen student writers and teachers.

The five essays in part 1, "Defining First-Generation Students," highlight difficulties in defining, identifying, and assisting first-gen students particularly from marginalized populations, even in the face of technological and curricular advancements that are designed to be useful interventions into the college (or precollege) experience. DeGenaro and MacDonald open this part with their essay's critique of the term *first-generation student* as used in public commodity discussions, and they explore how having that critique as the basis for analyzing websites geared toward first-gen students on comprehensive university campuses exposes a definition of first-gen that is far less diverse than the student bodies utilizing these campus sites. Next, Jenny Rice examines the archives of two Kentucky institutions (Berea College and the University of Kentucky) to uncover patterns in pedagogical and institutional discourse surrounding Appalachian first-gen students. Her research shows that while Berea's programs integrated first-gen student identities and literacy practices into their design, the University of Kentucky's key scholarship program for first-gen Appalachian students failed to incorporate students' own regional identities as part of writing pedagogies. Snyder and Lee's essay focuses on initiatives undertaken at a rural Arizona community college (one that is a Hispanic-serving insitution) to address issues of first-generation student access, including institutional partnerships, family educational programs, and revamped curricular design, including the use of an accelerated learning program for basic writing courses, which was designed to thoroughly address equitable access to higher education. Snyder and Lee argue that the accelerated-learning-program model is most beneficial in combination with local faculty-driven first-gen initiatives and administrative supports. Ruecker's essay on first-gen Latinx students utilizes interviews and observations to identify three barriers to literacy and writing success for these students: high school preparation and educational policy, financial barriers and university retention policies, and the dual transition of heading off to college and leaving behind a close-knit small community. Rounding out part 1 is Towle's essay on the Purdue University Writing Lab and how it has been using big data to identify first-generation students on its campus, in order to develop more and better outreach for these students, who significantly benefit from the lab's services. Towle argues that writing programs, including writing centers, engage in the use of such data to promote an approach that is rooted in individual institutional contexts that help first-gen students to become less invisible to campus administrators and to subsequently succeed.

Part 2, "First-Generation Students in the First Year and Beyond," focuses on some of the innovative pedagogies and theories that have been designed to help first-gen students as they begin their literacy training experiences on campuses in summer programs or first-year writing courses. Moreland details the history of dual credit and dual enrollment at the University of Connecticut and its origins in recruiting "superior" students, an activity that, when extrapolated to the national context, is antithetical in mission to what such programs purport to accomplish for first-gen and other marginalized students today. Christina Saidy's essay examines a summer retention program for at-risk, first-gen humanities students alongside the composition course these students took in the fall semester, in order to illustrate the nuances of first-gen issues that arise in the writing classroom; Saidy's study stands in contrast to larger-scale studies that cross disciplinary boundaries. Following Saidy's investigation of paired writing, Larracey discusses writing instruction for first-gen students on two-year branch campuses of four-year institutions, arguing that both these students and the institutional type are underresearched in our field's literature. Larracey examines the transition of several students to the four-year campus and how their anxieties about writing abilities, expectations, and available resources affect that transition in ways that are downplayed in transfer discussions on such campuses.

Next, and representing student voices in the writing classroom and curriculum, Christie Toth, Cristina Guerrero Perez, Kathryn Henderson, Jose Loeri, Joseph Andrew Moss, Jacque Thetsombandith, Adilene Tolentino, and Clint Gardner narrate and analyze the experiences of several first-gen students who participated in a summer bridge program for students transitioning from Salt Lake Community College to the University of Utah. Six of Toth's seven coauthors are the students under study, and so this essay serves as an insightful autoethnography of their experiences in the context of field literature on the experience of first-gen students transitioning from community college to university. Moving then from two-year institutions to a four-year historically black university, and closing part 2, Shurli Makmillen's essay focuses on how African American vernacular speech and writing are employed by first-gen, Pell Grant–eligible African American students in Makmillen's first-year writing course, with attention to the tension between "resistance" and "compliance" and in the context of Students' Right to Their Own Language (SRTOL). Makmillen uses corpus analysis to illustrate the pitfalls and promises of SRTOL as well as what it reveals about the tensions between resistance and compliance in the college classroom.

Part 3, "Writing Contexts for First-Generation Students, Teachers, and Administrators," widens out from the first-year writing classroom and into sites of writing across campus, including writing-intensive programs and programs in writing across the curriculum and writing in the disciplines. Neil Baird and Bradley Dilger's opening essay in this part focuses on theories of transfer for first-gen students, an especially appropriate topic as related to moving between sites of writing on the university campus. Baird and Dilger argue that transfer influences the negotiation of student writers' developing professional identities, requires internal negotiation about the value of prior knowledge, and external negotiation with others about students' writing, pressuring decision-making about the value of prior knowledge required for transfer. Next is Schiavone's essay on workplace writing as viewed by first-generation students at a large, public, research-intensive university. Schiavone reveals findings that challenge traditional views of the work-school balance, positing that students in her study had positive experiences with workplace writing done across labor, service, and professional settings while they were in school. Her study aims to help writing teachers highlight the positive attributes of various kinds of workplace writing, since first-generation students tend to "explicitly [value] the writing they [do] at work but less so than they [value] their academic writing."

Next, Christine Alfano, Megan Formato, Jennifer Johnson, and Ashley Newby discuss the Leland Scholars Program at Stanford University, a four-week summer residential program focusing on problem-solving in chemistry and academic writing, and how a reenvisioned curriculum focusing on cross-disciplinary discourse and mentorship cultivates the cross-disciplinary researcher identity of first-generation students as they transition from high school to college. Heather Falconer next examines discourse expectations in science that can "push students from, or pull them toward, the discipline." Her research follows a nontraditional Latino male student and a traditional white female student as they navigate study in a STEM-focused undergraduate research program at John Jay College. Following Falconer's student-centered essay, Nancy Mack focuses on student uptake of the genre of the literacy narrative, to examine the role of narrative writing assignments in identity building for first-gen students. Mack focuses on three areas: how much writers risk when selecting a topic, how identity is represented in these writers' texts, and how different genres afford opportunities for agency for first-gen writers. She argues that first-generation writers can take emotional agency against the internalized beliefs that they are unwelcome or out of place at the university. Finally, Courtney Adams Wooten and Jacob Babb close part 3 with their discussion of writing program administrators who were first-gen college students and how this background, which they share, influences how they design and manage their own writing programs. Using survey and interview data from other first-gen writing program administrators, Wooten and Babb also build on work on the subjectivities of writing program administrators and writing center directors to focus on this positionality heretofore unexamined in our field literature.

To close the book, Maimon's afterword is from the writer's vantage point as outgoing president of Governors State University and is on how first-gen students are part of the "new majority" in higher education. Drawing on national research, including by the Modern Language Association's Task Force on Doctoral Study in Modern Language and Literature, Maimon argues for stronger local and national attention to the specific needs of first-gen students across the curriculum.

I hope that in the rich range of perspectives, research methods, and insights in these essays, readers find valuable strategies for helping first-gen students go beyond just fitting in in our writing classrooms, on our campuses, and in our intellectual communities.

Notes

1. The general wisdom is that on-campus living improves retention and academic performance for all students, which can be true on particular campuses, but see Turley and Wodtke for a detailed discussion of the noted benefits of on-campus

housing for two distinct groups: African-American students and students attending liberal arts colleges. Such research is more pertinent than ever given the rise of remote learning during the COVID-19 pandemic and the increase in online programming that students have been required to participate in from their home (off-campus) environments.

2. These collections of course complement other important works on social class and literacy and language such as Peckham; Watkins; Lindquist; Deborah Brandt's *The Rise of Writing*; Rose; and Heath, as well as the work of Jean Anyon and of Michael Apple and notable articles by James Zebroski, Lynn Bloom, and William Thelin.

3. According to the Postsecondary National Policy Institute, as of 2017, "Minority students were more likely than white students to be first-generation students: 42% of black students and 48% of Hispanic students were first-generation students, compared to 28% of white students" ("Factsheets: First-Generation Students").

4. Data show that first-gen students take remedial courses at a higher rate but are not the only population to need remedial instruction (in mathematics, reading, or English), nor are their needs dramatically different from those of students whose parents completed some college but stopped short of receiving a degree. According to Chen and Carroll, of the first-generation students in their research group of 7,400 students, "[a]mong those with bachelor's degree goals who attended 4-year institutions, 45 percent of first-generation students took at least one remedial course, compared with 21 percent of students whose parents had at least bachelor's degrees." They also noted that "taking remedial courses in college was also common among students whose parents had just some college experience: 44 percent of these students took at least one remedial course, and close to one-third took at least one [remedial] mathematics course during their college years" (12).

5. Christie Toth is one scholar of rhetoric and composition who has explicitly taken up this call in her 2013 article "Beyond Assimilation: Tribal Colleges, Basic Writing, and the Exigencies of Settler Colonialism." In 2018, 89.5 percent of Native American students in college were studying at a tribal college. Further, according to the Postsecondary National Policy Institute, "only 16% of Native Americans attain a bachelor's or higher and only 9% attain associate degrees" ("Factsheets: Native American Students"). For an extended look at Native American students in first-year composition courses per se alongside Olivas's work, see Gardner.

6. See Biden's plan, which hails the original 2015 proposal and promises to make two years of community college free for "every hard-working individual, including those attending school part-time and DREAMers (young adults who came to the U.S. as children)" ("Biden Plan").

7. As evidence that some things never change regarding the information flow about higher education, according to the Office of Admissions at the University of

Illinois, Urbana-Champaign, many prospective applicants interpreted the Illinois Commitment program—which included aggressive marketing at "L" train stops throughout Chicago and on billboards lining the city's major expressways—to mean that regardless of academic qualifications, a student under a certain income level would be automatically admitted to the university under this new program. The many calls and e-mails from parents and students expressing this interpretation were met with patient explanations from admissions counselors who directed them to resources about academic requirements on the university website. The confusion over the program's mission and requirements exposes the need for more community education for students whose families have no prior knowledge of or experience with college admissions.

8. This echoes Tessa Wood's September 2020 op-ed in the *Harvard Crimson*, in which she states, "Harvard culture offers few incentives for professors to try to relate to students who aren't from the same background as they are. I wish the teaching staff would take a moment to remember that just because a student doesn't immediately introduce themselves as low-income doesn't mean they're not. I wish they would realize that it's hard to describe yourself with terms like 'first-gen' when you have never heard this term before, much less heard it defined."

9. Those students who took Advanced Placement exams in spring 2020, for example, experienced severely truncated exams that were designed to limit time spent online and to thwart Internet-based cheating. After taking their exams, many students learned that their scores had been invalidated because of technological glitches. Other students, frustrated by the new format and disconnected from support systems designed to help them prepare for the tests, chose not to take them at all. These testing outcomes only highlighted existing privileges afforded to high school students of means and have resulted in significant backlash against the College Board, including class-action lawsuits. College Board thereafter preempted its plan to put the SAT exam online, which further threw into turmoil the plans of many high school juniors who could not take the test in spring 2020. The College Board's decision has had the positive effect, however, of forcing colleges and universities to more seriously consider test-optional admissions practices that have been shown to increase applications from underrepresented groups. The entire University of California system led the way in making testing optional beginning with applicants seeking to matriculate in fall 2021. The University of Illinois, Urbana-Champaign, and countless others soon followed suit, and it appears that going forward, the inclusion of ACT and SAT testing requirements will likely be the exception in college admissions nationwide. This shift will help remove one significant barrier for students from underserved communities, but it will not erase ongoing socioeconomic inequities once these students arrive on campus.

10. For an excellent discussion of retention as applicable to first-year writing classrooms in particular, see Powell.

11. For example, at the University of Illinois, fifty percent of students come to campus with AP, International Baccalaureate, or SAT (evidence-based reading and writing) scores sufficient to exempt them from first-year writing, and many others still are exempted from first-year humanities courses, including English literature, as well as other general education courses.

12. These two tenets are further analyzed in Conley, *Being Black*, *Honky*, and *Pecking Order*.

13. Similarly, students responding to the question about intended college major on the SAT exam intake form historically and disproportionately choose fields such as engineering, business, computer science, and biological sciences, which have high-paying or distinct professional career paths.

Works Cited

Armstrong, Elizabeth A., and Laura T. Hamilton. *Paying for the Party: How College Maintains Inequality*. Harvard UP, 2015.

Bennet, Jesse, et al. "Are You in the Middle Class? Find Out With Our Income Calculator." *Pew Research Center*, 23 July 2020, www.pewresearch.org/fact-tank/2018/09/06/are-you-in-the-american-middle-class/.

"The Biden Plan for Education beyond High School." *Biden Harris Democrats*, joebiden.com/beyondhs/.

Boiarsky, Carolyn, Julie Hagemann, and Judith Burdan. "Working-Class Students in the Academy: Who Are They?" *Academic Literacy in the English Classroom*, Heinemann, 2003, pp. 1–21.

Brandt, Deborah. *The Rise of Writing*. Cambridge UP, 2015.

Carnevale, Anthony P., et al. *The College Payoff: Education, Occupations, Lifetime Earnings*. Georgetown University Center on Education and the Workforce, Aug. 2011, www2.ed.gov/policy/highered/reg/hearulemaking/2011/collegepayoff.pdf.

Carnevale, Anthony P., et al. *Learning While Earning: The New Normal*. Georgetown University Center on Education and the Workforce, 2015, cew.georgetown.edu/wp-content/uploads/Working-Learners-Report.pdf.

Cataldi, Emily Forrest, et al. *Baccalaureate and Beyond: A First Look at the Employment Experiences and Lives of College Graduates, Four Years On*. US Department of Education, National Center for Education Statistics, 2014, nces.ed.gov/pubs2014/2014141.pdf.

Chen, Xianglei, and C. Dennis Carroll. *First-Generation Students in Postsecondary Education: A Look at Their Transcripts*. US Department of Education, National Center for Educational Statistics, July 2005, nces.ed.gov/pubs2005/2005171.pdf.

Collier, Peter J., and David I. Morgan. "Is That Paper Really Due Today? Differences in First-Generation and Traditional College Students' Understanding of Faculty Expectations." *Higher Education*, vol. 55, 2008, pp. 425–46.

Conley, Dalton. *Being Black, Living in the Red*. U of California P, 2009.

———. *Honky*. Vintage Books, 2001.

———. *The Pecking Order: A Bold New Look at How Family and Society Determine Who We Become*. Vintage Books, 2005.

Cottom, Tressie McMillan. *Lower Ed: The Troubling Rise of For-Profit Colleges in the New Economy*. New Press, 2017.

Crowley, Sharon. *Composition in the University: Historical and Polemical Essays*. Pittsburgh UP, 1998.

Denny, Harry. *Facing the Center: Toward an Identity Politics of One-to-One Mentoring*. Utah State UP, 2010.

"Factsheets: First-Generation Students." *Postsecondary National Policy Institute*, Aug. 2018, pnpi.org/first-generation-students. Accessed 2 January 2019.

"Factsheets: Native American Students." *Postsecondary National Policy Institute*, 17 Nov. 2020, pnpi.org/native-american-students/.

Gardner, Rebecca Lyn. *Rhetorical Agency and Survivance: American Indians in College Composition*. 2012. PhD dissertation, U of North Dakota.

Hamilton, Laura T. *Parenting to a Degree: How Family Matters for College Women's Success*. U of Chicago P, 2016.

Heath, Shirley Brice. *Ways with Words: Language, Life, and Work in Communities and Classrooms*. Cambridge UP, 1983.

Hudson, David. "The President Proposes to Make Community College Free for Responsible Students for Two Years." *The White House*, 2015, obamawhitehouse.archives.gov/blog/2015/01/08/president-proposes-make-community-college-free-responsible-students-2-years.

"Illinois Commitment." *University of Illinois Urbana-Champaign*, admissions.illinois.edu/commitment.

Jack, Anthony Abraham. *The Privileged Poor: How Elite Colleges Are Failing Disadvantaged Students*. Harvard UP, 2019.

Lee, Elizabeth M. *Class and Campus Life: Managing and Experiencing Inequality at an Elite College*. ILR Press, 2016.

Lindquist, Julie. *A Place to Stand: Politics and Persuasion in a Working-Class Bar*. Oxford UP, 2002.

Ma, Jennifer, et al. *Education Pays: The Benefits of Higher Education for Individuals and Society*. College Board, 2019, research.collegeboard.org/pdf/education-pays-2019-full-report.pdf.

Mann, Sharmilla, et al. *Advanced Placement Access and Success: How Do Rural Schools Stack Up?* Education Commission of the States / College Board, Aug. 2017, www.ecs.org/wp-content/uploads/Advanced-Placement-Access-and-Success-How-do-rural-schools-stack-up.pdf.

"Mayor to Announce Plan to Help Kids Meet New CPS High School Graduation Requirement." *CBS Chicago*, 16 Jan. 2018, chicago.cbslocal.com/2018/01/16/cps-high-school-graduation-requirement/.

McMillan, John, et al. *Coming to Class: Pedagogy and the Social Class of Teachers*. Heinemann, 1998.

Mettler, Suzanne. *Degrees of Inequality: How the Politics of Higher Education Sabotaged the American Dream*. Basic Books, 2014.

Mullen, Ann L. *Degrees of Inequality: Culture, Class, and Gender in Higher Education*. Johns Hopkins UP, 2011.

Olivas, Bernice. *Supporting First-Generation Writers in the Composition Classroom: Exploring the Practices of the Boise State University McNair Scholars Program*. 2016. PhD dissertation, U of Nebraska.

Peckham, Irvin. *Going North, Thinking West: The Intersections of Social Class, Critical Thinking, and Politicized Writing Instruction*. Utah State UP, 2010.

Perez, Juan, Jr. "City Colleges to Provide Counselors to Help CPS with New Graduation Requirement." *Chicago Tribune*, 18 Jan. 2018, www.chicagotribune.com/news/ct-met-city-college-chicago-public-schools-graduation-requirement-counselors-20180118-story.html.

Pinsker, Joe. "Rich Kids Study English." *Atlantic Monthly*, 6 July 2015, www.theatlantic.com/business/archive/2015/07/college-major-rich-families-liberal-arts/397439/.

Powell, Pegeen Reichert. *Retention and Resistance: Writing Instruction and Students Who Leave*. Utah State UP, 2013.

Rivera, Lauren. *Pedigree: How Elite Students Get Elite Jobs*. Princeton UP, 2015.

Rose, Mike. *Lives on the Boundary*. Penguin Books, 1999.

Ruecker, Todd. *"Transiciones": Pathways of Latinas and Latinos Writing in High School and College*. Utah State UP, 2015.

Smith, Buffy. *Mentoring At-Risk Students through the Hidden Curriculum of Higher Education*. Lexington Books, 2015.

Stich, Amy. *Access to Inequality: Reconsidering Class, Knowledge, and Capital in Higher Education*. Lexington Books, 2012.

Stuber, Jenny M. *Inside the College Gates: How Class and Culture Matter in Higher Education*. Lexington Books, 2012.

Thelin, William, and Genesea Carter. *Class in the Composition Classroom: Pedagogy and the Working Class*. Utah State UP, 2017.

Toth, Christie. "Beyond Assimilation: Tribal Colleges, Basic Writing, and the Exigencies of Settler Colonialism." *Journal of Basic Writing*, vol. 32, no. 1, 2013, pp. 4–36.

Tough, Paul. *The Years That Matter Most: How College Makes or Breaks Us*. Houghton Mifflin Harcourt, 2019.

Trejo, Sam. "Two Roads in a Wood: An Econometric Analysis of the Major Choice of First-Generation College Students." *The Developing Economist*, vol. 3, no. 1, 2016, pp. 37–56.

"Tuition-Free Degree Program: The Excelsior Scholarship." *New York State*, www.ny.gov/programs/tuition-free-degree-program-excelsior-scholarship.

Turley, Ruth N. Lopez, and Geoffrey Wodtke. "College Residence and Academic Performance: Who Benefits from Living on Campus?" *Urban Education*, vol. 45, no. 4, 2010, pp. 506–32.

Ward, Lee, et al. *First-Generation College Students: Understanding and Improving the Experience from Recruitment to Commitment*. Jossey-Bass, 2012.

Watkins, James Ray. *A Taste for Language: Literacy, Class, and English Studies*. Southern Illinois UP / NCTE, 2009.

Westover, Tara. *Educated: A Memoir*. Random House, 2018.

Whitley, Sarah, et al. *First-Generation Student Success: A Landscape Analysis of Programs and Services at Four-Year Institutions*. Center for First-Generation Student Success, 2018.

Wood, Tessa. "Students Shouldn't Have to Educate Professors." *Harvard Crimson*, 2 Sept. 2020, www.thecrimson.com/article/2020/9/2/wood-students-should-not-educate-professors/.

Yosso, Tara. "Whose Culture Has Capital? A Critical Race Theory Discussion of Community Wealth." *Race, Ethnicity and Education*, vol. 8, no. 1, 2006, pp. 69–91.

Part One

Defining First-Generation Students

A Keyword Analysis of Websites That Support First-Generation Students

William DeGenaro and Michael T. MacDonald

As higher education increasingly recognizes the presence of first-generation students, institutions are using a wide array of rhetorics to describe this relatively new identity marker. For instance, needs-based discourses group first-gen students with other at-risk or marginalized populations and consider the efficacy of programming meant to support their learning. Critical and advocacy-based discourses highlight intersections among these groups and acknowledge systemic barriers to success. Consumerist discourses construct first-gen students as stakeholders, customers, and revenue streams. There is no single articulation of what we talk about when we talk about first-gen students, and no single way that colleges and universities reach out to this population. Some institutions create social and student life programs, some build academic support structures, and some do both. Finally, no single definition of first-gen students exists. They may be defined as the first in their immediate family to attend a four-year college or university, as the first to attend any college, or as students whose parents did not complete a four-year degree, to name the most common definitions. The fact that the term *first-gen students* is contested contributes to the diversity of rhetorics surrounding these students in higher education.

We come at these questions of who first-gen students are and how we might support them as teachers of writing with strong teaching and research interests in basic writing. We are faculty members at a regional campus of our state university system, a campus that has historically served large numbers of first-gen, working-class college students. In recent decades, the definition of first-gen students on our campus has broadened to include mostly monolingual students from white working-class suburbs, students of other racial and ethnic backgrounds from urban areas and suburbs with greater diversity, and multilingual immigrant and generation 1.5 students from Arab American and Hispanic enclaves in the metro area. Because we work in a context where the definition of first-gen students is expanding in terms of culture and language, the ideological work done by this shifting and dynamic category concerns us. In this essay, we examine college and university websites focused on programming for first-gen students, or what Nicole Stephens and colleagues call "university cultural products" (1181), in order to critique how institutional voices capture the construction of the term *first-gen students*. The inconsistent usage suggests that the term is slippery, fitting into Raymond Williams's notion that the most equivocal and contested terms signal spaces where we can glimpse cultural logics most clearly. In the introduction to *Keywords*, Williams suggests that words with "developing meanings," that is, words whose significations are in flux, reveal "many of our central experiences" (15). In that vein, we find that the lack of a consistent definition of the term *first-gen students* on these websites leads to a reliance on neoliberal abstractions that inform the ways these websites appeal to various audiences.

Locating First-Generation Community

College and university websites often attempt to bring together multiple audiences: first-gen students, first-gen alumni, their parents, their instructors, and faculty and staff members who also identify as first-gen. We found it noteworthy that these websites are meant not just to disseminate information but also to establish the legitimacy of the marker *first-gen*, fostering first-gen communities and affirming to these audiences that the marker invokes something meaningful. Similarly, web pages devoted to first-gen students are housed in varied places on institutional websites: under the library, counseling, student life, or academic affairs landing pages. The lack of a consistent location for these pages suggests that institutions aren't sure where to metaphorically put first-gen students. This placement also reflects the array of functions these sites serve: as clearinghouses for support services, resources that answer frequently asked questions about first-gen students and that are geared toward various campus and community audiences, repositories of college-life narratives, community builders and meeting places for anyone identifying as first-gen, sources for arguments for the utility and value of the *first-gen* marker. Some of these pages are part of the official web presence of initiatives for first-gen students, while others are attempts on the part of other campus bodies (e.g., the counseling office) to disseminate information about or for first-gen students. Despite this range, first-gen student support web pages have some relatively stable conventions: a definition of first-gen students; data on the percentage of first-gen students on campus; a mission or vision statement; links to campus resources deemed relevant or helpful to first-gen students; links to programs (social, academic, professional, and civic) specifically for first-gen students; testimonials from first-gen students, alumni, faculty, or staff; photos of, presumably, first-gen students that show visible diversity; and tips for first-gen students and occasionally for other audiences. We limited our study to websites of medium-sized state schools (either regional comprehensive schools or degree-granting branch campuses) because these are peers to our own university and because these campuses serve large numbers of first-gen and working-class students.

Defining *First-Gen* as a Keyword

In order to examine the term *first-gen*, we did an ideological critique of website language, looking for keywords and patterns of discourse. We wanted to study language meant for the public that articulates goals and defines *first-gen*. According to Marshall and Rossman, this kind of content analysis "is unobtrusive and nonreactive: It can be conducted without disturbing the setting in any way" (108). As public artifacts, college and university websites can be thought of as intersections of interests and audiences. Looking at these intersections through the lens of ideology (i.e., a critical awareness of the hegemonic forces maintaining cultural myths) is essential for understanding the place of first-gen students within larger contexts. One drawback of this kind of analysis is that it relies heavily on our interpretations. Marshall and Rossman also argue that "[c]are should be taken, therefore, in displaying the logic of interpretation used in inferring the meaning from the artifacts" (108). In this section, we articulate our logic for interpreting the website language in relation to the themes we uncovered and our other findings.

We identified fourteen peer institutions that have fairly robust web pages dedicated to supporting first-gen students. Four-year regional comprehensive schools like ours tend to attract a larger first-gen population than R1 universities do but are often part of the same university system. A 2018 US Department of Education report notes that studies by Paul Skomsvold as well as by Sandra Staklis and Xianglei Chen showed that thirty-three percent of students enrolled in higher education were categorized as first-generation (Cataldi et al. 1). At regional campuses, first-gen student enrollment is often between thirty-five percent and fifty percent.[1] Analyzing discourse about first-gen students at regional campuses also allows us to connect that discourse's foregrounding of access and inclusion to the ways the field of rhetoric and composition (particularly basic writing studies) has historically taken up those themes. Websites can be infrequently updated and do not necessarily give a full picture of how a university supports first-gen students. But a website can also provide useful examples of educational marketing, of an institutional voice, and of how institutions frame friendliness to first-gen students or their presence on campus as a selling point for prospective students.

Our intention in this essay is to treat excerpted language from the websites we studied as anonymized, aggregated discourse. That is, our critique is not aimed at any one institution, but at trends in how institutions of this type talk about first-gen students. We separately read and notated the websites in our study in order to practice a kind of intercoder reliability. Before conferring, we made notes, created tentative codes, and identified relevant excerpts; next, we synthesized our notes and entered revised codes into the software program *NVivo* 12 in order to generate themes. We analyzed excerpts from the websites using a grounded theory approach (Charmaz), using the language of the websites to form more precise codes. For instance, when examining how first-gen students were defined by a given institution, we highlighted phrases like *first in their family to pursue a four-year degree* and *whose parents might not otherwise have been able to pursue a college career* and combined similar codes under categories like "definition," "accountability," and "college culture."

Table 1 details six themes that emerged from our study, as well as example codes, frequency of occurrence, and excerpts from the websites. Themes in the table represent generalized categories. For instance, phrases from web pages like *legacy*, *professional development*, and *self-reliant* were grouped under categories like "future-oriented" and "accountability," which we then combined with other categories for the broader theme of neoliberal discourse. We drew from established scholarship on first-gen students to lay our codes and excerpts alongside those from other studies. Terms like *college culture*, *cultural capital*, *affect*, and *neoliberal* did not necessarily appear on the websites but were prominent in the literature, and the ideas they represent were manifest on the websites. The themes in Table 1 identify commonly used discourses and are the themes that we urge faculty, staff, and administrators to pay close attention to as they work on their own messaging to and recruitment of first-gen students. We also invite our readers in rhetoric and composition—including those at both open-admissions and regional or two-year institutions and at large R1 schools—to consider ways that the rhetoric of these websites embodies a familiar tension between assimilation and pluralism. We maintain that just as the teaching of academic literacies can open up new possibilities for students from underrepresented communities while also asking them to conform to dominant cultural norms, so too can broader college and university programs geared toward the success of first-gen students. We also leveraged these themes to roughly categorize the schools themselves. On regional campuses thirty-five to fifty percent of enrolling students are first-gen students, and we can use this finding to show which of these

Table 1. Themes, codes, frequency, and excerpts from institutional web pages about first-gen students

Theme	Sample codes	Frequency	Sample excerpts
Normalizing and institutionalizing definitions	Definition, need, race, social class, not having knowledge, minimal college experience	93 references across all 14 websites	"Are you the first person in your family to attend college?" "[I]f a student has only had close contact to people with minimal college experience . . ."
Neoliberal discourse	Arrive on time, get involved, positively contribute, take advantage of resources	89 references across 12 websites	"To underscore the necessity of positively contributing to their communities . . ." "Through this network, we enhance the academic success, professional growth, and personal development of first generation students."
Affect of care	Creativity, empowerment, resilience, special, self-actualization	67 references across 13 websites	"First-generation students are some of our favorites." "Being first is something to take pride in and celebrate."
College culture	Adjustment, balance, network, new, relate, journey, how to do college	59 references across 13 websites	"If college language is new to you . . ." "Feeling the pressure of being an academic pioneer . . ."
Community and collectivism	Campus community, peer mentor, role of faculty	38 references across 12 websites	"You have entered into a collective group whose sole purpose is your success." "Professors are one of your most valuable college resources."
Inclusion	Diversity, dialogue, multilingual, cultural concerns, identity	30 references across 7 websites	"We pledge ourselves to creating and maintaining an environment that honors diverse traditions, heritages, and experiences and we do this with compassion and care." "[S]upport them with specific programs as well as an overall sense of community and inclusiveness on our campuses."

schools promote supportive messaging about first gen-students (i.e., are first-gen-friendly schools) and which offer more robust material support to those students (i.e., are first-gen-priority schools).[2]

Table 2 shows how the websites of first-gen-friendly and first-gen-priority institutions address potential audiences (such as students, student families, community members, and staff or faculty members) who might use the sites to support or understand first-gen students. If a given school seemed first-gen-friendly, we questioned to what degree the school emphasized an affect of care combined with neoliberal discourses of accountability. To identify

Table 2. Characteristics of first-gen-friendly and first-gen-priority institutional websites

First-gen-friendly institutional websites	First-gen-priority institutional websites
Appear to outsource some support to external websites such as scholarships.com, imfirst.org, and gocollegenow.org.	Provide information on campus resources specifically for first-generation students.
Emphasize mental health.	Offer a peer mentoring program.
Link to campus resources available to all students.	Offer other programs for underrepresented students like summer bridge programs.
Link to tips and FAQ pages.	Describe a first-generation student organization.
	Link to scholarships reserved for first-generation students.

first-gen-priority schools, we looked to see if schools publicized resourced programs and offered material support through scholarships, peer mentoring, or bridge programs. Several schools outsource support by linking to external websites like Imfirst.org, which partners with institutions to offer online mentoring, and we identified these schools as first-gen-friendly. In addition to having less emphasis on material support structures, first-gen-friendly schools also paid less attention to local contexts, as their outsourcing of information indicates. If peer mentoring, for instance, is conducted online, matching students across institutions, then important local aspects of college culture are more difficult to learn.

Scholarly Conversations That Center Student Needs

The work of identifying and interpreting themes in our corpus of websites was informed by both our own subject positions and institutional affiliation and by scholarly conversations. The literature affirms how the web pages we studied tend to place the onus on students to conform and adapt to institutional norms. As colleges reckon with the best ways to support the success of first-gen students, they often emphasize the imperative to inculcate the largely working-class first-gen students with the literacy skills commonly associated with academic discourse (see especially Bollig). Indeed, research in literacy studies, higher education, and social psychology has explored first-gen students' real and perceived deficits. And though this literature narrates well-intentioned programs geared toward addressing the so-called needs of students, a portrait emerges of assimilationism. To be sure, empirical work has established that programs designed around orienting first-gen students to the academic and cultural conventions of higher education can lead to moderate increases in success; for instance, Julian Mendez and Sheri Bauman found that a bridge program they studied for first-gen Latinx students fostered resilience and connectedness in demonstrable albeit modest ways (199). Similarly, Carla Gonzalez and colleagues point to programs accomplishing more in terms of social integration than academic performance (63). Melinda Gibbons and colleagues write that some first-gen students lack "self-efficacy" (490), leading to the recommendation that first-gen students engage in reflection and self-assessment (505); notably, this model emphasizes the role students play in their success and largely backgrounds the role of institutions—students must conform to institutional norms rather than institutions themselves adapting. Our own sense of the institutional web pages we examined about first-gen students, which often lay out prescriptive tips on subjects ranging from interactions with professors to aspects of campus etiquette, largely confirms the notion that first-gen students are most in need of awareness of how to adapt to social norms, or what we call college culture.

Of course, college culture has a largely class-based definition. Compositionists have explored how our roles as teachers of academic discourse are wrapped up in gatekeeping middle-class decorum (Bloom; O'Dair; Stuckey; Trimbur). But academic writing is only one example of how higher education serves as a normalizer. Departments of Academic Affairs and Student Life often work in tandem to remediate real or perceived deficits in students. As institutions increasingly identify first-gen students as a demographic, we need to parse resonance of this demographic in the context of higher education's class values. Stephens and colleagues identify academic and cultural challenges faced by first-gen students and argue that the divide between first-gen and continuing-gen students is rooted in class. They find that first-gen students are largely working-class and often value "interdependence" and community over the individualism of higher education (1179): "American universities are in fact organized according to middle- and upper-class cultural norms of the game" that "constitute an unseen academic disadvantage for first-generation college students" (1192). If "university cultural products" reproduce and circulate norms of college culture (1181), we suggest that student support websites serve a similar function. Indeed, we find that these websites at times even overtly name the class values, like individualism versus collectivism, that Stephens and colleagues explore. Sometimes this move by such websites can do at least some of the work of calling attention (albeit in sometimes problematically monolithic ways) to a cultural divide between the institution and the (working-class) student body.

The identification of first-gen students as a demographic seems to promote a productive degree of transparency regarding these norms and represents potential praxis. Gonzalez and colleagues critique "institutional barriers to . . . full integration" (66), noting that many first-gen students of color both perceive the academy as having a monolithic view of them and perceive themselves as outsiders to institutional norms, and so the researchers emphasize the imperative for community and for mentors "with similar identities" (72). Gray and colleagues note that first-gen students must find strategies for coping with pervasive "microaggressions" in a racist and classist "hostile environment" on campus (1229). They point to the "identity work" (both productive and otherwise) such students do, including validating their identities, forming peer communities with like students, and even dressing and talking in ways that mask or downplay core identity markers (1228). Bernice Olivas helpfully explains that sometimes acknowledging the hostility first-gen students experience on campus is difficult because they are both "privileged and marginalized" (25), othered but also in the midst of what they perceive to be "upward mobility" (48). She argues for the need for effectual literacy sponsors who recognize the agency of first-gen students.

It seems that Lynn Z. Bloom's observation that higher education is largely a "middle-class enterprise" is still relevant, both within and beyond first-year composition and basic writing courses (655). In a critique of Australian and British schools that resonates with trends in schools in the United States, Sarah O'Shea and colleagues theorize institutional developments that construct first-gen students as "independent learner[s]" who need to display initiative (7), rhetoric they argue that implicitly works to justify students' taking on increasing financial burdens to enroll (6–8). Contrary to this meritocratic and individualistic rhetoric, the researchers argue that the presence of first-gen students on campus is a "social as much as an individual act" (99) and that these students often attend college to improve not just themselves but also the material conditions of their families and communities. O'Shea and colleagues conclude that first-gen students are not "the solo neo-liberal subject" but rather "embedded in . . . relationships" and "networks" across family, occupational, and civic contexts (204).

Composition scholarship on first-gen students reinforces these problematics of naming. Chase Bollig argues for the need to reflect on how the term *first-gen* resonates "as a marker of difference" (23), urging intersectional approaches that avoid decentering race, which the term sometimes does (26–27). Bollig makes a compelling case that the term also does productive work: it "situates these individuals within narratives of value" (28), establishes solidarity and community, and connects students to literacy sponsors. Naming oneself a first-gen student "acknowledges the constraining influence of material difference in social interactions" (29). Students invoke these differences while also stating their desire for mobility (31). Bollig links the term *first-gen* to pedagogies of social class, which can foster analysis or critique but don't always serve a transformative role, in part because they "privilege adaptation" (32). Ultimately, agency and transformation come not from being a first-gen student but rather from claiming an identity as one—there is power in naming oneself. Similarly, Ann M. Penrose argues that first-gen students often feel the "contrast between their old and new surroundings" (442). Statistically, they tend to have poorer college preparedness and negative perceptions of their own literacy skills. Penrose finds that their perceptions, including forms of impostor syndrome, can contribute to low retention rates despite there being no statistical difference in the GPAs of first-gen students and those of their peers or in their and other students' performance in required writing classes. All of us invested in working with first-gen students should be aware of the paradoxes of identifying as a first-gen student: namely, the potential that the identity has to empower students but also the lingering doubts that first-gen students often have about whether they belong on campus. It is with an awareness of this paradox that we read our corpus of websites.

Legitimizing Discourse about First-Generation Students

Websites for first-gen students face a rhetorical challenge because this identity group lacks the immediate name recognition of other identities. Websites for African American student unions or women's resource centers on campus can convey a stronger sense of clarity to readers; most audiences know who is served by such offices and their attendant websites, though the terms *African American*, *woman*, and *first-gen* are all indeed contested. So, it's unsurprising that most websites in our corpus present a definition of first-gen students in a prominent place like on the main splash page. Often these definitions are institution-specific and have slight variations or levels of specificity when it comes to what constitutes a first-gen student: the first in the family (or immediate family) to attend a four-year college, the first to attend any college, the member of a family in which no one has graduated from college, and so on. Some variations seem nominal while some have material import, such as when they delineate who qualifies for a scholarship or when they count as first-gen those students whose family members have attended college outside of the United States.

Normalizing Definitions: Community and Collectivism

Beyond doing the work of clarifying institutional practice, definitions of first-gen students assert the existence of this identity marker. One way is through prominent discussion of the high percentage of students on campus who are first-gen. Sites assert first-gen students as a category through needs-based discourses, using phrases like "unusual challenges" and "achievement gaps" to foreground the deficits and barriers these students face. The sites often establish that first-gen students share certain traits by emphasizing their unfamiliarity with the norms and practices of academe. Bollig argues that labeling first-gen students authorizes an institution to sponsor literacy in particular ways and enables first-gen students to make sense of their "marginalization," to use the label to constitute their own sense of their literate selves in relation to their campuses (27).

The economist Michael Zweig points out in *The Working Class Majority* that there are conceptions of working-class identity rooted in labor and conceptions rooted in culture. Similarly, the identity of first-gen students as depicted in our corpus is sometimes rooted in materiality (e.g., when websites provide links to financial aid offices and scholarship programs) and sometimes in familiarity with campus culture (e.g., when websites include glossaries of terms related to academe). The term *first-gen students* invokes Bloom's analysis of the middle-class "values" and folkways that first-year composition inculcates (658). So just as we in the United States often have to ask, Who is the working class? we also might ask, Who are first-gen students? Invoking either of these categories constitutes an implicit argument about their utility and the legitimacy of the presence of individuals who fit into them. To name oneself working-class in the United States is to acknowledge the existence of the working class. There's a sense on these websites that the term *first-gen students* establishes the existence and presence of such students on campus.

College and university websites also tout programs on their campuses that establish a first-gen community and that respond to the imperative to assist first-gen students in creating social bonds so they can persist and succeed (see Gonzalez et al.; Mendez and Bauman; O'Shea et al.). Some of these programs convene students, faculty, and staff for socials, discussion circles, and mentoring sessions—bringing together groups who rarely interact in officially sanctioned ways (it's rare to have campus programs designed for undergraduates, their professors, and office staff). The websites use affirming rhetoric: "We are here to help with faculty and staff members who once were first-generation students and can offer advice, support and direction." Another institution calls a program in which first-gen students, faculty, staff, and alumni tell their college stories its "I Relate . . ." program.

These websites use discourses of community and social bonding to promote first-gen and working-class values as less individualistic and more collectivist. Recall Bloom's argument that one of a college or university's "middle-class virtues" is "self-reliance" (658). Some of the websites acknowledge this virtue, warning that the individualism of campus culture can feel alienating to first-gen students and lead to their attrition. In our analysis, for instance, the word *self* appeared seven times on the websites we examined, and discourses of accountability more broadly were referenced thirty-six times across ten of the fourteen institutions. One website provides a list of "first-gen friendly" faculty and staff members, so first-gen students will know who to contact if they need assistance from mentors who share their experience. Another site tells first-gen students that the university understands that their attendance "is not just for yourself, but also for the entire family and/or community." The tone of written material on the sites sometimes suggests a class consciousness, albeit a nonradical version thereof, asserting not just a surface definition of first-gen students but a granular characterization of them as collectivist and in search of community. In addition, the programs advertised on the websites often encourage assimilation to middle-class values in fairly overt ways, such as the workshops in etiquette offered to first-gen students at one institution.

The question remains as to whether the category of first-gen students resonates across intersectional identities. Bollig suggests that the first-gen marker "both describes and obscures intersectional marginalization" (27), arguing that it affirms students and provides support but also too readily becomes a generic "umbrella" term (27) that is analogous to "working-class" and that sometimes invokes "white working-class" (26), further othering students of color. Teachers, too, can sometimes slip into what Bollig calls "narratives of transformation through literacy" (33), a self-congratulatory move focused more on celebration of students' assimilation than on social change. Insomuch as literacy instruction perpetuates myths of transformation, the concept of literacy is "violent" and rooted in "oppression" (Stuckey 64). Catherine Chaput analyzes how higher education engages in "the circulation of multicultural texts" in ways that commodify students of color and the construct of "multiculturalism." According to Chaput, "Cultural difference is integral to university work, but it most frequently functions as a depoliticized form of multiculturalism compatible with the agenda of economic globalization" (217). This dynamic plays out on institutional websites for first-gen students that leverage student difference for the purpose of public relations.

Addressing College Culture: Affect of Care and Neoliberal Discourse

A common theme in scholarship on first-gen students is the idea of college culture. Relevant scholarship indicates how first-gen students struggle because of a lack of certain forms of social and cultural capital, and how gaining this capital is an important access point to college culture (Stephens et al. 1180). Definitions of college culture within our corpus are largely implicit, so we worked to identify language that described how college culture was being imagined. At the same time, we noticed that *college culture* is a vague term, implying an abstract concept more than a concrete set of practices or experiences. Even after our close examination of website content, the meaning of the term remained unclear, but definitions tend to evoke both campus life and academic bureaucracy.

Some websites acknowledge race but sometimes in ways that are absolute or demeaning. One site touts workshops that "provide African Americans, Latino, Samoan, and Native American youth positive strategies to combat and overcome the debilitating environment and conditions they face daily at school and on the streets." In an effort to support students, this site uses colonialist terms like "combat" and "debilitating" that place college culture in an adversarial relationship with students' home communities. Elsewhere, racial inequality is neutralized by terms like "identity" or "cultural concerns." Indeed, Gonzalez and colleagues point out how students experience social isolation, noting that white students belong because they are confident about the culture of campus (67). What we see in looking at the language of support sites for first-gen students alongside the findings of Gonzalez and colleagues is not so much that home communities create barriers for students to overcome, but that the white spaces on campus—and the feeling that space on campus is reserved or mainstreamed in racialized ways—are the actual "debilitating environment" students must "combat." From this point of view, we see how first-gen-friendly schools describe identity in more neutral, abstract terms or treat student backgrounds as a deficit rather than a resource.

The idea of college culture is communicated to students (and others) through neoliberal discourses and a general affect of care. For instance, some sites emphasize balance and the affective benefits of maintaining family ties. This content reflects studies that find first-gen students "struggle with college adjustment," have "[l]ower self-esteem," and face "challenges understanding college culture" (Gibbons et al. 489). An affect of care is often used to express support for first-gen students and to acknowledge they may face challenges: "You are in a new environment with new teachers, new classmates and new challenges, but you are not alone and you are not without resources." Perhaps to complement neoliberal messages urging "self-reliance" and "personal development," sites also express affirmation, stressing that students are not alone in their struggles. In other examples, an affect of care encourages students to "advocate" for themselves, celebrating first-gen students for their "creativity," "determination," "persistence," "perseverance," and "resilience." One school's site exclaims that "[f]irst-generation students are some of our favorites, because they often come to higher education with unmatched energy and excitement." Further, Olivas helpfully points out that "self-care" is a mentoring topic for the McNair Scholars program for first-gen students (34). Recall Penrose's findings that first-gen students' struggles with self-perception and the adjustment to the culture of higher education most markedly contribute to lower retention. It's clear then that institutions are largely justified in adopting an affect of care to counter these negative self-perceptions. This also maps onto the field's ethic of student success, evident especially in the literature on basic writers.

Sites also describe a lack of certain kinds of knowledge. One states, "Because first generation college students don't have immediate family members to give them inside tips on what to expect in college, they may find it harder to adapt to campus life." Knowledge of campus culture extends to financial aid, work study, and what kinds of support to expect from faculty members, like office hour consultations. Some of the services mentioned on the websites seemed in our eyes more related to culture, while others are more about access to technical knowledge about how college works, yet the holistic, all-inclusive conception of culture further signifies these websites' affect of care.

A common neoliberal refrain is the idea that students should "get involved," "make connections," "reach out," find ways to "connect" with others on campus, "take advantage of resources," and "positively contribute to their communities." Although some of this language imagines campus as welcoming, these messages also link to discourses of self-help, self-reliance, and accountability. First-gen-friendly schools emphasize such messages in lieu of connecting students and their families to material resources like peer mentoring programs. These schools seem to expect that first-gen students will transform themselves in order to adapt and overcome. This kind of expectation reflects what Bloom has said about the middle-class values of first-year composition: "such stories embody what American education has historically been dedicated to . . . enabling the transformation and mobility of lives across boundaries, from the margins to the mainstreams of success and assimilation on middle-class terms." Transformation in itself is not necessarily problematic, but the terms of this transformation are set by middle-class, neoliberal ideologies that place the burden of self-reflection solely on students to join the "mainstreams of success" (668). This is a message we take issue with. Institutions can and should engage more in transforming college culture. We cannot forget that the recruitment of first-generation students serves two purposes: to increase access to education in an effort to foster upward mobility, and to enable universities to access streams of tuition revenue. This dual purpose is embedded in the inconsistencies and imperatives we see in discourses about college culture.

Beyond Fitting In

Demographic terms like *first-gen students* both empower and marginalize, particularly when used in institutional contexts like on college websites. These terms can invoke identity, consciousness, and the imperative to acquire resources; they can also be co-opted for public relations purposes. Higher education professionals across institutional types should remain conscious of the shifting resonances of the term *first-gen students* and consider who is benefiting from the use of the term. Just as institutional identity can shift with student demographic changes (e.g., greater numbers of multilingual students), so too can the meaning of *first-gen students*. The term can connote white monolingual working-class students in some contexts; in others, it suggests multilingual immigrant students and students of color. Looking at the term on your school's website or in other promotional materials, you might ask how your campus serves first-gen students, what material resources for them are earmarked on the website, how the institution assesses these students' needs, the degree to which the construction of these students' identity on the site acknowledges or engages intersectional identities, whether the site reveals the presence of biases and assumptions, and how it navigates the tension between asking students to assimilate to higher education's conventions and asking the institution to evolve its worldview to account for multiple sets of norms.

The growing number of websites for first-gen students reflects the always-in-flux student bodies we serve, the multivalent ways our campuses engage these populations, the visibility of first-gen students, and more broadly the move to affirm and acknowledge diversity. As we suggest, these populations are especially visible at regional campuses like ours, but they are not unique to our institution type. The term *first-gen students* does important rhetorical work, as Bollig and others have argued. Indeed, Bollig finds that first-gen students are "leveraging identification (rather than identity)" to aid in their acquisition of new literacies and new forms of capital (35), claiming agency more from the rhetorical use of the term than from the identity itself. If the term *first-gen students* has similar resonances as the term *working-class students*, then scholarship on the performance of working-class identity is instructive. LeCourt and Lindquist both emphasize the performativity of working-class identity: LeCourt argues that academic discourse and working-class discourse aren't opposed to one another; rather, working-class student identity is a performance and is "always being negotiated," such as in academic writing, in the context of other power structures and rhetorical situations (45). Lindquist says that teachers too might productively perform affective discourse in a way that working-class students "find authentic and valuable" (188), to sponsor their literacy development and give them more agency to engage in open-ended and productive inquiry. Given Bollig's findings about the potential of the invocation of the term *first-gen students* and our own findings suggesting the potential for the use of the term to transform campus culture, how might we support performances of different kinds of identities on campus? Writing studies professionals have long been interested in providing students with tools to enter critically into multiple discourse communities in service to their own objectives. Certainly, diverse units across campus can engage in these kinds of capacity-building programs with first-gen students (and others interested in performing various identities).

At the same time, even the term's abbreviated nature ("gen" for "generation") aligns the term with a kind of branding. It's a catchy keyword. It supports discourses of affirmation, celebration, and care while also legitimizing the identification of students. It also can entrench neoliberal discourses of accountability and transformation. Identifying students as first sets them apart from others in their cohort and establishes important knowledge about the vagaries of college culture as the dividing line between them.

Providing services for first-gen students also aligns with the democratic ideals of diverse colleges and universities like those we surveyed and the one where we work. Questioning the rhetorical work done by the keyword *first-gen students* allows us to consider how institutions can foster agency but fail to account for their own top-down ideologies of individuality. We are reminded of the observation by Stephens and colleagues that "university cultural products" send messages about "the importance of finding yourself, paving your own path, and developing your own interests" (1181). Such products ask first-gen students to accommodate college culture. Stephens and colleagues point out that students who identify as "first-gen" or "working-class" are often more familiar with ideologies of "interdependence," in which all the parties adjust to the others' needs (1180). University messaging relies on the assumption that only first-gen students should adjust. Programs are put in place to support that adjustment. One alternative to this accommodationist mode is to ask institutions to adapt themselves to first-gen perspectives in order to promote interdependence and collaboration. Some programs seem to accomplish this shift, in particular, ones that ask students to work with peer mentors or that bring together first-gen faculty, staff, and students.

The websites we studied suggest that institutions are thinking about how to go beyond asking first-gen students to fit in. Yes, they often foreground middle-class values, assimilation, and the imperative to be the model first-gen students (think model-minority discourses). But there's also evidence of reciprocity, a sense that the institutions have assessed and are acknowledging first-gen values. For example, some of these websites construct community broadly to include anybody on campus who claims first-gen identity, and some acknowledge intersection of first-gen students with other marginalized populations. This inclusivity suggests that institutions are accommodating a population they believe to be less individualistic. Similarly, some of these websites claim first-gen identity as an institutional identity: one even tells first-gen students who might be experiencing impostor syndrome that the institution knows "what it's like to thrive amid those who have been around for a while."

Williams suggests that slippery, equivocal terms reveal insights about ideology. For Williams, the problem of ideology is a "problem of *vocabulary*" (15). The term *first-gen students* reproduces particular cultural logics. First is the market logic of commodities: the terms *first-generation students* and *first-generation immigrants* often frame the two groups as demographics whose presence is assessed according to the potential to be an emerging market. (See also similar product terms like *first-generation iPhone*.) Second is a logic of mobility in which narratives support bootstraps myths and political arguments about access. Third is a top-down logic of aid that frames traits as deficits and that positions students as objects needing diagnosis and best practices. Across these logics, we see some unacknowledged contradictions that help secure dominating ideologies.

At our own school, the term *first-gen students* can signify not just the United States–born, mostly monolingual, and mostly white working-class students who have matriculated here since the founding of the branch campus sixty years ago but also multilingual students from the Middle East. So the keyword *first-gen student* locally connotes a white student from downriver suburbs, an African American student from Detroit or one of the racially diverse suburbs, a Yemeni student who perhaps came to the United States just a few years prior, other international students, and many more. Further, just as we found the term to be defined differently by different institutions (e.g., as referring to the first person in a family to attend a four-year college versus the first person in a family to receive any higher education), we might imagine locally that students from, say, Lebanon, who are the first in their families to attend college or university in the United States, are essentially first-gen students, in that they are as likely as other first-gen students to be unfamiliar with the norms and practices of campus life at a US college. The point is that first-gen identity is always in flux and always contingent on materiality and locality.

Notes

1. For example, the proportion of first-gen students at regional and midsized campuses in our study was as follows: twenty-seven percent at Kutztown University; thirty-eight percent at Grand Valley State University; thirty-five percent at Northern Michigan University; about half at San Jose State University; just over half at Purdue University, Fort Wayne; nearly half at the University of Cincinnati,

Blue Ash College; thirty percent of new students at University of Central Arkansas; and 39.6% of students at Winona State University.

2. In our research we identified the following as first-gen-friendly institutions: California State University, Monterey Bay; Indiana University–Purdue University, Indianapolis; Kutztown University; Northern Michigan University; Purdue University, Fort Wayne; San Jose State University; Towson University; University of Cincinnati, Blue Ash College; and Washburn University. We identified the following as first-gen-priority institutions: California State University, San Marcos; Emporia State University; Grand Valley State University; University of Central Arkansas; and Winona State University.

Works Cited

Bloom, Lynn Z. "Freshman Composition as a Middle-Class Enterprise." *College English*, vol. 58, no. 6, 1996, pp. 654–75.

Bollig, Chase. "'People Like Us': Theorizing First-Generation College as a Marker of Difference." *Literacy in Composition Studies*, vol. 7, no. 1, 2019, pp. 22–43.

Cataldi, Emily Forrest, et al. *First-Generation Students: College Access, Persistence, and Postbachelor's Outcomes*. US Department of Education, National Center for Education Statistics, Feb. 2018, nces.ed.gov/pubs2018/2018421.pdf.

Chaput, Catherine. *Inside the Teaching Machine: Rhetoric and the Globalization of the U.S. Public Research University*. U of Alabama P, 2008.

Charmaz, Kathy. "Grounded Theory: Objectivist and Constructivist Methods." *Handbook of Qualitative Research*, edited by Norman K. Denzin and Yvonna S. Lincoln, 2nd ed., Sage Publications, 2000, pp. 509–35.

Gibbons, Melinda M., et al. "How First-Generation College Students Adjust to College." *Journal of College Student Retention: Research, Theory, and Practice*, vol. 20, no. 4, 2019, pp. 488–510.

Gonzalez, Carla, et al. "'They Say They Value Diversity, but I Don't See It': Academic and Social Experiences of First Generation Latinx Students at a Predominately White Midwest Institution." *Perspectives on Diverse Student Identities in Higher Education: International Perspectives on Equity and Inclusion*, edited by Jaimie Hoffman et al., Emerald Publishing, 2018, pp. 61–73.

Gray, Barbara, et al. "Identity Work by First-Generation College Students to Counteract Class-Based Microaggressions." *Organization Studies*, vol. 39, no. 9, 2018, pp. 1227–50.

LeCourt, Donna. "Performing Working-Class Identity in Composition: Toward a Pedagogy of Textual Practice." *College English*, vol. 69, no. 1, 2006, pp. 30–51.

Lindquist, Julie. "Class Affects, Classroom Affectations: Working through the Paradoxes of Strategic Empathy." *College English*, vol. 67, no. 2, 2004, pp. 187–209.

Marshall, Catherine, and Gretchen B. Rossman. *Designing Qualitative Research.* 4th ed., Sage Publications, 2006.

Mendez, Julian J., and Sheri Bauman. "From Migrant Farmworkers to First Generation Latina/o Students: Factors Predicting College Outcomes for Students Participating in the College Assistance Migrant Program." *The Review of Higher Education*, vol. 42, no. 1, 2018, pp. 173–208.

O'Dair, Sharon. "Class Work: Site of Egalitarian Activism or Site of Embourgeoisement?" *College English*, vol. 65, no. 6, 2003, pp. 593–606.

Olivas, Bernice M. *Supporting First-Generation Writers in the Composition Classroom: Exploring the Practices of the Boise State University McNair Scholars Program*. 2016. U of Nebraska, PhD dissertation.

O'Shea, Sarah, et al. *First-in-Family Students, University Experience and Family Life: Motivations, Transitions and Participation.* E-book ed., Palgrave Macmillan, 2017.

Penrose, Ann M. "Academic Literacy Perceptions and Performance: Comparing First-Generation and Continuing-Generation College Students." *Research in the Teaching of English*, vol. 36, no. 4, 2002, pp. 437–61.

Stephens, Nicole M., et al. "Unseen Disadvantage: How American Universities' Focus on Independence Undermines the Academic Performance of First-Generation College Students." *Journal of Personality and Social Psychology*, vol. 102, no. 6, 2012, pp. 1178–97.

Stuckey, J. Elspeth. *The Violence of Literacy.* Boynton Cook, 1991.

Trimbur, John. "Articulation Theory and the Problem of Determination: A Reading of *Lives on the Boundary*." *Composition Theory for the Postmodern Classroom*, edited by Gary A. Olson and Sidney I. Dobrin, State U of New York P, 1994, pp. 236–53.

Williams, Raymond. *Keywords: A Vocabulary of Culture and Society.* Rev. ed., Oxford UP, 1985.

Zweig, Michael. *The Working Class Majority: America's Best Kept Secret.* 2nd ed., Cornell UP, 2011.

Integrated Regionalisms and First-Generation Students: A Place-Conscious Heuristic

Jenny Rice

It might seem strange to begin an essay on first-generation students with a discussion about the Appalachian Mountains, but for those of us who teach in this region, there is a real connection between our students and the mountains that stretch across eastern Kentucky, West Virginia, Tennessee, and North Carolina. I teach at the University of Kentucky (UK), where many students come from the eastern part of the state, better known as coal country. This area has been overwhelmingly shaped by what Todd Snyder calls "extractive industry economies" (79). The industries in this area include coal mining, mountaintop removal, logging, and deforestation. Coal mining and logging have quite literally shaped where and how generations of Appalachians have lived. As Snyder writes, Appalachian coal mining towns "were deliberately established for a noneducated workforce" (82). Mining and logging companies built the houses, stores, and churches and even provided a police force for the towns. According to historian Ronald L. Lewis, "The unincorporated company town become one of the defining features of life in the region" (34). Passable roads were not built across the mountains of eastern Kentucky simply because it was more profitable for each "company town" to ensure that its residents did not need to (and could not) leave.

Today, eastern Kentucky very much remains coal country. Yet, as mountaintop removal and strip mining have depleted much of the resources, the coal industry does not offer the secure employment it once did. According to a 2019 report by the Appalachian Region Commission, the poverty rate in Appalachian Kentucky was 25.5%, compared with around twelve percent for the national average (Pollard and Jacobsen 121). Similarly, around twenty-two percent of Appalachian Kentuckians hold less than a high school diploma, compared to a 12.7% national average. Even as I write, the Harlan County coal miners are blocking a railroad and the trains delivering coal as part of their ongoing strike after their paychecks bounced from Blackjewel, their employer, which declared sudden bankruptcy. Even if the miners eventually receive back pay, however, Blackjewel's bankruptcy has left a thousand coal miners in the region without jobs.

My experience teaching Appalachian students echoes the experience of Snyder, who was a first-generation college student from Kentucky's coal country. He writes, "For most first-generation college students from rural Appalachia, the process of preparing for and transitioning into college life is fraught with anxiety and indecision" (79). Gloria Gammell argues that Appalachian students, coming from a nondominant culture, experience a kind of "biculturalism" when they enter higher education (12). She quotes James Branscome's 1970 essay in the short-lived journal *The People's Appalachia*, which boldly declares that "no institution of American society . . . is more divorced from Appalachia than the higher educational system residing within it" (13). While explaining the experience of first-generation Appalachian students in terms of the mountains where they live is simplistic, there is something quite important about paying attention to place.

Indeed, place is remarkably important in the lives of many first-generation students. For example, a significant percentage of first-generation students attend colleges close to home. According to one 2005 study by the Higher Education Research Institute at the University of California, Los Angeles, almost half of first-generation students live fifty miles or less from home, whereas only 35.2% of continuing-gen students live that close to home (*First*). On my campus, nearly seventy percent of UK's 15,187 undergraduate students are from Kentucky. When we consider the additional fact that approximately thirty percent of the university's undergraduates are first-generation students, it seems safe to say that many of the university's students have strong ties to the region. Furthermore, at neighboring regional institutions, such as the University of Pikeville in eastern Kentucky, the numbers are even more significant. Seventy-four percent of the students in Pikeville's 2018 freshman class were classified as "Appalachian Region Residents," and almost forty percent of them were first-generation students (*2020 Fact Book*).

When first-generation students step foot on campus, they are met with a certain cosmopolitan rhetoric that celebrates their roles as global citizens and members of the campus community. While there is much to be said for encouraging all students to see themselves in broader terms, I join a number of other literacy and writing studies scholars who insist that we must not lose sight of how students are shaped by material places and spaces. Johnathon Mauk, for example, calls for us to develop "a pedagogy and theoretical lens that accounts for and engages the spatial and material conditions that constitute the everyday lives of students" (370). Similarly, Robert Brooke's "place-conscious" pedagogy encourages writing teachers to consider how our classrooms exist always in the context of specific places, which means that writing pedagogies do not necessarily have a universal (or placeless) application. As Brooke writes, "Place-conscious education asks us to think of the intradependence of individual, classroom, community, region, history, ecology—of the rich way local place creates and necessitates the meaning of individual and civic life" (10). In short, pedagogies rooted in concepts of place must understand the landscape itself as an important part of our literacy practices. Place matters, even if it matters differently depending on the institution.

It is worth asking how our concepts and theories of place affect how we approach first-generation literacies. However, the notion of place can sometimes be so vague as to be unhelpful. Therefore, in order to find useful tools for enhancing our approach to literacy pedagogies for teaching first-generation students, I push past the imprecision of place as a concept. Instead, I suggest a framework that works through the lens of *critical regionalism*, a theory with a complex history (see Rice). I refer to critical regionalism in its pedagogical sense, following Douglas Reichert Powell, who calls for us to develop "critical strategies capable of recognizing conflict and struggle in forms unique to specific landscapes, and implementing tactics for intervention and action specific to those landscapes" (21). Karen Hall likewise argues that critical regionalism can inform pedagogy by calling attention to "the material conditions of a regional location, engagement with the specific histories of that location, and, additionally, its interconnections with other territories." As a pedagogical framework, Hall continues, "critical regionalism functions as a call for a sensitive, nuanced, flexible and situated engagement with place as geographic and cultural location" (32). The strategic discourse of critical regionalism draws attention to those forms unique to specific landscapes our students are from.

In this essay, I propose a heuristic for thinking strategically about how regionalism can be used to enrich literacy pedagogies for teaching first-generation students. Throughout this piece, I describe two different strands of regionalism—*integrated regionalism* and *disintegrated regionalism*—to develop a usable heuristic that accounts for the interdependence of students and their classrooms, communities, regions, and histories. Drawing on archival research spanning a century, I trace three historical examples of how regionalisms have informed pedagogical and institutional approaches to literacy instruction for first-generation students in Appalachia. While this region is significant to me (since it is my home), my larger goal here is to explore what critical regionalisms can show instructors, wherever they are, about their own pedagogical literacy practices.

Bad Roads and Moonlight

When discussing Appalachian literacy pedagogies, it is nearly impossible to ignore the history of moonlight schools in eastern Kentucky. Founded in 1911 by Cora Wilson Stewart, superintendent of Rowan County Schools, the moonlight schools were initially designed to help adult Appalachians gain literacy skills. After working all day, adults walked across the mountains to attend Stewart's schools. It was not uncommon to see children sleeping in the back of the school room as their parents took lessons on reading and writing. The moonlight schools saw incredible success in Rowan County, and eventually, they began popping up outside of Rowan County, and soon even outside of Kentucky and Appalachia. According to state records, around a hundred thousand Kentuckians learned to read thanks to moonlight schools (Greer 216).

Arguably, part of the success of these schools is due to how Stewart folded a sense of regionalism into her pedagogy. For Stewart, understanding the region requires a concrete understanding of its landscape. Even the name of Stewart's first school, Moonlight School, reflects a strongly material sense of the region. In her later reflections, Stewart notes that she was keenly aware of the obstacles to literacy education in the Kentucky mountains. Walking to schools in the evening presented difficulties, she writes, because of "bad roads with innumerable gullies, high hills and unbridged streams." Moreover, she writes that Rowan County was widely known as a "feud county and [that] the people were not accustomed to venturing out much after night" (*Moonlight Schools* 14). For these reasons, she explains, literacy classes were to be held only on moonlit nights, so that there would be enough light to help students navigate the terrain.

The original textbook for the moonlight schools, *Country Life Readers*, was written with Appalachian life in mind. Like many textbooks designed for beginning literacy, it includes only simple and basic readings. The subjects were contextualized for readers who lived in rural areas of Appalachia. As Stewart writes, *Country Life Readers* "tells about good roads and bad roads; about raising good cattle; . . . lessons on Corn Clubs and Tomato Clubs are given; the value of testing seed; . . . forest values and the great loss occasioned by forest fires are explained" (*Country Life Readers* advertisement). While these might seem like trivial subjects to some readers, they carried special significance for students in the moonlight schools who lived in the eastern Kentucky mountains.

The fact that roads are the subject of one of *Country Life Readers'* first lessons is, therefore, not an insignificant detail. Stewart understood quite well how the poor roads in eastern Kentucky (the few that there were) shaped life for generations of residents. Because travel was more difficult between counties, many Kentucky counties remained relatively isolated. This fact, in turn, reinforced both seclusion and a strong sense of the communal ties in local areas, as well as an economy that depended on working the land in place. The "bad road" was therefore a familiar figure in this region. One of the earliest readings in *Country Life Readers* articulates this familiar sentiment:

See the bad road!
It will waste my time.
It will hurt my team.
It will hurt my wagon.
The bad road is my foe.
I will get rid of the bad road. (Stewart, *Country Life Readers* 11)

Stewart's focus on weaving the everyday experience of regional landscape into her pedagogy was no accident. She saw literacy as having an intricate connection to region. One cannot be fully understood without the other.

Other scholars have rightly noted that Stewart's public discourse was often infused with nativist and other problematic rhetoric (Greer), but in this brief sketch, I highlight the integrated regionalism at work in the moonlight schools. In integrated regionalism, region is more than an identity marker. Rather, it informs pedagogical practices and frameworks. This kind of regionalism encourages a literacy not just *in* place or *for* place but *through* place. More specifically, it adopts an ecological approach to a given region whereby geological landscape, cultural history, economic history, and the students who live in the region all exist in a mutually shaping relationship. In other words, pedagogy informed by integrated regionalism is multidimensional, and in it each element affects the others. Because these elements are not static, moreover, such pedagogical orientation requires teachers to continually ask how changes in any one of these elements affects the others. When the landscape evolves or economic conditions shift, for example, integrated regional pedagogies must consider how these changes affect the students' cultural conditions and students themselves. In turn, this ongoing reflective inquiry affects how, when, where, and why instructors choose to teach particular literacy practices in a given space and time.

This integrated regionalism can also be seen in the moonlight schools that were eventually founded elsewhere in the United States. As I reviewed Stewart's papers in the UK archives, I was shocked to find significant archival material of a moonlight school founded in Browning, Montana, on the Blackfeet Indian Reservation. This reservation is where my mother, who is Blackfeet, and her family lived for generations. Although Stewart was born and raised in Rowan County, Kentucky, she understood that any literacy education among the Blackfeet required an understanding of their cultural, economic, and regional ecologies. As Samantha NeCamp writes, Stewart emphasized that Indian literacy must be seen as a complex and fluid concept. According to NeCamp, teachers in all reservation moonlight schools "documented students' language and literacy in *all* languages, not only English, resulting in an impressive recognition of the cultural diversity within (as well as among) reservations" (159).

Rather than using the quite successful *Country Life Readers* with the Blackfeet, therefore, Stewart created a textbook specific to the landscape, economic context, and cultural conditions on the reservation in northern Montana. The textbook doesn't discuss bad roads, for instance, because the Blackfeet students would find the idea of selling land more relevant.

> I have land.
> I will keep it.
> I will keep it for my children.
> Some men want to rent my land.
> Some men want to buy it very much.
> They offer me much money.
> My friend wants me to keep it.
> He says if I do not sell it quick some men will offer me more money.
> I will keep my land. (Manuscript)

I know firsthand how the thought of selling land has long been an important and often heated subject on the reservation. I recall intense conversations about this subject with my grandmother and great-aunts and uncles. By creating literacy readings that drew upon the specific conditions in which the Blackfeet students lived, Stewart recognized that literacy—and the prospect of gaining knowledge—does not mean the same thing for each community. Such integrated regionalism requires those who teach to constantly take stock of their region's history, characteristics, changes, and so on.

Teachers in the Mountains

Several decades before Stewart created the moonlight schools, Berea College was founded by a band of abolitionists, including John Gregg Fee and Cassius Marcellus Clay. Established in 1855 in Berea, Kentucky, the college was designed for first-generation Appalachian students. Berea College's history is remarkable in many aspects, especially for the ways that the region's complex ecology was thoroughly integrated into the college's mission from the start. While other colleges at the time claimed to serve citizens of their respective regions, few of them admitted students who fully reflected the regional ecology. Yet Berea's student body was both coed and racially integrated. The multiracial makeup of Berea's student body was undoubtedly driven by the abolitionist beliefs of the college's founders, but it also reflects a commitment to serving the region.

From Berea College's earliest days, the college's founders regularly articulated the concept of region as being multifaceted. Steve Gowler writes, "Unlike many colleges that are the product of nineteenth century social activism, Berea cultivates communal memory of its past and attempts to develop in a way that is consistent with its roots." Gowler notes that this cultivated communal memory is explicitly related to the Appalachian region and its history (388). In the writings of Berea College's early founders, region always figures centrally. As Fee remarked in an 1869 address, the aim of Berea was to educate the people of Appalachia in order to strengthen the region: "[T]here must be raised up on the soil, native defenders of the truth—men and women—acquainted with the habits of the people, and allied to them in interests, relationship and association" (qtd. in Fairchild 3). Similarly, William Goodell Frost, president of Berea College from 1892 to 1920, repeatedly stressed that the mountains are more than a backdrop. Frost explicitly called for Berea's teachers to think of themselves as "mountain teachers."

Berea College's founders stressed the notion that pedagogy must be contextualized within real material conditions of place. As John A. R. Rogers, one of the school's original founders, puts it in his book about the college's creation: "In order to better understand the history, work and mission of Berea College, it will be needful to consider briefly the geography and people of Eastern Kentucky" (3). Rogers then details the geological characteristics of the local valleys, waterways, and mountains. For Rogers, as for other early chroniclers of the college, this landscape is important to understand because the conditions—steep, rocky, and difficult to traverse—explain part of what makes life in eastern Kentucky unique. Education at Berea was meant to be not merely in a place, nor merely for a place, but through and with a place.

Nearly two centuries after Berea College's founding, this same complex sense of region continues to inform programs and practices for the school's largely first-generation student body. One example is Berea's decision in 2000 to transform its significant Appalachian artifacts collection from a museum exhibit into a teaching collection available for use in courses. The Appalachian Studies Artifacts Teaching Collection features artifacts, images, and other archival materials that span over a century. Notable collections include objects depicting the stereotype of the hillbilly, historical Appalachian quilts, and other handmade crafts. Since the transformation, Berea faculty members have integrated the collection's materials into their courses, thereby developing a place-based literacy shaped by the same material cultures that have also shaped students themselves. One recent course, Quilts: Geometry, Art, History, integrated Berea's vast Appalachian quilt collection as a way to discuss social change, women's history, and activism through the lens of quilting. By learning the political history of geometric quilt designs—such as the patterns used on abolitionist friendship quilts—students may have also gained a new perspective on the quilts (and quilters) in their own communities. Such pedagogical approaches to first-generation literacy are examples of "critical strategies capable of recognizing conflict and struggle in forms unique to specific landscapes," as Powell puts it (21). Yet this work also requires institutions to see students in their relationship to the shifting landscapes, cultures, and economics of place.

Students or Trees

Although there is only a short distance between Berea College and UK, the two institutions can sometimes feel like separate worlds. There are obvious reasons for this, of course. UK is a large public university, with enrollments that dwarf those of tiny liberal arts colleges like Berea. However, the student populations of both institutions do share certain characteristics. One 2011 report estimated that nearly thirty percent of incoming UK students are first-generation (Peabody et al.). Additionally, UK's official demographics collected between 2011 and 2021 show that in-state student percentages have steadily hovered around seventy percent. Much like Berea College, therefore, the university must be aware of the unique needs of both first-generation and Appalachian students.

One UK program in particular was designed to support students who fall into both categories. The Robinson Scholars Program, established in 1997, selects low-income, first-generation students from twenty-nine counties in eastern Kentucky to receive a scholarship that covers all tuition and personal expenses for ten semesters at the university. To overcome barriers to success, the Robinson Scholars Program identifies promising students as early as eighth grade and helps them develop to be college-ready by the time they graduate high school. Or, in the less-than-ideal words of UK officials who first introduced the program, Robinson Scholars were imagined as "first generation college students who lack hope, interest, motivation, knowledge, academic preparation, and/or financial means to pursue a college degree" ("Minutes" [2000] 11). As part of the program, students attend workshops, meet with advisers at least twice, and complete a minimum of ten hours of community service.

Over the years, the Robinson Scholars Program has faced several challenges. According to one report, "Only 23.8 percent of the scholars are still enrolled by their eighth semester, so most of the students are not remaining in college long enough to obtain a bachelor's degree. . . . The Robinson Scholars Program may be getting a considerable number of these students to college, but it is not getting them to walk across the stage after four years" (A. M. Dunn 18). At the same time, the program reports high retention rates for students transitioning from their first to their second year. Those who graduated as Robinson Scholars are quick to credit the program's support as a key factor in their success. As one former Robinson scholar puts it, “Higher education is hard to come by for low-income, first-generation students. It was a life-changing experience, because this program is really based around a culture of leadership, preparing students not just for college but for success” (qtd. in Blackford and Wright).

Yet the program received its most significant blow in 2018 when Governor Matt Bevin announced that he would cut funds for the Robinson Scholars Program as part of his state budget plan. As it was, the program had already been slowly losing funding, resulting in scaled back implementations and reduced staff. The outcry from program supporters eventually resulted in some lawmakers calling for its restoration, yet it became clear that the Robinson Scholars Program was not likely to ever grow in influential ways.

The financial threat to the Robinson Scholars Program is yet another testament to how first-generation students are often overlooked and underserved. But the story of the program also reveals an important lesson about how a pedagogical approach to region can become a kind of disintegrated regionalism. On the face of it, the Robinson Scholars Program seems to be driven above all by a regionalist approach to first-generation students. Nevertheless, its history highlights some of the ways that regionalism can sometimes fall short.

The Robinson Scholars Program was named after Robinson Forest, a 14,786-acre forest stretching across Breathitt, Knott, and Perry Counties in eastern Kentucky. The environmental writer Erik Reece describes the forest as “one of the last, largest examples of the oldest, most biologically diverse ecosystem in North America—the mixed mesophytic.” Robinson Forest has a lengthy and complicated history. At the beginning of the eighteenth century, Robinson Forest was home to the Cherokee and other tribes. By the century’s end, however, the logging and timber industries had claimed much of the land for industrial purposes. Reece describes how the Mowbray and Robinson Lumber Company cleared a significant portion of the land by the 1920s, stripping bare a nearly twenty-three-square-mile portion of the forest. After the company had clear-cut all they could, they turned over the property to UK in 1923. Before the university could begin to use the land, however, its first order of business was tearing down the homes of loggers and impoverished families who were squatting on the land. According to the minutes from a 1923 meeting of the university’s board of trustees, a local man named Tony Cheney was hired to dismantle “houses and camp sheds in and around Buckhorn, Kentucky,” in order to kick out the squatters (“Minutes” [1923] 10–11). As payment, Cheney was allowed to keep all the materials left from the dismantling process.

Soon after the university received the land, it began to strip-mine the forest for valuable minerals that lay underground, causing considerable damage to the landscape that surrounded the forest. Eventually, the university sold coal and timber rights to four thousand acres of Robinson Forest. A portion of the proceeds—$37 million—was then used to establish the Robinson Scholars Program and to offer scholarships to students whose families had lived near Robinson Forest for generations. Unfortunately, the earnings from the program's endowment dwindled over time. "By 2003, the Robinson Scholars endowment was earning less than it cost to sustain the program," Reece writes. "The solution, coal operators were quick to point out, was to mine more of Robinson Forest. 'What's more important,' went the argument, 'trees or young people?'" And with that, Robinson Forest continued to see rampant mining, deforestation, and environmental devastation.

At every stage of Robinson Forest's history, many UK students and faculty members vocally objected to the university's decisions. Students organized to form Students to Save Robinson Forest, a group that held protests and called for statewide action. In a speech to the group, the famed Kentucky writer Wendell Berry summed up the group's core argument to the university's administration: "The principle that you may destroy the land of Kentucky in order to promote the education of Kentuckians is a false principle, and a dangerous one." Other students objected to the fact that the areas being destroyed were their hometowns. Cathy Dunn, an undergraduate at UK, wrote an impassioned letter in 1982 that articulates sentiments shared by many students and faculty members: "I was raised in Pike County where people experience temporary alleviation by coal industry, but after the land is spoiled, and a pitifully small excise tax is returned to the Commonwealth what have we left for future generations? Very little hope." Meanwhile, student protesters also expressed frustration at the disconnection between the university and the land itself. In his dissertation on the Robinson Forest debacle, David Barrett Gough writes: "To the extent that any of [the university administrators] knew the region directly it was through work as a coal operator. . . . This contrast between conceiving of Robinson Forest as an abstraction, a piece of real estate on the university's ledger sheet versus intimate knowledge gained through labor in the forest led to radically different interpretations of the stakes of mineral extraction" (197). While strip-mining Robinson Forest provided a sizable revenue source, the lasting damage to eastern Kentucky was hard to ignore for those who call that area home.

It is difficult to think about the Robinson Scholars Program without also thinking about the landscape and economic conditions in eastern Kentucky. Indeed, without strip-mining and timber clearing, there would arguably be no Robinson Scholars. However, while place is central to the program, students participating in the program are strangely disconnected from the place. The program emphasized college readiness, but it did very little in the way of thinking about regionality and its role in the lives of the students. Thus, the story of Robinson Forest is sadly ironic. First-generation students in the program have been negatively affected by the "extractive industry economies," and yet those extractive economies are also what helped them attend college (Snyder 79).

The history of the Robinson Scholars Program also reveals how place is missing from a broader strategy to address first-generation students. An integrated regionalist framework calls for explicit reflections on the interrelationships between landscape, economic conditions, cultural conditions, and the students, yet the Robinson Scholars Program was created out of a glaring disconnection between students and landscape. This is not to say that the aims of the program are bad or unimportant. Many first-generation students from eastern Kentucky have benefited as a result of it. However, we might ask how those students might also benefit from pedagogies and programs that offer a richer sense of literacy. The idea that we can only help first-generation students at the cost of destroying their land is a troubling equation that erroneously suggests that landscape, economics, and culture do not shape the identities of these students. This is an example of what I call disintegrated regionalism, which inevitably contributes to disintegrated literacies.

A Critical Regionalist Heuristic

Of course, the Robinson Scholars Program is not the only example of disintegrated regionalism. Furthermore, there is nothing necessarily harmful in pedagogies or programs that do not reflect on the interconnections between place and literacy. However, as Nedra Reynolds reminds us, "*Where* writing instruction takes place has everything to do with *how*" (20; my emphasis). Although I have focused here on Appalachian literacy, my point is not really about this particular region, which others have covered adequately. Rather, I am trying to make the case that not only is regionalism important to account for in our pedagogical and institutional programs but that we must also ask ourselves what kind of regionalism informs our work. While not every institution has the same degree of concentrated regional populations, there is something productive in questioning how regionalism can be part of the first-generation student experience. Such reflection is central to supporting literacy practices.

As an example of how critical, integrated regionalism can inform writing pedagogy, I want to highlight Steven Alvarez's UK course Taco Literacy. Alvarez's course encourages students to see themselves "as ethnographers exploring the affective foodways of Mexican immigrants in the U.S. South—the region of the nation experiencing the fastest growth of Mexican migration" ("Taco Literacies"). Alvarez describes how this course grew out of an earlier course focusing on "Mexington, Kentucky," which took students "into the field," visiting "the *barrios* of Kentucky to explore a local bakery, a western wear store, a family-owned grocery store, a bilingual library, and a local *taquería*" ("Taco Literacy" 153). Alvarez uses food as a way for students to inquire about the existing and changing places they call home. The UK student body is largely white and southern, and students from eastern Kentucky and rural counties who took the earlier course may have been unfamiliar with many of the places they visited as part of the "Mexington" tours, yet this lack of familiarity is precisely what created learning opportunities for these students.

I was fortunate enough to be colleagues with Alvarez while he was teaching these classes. Hearing about the work his students were doing, I often wondered what "taco literacy" might look like in my Texas home region, where I grew up around Mexican bakeries and taquerias. How would the class change in a different regional ecology? How might the class have changed if it had been taught prior to 1990? As Alvarez notes, between 1990 and 2015, the Latinx population (primarily Mexican) tripled in Kentucky. He explains that many migrant families settled in Kentucky after 1990 after leaving other southern states where anti-immigrant sentiment was overwhelming ("Taco Literacy" 153). Regardless of where or when a course like Taco Literacy might be taught, the different landscapes, cultures, and economies of a given region present different challenges and opportunities. It falls to those of us who design such courses or programs to carefully reflect on how all those elements are working together at this moment.

The course Taco Literacy is only a small example of how regionalism can be pedagogically generative. In order to create richer literacy practices for first-generation students (who often come with strong connections to place), instructors can use the four parts of integrated regionalism—landscape, economic conditions, cultural conditions, and students—as a useful heuristic, or a starting point for reflection. This simple heuristic breaks down these four parts into related questions:

Landscape: What are the physical conditions of this region? What other regions are students connected to? How do students travel between campus and home? What affordances does this landscape provide? What kinds of movement or work are inhibited by this landscape? What are the spaces on and off campus that students move through? One excellent model for how institutions might help engage these questions is Berea College's Appalachian seminar and tour for new faculty members, which includes a five-day road trip across eastern Kentucky. During this tour, new faculty members have an opportunity to physically encounter rural and urban Appalachia, as well as to hear talks from representatives from the local communities.

Economics: What are the region's current and historical economic conditions? How have these economic conditions been shaped by the landscape? What are the economic opportunities or limitations within the region? What kinds of demographic changes are happening? These questions also require that faculty members (new or seasoned) become familiar with the region's economic history. In many regions, certain industries that once existed are no longer thriving, yet the effects of such industries (and their erasure) continue to shape students' ideas of what literacy means.

Culture: What are the current and historical populations in this region? How is the region divided according to race, class, or ethnicity? How diverse or homogenous is the population? What kinds of public narratives are told about this region? What kinds of practices, habits, and traditions are shared in this region? These questions encourage faculty to become curious about the stories that remain untold in the demographic data about the region. Again, institutions can help facilitate learning about local culture by actively promoting these stories. For example, at UK, new faculty members often, and correctly, assume that Kentucky is an overwhelmingly white state, with less diversity than many other places. However, in recent years, the university has actively spotlighted the work of poet and faculty member Frank X. Walker, whose work calls attention to "Affrilachian" identity. Walker coined this now popular term as a way of speaking about the black Appalachian experience, something that might easily be overlooked in many narratives about the region. Indeed, the presence of Affrilachian identity is literally embedded in the walls of UK's new student center, which features a fragment from one of Walker's poems written in large letters at the entryway.

Students: Are students close to home when they are on campus? What kinds of linguistic characteristics are common to students' home region? What kinds of narratives about learning are familiar to students in this region? How mobile are students in their home region or at school? While many instructors are familiar with literacy narratives, they might also encourage students to reflect on how place enters into their ongoing experiences of literacy. The introduction of place-conscious literacy narratives at the beginning of a semester can help teachers create classroom environments that meet the needs of their students at a particular time and in a particular place.

Of course, these are only a handful of suggestions for how we might reflect on regionalism. Importantly, the questions cannot simply be asked and answered one time; the elements in regional ecologies are constantly in flux. Even so, integrated critical regionalism is worth the time such inquiry demands. Whether instructional materials are being designed for first-generation students in a single course or in an entire program, the questions raised by integrated critical regionalism may indeed lead to more effective and influential outcomes. At the very least, this regionally focused heuristic can, in the words of Powell, help us "not only to criticize but also to plan, to envision . . . more just and equitable landscapes" (25). It is one step toward creating literacies not merely in place but also with place.

Works Cited

Alvarez, Steven. "Taco Literacies: Ethnography, Foodways, and Emotions through Mexican Food Writing." *Composition Forum*, vol. 34, no. 1, 2016. compositionforum.com/issue/34/taco-literacies.php.

———. "Taco Literacy: Public Advocacy and Mexican Food in the U.S. Nuevo South." *Composition Studies*, vol. 35, no. 2, 2017, pp. 151–66.

Berry, Wendell. "Wendell Berry Speech, September 14, 1982." Students to Save Robinson Forest Records, 1981–84, U of Kentucky Special Collections, box 1, folder 9.

Blackford, Linda, and Will Wright. "Why This 'Life-Changing' Program That Sends Eastern Kentucky Students to UK May End." *Lexington Herald-Leader*, 25 Jan. 2018, www.kentucky.com/news/local/education/article196571424.html.

Brooke, Robert E., ed. *Rural Voices: Place-Conscious Education and the Teaching of Writing.* Teachers College Press, 2003.

Country Life Readers advertisement. Cora Wilson Stewart Papers, 1869–1979, U of Kentucky Special Collections, box 36, folder 4.

Dunn, Amanda Michele. "Factors Affecting the Success of Robinson Scholars." 2010. uknowledge.uky.edu/cgi/viewcontent.cgi?article=1114&context=mpampp_etds. U of Kentucky, MPA/MPP Capstone Projects 127.

Dunn, Cathy. Letter. Students to Save Robinson Forest Records, 1981–84, U of Kentucky Special Collections, box 2, folder 1.

Fairchild, E. H. "Spent Arrows: Extracts from the Speeches and Writings of William G. Frost with Inaugural Address." Awards, Conferences and Programs: Presidential Inaugurations 1869–2013, Berea College Special Collections and Archives, RG 11/11.14, box 1, folder 1.

First in My Family. Higher Education Research Institute, May 2007, www.heri.ucla.edu/PDFs/pubs/briefs/FirstGenResearchBrief.pdf.

Frost, William Goodell. "For the Mountains: Our Aims and Strategic Principles." Berea College Special Collections and Archives, William Goodell Frost Papers, box 15, folder 25.

Gammell, Gloria Ruth. *The Transition to College Experience for First-Year Appalachian Students*. 2006. Peabody College of Vanderbilt U, PhD dissertation.

Gough, David Barrett. *The Value of the Commonwealth: An Ecocritical History of Robinson Forest*. 2013. University of Iowa, PhD dissertation.

Gowler, Steve. "The Habit of Seeking: Liberal Education and the Library at Berea College." *Library Trends*, vol. 44, no. 2, 1995, pp. 387–99.

Greer, Jane. "Expanding Working-Class Rhetorical Traditions: The Moonlight Schools and Alternative Solidarities among Appalachian Women, 1911–1920." *College English*, vol. 77, no. 3, 2015, pp. 216–35.

Hall, Karen. "Starting in Place: A Preliminary Investigation of First Year Curriculum Design in Response to Critical Regionalism." *Places and Spaces*, 2014, pp. 30–36.

Lewis, Ronald L. "Beyond Isolation and Homogeneity: Diversity and the History of Appalachia." *Back Talk from Appalachia: Confronting Stereotypes*, edited by Dwight B. Billings et al., UP of Kentucky, 1999, pp. 21–43.

Mauk, Johnathon. "Location, Location, Location: The 'Real' (E)states of Being, Writing, and Thinking in Composition." *College English*, no. 65, no. 4, 2003, pp. 368–88.

"Minutes of the University of Kentucky Board of Trustees." 11 Nov. 1923.

"Minutes of the University of Kentucky Board of Trustees." 6 Aug. 2000.

NeCamp, Samantha Hope. *The Moonlight Schools: Adult Literacy Education in the Age of Americanization*. 2011. U of Louisville, PhD dissertation.

Peabody, Michael, et al. *First-Generation College Students at the University of Kentucky*. U of Kentucky, 2011.

Pollard, Kelvin, and Linda A. Jacobsen. *The Appalachian Region: A Data Overview from the 2013–2017 American Community Survey*. Appalachian Regional Commission, 21 May 2019, www.arc.gov/wp-content/uploads/2020/06/DataOverviewfrom2013to2017ACS.pdf.

Powell, Douglas Reichert. *Critical Regionalism: Connecting Politics and Culture in the American Landscape*. U of North Carolina P, 2012.

Reece, Erik. "The Cleanest Stream in Kentucky." *Still*, www.stilljournal.net/erik-reece-nonfiction.php.

Reynolds, Nedra. "Composition's Imagined Geographies: The Politics of Space in the Frontier, City, and Cyberspace." *College Composition and Communication*, vol. 50, no. 1, 1998, pp. 12–35.

Rice, Jenny. "From Architectonic to Tectonics: Introducing Regional Rhetorics." *Rhetoric Society Quarterly*, vol. 42, no. 3, 2012, pp. 201–13.

Rogers, John Almanza Rowley. *Birth of Berea College: A Story of Providence*. HT Coates, 1903.

Snyder, Todd. "The Transition to College for First-Generation Students from Extractive Industry Appalachia." *Rereading Appalachia: Literacy, Place, and Cultural Resistance*, edited by Sara Webb-Sunderhaus and Kim Donehower, UP of Kentucky, 2015, pp. 77–98.

Stewart, Cora Wilson. *Country Life Readers: First Book*. B. F. Johnson Publishing, 1915.

———. Manuscript for book on Indian education. U of Kentucky Special Collections, box 28, folder 3.

———. *Moonlight Schools for the Emancipation of Adult Illiterates*. E. P. Dutton, 1923.

2020 Fact Book. U of Pikeville, www.upike.edu/wp-content/uploads/2020/03/PC-FactBook-2020-Ed-FULL.pdf. Accessed 1 Feb. 2021.

Walker, Frank X. *Affrilachia*. Old Cove Press, 2020.

First-Generation Students in an Accelerated Learning Program at a Community College

Sarah Elizabeth Snyder and Eric S. Lee

This essay addresses issues of first-generation student access and success through the institutional initiatives, partnerships, and curriculum design at Arizona Western College (AWC), a 71.1% Hispanic-serving institution (HSI), open-access community college in the southwestern United States that serves about eleven thousand students. AWC institutional initiatives support first-generation student populations by building essential pipelines from high schools directly to colleges and to university partners serving the geographic area through satellite campuses, by reducing tuition barriers, by educating first-generation families, and by creating a college-going culture in a depressed economic area. Specifically, AWC's composition program has made large strides in restructuring the developmental composition sequence in the curriculum. This essay investigates the success (passing) rates of first-generation students enrolled in the college's version of the Accelerated Learning Program (ALP) model and shows how the ALP model supports first-generation students through their first-year composition (FYC) journeys.

Before we can address first-generation writing and literacy strategies, we need to address the often ignored question in the larger discussion of first-generation Latinx education: How do educational institutions increase the enrollment and success rates of Latinx students, especially in rural, economically depressed areas like those that many community colleges serve? The National Center for Education Statistics reports, "[B]etween 2000 and 2016, Hispanic undergraduate enrollment more than doubled—a 134 percent increase from 1.4 million to 3.2 million students" (de Brey et al. vi). While this trend is promising, many colleges and universities are scrambling to deal with the changing demographics of their student populations. In contrast, HSIs in economically depressed areas like that around AWC serve student populations that were more than sixty-two percent first-generation and sixty-eight percent Latinx in 2018–19 (Lopez et al. 3). Ostensibly, AWC's student population serves as a case study for the numerous challenges and opportunities that many institutions will face in the coming decades.

The Accelerated Learning Program Model

The Community College of Baltimore County's ALP model is an innovative approach to accelerating developmental education for students who test into the course below a typical FYC class (Adams et al.). ALP supplies additional support concurrently with the FYC course rather than requiring students to take a prerequisite course. Peter Adams and his colleagues discovered through developing and implementing this model that many students with the extra support were able to complete the first semester of FYC regardless of how they had initially tested into developmental coursework. This model has been put into competition with the Stretch model (a model of FYC that stretches the first-semester class over two semesters) because it claims to prevent persistence-related issues as it creates an intensive learning experience that does not lengthen the time required (in terms of semesters) for students to complete the FYC classes that are often prerequisites for their major coursework. Inherent to the ALP model is an intensive number of credits, perhaps in the form of a developmental class that is attached to the first course in the composition sequence, but the model has taken many forms across the country. In studies by the Community College Research Center, the ALP model has been shown in general to be cost effective and successful in accelerating students through developmental class sequences (Jenkins et al.; Cho et al.).

The ALP model also seems to be in line with many of the existing recommendations for ensuring first-generation student success. Jeff Davis, in his 2010 book *The First-Generation Student Experience*, recommends almost a dozen research-based principles to keep in mind when planning for first-generation student success in higher education. Davis suggests a myriad of recommendations to help first-generation students persist and succeed in college, specifically in their developmental coursework. The most important finding was to limit class size so that first-generation students can receive the attention they need. Davis goes on to further argue for these conditions explicitly: "If this enlightened attitude toward teaching [developmental] courses is coupled with smaller class sizes, colleges and universities will see not only higher graduation rates but also improved academic performance across the board" (182).

The ALP model creates the conditions for these best practices in two ways. Normally, preparation requirements for instructors of prematriculation classes for credit are less stringent for many accreditation bodies, including the Higher

Learning Commission that accredits AWC. This means that at the community college level, many developmental classes can be taught by those who ostensibly have less training in composition and rhetoric, developmental writing theory, multilingual writing theory, and the like. The ALP model, however, requires that both the developmental classes and those for matriculated students (FYC classes) be taught by the same instructor, for continuity of instruction, which by default raises the required training level to that for instructors who are also allowed to teach the college-level class. The ALP model also stipulates that half of the students in the FYC class be traditional, matriculated students and that half be developmental-level students. At AWC, the normal FYC course is capped at twenty-four students, so the corresponding developmental course is capped at twelve students. This reduced class size allows the instructor to give extra attention to each ALP student.

The ALP model, like the Stretch model, in theory allows more time for students to make personal connections with professors. As Davis reiterates, the scholarship suggests that

> developing a personal relationship with a faculty member is an extremely important factor in becoming comfortable in the postsecondary environment and is highly correlated with academic success among first-generation students. The symbolic impact of being able to say, "I know Professor Smith," cannot be underestimated. Many parents (as well as friends and other family members) of first-generation students will regard postsecondary professors with such respect that any such report from their child will be received as proof that he or she is a full-fledged college student. (196–97)

Ostensibly, with more time per student, the instructor has more opportunities to make personal connections with students through assignments that encourage what Edward White calls "looking in," or self-discovery and sharing with the professor. In a community college setting, though, the best practice of forming a personal connection with students may still be hard to achieve with regular teaching loads of five classes or more per semester. At the very least, the professor in the ALP model has fewer students than a professor in the Stretch model with an equivalent teaching load. Furthermore, Davis suggests making study groups and academic skills instruction mandatory, addressing impostor syndrome within the classroom, and creating orientation classes and events. While multiple models can allow for these suggestions, the ALP model at AWC creates this space with the extra three credits for the developmental course that students take along with the three-credit FYC course, allowing instructors to address quality with a deep dive into the content of the college-level class and into the process of writing. In contrast, the Stretch model emphasizes quantity in FYC classes through a longer survey of different types of materials and exercises, which normally leads students to do double the number of writing assignments (Glau, "Bringing" and "'Stretch'").

Theoretically, as a program design, and assuming an informed, equal contribution from the curriculum, the ALP model should be serving first-generation students well. Our data, discussed below, compare the success of first-generation and continuing-generation students in the ALP with those in the traditional first-year writing program at AWC.

The Community College Context

In fall 2018, AWC served 11,521 students in two counties,[1] Yuma and La Paz, covering a large geographic area on the border of Mexico, California, and Arizona. According to the Hispanic Association of Colleges and Universities, AWC was designated a 72.1% HSI in 2018, and sixty-eight percent of the student population at AWC self-identified as "Latino" in 2019 (Lopez et al. 3). AWC defines "Hispanic/Latino" as "[a] person of Cuban, Mexican, Puerto Rican, South or Central American, or other Spanish culture or origin, regardless of race" (Lopez et al. 63). AWC indicates that sixty-two percent of the student population self-reported as first-generation (3). At AWC, students self-report their first-generation status, defined by the college as when neither parent has finished a baccalaureate degree. During the application process, which is in both English and Spanish, each student is asked whether either of their parents has a bachelor's degree. Complications with self-reporting aside, the percentages of Latinx and first-generation students may be higher than reported.

To further complicate the context, definitions of first-generation students vary in the literature, such as in the book by Davis and in work by Jennifer Engle and Vincent Tinto, who consider first-generation students to be those whose parents or guardians have not attained a four-year degree; in work by Ernest Pascarella and colleagues, whose three-part definition differentiates between students whose parents have high and moderate levels of postsecondary educational experience and those whose parents have no postsecondary achievement; and in the work of scholars who define first-generation students more generally as those who may not feel they have the cultural capital to navigate higher education (Dumais and Ward 263). However, the reality is that eleven percent of residents in La Paz County and eighteen percent of residents in Yuma County have achieved a bachelor's degree, compared to the national average of thirty-one percent, which is similar to the statistic for the Phoenix metropolitan area ("Yuma").

When looked at in concert, the bachelor's degree achievement rates for first-generation, low-income, and Latinx students are particularly grim. Numerous studies (Engle and Tinto; Schak and Nichols; Fink et al.) demonstrate significant gaps in degree achievement between first-generation, low-income, or nonwhite students and continuing-generation, higher socioeconomic, or white students. The majority student population of AWC represents each of these risk factors to degree completion. The AWC Communications Division took the initiative to make curricular changes based on studies such as those above, especially after receiving the following information from the college's Office of Institutional Effectiveness and Research: as of 2018–19, over twenty-two percent of our student body (2,543 students) was taking remedial English, mathematics, or both. An internal AWC study revealed that over fifty-five percent of all students placing into developmental English classes from 2006 to 2012 never attempted the college's first-semester FYC class.

While there are numerous noncurricular reasons why these students never took the standard FYC class, it is not unwarranted to believe that students who place into remedial, noncredit classes are far more likely than their nonremedial peers to drop out. In addition, there is the increasing cost of tuition, and no matter how the economy behaves, students of low socioeconomic status face increasing pressure from their families to pursue jobs and thus to delay their graduation or to drop out altogether to help support their families. This reality is reflected in a four percent increase in part-time enrollment, a trend that needs to be reversed (Lopez et al. 5, 43). Unfortunately, this issue is not unique to AWC's geographic locality. A recent report from the Southern Regional Education Board also cited the growing economy and the increasing cost of college tuition as likely factors in declining enrollment (Lounsbury and Datubo-Brown).

In order to combat these growing concerns, the FYC faculty, division chair, and writing program administrator at AWC made numerous suggestions for improving student success, including the lowering of student caps to reach for the guidelines listed in "ADE Guidelines for Class Size and Workload for College and University Teachers of English" and in the Conference on College Composition and Communication's "Principles for the Postsecondary Teaching of Writing," reducing the number of FYC sections that the faculty taught per semester, streamlining the developmental reading and writing program, and investigating the ALP model in either a one-credit or a three-credit module to help streamline students in need of some developmental education directly into the first-semester FYC course.

While lower caps and teaching loads are still being pursued, and the restructuring of the developmental English curriculum is complete, the numerous challenges rural community colleges face include a lack of appropriate state funding and a dearth of highly qualified faculty and staff as defined by current Higher Learning Commission standards. Thus, the AWC writing program's first move toward removing barriers to educational success in English was to pilot the ALP model after reviewing the literature. Ultimately, the department chose to implement the ALP model through a six-credit, corequisite pair of classes taken in the same semester that allowed students to earn credit for both a developmental composition class (for prematriculation students but offering college-level credit) and the FYC class (which offers transferrable credits). Early results of the pilot program looked promising, but success metrics were not initially distinguished by first-generation or socioeconomic status or by ethnicity. In this essay, we delve deeper into this data.

Method

There is a history of analyzing pass and persistence rates in composition courses to compare program structures for evidence of program success (e.g., Glau, "Bringing" and "'Stretch'"), and there is also a newer movement to further analyze those rates with a technique for disaggregating certain populations (e.g., Inoue; Snyder, *Stretch Model*). Greg Glau started his inquiry into the Stretch model at Arizona State University, making the argument that it was retaining students more efficiently than requiring students to attend area community colleges for the developmental sequence of classes before entering university ("Bringing"). Glau's study established baseline data that were then compared to the next decade's worth of data, which showed through the Step model analysis that Stretch students were passing at higher rates than the traditional FYC students at the college. Sarah Elizabeth Snyder added another set of data from the next decade and disaggregated those results specifically for second language writers in the Stretch program, showing that the rates of success were somewhat different, albeit positive, for second language writers in the Stretch program—in fact they had the highest rates of success of all students in the program. However, one facet of the Stretch program that has proved problematic is the persistence of students from class to class (Snyder, "Retention Rates"; Glau, "Bringing"), and this issue has been shown to lengthen the time to degree by as much as a semester (Snyder, *Stretch Model*).

This essay uses the Step model to analyze student success for the ALP model at AWC while disaggregating for first-generation students. The Step model calculates success within cohorts using the number of students who passed in the previous semester as the new denominator for the next class. We define success as a final passing grade of A, B, or C at the end of the semester. Grades of D and F, for "fail," are the opposite of the passing grades. Grades of W, for "withdrawal," and I, for "incomplete," were not included in the data set. Although persistence (defined most often as enrollment in the subsequent semester's class) is normally a metric reported with success, it was not analyzed as it was out of the scope of this study. All students enrolled in the college's FYC class were included in the sample, and they were disaggregated by first-generation and continuing-generation status as the college collected that data.

First-Generation Student Success in an Accelerated Learning Program Model

In total, this study reports on 3,823 students at AWC from fall 2017 to spring 2019, excluding summer and winter terms. The ALP cohorts were a fraction of the size of the traditional cohorts, as they were still in midpilot stage; given the limited instructor resources, only about eight to ten sections in the ALP could be offered in any semester. ALP students represent nine percent of the data set and number 323 students over two years. Unlike the enrollment fluctuation that is seen in the traditional FYC classes, where there is normally double to triple the enrollment in fall compared to spring because of demand, the ALP population steadily rose as the pilot was scaled up and as more instructors were recruited to teach the ALP sections.

To compare the two cohorts, the average success rates for students in the ALP and traditional FYC sections are reported in table 1 in aggregate. The ALP model shows greater or about equal success rates as the traditional course, which is impressive since the test scores for all the ALP students placed them in developmental classes rather than in traditional FYC classes, indicating that these students would not be successful in a traditional FYC course. Without running a statistical test to determine the power of the results reported in table 1, they still look promising.

Table 2 shows the data disaggregated for first-generation and continuing-generation students within the ALP. When the ALP was in the early stages of

Table 1. Success rates in accelerated learning program and traditional first-year composition classes

	Percentage of successful students in the classes (number of successful students)			
	Fall 2017	**Spring 2018**	**Fall 2018**	**Spring 2019**
ALP classes	80% (70)	73% (67)	68% (95)	71% (91)
Traditional FYC classes	68% (1,257)	56% (455)	69% (1,166)	73% (622)

Table 2. Success rates of accelerated learning program students disaggregated for first-generation status

	Population		Success rate	
	Student cohort	Percentage of the class (number of students)	Percentage by cohort	Number of students by cohort
Fall 2017	First-generation	53% (37)	89%	33
	Continuing-generation	47% (33)	70%	23
Spring 2018	First-generation	69% (46)	78%	36
	Continuing-generation	31% (21)	62%	13
Fall 2018	First-generation	75% (71)	68%	48
	Continuing-generation	25% (24)	71%	17
Spring 2019	First-generation	45% (41)	63%	26
	Continuing-generation	55% (50)	78%	39

Table 3. Success rates for accelerated learning program and traditional first-year composition students disaggregated for first-generation status

	Percentage of successful students in each cohort				
Student cohort	Fall 2017	Spring 2018	Fall 2018	Spring 2019	Average
ALP first-generation	89%	78%	68%	63%	75%
ALP continuing-generation	70%	62%	71%	78%	70%
Traditional first-generation	68%	61%	70%	74%	68%
Traditional continuing-generation	68%	50%	69%	72%	65%

its pilot, the data showed that nineteen percent more first-generation students in the ALP were achieving success than continuing-generation students in the program. The disaggregated success rates for ALP students in subsequent semesters seem to fluctuate throughout the scaling of the ALP pilot, which could be the result of many factors, including the diversification of instructors and the solidification of the curriculum implemented in the ALP model. Many curricular changes, including a writing-program-wide student learning outcome assessment, may have temporarily altered the strength of the ALP model through changes to the curriculum. Regardless of fluctuations in semester success rates, table 3 shows that the average rate of success of first-generation students over the first two years in the ALP is seventy-five percent. This is currently the highest rate of success in composition at AWC, even when compared to first-generation students who tested into traditional FYC classes, whose average success rate is sixty-eight percent. Students who did not identify as first-generation in both the ALP and traditional FYC classes are achieving success at slightly lower rates (seventy percent and sixty-five percent, respectively) than their first-generation counterparts.

The National Context for Interpreting Success in Composition Models

First-generation students are exhibiting higher levels of success in the ALP model at AWC, and when these rates are compared with those of first-generation students across the nation, we see that using the ALP model with first-generation populations seems to make the model competitive. The Community College Research Center reported an eighty-two percent success rate in the ALP cohort studied by Davis Jenkins and colleagues (13), and Sung-Woo Cho and colleagues found that ALP students were passing FYC in the fall semesters from 2007 to 2010 at 74.66%—almost exactly the average success rate of first-generation students in the ALP at AWC (7). While Cho and colleagues describe their study population in many ways, they do not use the label *first-generation*. Regardless, a program model that can consistently reproduce success at community colleges across the nation with somewhat different populations is worth encouraging.

When we compare these results to Snyder's 2018 study of the Stretch program at Arizona State University (ASU), one of the most influential university transfer partners of AWC, it seems there is still a disparity between success rates at the community college and at the university. According to Snyder, the Stretch program at ASU reports success rates as high as 93.58% and 91.24% for traditional FYC (*Stretch Model* 52). However, Snyder found that there are issues with comparing success rates using the Step model of analysis and with what may be understood to be the yield model of analysis, which may be altering the understanding of program success data. Glau's Step model differs from the traditional yield model, as the denominator in the yield model does not change, but the denominator in the Step model does. The denominator in the Step model reconfigures to only include the number of students who started or persisted to the course, with the numerator being the number of students who passed the course. Therefore, comparing results from the ASU Stretch program and AWC's ALP using the Step model would be more congruent if the success rates of the first FYC class in AWC's ALP were compared to the developmental FYC class in ASU's Stretch program. The average success rate for FYC classes at ASU between

2007 and 2014 was 87.98%, but after that, using a yield model, the pass rate of the second FYC class at ASU is calculated to be 73.63% (Snyder, *Stretch Model* 52).

This analysis suggests, on the surface, that both the ALP and Stretch models are congruent, but their numbers still may mean vastly different things that high HSI, high first-generation, and low socioeconomic status may help us see. As ASU is not officially an HSI, this factor cannot be directly compared, but 24.64% of the Stretch population at ASU self-identified as "Hispanic/Latino" (Snyder, *Stretch Model* 20). ASU's first-generation population is about thirty percent for first-time freshmen and thirty-five percent in the general enrollment (Faller). As AWC has nearly double this proportion of first-generation students, one might expect the AWC success rates to be lower than ASU's. Compound that difference in student demographics with the fact that Yuma County, where AWC is located, is a rural, depressed area, whereas Maricopa County, where ASU is located, is one of the largest metropolitan areas in the United States, and the success rate of AWC first-generation students in the ALP program seems like much more of an accomplishment.

In general the comparison of success rates for individual courses is more appropriate than a comparison of graduation rates at, say, a community college and an Ivy League school. Patrick Sullivan rightly has reservations about comparing graduation success rates at an open-access community college with high numbers of first-generation students to other populations ("Measuring 'Success'"). We do not use graduation as a metric of success for first-generation students participating in the ALP at AWC because doing so is beyond the scope of this study. Also, the AWC ALP cohort has only been in place since 2017, and as of this writing we do not have four-year graduation statistics for these students. One hypothesis for how the graduation metric might look is that because of the ALP's intensive structure, which fits six credits into one semester, students might not have their time to degree lengthened by one semester, as the Stretch data showed. This topic requires further study.

Other data show positive trends in junior-year GPAs for AWC students. In the academic year 2018–19, 143 students who transferred from AWC to an Arizona university with twenty-four or more credits had an average GPA of 3.28, indicating some success overall (AZ Transfer Assist). To further contextualize this population, two-year graduation rates at AWC for first-generation students dropped (from 944 graduates in 2014–15 to 510 graduates in 2018–19), and the average time to completion increased from 4.5 years in 2014–15 to 5.8 years in 2018–19 (Lopez et al. 51). As AWC has the highest transfer rates in Arizona, we would like to push back (much like Pascarella et al.; Chen and Carroll; and Davis) against the notion, albeit well supported by the data, that "a large number of low-income, first-generation students began—and ended—their studies at public two-year and for-profit institutions" (Engle and Tinto 2) and that therefore it is better for these students to attend four-year institutions immediately rather than going to a community college. Further study will be conducted to see if the ALP affects the time to graduation for first-generation students in comparison with other cohorts at the college.

First-Generation Student Considerations for the Accelerated Learning Program Model

Although the ALP model shows promise for first-generation students' success, there is still one major concern: the cost of the program for students, which is also a concern of the Stretch program as well as of developmental education more broadly. Both programs require students to register and pay for six credits rather than three. As Snyder found in her 2018 dissertation about the Stretch program, students who are the least prepared for FYC, as shown by placement test scores, are also most often economically disadvantaged students, and so these programs create something of a tax on the students who can least afford it (*The Stretch Model*). In kind, the literature on first-generation students repeatedly cites the economic situation of many students in our scenario. Davis says,

> The desire to work, the need to make money, may be the single biggest impediment to first-generation students' participating in campus life activities. Because of their backgrounds, many first-generation students work more than their non-first-generation counterparts. Also given their backgrounds, I do not think it is unreasonable to conclude that many work even when they do not really *need* to work, when it would be better to take out a student loan, for instance. (194; see also Somers et al.)

While the decision to take out a student loan or work during college is highly personal, we know anecdotally from classroom observations, from the literature, and from experience advising students that their work schedules pose the greatest risk to their college success and that they are intensely feeling financial stress (Mehta et al.). More students are working full-time, or working two or more part-time jobs, while also attending school. As the economy fluctuates and students, especially in low-income areas, are encouraged to work or find that they need money to pay for medical bills or to raise their families, fewer hours in the day are available for class and homework, neither of which cry out from hunger or repossess a vehicle. When work and school schedules conflict, students are caught between keeping their jobs and being successful in school. Davis makes a recommendation in this regard, encouraging first-generation students to work on campus (194). This may be the safest place to encourage students to work because their supervisors will undoubtedly be sympathetic to the student's school schedule and will limit their working hours (along with, unfortunately, their earning potential). Paradoxically, it may also be the most difficult place to persuade first-generation students to work, as they disproportionately experience impostor syndrome and may not feel qualified to be, say, a writing tutor or an academic assistant. The extra time spent by instructors with this population encouraging them to identify as college students will undoubtedly help first-generation students succeed to the desired level of coursework. Ultimately, colleges and universities might not be able to eradicate the need for first-generation students to work, but they can lessen the need to work by eliminating financial barriers to college.

At this time in the pilot, the ALP model makes a convincing argument for first-generation students at our institution. It creates an opportunity for students who may be disincentivized by a longer developmental education sequence to jump right into their FYC course. It protects students' time for their coursework and creates the space for them to devote extra attention to academic skills. It allows the institution to reserve its most prepared faculty members' time for those students who may need it most. The ALP model also can be a space for rejuvenating teaching practices through professional development that supports the professors in this venture in serving first-generation students and other populations such as multilingual students. AWC is preparing to pilot multilingual sections of the ALP to pair with the multilingual composition courses being offered, as this approach to teaching multilingual students was found to be successful at Queensborough Community College (Anderst et al.). Future studies will examine the longitudinal success of first-generation students, including multilingual students in the multilingual ALP course sequence, and will try to replicate these results across the country. Furthermore, future research should examine the writing that these students are producing for analysis.

Fostering First-Generation Student Success beyond the Accelerated Learning Program Model

Although AWC demonstrates initiative in exploring the success of first-generation students in the ALP model, even highly motivated writing program administrators and division chairs cannot adequately address issues of student access or foster radical curricular change to address these issues if changes are not supported by administrative leadership. AWC leadership supports these efforts to improve access for first-generation students through a multipronged approach. The first bold move AWC made under President Daniel Corr was to embark on a strategic plan that addressed the future direction of the college, and a point of pride was that of including first-generation students in that direction. By rewriting the college's mission and vision statement in spring 2017, Corr and the District Governing Board set the tone by making it the vision of the college to "[c]ultivat[e] generations who value knowledge, foster independence, *eliminate poverty*, and create vital, equitable and sustainable communities" (*Growing*; our emphasis). To this end, the college has implemented a four-pronged campaign for first-generation accessibility and success that we might suggest as an approach for other colleges as well: raise awareness of first-generation student identity and issues on campus, build the high-school-to-college pipeline through concurrent and dual enrollment initiatives, eliminate financial barriers to college, and create education initiatives for the families of first-generation students.

First, in an easily replicable initiative, AWC has launched a massive awareness campaign to encourage students to want to identify as first-generation and to be proud of this identity. Corr, once a first-generation student himself, brought his story to the campus. AWC's #firstgeneration campaign includes proclaiming November 8 First-Generation Day and hosting a large annual event on that day that families, high schools, and community partners take part in ("AWC to Proclaim"). Specific awareness merchandise is distributed at events like this one, such as buttons, shirts, and laminated plaques that have positive messaging about being first-generation at AWC, and there is a special white stole for first-generation students to wear at graduation. The simplest, yet most influential portion of the awareness campaign is encouraging faculty members to identify as first-generation. Faculty members at AWC can put up signs proclaiming "First-Gen Faculty" on their doors or in their offices, as well as wear campaign apparel and celebrate the accomplishments of the first-generation students in their classes and across campus. When faculty members are open about their first-generation identities, students have the opportunity to gain mentors who may help them overcome barriers to their education. Begun in 2017, the awareness campaign has made an impact and motivated researchers at the college to explore this population in a data-driven manner.

Second, AWC is innovatively and responsibly building the high-school-to-college pipeline. AWC has been good at enrolling local high school graduates. Thirty-eight percent of all high school graduates districtwide and up to seventy-five percent in San Luis attend AWC after graduation, but over twenty percent of all new students at the college tested into developmental English, mathematics, or both. The college determined, on further investigation, that only six percent of students from the district were taking advantage of concurrent and dual enrollment programs even if they were eligible. It seemed clear in the early phases of strategic planning that the institution needed to build and accelerate educational pipelines and opportunities for students to earn transferrable credit while they completed their high school diplomas and to prepare them for the rigor of college education.

The third part of the campaign, eliminating financial barriers to college, dovetails with building the pipeline. AWC reduced tuition to twenty-five dollars per credit hour for students eighteen and under, which spiked enrollment nearly three hundred percent over two academic years, from 5,182 credit hours to over 15,205 credit hours. Even then, some families reported financial hardship when paying that more modest tuition. To alleviate this issue, the Communications Division chair successfully petitioned the college president to provide microscholarships by partnering with local community businesses and the Arizona Western College Foundation to ensure that financial barriers would be eliminated for any student who was academically eligible to enroll in college classes. The college also sent scholarship letters to students who had eligible scores on the ACT, encouraging them to enroll.

Still, there were potential issues with the high school ecosystem: academically eligible, high-achieving students taking Advanced Placement classes were disincentivized from enrolling in classes where they would earn transferrable college credits because the Advanced Placement classes were weighted on a five-point scale, whereas AWC's classes were only weighted on a four-point scale. The highest grade in an Advanced Placement class would count more toward a student's GPA than the highest grade in an AWC class. High school students were interested in classes that would potentially earn them a higher GPA because they might then receive more merit-based scholarships for college—even though they would eventually have to take FYC and college-level math classes at higher tuition rates (depending on enrollment at their college or university) and delay their graduation by at least a semester, as most students at Arizona universities who want a bachelor's degree have to take the two-semester FYC sequence. The AWC college president and the superintendent of the high school union worked together to rectify this issue. Composition and math college credits are now on a five-point scale so that they compute into high school GPAs at the same rate as Advanced Placement credits do. However, even when AWC did offer full scholarships, buy books, and create equitable exigencies for high school students to take these classes, a number of academically eligible students still did not take advantage of the program because outreach efforts were not yet in place and knowledge of the program was limited.

Finally, the Yuma Promise and La Paz Promise, AWC's newest initiatives to encourage college access and attainment, ensure that district high school graduates will receive reimbursement for all out-of-pocket expenses for their associate's degree pending the following conditions: FAFSA completion, full-time enrollment, graduation within five semesters, and enrollment in a bachelor's degree program with one of the college's state university partners located on the Yuma campus. The hopes for these two initiatives are manifold, but increased baccalaureate attainment and building a homegrown educated workforce are the most cited. Future research will be conducted to see the impact of these two initiatives on first-generation students.

Call to Action

While many of these recommendations will improve outcomes for first-generation, low-income, and underrepresented students at individual progressive institutions, ultimately these measures will do little until the underlying societal issues are addressed at the state and national levels.

We need to work across traditional academic boundaries to provide a concerted effort in support of all students. After all, what good are streamlined ALP models if one out of five students walk into our classrooms unsure of where their next meal is coming from? What use are tuition reductions and promise initiatives when we do not have enough high school counselors to educate students and their families about the plethora of educational opportunities and certificate programs and degree pathways that are available? Currently, according to College Success Arizona, a higher education policy advocacy group, Arizona ranks forty-ninth in FAFSA applications ("Current FAFSA Completion Rates") and has a paltry 903:1 student-to-counselor ratio compared to the national average of 464:1. In addition, from 2008 to 2017 there was a "-53.8% change in state spending per student on higher education" and a corresponding "90.9% [t]uition increase in Arizona for public 4-year institutions" during the same ten-year period ("Need"). College is increasingly underresourced, and the students and their families are bearing the brunt of the cost—or are unable to attend. Access means nothing without financial ability, which is why AWC's definition of accessibility includes "[e]liminat[ing] cultural, financial, time and place barriers to education" (*Growing*).

As educators, we need to reenvision ourselves as teacher-scholar-activists (see, for example, Andelora; Sullivan, "Two-Year College Teacher-Scholar-Activist"; Jensen and Toth; Toth et al.) and work with our national organizations (the National Council of Teachers of English, Conference on College Composition and Communication, and Two-Year College English Association) to be active in education policy nationwide to represent student populations currently being underserved by our institutions. In his summary report for the National Student Clearinghouse Research Center that examines college enrollment, persistence, graduation, and other success metrics from five thousand public high schools in the United States, Michael Nietzel finds damning disparities for our students based on degree of poverty and minority status. The six-year graduation rate from low-poverty schools (fifty-three percent) was more than double that of high-poverty schools (twenty-one percent). Minoritized, low-income students fared the worst, with a six-year graduation rate of twenty-seven percent compared to their nonminority, higher-income peers, whose rate was fifty-one percent. Nietzel correctly points out that

> [t]he income gap in college success continues to be one of our nation's greatest shames, a stubbornly cruel obstacle to the economic mobility that education should provide. It's our big bad sort—a harsh divide where children who are born into poverty or who are educated in America's poorer schools face distressingly long odds to realize educational goals and lifetime dreams.

As we have demonstrated, economic barriers to success, particularly with first-generation students, are real.

And while we, in writing this essay, are reluctant to tie college access and success initiatives to the increasingly common rhetoric of college as career training, or to the imperatives of economic growth, the fact remains that it would be naive to believe that state and national policy makers will be swayed by anything other than the potential impact to their bottom lines. Cultivating generations of students who value knowledge, fostering their independence, and eliminating poverty is an aspirational vision and should be properly lauded, but efforts to lobby funding for higher education will be largely ignored unless they demonstrate the economic impact of initiatives based on such a vision and the detriment to the public good if these initiatives are ignored. That being said, even with Arizona's anemic FAFSA completion rate, the total amount of money directed to in-state students through FAFSA is $4.5 billion a year. Imagine what this amount could be if more students and their families filled out the FAFSA. With activism from teacher-scholar-activists, the narrative could be greatly improved.

Given its high HSI status, multilingual populations, and class strata, AWC ostensibly serves as a case study for what many institutions currently look like, or will look like in the not-too-distant future. Replicating the work of AWC and its various allies, such as the American Dream Academy, Achieve60AZ, and College Success Arizona, will go a long way in forcing policy makers to reexamine the consequences of continued reductions in high school and college funding.

The ALP model, in conjunction with multiple initiatives that increase awareness of first-generation students and their needs, creates a positive atmosphere where students can flourish. In terms of writing instruction, the ALP model affords first-generation students with access to a highly skilled professor for more demanding developmental work, limited class sizes to encourage the development of a personal relationship with the professor, more individualized instructional time, and support for academic skills, including peer tutoring embedded in the course model. The benefits of the ALP model are not only for the student. The ALP model allows for a more reasonable workload for professors who are engaging with the most vulnerable populations in colleges. Through these reduced workloads, professors have more opportunities to recognize the behaviors of first-generation students, such as succumbing to pressure to work rather than attend class. Professors who have deeper relationships with their students are a line of defense against other factors that might impede first-generation student success.

While not every recommendation will suit every institutional context, we strongly emphasize that any ALP or initiative for first-generation students needs to be faculty-driven and supported by the administration through adequate funding and release time to develop, support, and sustain the responsible reproduction of theoretical models appropriate to each campus and student body. Even with the successes that AWC has achieved for its first-generation student population, the national context proves that there is always more work to be done.

Notes

Our deepest gratitude goes to our colleagues in the Communications Division at AWC and to Daniel Corr, Linda Elliott-Nelson, Lori Stofft, Betty Lopez, and Laura Corr for their support of our research.

1. The number of students served reflects an unduplicated head count, which means that a student may have enrolled in more than one course but was counted only once (Lopez et al. 3).

Works Cited

Adams, Peter, et al. "The Accelerated Learning Program: Throwing Open the Gates." *Journal of Basic Writing*, vol. 28, no. 2, 2009, pp. 50–69. *JSTOR*, www.jstor.org/stable/43443881.

"ADE Guidelines for Class Size and Workload for College and University Teachers of English: A Statement of Policy." *Association of Departments of English*, Modern Language Association of America, Sept. 2020, www.ade.mla.org/Resources/Policy-Statements/ADE-Guidelines-for-Class-Size-and-Workload-for-College-and-University-Teachers-of-English-A-Statement-of-Policy.

Andelora, Jeffrey. "Teacher/Scholar/Activist: A Response to Keith Kroll's 'The End of the Community College English Profession.'" *Teaching English in the Two-Year College*, vol. 40, no. 3, 2013, pp. 302–07.

Anderst, Leah, et al. "Assessing the Accelerated Learning Program Model for Linguistically Diverse Developmental Writing Students." *Teaching English in the Two-Year College*, vol. 44, no. 1, 2016, pp. 11–31.

"AWC to Proclaim Nov. 8 First-Generation College Student Day." *Arizona Western College*, 6 Nov. 2017, www.azwestern.edu/about/news/awc-proclaim-nov-8-first-generation-college-student-day.

AZ Transfer Assist. "Arizona Western College Average Junior Year GPA of New Transfers: Compared to New Freshman and Other Transfers." Sept 2019. PDF.

Chen, Xianglei, and C. Dennis Carroll. *First-Generation Students in Postsecondary Education: A Look at Their College Transcripts*. US Department of Education, National Center for Education Statistics, 2005, nces.ed.gov/pubs2005/2005171.pdf.

Cho, Sung-Woo, et al. "New Evidence of Success for Community College Remedial English Students: Tracking the Outcomes of Students in the Accelerated Learning Program (ALP)." Community College Research Center, 2012, ccrc.tc.columbia.edu/media/k2/attachments/ccbc-alp-student-outcomes-follow-up.pdf.

Conference on College Composition and Communication. "Principles for the Postsecondary Teaching of Writing." National Council of Teachers of English, 2015, cccc.ncte.org/cccc/resources/positions/postsecondarywriting.

"Current FAFSA Completion Rates by State." "FAFSA Tracker—National." *FAFSA Tracker*, national.fafsatracker.com/currentRates.

Davis, Jeff. *The First-Generation Student Experience: Implications for Campus Practice, and Strategies for Improving Persistence and Success*. E-book ed., Stylus Publishing, 2010. *ProQuest Ebook Central*, ebookcentral-proquest-com.ezproxy1.lib.asu.edu/lib/asulib-ebooks/detail.action?docID=911903.

de Brey, Cristobal, et al. *Status and Trends in the Education of Racial and Ethnic Groups, 2018*. US Department of Education, National Center for Education Statistics, 2019, nces.ed.gov/pubs2019/2019038.pdf.

Dumais, Susan A., and Aaryn Ward. "Cultural Capital and First-Generation College Success." *Poetics*, vol. 38, no. 3, June 2010, pp. 245–65.

Engle, Jennifer, and Vincent Tinto. *Moving beyond Access: College Success for Low-Income, First-Generation Students*. Pell Institute, 2008, files.eric.ed.gov/fulltext/ED504448.pdf.

Faller, Mary Beth. "Cultural Connections Key to Success of ASU's First-Generation Students." *Arizona State University*, 6 Nov. 2020, universitycollege.asu.edu/cultural-connections-key-success-asus-first-generation-students.

Fink, John, et al. *What Happens to Students Who Take Community College 'Dual Enrollment' Courses in High School?* Community College Research Center, 2017, ccrc.tc.columbia.edu/media/k2/attachments/what-happens-community-college-dual-enrollment-students.pdf.

Glau, Gregory R. "Bringing Them Home: Arizona State University's New Model of Basic Writing Instruction." Conference on College Composition and Communication / ERIC Clearinghouse, 1996.

———. "'Stretch' at 10: A Progress Report on Arizona State University's 'Stretch Program.'" *Journal of Basic Writing*, vol. 26, no. 2, 2007, pp. 30–48.

Growing Our Communities: Strategic Plan 2025. Arizona Western College, 2019, www.azwestern.edu/sites/default/files/awc/office-of-the-president/AWC_Strategic_Booklet_SR_Fall_2019.pdf.

Inoue, Asao B. *Antiracist Writing Assessment Ecologies: Teaching and Assessing Writing for a Socially Just Future*. WAC Clearinghouse, 2015.

Jenkins, Davis, et al. "A Model for Accelerating Academic Success of Community College Remedial English Students: Is the Accelerated Learning Program (ALP) Effective and Affordable?" Community College Research Center, 2010, ccrc.tc.columbia.edu/media/k2/attachments/remedial-english-alp-effective-affordable.pdf.

Jensen, Darin L., and Christie Toth. "Unknown Knowns: The Past, Present, and Future of Graduate Preparation for Two-Year College English Faculty." *College English*, vol. 79, no. 6, 2017, pp. 561–92.

Lopez, Betty, et al. *2018–2019 Arizona Western College Fact Book*. Arizona Western College, 2019, www.azwestern.edu/sites/default/files/awc/institutional-research/2018-2019%20Fact%20Book-Final%20Complete.pdf.

Lounsbury, Susan Campbell, and Christiana Datubo-Brown. *Fact Book on Higher Education: U.S. Regions and Fifty States in Perspective*. Southern Regional Education Board, 2019, www.sreb.org/sites/main/files/file-attachments/2019factbook_web.pdf?1561062852.

Mehta, Sanjay S., et al. "Why Do First-Generation Students Fail?" *College Student Journal*, vol. 45, no. 1, 2011, pp. 20–35.

"The Need to Increase College Access and Attainment in Arizona." *College Success Arizona*, 2019, o5otc2v1fzo3zjgc0kr72fml-wpengine.netdna-ssl.com/wp-content/uploads/2019/06/College-Success-Arizona_Updated_POLICY-PRIORITIES-ONEPAGER_11019.pdf.

Nietzel, Michael T. "New Report Shows Large Gaps in College Progress Based on Whether Students Attend High- or Low-Income High Schools." *Forbes Magazine*, 8 Oct. 2019, www.forbes.com/sites/michaeltnietzel/2019/10/08/new-report-shows-large-gaps-in-college-progress-depending-on-whether-students-attend-highor-low-income-high-schools/#159124e42c13.

Pascarella, Ernest T., et al. "First-Generation College Students: Additional Evidence on College Experiences and Outcomes." *The Journal of Higher Education*, vol. 75, no. 3, 2004, pp. 249–84.

Schak, Oliver J., and Andrew Howard Nichols. "Degree Attainment for Latino Adults: National and State Trends." The Education Trust, 2017, edtrust.org/wp-content/uploads/2014/09/Latino-Degree-Attainment_FINAL_4-1.pdf.

Snyder, Sarah Elizabeth. “Retention Rates of Second Language Writers and Basic Writers: A Comparison within the Stretch Program Model.” *Retention, Persistence, and Writing Programs*, edited by Todd Ruecker et al., Utah State UP, 2017, pp. 185–203.

———. *The Stretch Model: Including L2 Student Voices*. Arizona State University, 2018, arizona-asu-primo.hosted.exlibrisgroup.com/permalink/f/chl6tq/01ASU_ALMA51106828987000384l. PhD dissertation.

Somers, P., et al. “Pushing the Boulder Uphill: The Persistence of First-Generation College Students.” *NASPA Journal*, vol. 41, no. 3, 2004, pp. 418–35.

Sullivan, Patrick. “Measuring ‘Success’ at Open Admissions Institutions: Thinking Carefully about This Complex Question.” *College English*, vol. 70, no. 6, 2008, pp. 618–32.

———. “The Two-Year College Teacher-Scholar-Activist.” *Teaching English in the Two-Year College*, vol. 42, no. 4, 2015, pp. 327–50.

Toth, Christie, et al. “Two-Year College Teacher-Scholar-Activism: Reconstructing the Disciplinary Matrix of Writing Studies.” *College Composition and Communication*, vol. 71, no. 1, 2019, pp. 86–116.

White, Edward. “Fifty Years of Curriculum Changes: Looking In and Looking Out in College Writing Classes.” *Talking Back: Senior Scholars and Colleagues Deliberate the Past, Present, and Future of Writing Studies*, edited by Norbert Elliot and Alice S. Horning, Utah State UP, 2020, pp. 359–75.

“Yuma, Arizona Education Data.” *Town Charts*, 2019, www.towncharts.com/Arizona/Education/Yuma-city-AZ-Education-data.html.

Rural First-Generation Latinx Students and College Access: Considerations for Writing Instructors and Administrators

Todd Ruecker

Though much attention to Latinx student populations has concentrated on urban areas, many rural and small-town communities across the United States are rapidly diversifying. The percentage of minoritized students in rural schools rose from 16.4% in 2000 to 26.7% in 2013, and rural schools now serve more than 2.6 million minority students and around 300,000 students classified as English Language Learners (Johnson et al. 11, 27). Data indicate that fifty-two percent of Latinx immigrants have parents who never attended college, compared to only thirty-three percent of all undergraduates (Arbeit et al.). In a study focused on the perceived educational barriers of rural youth, Matthew J. Irvin and colleagues found that Latinx youth, youth whose first language was not English, and youth with lower levels of parental education perceived greater barriers to accessing and succeeding at college (80). With these numbers in mind, it is vital for writing faculty members and program administrators to consider the uniqueness of rural immigrant youth and how to better facilitate their access to and success in college. Drawing on interviews with Latinx first-generation college students from five rural high schools as well as on situated ethnographic work, this essay explores the challenges rural Latinx first-generation students face in transitioning to college along with the ways they have been able to transition successfully.

Data on Latinx Students and College Access

Statistically, rural first-generation students face several barriers to pursuing higher education that their suburban and urban continuing-generation counterparts do not. Rural areas tend to be poorer than many urban and suburban areas and are often home to higher numbers of first-generation students. According to the Postsecondary National Policy Institute, first-generation first-semester college students come from families with a $37,565 median income, compared to $99,635 among continuing-generation first-year students ("Factsheets"). Income level and first-generation status often correlate with test scores as well. For instance, in an April 2014 ACT study, rural first-generation, low-income students averaged 16.9 on the ACT, whereas rural continuing-generation, low-income students averaged 18.5, and rural continuing-generation, higher-income students averaged 21.1. Urban and suburban continuing-generation, higher-income students had the highest average ACT scores: 22.1 and 22.7, respectively (Buddin). These scores play an important role in shaping not only which colleges students are admitted to but also the scholarships they have access to. While the University of New Mexico (UNM), the university where the focal students in this essay were studying, is largely open access and does weigh ACT and SAT scores heavily in admissions, these scores have other implications. The most generous and prestigious scholarship offered by UNM, the Regents' Scholarship, reports that award recipients need a score of 31 on the ACT; another valuable scholarship, the Presidential Scholarship, requires a score of 25 on the ACT ("Scholarship Office").[1] These scores are also used for writing placement: students who score below a 15 on the ACT English or a 430 on the SAT Language portion are required to take a developmental stretch writing class.

Although a Pennsylvania study reports that rural students enroll in college at higher rates than their urban counterparts, they tend to lag behind students from town and suburban areas with similar demographics (Howley et al. 4). The aforementioned nationwide study of seven thousand youth in seventy-three high schools across thirty-four states similarly found that rural youth from minoritized backgrounds reported more barriers to accessing college than their rural white peers, a finding that also has been found repeatedly among nonrural youth (Irvin et al. 80). Especially relevant for this study, students who reported a native language besides English and lower levels of parental education perceived more barriers to pursuing a college education. Researchers have reported other barriers, such as prejudice against Latinx immigrant families in small communities and inconsistent ad hoc support for language and literacy learning in schools with recent increases in immigrants (E. Martinez; Bruening).

Educational Foundations and Financial Barriers

As I detail later in this essay, it is clear that financial barriers are one of the most significant barriers standing in the way of rural Latinx students pursuing higher education. The students I talked with almost all benefited from the state lottery scholarship, which traditionally paid full tuition for students who graduate from a New Mexico high school with a certain minimum GPA and who meet other requirements like immediately enrolling in college after high school and maintaining a full-time load of college courses. However, in recent years, the amount of funding has been cut, and *full-time* has been redefined from twelve credit hours to fifteen credit hours. This push for fifteen credit hours has translated into additional policies at UNM that have made it cheaper for students to take fifteen instead of twelve hours.

As I have noted elsewhere, these policies have been aggressively promoted by foundations like Complete College America, which has an initiative titled Fifteen to Finish. As indicated by language on the foundation's website, initiatives like this are supported in part by a narrow reading of retention research: "The vast majority of college students aren't taking the credits needed to graduate on time, despite research showing the significant benefits of doing so—including better academic performance, higher retention rates and the increased likelihood of completion" ("Fifteen"). Organizations like Complete College America treat a four-year graduation rate as the norm despite the fact that only 40.6% of students nationwide graduate in four years; this number is 45.2% for white students and drops to 31.7% for Latinx students and 21.4% for African American students ("Table 326.10").

While organizations like Complete College America are well-intentioned, the policies they promote, centered around a white middle- and upper-class norm, have the potential to erect further barriers for rural Latinx first-generation students. For instance, this obsession with boosting four-year graduation rates has led to a related policy instituted at UNM and a growing number of public colleges and universities around the country that requires first-year students to live in campus housing unless they live within commuting distance of the university or demonstrate financial hardship. Residency requirements ignore the fact that on-campus room-and-board plans place increased financial burdens on students and their families. While there is an exemption for those with financial hardships, this exemption places the burden on students to apply for it and to navigate a system they already might be overwhelmed by as first-generation students.

Methodology and Theoretical Framework

This essay is based on a study focused on the literacy- and language-learning experiences of immigrant students in rural high schools. During the study, I visited six rural schools, five in New Mexico and one out of state, for three to four weeks at a time, observing classes in English as a second language, English language arts, and Spanish and interviewing teachers, students, and administrators. After visiting the five New Mexico schools, I obtained lists of graduates from those schools who were attending UNM. Based on teacher recommendations of students who likely came from bilingual households, I reached out to invite them to be interviewed. These interviews are the primary data used in this essay. It is important to note that, despite my focus on immigrant students, I had a difficult time finding immigrant students who had graduated from the high schools I studied and who had matriculated into UNM. In general, the college interviewees were second-generation immigrants who were never in an English as a second language program or only in one in younger grades. This fact raises questions of college access for first-generation rural Latinx immigrant students, and it is important to recognize that their voices aren't well represented here. I ended up interviewing an average of four to five college students from the five New Mexico high schools I visited, for a total of nineteen students interviewed for this portion of the study. Details about the five schools, the number of their college participants, and their towns may be found in table 1.[2]

Table 1. School characteristics and town demographics

	Characteristics of each school			Demographics of the town for each school			
	Size	Percentage of English language learners in the district	Students enrolled in college	Size	Ethnicity and foreign-born status	Poverty rate and median income	Economy
Northern High School	~120	10%	4: 3 male, 1 female	~1,500	82% Latinx 1.3% foreign-born in 2000, 1% in 2015	~20% $32,000	Mining, agriculture, service jobs
Leon High School	~900	23%	2: 1 male, 1 female	~10,000	90% Latinx 7.3% foreign-born in 2000, 11.8% in 2015	~30% $30,000	Service jobs, federal lab or base
Rio High School	~350	43%	4 female	~1,500	90% Latinx 38.4% foreign-born in 2000, 36.8% in 2015	~30% $30,000	Agriculture
Flatlands High School	~300	18%	5: 4 male, 1 female	~1,500	75% Latinx 18.1% foreign-born in 2000, 21.7% in 2015	15% $45,000	Agriculture
Mineral High School	~200	16%	2 female	~1,500	80% Latinx 9.6% foreign-born in 2000, 12.8% in 2015	20% $35,000	Mining

Source: *United States Census Bureau*, data.census.gov/cedsci.

All interviews were transcribed by a research assistant and verified by the researcher. During the verification and coding process, I drafted analytical memos that summarized key points from each interview, including excerpts that stood out. I inductively developed codes as I read through transcripts during the verification process, creating codes in four major categories (background, family, high school, and college), with seven to sixteen subcodes in each. For instance, the category *background* captured my discussions with students around their college decision-making, the use of English and Spanish in their personal lives, their opinions of themselves as students and of living in a town or rural area versus in a city, among other topics. The category *family* captured issues such as students' first-generation status, parental work, and negative and positive support. The categories *high school* and *college* captured issues such as students' writing experiences, favorite teachers, strengths, weaknesses, and perceived barriers.

Community Cultural Wealth and Family Capital

As noted in the introduction of this book, some of the existing research on first-generation students and minoritized student populations accessing college uses a deficit perspective, aided by theories such as Pierre Bourdieu's on social and cultural capital. The narrative promulgated by this perspective is that first-generation Latinx students in the United States lack the capital to succeed in college: their parents don't know how to navigate higher education because they've never attended, Latinx students may lack the standardized variety of English privileged in the education system, and they lack the financial resources needed to afford college. In order to avoid this trap, especially as a white scholar writing about students of color, I have long situated my work in critical race theory, which works from the perspective that existing social institutions have been constructed to privilege white people at the expense of people minoritized by these systems (A. Martinez). Along with many others, I have found Tara Yosso's theory of community cultural wealth to be especially useful in exploring the experiences of minoritized students, as it shifts the lens:

> A traditional view of cultural capital is narrowly defined by White, middle class values, and is more limited than wealth—one's accumulated assets and resources. [Critical race theory] expands this view. Centering the research lens on the experiences of People of Color in critical historical context reveals accumulated assets and resources in the histories and lives of Communities of Color. (77)

Yosso defines several areas of community cultural wealth that communities of color possess: aspirational, familial, social, linguistic, resistant, and navigational capital. While I find it important to still draw attention to the barriers and challenges that students face, in making recommendations I place the burden for change primarily on the institutions and systems that help perpetuate oppression and inequality.

Exploring Student Experiences

This section discusses the participants' experiences in several areas: exploring college options, nonacademic aspects of their transitions, their high school and college writing experiences and expectations, and any heritage language instruction they received.

Choosing a College

It was clear that financial concerns strongly influenced students' considerations on where to attend college. As noted earlier, first-generation college students tend to come from lower-income families than their continuing-generation counterparts. The students in this study arguably have the additional challenge of coming from rural areas that tend to be poorer than their urban or suburban counterparts. A number of their parents worked in agriculture, whether in dairies, vegetable processing sheds, or in the fields picking crops, in professions that tend to involve long, variable, and poorly paid hours with minimal benefits. The limited money in their communities created a general aversion to taking out loans, which meant that students would base their college choices solely on financial decisions or attend college on and off, working to save up money to attend future semesters.

Over and over, I heard stories of students starting out with ambitions to attend a respected out-of-state university only to quickly moderate their expectations and end up at one of the major state universities. Lorenzo, who graduated as the valedictorian from Flatlands High School, described this shift: "early in my high school, I was like, I wanna go to UCLA or Stanford or somewhere . . . but I started realizing, you know, how competitive it is and how ACT scores matter and then scholarships and stuff like that" (ellipsis in source). Daniel, from the same school, described a similar realization: "Sophomore year, I really wanted to go to UCLA, but I saw all the things wrong with my hypothesis." Students were often disappointed with their ACT scores, which limited their scholarship access and made them question their ability to get admitted to more selective institutions. As touched on earlier, while rurality doesn't appear to correlate too closely with ACT scores, income and first-generation status certainly do (Buddin).

Even when students were not overly focused on the financial implications of moving out of state, they reported being surrounded by a culture of low expectations built in part by counselors, teachers, and other community members. Lorena from Rio High School explained that she began looking at schools on the East Coast and that her college counselor essentially told her that "[s]tate would be fine . . . for you." She also explained this negativity as a reason for why she didn't apply to a program at UNM that gave admitted students a scholarship and guaranteed their admission to medical school as long as they met certain requirements.

Personal Transition

If students are able to overcome financial barriers or other negative barriers mentioned in the previous section, then they make both a personal and an academic transition to college that can be shaped by their proximity to their families and communities, their high school academic preparation, and the type of support and instruction they receive in college.

Because rural students usually have to move away from their towns and families to attend a four-year institution, they do not have the same choice that suburban and urban students often do to attend college in their hometown. At the same time, they have to transition from a small, close-knit community to one where they are surrounded by new people, both around town and in the large lecture halls common at large four-year research institutions. Some, like Joanne from Mineral High School, noted how living in a large city presented challenges like increased crime. Homesickness seemed to claim a lot of the students who went off to college, and students like Susanna from Northern High School shared stories of students returning home after a year or so.

The desire to return home was shaped in part by students' families. Most were positive, encouraging their children to go away in order to seek opportunity; on the other hand, some were sad to see their children go. Guadalupe from Rio High School described this tension and how her mom encouraged her to go: "she didn't want us to leave all the way to another county cause, that's kinda Mexican ties: you want your family to be close, but you also don't want them just to end up exactly where she was. She didn't want us just to be where you're just working [as a farmworker] shed by shed and season by season." Another Rio High School student, Leticia, explained how her single mother, whom she saw as an independent feminist, initially failed to support her decision to head off to college: "she didn't want me to leave, . . . and I told her I got accepted to UNM. It was the happiest moment for me, but seeing sadness in her face kind of was hard for me. My first semester was really hard. I didn't feel the support from her. At one point I was just like, no, I don't think she wants me here, and there was a point where she did tell me like, 'You left me.'" One could imagine how being accused of abandoning their family could make students feel more intensely homesick and a stronger desire to return home. While the first-generation college students I interviewed made overwhelmingly positive references to how their families encouraged them to seek a better future in college, it is important to note that these students are the minority in that they made the decision to attend college away from home and had persisted through at least a year of college by the time I talked with them.

Several interviewed students participated in the College Assistance Migrant Program (CAMP), which is a federally funded scholarship program for children of migrant farm workers that aims to facilitate their transition to college. This program focuses on building a learning community, and CAMP students are placed in classes with other CAMP students, take a few classes in their first summer together, and receive special tutors and financial support. Those who participated in the program found it vital to their first-year success in part because of the personal connections they made, as evident in this comment by Leticia: "I've made really great friends, and I feel like we all come from rural high schools, so we were able to work things out together." Nonetheless, the program, like any program supporting college transitions, does not have a perfect success rate. Leticia noted that the other two students from Rio High School who participated in CAMP with her left college during their first year. While the CAMP program focuses on the first year of college, there are other college pipeline programs that work earlier in students' educational pathways to promote successful transitions—two more common federally funded programs are Gear Up and Upward Bound. Both are aimed at students from low-income backgrounds, and Upward Bound is also dedicated to serving first-generation students.

Writing in High School

The students I interviewed often found their academic preparation to be more lacking in the sciences and in math than in English and writing. As Leonardo explained, "[I]in some aspects, I felt really prepared, especially when it came to my writing skills and stuff like that, but math—it was one thing the school district in general struggles with." He expanded on this: "[My English teachers] did a really good job of preparing us. There were a lot of things that kids were struggling with in 101 and 102, like . . . constructing the paper, . . . having it concise, having a thesis and everything tied into the thesis and stuff, and honestly, every time, I try and go visit [my teacher] every time I go back, and every time I tell her 'You completely prepared me for college.'" As evident from Leonardo's comment, the quality of individual teachers makes an important difference. Rural students often have more limited access to advanced and dual credit classes. One study reports that forty-seven percent of rural districts did not have students enrolled in Advanced Placement (AP) classes, compared with five percent of suburban and three percent of urban districts (Gagnon and Mattingly 1)—and even when such classes were offered, students in advanced classes sometimes reported instruction of mixed quality. For instance, Concepcion from Rio High School said that she took dual credit classes but that they "really just babied us cause we were high schoolers." Similarly, Martin from Flatlands High School was disappointed in his AP English class: "I think the only AP class we had was English. And the school actually paid for us to take the AP exam, and they didn't prepare us at all for the exam. The professor wasn't the best by no means, he was very tangential and didn't really hit the bullet points for what an AP class should be hitting." On the other hand, Raul from Flatlands recalled that the teacher of his gifted class prepared him well for college writing expectations:

> [If] your only strategy is [to] give me a five-paragraph essay with an introduction and conclusion at the end, what are you gonna produce? Who knows. But if you're really explicit about how many sources you want and, oh, a paragraph doesn't have to be five sentences, you can actually organize your paper by themes or follow a logical argument, or maybe make a list, or do a description. There's different types of expository text. And, you know, I didn't know that until Miss showed me.

It is evident from these comments that individual teachers can make a huge difference in students' preparation for college.

Students primarily reported writing in high school about literature and not about topics tied to their small-town identities. Some, like Guadalupe, supported this outside focus because reading literature about different people exposed them to new ideas: "I was more interested in the basic literature. I was more excited reading about Shakespeare and everything else about that than about a small-town farming community, I guess because partially maybe I was just already living in one, so I was just like, I wanna explore something else that I don't have to see on a daily basis."

Writing in College

The differences between writing in high school and in college varied for the students I talked to, and their experiences were shaped not only by their high school preparation but also by their major in college. As noted elsewhere (Applebee and Langer; Ruecker, *Transiciones*), high school students tend to write much shorter essays than their counterparts in college. Multiple students explained that they wished they had written longer essays in high school. Martin, a highly accomplished student who was finishing medical school at the time of our interview and who had been used to getting As in high school, was shocked when asked to write a twenty-page essay in one of his first college classes. He explained that "I probably wrote more in that paper than I did in all of high school" and was surprised to end up with a C.

On the other hand, some students did not find writing in college to be as different as anticipated. Joanne explained that it was a bit more advanced, but not completely different: "It hasn't been too different, but it has been a little bit more difficult because you actually have to research a little bit more. You have to go in depth and discuss. This past semester I did a report. We have to have our introduction, of course, our results. That was different. The way it was set up was different, so I guess you would say it's a little bit difficult." The length of assigned papers and increased research expectations were cited by other students, such as Lorenzo, as the main difference between writing in high school and in college.

Maria from Flatlands High School said she didn't have to write much in college, except for some writing in her composition, art history, and history classes. She was somewhat surprised about the lack of writing assignments but noted that she was majoring in science, so it made sense why she was not writing as much as anticipated. Elsewhere, Guadalupe noted that in college she had to do a "lot less writing than [she] expected," in part because she had credit for her first-year writing classes. In contrast, Jesus from Leon High School explained that he wrote a lot in college because it was a strong focus in his major: "I'm a history and political science major, so that's all we do." Consequently, the need to become a good writer was more urgent for him: "it's just hard to have a major where all your work is judged by how good you write."

An important part of first-generation student experiences, especially for first-generation minoritized students, is feeling that one is not as good or as prepared as other students at the university—this impostor syndrome can be exacerbated by the deficit discourses surrounding these students during their education (Shapiro). Concepcion felt like one of the weaker links in her study group in her engineering classes. As she struggled with some of the more advanced classes, she received discouraging feedback: "[I] got told a lot last year to switch my major, so that didn't help either because it's like, well, . . . I don't already believe in myself, and if you guys don't believe in me, then well, maybe you're right, maybe I should switch my major." Elsewhere, Miguel from Rio High School explained that his first-year writing class was easier than his high school English classes but that he did a college honors class that was much harder than what he had experienced in high school, and in it he recognized that he was behind his peers: "I didn't do very well on my essays. They weren't at the level that they needed to be [for] a college student. So yeah I did struggle. I had to work. I feel like I had to work extra hard than the rest of my peers to get at that level that I needed to be just to get the credit for the course."

Heritage Language Development

In general, bilingual students did not recall much development of their Spanish throughout their K–12 schooling. Concepcion didn't mind this, saying that she was able to maintain and develop her Spanish at home. Similarly, Daniel recalled deliberately doing poorly on his college language placement exam so he could be in the easier Spanish class. However, others expressed sadness and frustration that the school system did not take their first language literacy development more seriously. Leticia described her emotions when struggling in an AP Spanish class:

> [A] lot of the material was too advanced for me, I feel. And the only time that when I would go home, I would just practice my Spanish, and it was sad. It would get to a point where there was words that I didn't know in Spanish, and I felt frustrated because I couldn't tell them to my mom. I was kinda losing my Spanish in a way, and I wish there would have been more literature where I could have read in Spanish.

At UNM, Leticia was a Spanish and Chicanx studies major. In our interview she noted how her college classes really helped her to open her eyes to some of her previous experiences and to develop a criticality toward race, language, and culture that she did not have the opportunity to develop in high school. While Lorena from Leon High School didn't express sadness in the way that Leticia did, she found the Spanish class she took at UNM eye-opening: "So going into those classes, it was definitely interesting because I was learning more of the technical side of [Spanish]. It wasn't just speaking and reading it. I was learning actually how to write it, which was a little bit of a challenge at first, especially because I had so many bad habits that I didn't realize I had." Lorena is another example of a student who struggled with reading and writing in a language she had grown up with because it had been ignored in her schooling so long. While a failure to support students' heritage language development is not confined to rural schools, schools may be limited in their ability to develop dedicated classes for students if there are only a few students in a school that speak a particular language at home. Mineral High School worked around this restriction by offering an online AP course. The assistant principal described the positive impact of this course: "a lot of kids honestly did not realize being bilingual was a gift, and when we first started introducing that AP Spanish class . . . it made them feel wonderful, so we need to embrace that."

The Cultural Wealth That Supports First-Generation Latinx Student Success

The students I interviewed, the ones who decided to attend UNM and were successful there, were not the norm in their communities. For these students, the following seemed to be the most important factors shaping their cultural capital: people who push them to pursue continued education, scholarship programs, and internal motivation. Leticia offered an example of the first factor when she responded to my query about what made her successful: "Definitely the opportunities given to me such as the CAMP program but also having people, you know, that care about me and have pushed me, like my family. I feel it has been the most important thing after my mom realized the good things I was doing here. I feel like now she's like, 'No, don't worry, don't call me; you go do your homework.'" Although Leticia drew on a variety of sources of cultural capital to succeed in college, her family is at the heart of her statement. As noted earlier, her mom initially discouraged her but later helped build familial capital by supporting her and encouraging her to focus on college. Programs like CAMP and Upward Bound, which build social and linguistic capital by surrounding students with an encouraging community of learners and tutors, clearly made a difference in some of the participants' lives. Students also benefited from the navigational capital provided by these programs, where they received more specialized advising that helped them figure out what classes to register for as well as personalized tutoring. Various students also talked about individual classes or teachers that helped boost their linguistic capital, whether it was the Spanish classes they took in college or a particularly supportive writing teacher they had in high school. Raul, for example, grew a lot as a writer in a particular high school class, learning that there was a world of writing beyond the five-paragraph essay.

As described earlier, financial concerns were at the forefront for many students, who consistently reiterated that the state lottery scholarship, and in a few cases, a more prestigious one like UNM's Presidential Scholarship, helped alleviate some of their financial concerns. Even among the students I interviewed, there was a general aversion to student debt, so it is evident that whatever institutions can do to help students avoid debt is useful. Unfortunately, in part because of poor advising, many students didn't know about the scholarships available to them. However, the successful students I interviewed referred to some areas of social capital that helped give them access: a teacher who took the initiative to inform them, a visit by a CAMP or other scholarship program recruiter, a sibling who attended college before them, or sometimes just their own initiative. Concepcion remarked that "no one told me about the Daniels Fund scholarship or any of that that's offered here. I had to like, I literally just typed in scholarships for high school students, which is kinda sad because I wish I, like

I'm always on my sister's butt now, like you need to do community service, you need to go out there, you need to get good grades." Here, we see Concepcion passing this info on to her younger sibling, an accumulation of familial capital among siblings that will lift the whole family in pursuing college.

Although Lorena from Rio High School initially responded to my question about what made her successful by saying, "I don't think I'm very successful," after I questioned this, she responded more fully:

> I pride myself in saying that I did really well considering the background that I've had, and the help that I've had. I think I did better than most students. I think just the biggest reason is I don't really have the luxury of not being successful in what I'm doing. . . . I know I have to go to college and I have to go to work; I need the money and I need my education so that I can provide for my mom and for my sisters and for myself. Because if not, then what's the point . . . why did my parents struggle to bring me here and go through all that hard work and all that pain?

Students like Lorena emanated a capital of resistance that manifested as a resilience to succeed even as particular systems worked against them, and their aspirational capital was built and sustained through the sacrifices their families made to give them access to a better life. For students like these, seemingly negative factors often had a positive impact on their motivation and desire for success. For instance, Leonardo talked about how negative stereotypes surrounding his town motivated him to go out and resist them: "we don't like that people thought so bad of us. So like me especially, my goal was to not necessarily get out of the town, but go be somewhere else and be able to come back and maybe one day to try to make a change, maybe try and make it better for the future." Other students noted how having to work long hours in low-paying, physically demanding agricultural jobs motivated them to seek something better for themselves. When asked if his long work hours in a local dairy during high school and college hindered his success, Daniel strongly countered this assumption: "No, not at all. I think it actually it helped me a lot because, if you've ever worked in a dairy, it's awful, dude." While students like Daniel respected the sacrifices their parents made to pave a better future for them, they did not want to be stuck in the same labor conditions.

The Role of Writing Teachers and Administrators

It was encouraging to see that students generally found their English classes in high school helpful for writing they were expected to do in college. High school

English teachers also served other important roles as well, informing students about scholarship opportunities or mentoring them through the process of writing essays for scholarships or admissions applications. Nonetheless, it is evident that high school English teachers could have done more to prepare students for college expectations. Often high school district curricula focus on the quantity of writing experiences, having students write short essays regularly instead of providing a longer-term focus on a larger piece of writing, a trend that we see increasing in first-year college writing classes. Some of the teachers at Flatlands High School, for instance, expressed concerns about the rushed nature of writing tasks in their district curriculum. In another vein, a few students mentioned that they would have liked to have gotten a better sense of what college writing was like from their teachers. At the college level, there are several practices that writing program teachers and administrators can embrace to help their rural first-generation Latinx students transition to college.

Support Student Success in and beyond the Classroom

Students entering college were consistently overwhelmed when they experienced large classes and uncaring professors in an unfamiliar community. Writing classes may be the smallest classes first-year students will take, so it is vital that teachers make the most of this opportunity, building a strong community through regular conferencing and through collaborative activities like peer review. Additionally, several students explained how programs like CAMP helped them become more comfortable in college and overcome the challenges posed by homesickness. First-year learning communities are another, more widely available option that have often been integrated with writing programs (LaFrance). Michael Day, Tawanda Gipson, and Christopher P. Parker have detailed the creation of a peer advocate program that placed undergraduate students as mentors and advocates in first-year writing classes: in addition to attending weekly meetings with program coordinators and attending class regularly, peer advocates led study sessions and pizza parties and were able to support students in unique ways. Given the earlier discussion about ACT and SAT scores, first-generation rural Latinx students may be more likely to end up in developmental classes, and it is vital that writing programs continue their long tradition of innovating in this area, offering stretch and studio options that help students transition into college writing while obtaining academic credit for their work (Davila and Elder).

Offer Clear and Supportive Feedback

While some of the students I interviewed came into college confident about their writing abilities and surprised at the lack of writing they were asked to do, many expressed shock at the amount and type of writing they had to do and were frustrated when receiving lower grades than they were used to without receiving concrete guidance on how they might improve, a tendency that students encountered while writing across the curriculum. Fortunately, a recent survey of 216 students at a regional campus of a large Midwestern university found that the vast majority of first-year writing instructors are providing feedback and that their students are reading this feedback (ninety-four percent) for various reasons, including the desire to earn higher grades, to understand the grade they received, or to improve their writing overall (Cunningham 15, 30). As we have seen throughout this essay, first-generation Latinx students tend to come with strong aspirational capital that helps them succeed against the odds—thus, they are likely to take feedback to heart and use it to improve their writing.

Help Build Students' Navigational Capital

Rural first-generation students often don't have access to familial networks or sufficient advising in institutional settings to help them navigate the myriad college-related bureaucracies. Writing programs should be transparent with their placement processes and work to ensure students know their options—simply posting this information on a website is not sufficient. Similarly, the writing class should be a place where students are familiarized with tutoring services and other academic support opportunities as well as with learning management systems. Simply putting a note about the writing center or library resources on the syllabus is not enough; classes can visit the writing center and library, integrate tutoring within the class, or invite representatives from these different departments to come and talk with the class. The aforementioned peer advocacy program is another way that students may be introduced to campus resources (Day et al.). Chances are, students are not getting this support through advisers or in classes in other disciplines that may not have traditionally had as strong a focus on student success as our field has.

Help Students Critically Read Their Experiences

Rural communities tend to be politically and socially conservative, and as such, Latinx first-generation students likely won't have access to readings and discussions in their high schools that can help empower them and their communities in the face of prejudice. Consequently, writing programs and related programs at universities can help raise awareness of how certain populations have traditionally been excluded from the education system through various policies. One of the students I interviewed was able to identify a variety of inequalities in her town that other students didn't notice, such as who owned the farms versus who worked on them and which students took AP classes: "my eyes opened, you know, when I got here because of Chicano studies and how I was exposed to other things, and a lot of people were very radical, and I was exposed to their thoughts, and I had to really think about what is affecting me and how am I as a person or how am I a student of color in an institution that is not designed for us." From the Conference on College Composition and Communication's "Students' Right to Their Own Language" statement in the 1970s, to work by James Berlin and others in the 1980s, to the rise of translingual approaches in the most recent decade, writing scholars and teachers have been conscious of raising students' awareness of societal inequities while validating the different languages and cultures students bring to our classrooms.

Challenge Harmful University Policies

I have long been influenced by Linda Adler-Kassner's work promoting an activist stance among writing program administrators, which means engaging in story-changing work by articulating values and principles and building alliances to push back against misguided policies, a practice more likely to be successful at a local level (184). Based on my research and teaching experiences, I found that the policies promoted by organizations like Complete College America, such as the ones pushing students to take fifteen credit hours, privilege students who come to college better prepared academically and who come from higher socioeconomic classes. For instance, I regularly encountered students taking fifteen or eighteen credit hours while working thirty to forty hours a week—an unsustainable workload, especially for students who were adapting to the different academic expectations of college. I have sought to voice these concerns in various venues, ranging from provost-level committee meetings to editorials in local newspapers (Ruecker, "Lower Enrollment?"). Simply decrying the injustices of these policies in journals and at conferences is not enough.

Rural first-generation Latinx students have many challenges to accessing college and succeeding as college writers: financial and familial challenges, inconsistent writing instruction, the lack of first-language support in our education system, assessment bias, and other structural inequities. Nonetheless, the students profiled in this essay have shown that they can be adept at building the networks and cultural capital they need to succeed in college and beyond, and their successes have been supported through writing programs and classes designed to truly value and learn from the linguistic and cultural resources these students bring to our institutions and classrooms.

Notes

I would like to acknowledge funding from UNM's RAC Grant Program and from the Spencer Foundation and the National Academy of Education. Any opinions, findings, and conclusions expressed in this essay are my own.

1. In line with moves by other institutions during the pandemic, ACT and SAT scores do not currently appear to be required for scholarship eligibility but were in place when I conducted this study.

2. This research was approved by UNM's IRB and by the superintendent of each school district. All high school and participant names are pseudonyms. The quotations from student interviews included in this essay have been edited for readability.

Works Cited

Adler-Kassner, Linda. *The Activist WPA: Changing Stories about Writing and Writers.* Utah State UP, 2008.

Applebee, Arthur N., and Judith A. Langer. "EJ Extra: What Is Happening in the Teaching of Writing?" *The English Journal*, vol. 98, no. 5, 2009, pp. 18–28.

Arbeit, Caren A., et al. "New American Undergraduates: Enrollment Trends and Age at Arrival of Immigrant and Second-Generation Students." US Department of Education, National Center for Education Statistics, 2016, nces.ed.gov/pubs2017/2017414.pdf. Statistics in Brief.

Berlin, James. "Rhetoric and Ideology in the Writing Class." *College English*, vol. 50, no. 5, 1988, pp. 477–94.

Bruening, Erika. "Doing It on Their Own: The Experiences of Two Latino English Language Learners in a Low-Incidence Context." *Revisiting Education in the New Latino Diaspora*, edited by Edmund T. Hamann et al., Information Age Publishing, 2015, pp. 29–48.

Buddin, Richard. "ACT Composite Test Scores by Student Background and School Location." ACT, 2014, www.act.org/content/dam/act/unsecured/documents/Info-Brief-2014-17.pdf.

Conference on College Composition and Communication. "Students' Right to Their Own Language." 1974. National Council of Teachers of English, prod-ncte-cdn.azureedge.net/nctefiles/groups/cccc/newsrtol.pdf.

Cunningham, Jennifer M. "Composition Students' Opinions of and Attention to Instructor Feedback." *Journal of Response to Writing*, vol. 5, no. 1, 2019, pp. 4–38.

Davila, Bethany A., and Cristyn L. Elder. "Welcoming Linguistic Diversity and Saying Adios to Remediation: Stretch and Studio Composition at a Hispanic-Serving Institution." *Composition Forum*, vol. 35, 2017, compositionforum.com/issue/35/new-mexico.php.

Day, Michael, et al. "Undergraduate Mentors as Agents of Engagement: Peer Advocates in First-Year Writing Courses." *Retention, Persistence, and Writing Programs*, edited by Todd Ruecker et al., Utah State UP, 2017, pp. 237–56.

"Factsheets: First Generation Students." *Postsecondary National Policy Institute*, 2018, pnpi.org/first-generation-students/.

"Fifteen to Finish / Stay on Track." *Complete College America*, completecollege.org/strategy/15-to-finish/.

Gagnon, Douglas J., and Marybeth J. Mattingly. "Limited Access to AP Courses for Students in Smaller and More Isolated Rural School Districts." *Carsey Research*, vol. 80, 2015, pp. 1–5.

Howley, Caitlin, et al. "College Enrollment and Persistence in Rural Pennsylvania Schools." US Department of Education, Institute of Education Sciences / Regional Educational Laboratory Mid-Atlantic, 2014, ies.ed.gov/ncee/edlabs/regions/midatlantic/pdf/REL_2015053.pdf.

Irvin, Matthew J., et al. "Educational Barriers of Rural Youth: Relation of Individual and Contextual Difference Variables." *Journal of Career Assessment*, vol. 20, no. 1, 2012, pp. 71–87.

Johnson, Jerry, et al. *Why Rural Matters, 2013–2014: The Condition of Rural Education in the Fifty States*. Rural School and Community Trust, 2014, www.ruraledu.org/user_uploads/file/2013-14-Why-Rural-Matters.pdf.

LaFrance, Michelle. "Linked Writing Courses." Council of Writing Program Administrators, 2010, comppile.org/wpa/bibliographies/Bib14/LaFrance.pdf. WPA-CompPile Research Bibliographies 14.

Martinez, Aja Y. "Critical Race Theory: Its Origins, History, and Importance to the Discourses and Rhetorics of Race." *Frame: Journal of Literary Studies*, vol. 27, no. 2, 2014, pp. 9–27.

Martinez, Elias. "Fragmented Community, Fragmented Schools: The Implementation of Educational Policy for Latino Immigrants." *Education in the New Latino Diaspora: Policy and the Politics of Identity*, edited by Stanton Wortham et al., Ablex Publishing, 2002, pp. 143–67.

Ruecker, Todd. "Lower Enrollment? New Policies Push Students Out." *Santa Fe New Mexican*, 6 Oct. 2018, www.santafenewmexican.com/opinion/my_view/lower-enrollment-new-policies-push-students-out/article_1852a5bd-e553-547a-aaa7-b4f164a9b241.html.

———. *Transiciones: Pathways of Latinas and Latinos Writing in High School and College*. Utah State UP, 2015.

"Scholarship Office." *The University of New Mexico*, scholarship.unm.edu/.

Shapiro, Shawna. "'Words That You Said Got Bigger': English Language Learners' Lived Experiences of Deficit Discourse." *Research in the Teaching of English*, vol. 48, no. 4, 2014, pp. 386–406.

"Table 326.10." *Digest of Education Statistics. National Center for Education Statistics*, US Department of Education, 2017, nces.ed.gov/programs/digest/d17/tables/dt17_326.10.asp.

Yosso, Tara J. "Whose Culture Has Capital? A Critical Race Theory Discussion of Community Cultural Wealth." *Race, Ethnicity and Education*, vol. 8, no. 1, 2005, pp. 69–91.

Finding First-Generation Students through an Intersectional Approach to Institutional and Programmatic Data

Beth A. Towle

As one of the only native Hoosiers in my graduate program at Purdue University in Indiana, I assumed that many of the students I would see in my first-year composition classroom would be like I had been as a student: rural, working-class, and first-generation. Not many people from my small high school went to college, but of those who did, many of them went to Purdue to study agriculture or environmental sciences. However, many of my students at Purdue were actually quite well-to-do, hailing from the nicer suburbs of Chicago and Indianapolis. They wanted to study engineering partly because that was what their parents, many of whom were engineers, wanted them to study and partly because they thought they would make good money as engineers. They dressed in laid-back but expensive clothes, and most of them arrived at Purdue with banked Advanced Placement credits. One or two of my students each semester had what Harry Denny, the current director of the Purdue Writing Lab, calls "farm kid drag," a telltale slow walk and worn jeans that gave them away. Some of my students were also student athletes who openly talked about being the first person in their family to go to college. These working-class, first-generation students existed, but they hid in a crowd that looked just like the population at my previous institution, an elite private university. By walking into that first-year composition classroom at Purdue expecting first-generation students who looked like my former high school classmates, I wasn't seeing the first-gen students who were actually there.

In the Purdue Writing Lab, where I worked as a graduate tutor and administrative coordinator, I and other staff members found that our understanding of first-generation students at Purdue was caught up in issues of class and race that the larger university had mostly let go unexamined. Partnering with Purdue's Office of Institutional Research, Assessment, and Effectiveness (OIRAE) to assess our work with first-generation students made us realize that our assumptions were problematic and needed to be complicated by reality. It might be easy to assume that many of the students who come to a writing center are first-generation because of the misconception that writing centers primarily support remedial learning and that first-gen students usually need remedial learning. However, most writing centers are likely not collecting generational data as part of their regular assessment and record keeping, and so it can be hard to test such an assumption. At Purdue, we customized the online writing center scheduling tool *WC Online* so that students can provide their home languages, their preferred names, and their countries of origin when they register for writing center support. But we did not collect data about race, class, or gender through the *WC Online* intake form. These identifying categories are where OIRAE comes in. Using the writing lab's data to track anonymized student ID numbers alongside institutional data allowed us to see the types of identity markers that we would miss if we relied only on *WC Online* data.

However, identity was not the initial reason (or at least not the primary reason) that the writing lab collaborated with OIRAE. Upon his arrival in 2015 as the lab's new director, Denny ensured that we were able to partner with OIRAE to make the best case for the lab's presence on campus and to show how the lab affects patterns of retention, grades, and GPAs. Additionally, because the majority of students who come to the lab are international students and L2 writers, we wanted to make sure we could track grade and retention trends based on country of origin and language preparedness. Race, gender, and parental income levels, then, were merely other ways to organize and understand the data. But examining these demographic markers revealed to us the error in our assumption that we were seeing a lot of first-generation students in the lab.

In this essay, I explore how the lab has partnered with OIRAE to better understand student populations and track their success as it connects to their use of the lab. I focus in particular on how the lab has been able to better understand its work with working-class and other marginalized students, many of whom are first-generation, through the use of large-scale assessments, and how that work has both helped and hindered the ability of the lab to reach out to at-risk students. My goal is to complicate narratives of both assessment and first-generation student success to show how the term *first-generation* masks the reality of struggling students. Finally, I provide recommendations for writing programs that want to engage in ethical assessment plans that highlight marginalized or at-risk student populations. My hope is not that readers will model their assessments directly on the Purdue Writing Lab's assessment, but rather that they will use the framework provided by this essay for thinking about fair and insightful assessment efforts for individual writing programs and student needs.

First-Generation Students in Higher Education and Writing Programs

First-generation students face hardships that their continuing-generation peers simply do not, and many scholars and academic advising professionals recommend that they are best served by close mentoring relationships, which writing centers can provide. Yet providing that mentoring can be difficult because first-generation students are socialized to fear seeking out additional support, as doing so might make them seem less competent than their peers.

Definitions of first-generation students vary. Some institutions and researchers define first-generation students as students whose parents did not obtain a four-year degree but might have attended some college or earned an associate's degree. Others take the stricter view that first-generation students are those whose parents did not attend any college. Lee Ward and colleagues complicate these definitions by focusing on how first-generation students are often affected by three primary dimensions of the social structure: class, culture, and race or ethnicity. Ward and colleagues argue that the lack of cultural capital (using Pierre Bourdieu's definition) among students whose parents have no college education significantly affects their experiences in college (69). Additionally, first-generation students who are from lower socioeconomic backgrounds or are part of another marginalized minority group are doubly affected by disparities in education experiences. The National Center for Education Statistics, in its 2018 report on first-generation students, distinguishes first-generation students from two other groups: continuing-generation students whose parents attended some college, and students whose parents have earned bachelor's degrees (Cataldi et al. 2). Unfortunately, institutions do not always make these distinctions. When I was an undergraduate, I received the same first-generation student support as students who were upper-middle-class and whose parents had associate's degrees, even though I was from a working-class background and my parents had not attended college. My experience reflects the ways in which first-generation students can be made even less visible by institutional structures that erase their unique cultural backgrounds.

Additionally, definitions of first-generation students rely heavily on standard two-parent family structures. Students who may have an estranged parent with a college degree but who live and primarily interact with a parent with no college experience are as disadvantaged in terms of cultural capital as students with two parents who only graduated from high school. Nontraditional students, especially ones returning to college after years of working, also complicate definitions of first-generation students because parental influence no longer affects their lives as directly. Divorce, the death of a parent, foster care, and late-age adoption all profoundly affect the cultural capital of students entering college, which means that using a simplistic family model to define first-generation students is highly problematic. Therefore, we need to reexamine our definitions to better understand these unique student populations.

One of the foremost problems with the term *first-generation student* is that it often gets conflated with *low-income* or *working-class student* as a descriptor for students who come from poorer backgrounds. To avoid identifying students as poor when the word *poor* is so loaded in our political moment, institutions instead position these students as first-generation because many of them are, in fact, the first people in their families to attend college. As Ward and colleagues note, class is part of many first-generation students' identities (70), and so it makes sense that these two descriptors get conflated by institutions, researchers, and even students themselves. This type of conflation is unfortunate, and, as I argue later, a possible area in which writing and education scholars can push back by more directly addressing poverty. Additionally, the conflation of class and generational status further complicates our ideas of who counts as a first-generation student. All these problems of definition make data-driven assessments incredibly difficult, even at Purdue, where we struggled to figure out what we could track cleanly as an issue of either class or generational status.

Despite all these issues of definition, we do know that the lack of cultural capital for first-generation students profoundly affects their ability to succeed in college, especially on campuses where they are insufficiently supported. First-generation students struggle with finding and utilizing support and resources (Engle and Tinto), understanding assignment guidelines and instructor expectations (Collier and Morgan), and developing self-efficacy (Ramos-Sánchez and Nichols). Citing the National Center for Education Statistics, Emily Cataldi and colleagues report that first-generation students are less likely to attain a degree within six years and were significantly more likely to leave their institution than peers whose parents had earned a bachelor's degree (8–9). The statistics also reveal that first-generation students are less likely to attend college in the first place and have lower postsecondary graduation rates (6). First-generation students face an uphill battle before they even set foot on campus, and often they find the adjustment to college incredibly difficult.

Along with the financial and professional barriers first-generation students face, they also bear emotional burdens. First-generation students often suffer from impostor syndrome or self-esteem issues, and they struggle to fit into their new environments (London). Worse, their new lives as college students or graduates can alienate them from their home communities and families (Lubrano). First-generation students end up being squeezed out of their own comfort emotionally, physically, and culturally in ways that can be detrimental to their success in academia and beyond.

First-generation and working-class students can particularly struggle with writing or with courses that involve writing assignments. Their identifications with home or multiple languages, the cultural aspects of writing and literacy, and the fraught nature of language rights all make writing an especially vulnerable task for students who straddle the line between their home and new academic communities. Students from minority populations are at even higher risk for being affected by their institutions' classist and racist expectations of what counts as good academic writing (Guerra; Inoue). Meanwhile, writing centers, in their efforts to avoid being perceived as spaces for remedial education, are in danger of alienating students who are already marginalized by their universities (Denny et al.; Salem). The fear and shame of being seen as needing additional help to navigate academia can have a profound effect on first-generation students. While scholarship has taken a turn toward challenging the white supremacy and classism in writing programs (Inoue; Perryman-Clark and Craig) and writing centers (Denny; Greenfield and Rowan), the overwhelming majority of institutions and writing courses are still invested in Standard American English and its white, middle-class ways of communicating and writing. It is up to programs and their administrators to try to challenge those notions within their own spaces. Assessment is one way programs can attempt to better understand their own culpability in perpetuating the standards that undermine first-generation and other marginalized students in writing classes and writing centers.

First-Generation Students and Big Data

At Purdue, about twenty percent of incoming students are first-generation (Zehner 1), which is below the national average. These students come from a wide variety of places and backgrounds, including from suburbs and cities across America (especially the suburbs of large Midwestern cities) and, because of Purdue's strong engineering programs, from all over the world. Because Purdue is a land grant university with a strong commitment to agriculture, it enrolls in-state or Midwestern students who come from farms and small towns. The university also has some nontraditional domestic students. This vast range of student experiences means there is no one-fit model for first-generation students at Purdue, which is actually a positive thing in terms of shaping education to be universally designed and more aware of differences between students. However, this variety makes it hard for Purdue to track its first-generation populations, despite the best efforts of institutional research.

As higher education becomes more infatuated with big data—for both good and ill—Purdue has increased the number of ways in which it tracks student progress and success. Purdue became well-known in higher education in the early-to-middle 2010s for developing and using *Forecast*, a system that tracks students to predict their success. The university has the ability to track every time a student swipes their ID card at the gym, at campus events, and in the dining hall. And because most of the institutional information and forms that Purdue students access online are behind a log-in wall, student ID numbers are associated with many other services, including the writing lab's appointment system through *WC Online*, which students can only access through their Purdue student accounts. Using that information allows Purdue not only to study current patterns but to actually predict student success. So if, say, a student attends five visiting speaker events on campus, perhaps their GPA will be .05 better than their less engaged peers. This system has been criticized by faculty and students for treating students as data points rather than as complex beings whose successes or failures could be attributed to a huge range of personal and academic experiences. However, the university has claimed that this type of tracking has allowed it to improve the experience of students and contributes to increased GPAs, retention, and graduation rates.

The use of big data in higher education has made it easier to understand what contributes to student success and has also flattened the actual lived experiences of students. While it is helpful to see how student usage of campus resources affects GPAs and retention rates, these data do not account for how helpful students found those resources on a more personal level. Moreover, the university fails to track other day-to-day details of student lives that can contribute to or derail success, such as family problems, peer interactions, health issues, and emotional well-being. Because many of these external issues have a large impact on the experiences of marginalized students in particular, the use of success-tracking data can be especially problematic for students who are first-generation, working-class or impoverished, racial or ethnic minorities, or who have disabilities.

The use of large-scale, big-data assessments also contributes to students' and faculty's experiences of the university as a kind of surveillance state. The constant tracking of student IDs is legal and less ethically problematic than tracking students by name because IDs are dissociated from students' names. However, this does not mean that students' anonymity is completely protected. Issues of data security and breaches make it clear that someone could find and expose ID-name pairings, which would allow information about grades, retention, use of the gym and health center, and even the use of the writing center to be leaked onto the Internet. These concerns make universities complicit should something go wrong, and we must consider these ethical complications when it comes to using big data as a way of doing assessments.

While these ethical issues are important for how we track and engage with student data, there are also some benefits to the collection of institutional data. The annual common data sets that are regularly compiled by universities for public consumption help students, staff, faculty, and the community better understand student populations. Additional data about student preparedness and the forms of cultural capital they bring with them can also be helpful. For example, although Purdue has been seen as a school for the children of white farmers for many decades, the average family income for a white student at Purdue is close to $100,000, which makes many of these students relatively privileged compared to their peers at other state institutions. Meanwhile, the average family income for black students was about half that amount, which shows not only the astoundingly large gap in privilege between white and black students at Purdue but also the importance of understanding data through the prism of intersectionality, as defined by Kimberlé Crenshaw (1243). The link between in-state and out-of-state residential status is also revealing when examined through the data. Incoming in-state students at Purdue not only were at a greater socioeconomic disadvantage but also had lower SAT scores and high school GPAs on average. While Purdue may use a broad definition of first-generation students, using predictors related to class, education preparedness, and race and ethnicity can help us see which students are truly at-risk and lack the cultural capital that typically defines first-generation student experiences in college. Therefore, when we began doing assessments in the Purdue Writing Lab, we focused on looking at data through these prisms, rather than simply looking at first-generation students overall. In fact, simply looking at generational status did not tell us much about those students' needs.

Writing Lab Assessments

The assessment of writing programs, which includes everything from first-year writing to writing-across-the-curriculum programs and writing centers, has been a central part of writing program administration work since its inception,[1] although increased pressure to test and assess students in recent decades has made this work even more necessary and often propelled by external forces (Harrington). Assessment serves multiple purposes: it helps place students into writing courses, measures changes in a student's writing during a set period of time, and allows programs to see if students' results and progress match stated program goals and outcomes. Assessment for writing centers also includes tracking data such as center usage, types of written work brought to the center by students and from what courses and majors, and student satisfaction with the center. Neal Lerner notes the importance of this work in his influential article "Counting Beans and Making Beans Count," arguing that "[i]n the short term, our institutional survival is often dependent upon simple, straightforward numbers" (3). As dramatic as this statement sounds, it is true. At a time when programs are increasingly asked to demonstrate their usefulness to institutions undergoing austerity measures and when education is being undermined by political and social forces, writing centers, which are often run by non-tenure-track faculty and staff members and staffed by peer tutors, are especially vulnerable to the ax, and so they must justify their existence. Assessment, though, does not need to be performed under pressure. It can also reveal how writing centers set and reach their goals and how those goals reflect larger institutional missions (Schendel and Macauley; Thompson), allowing writing centers to reflect on their practices. Assessment can also be a form of research, and as writing center administrators are often disadvantaged in terms of the amount of labor they can allot to research, assessment can be an especially cost- and labor-efficient form of local research with the potential to reflect or even change practices in the larger field of writing studies.

The Purdue Writing Lab has been collecting and reporting on data since its inception in the mid-1970s. Early writing lab reports tracked the number of students who visited the lab, as well as repeat visits and reported instructor satisfaction. As new technology allowed the lab to better track specific numbers, annual writing lab reports focused on number of sessions, student languages, and majors, as well as types of written work seen and for what classes. When the writing lab finally moved away from a paper appointment schedule and note-taking forms and moved to *WC Online* in 2016, data became even more precise and customizable, which made for better reporting. However, the lab wanted to show it had an impact in terms of not only student visits but also the university's mission and goals: namely, higher retention rates and grades. To do that, the lab partnered with OIRAE to compare student ID numbers from lab visits with data about grades, GPAs, and retention. Additionally, doing this work enabled the lab to get data about student demographics that went beyond the simple demographic information *WC Online* collects. Now the lab has access to data about parental income levels, race and ethnicity, and in-state and out-of-state residence (which, as noted earlier, is a surprisingly good predictor of student preparedness and socioeconomic class). However, there is some information that Purdue does not allow us to access or track, including data that would help the lab a great deal, because of its interpretations of legal standards; in particular, the lab cannot track Pell Grant recipients, a major indicator for both socioeconomic class and generational status.

Despite the gaps that exist in the information the lab has been allowed to access, cross-analyzing the lab's data with OIRAE's lets the lab see its impact on retention rates for Purdue students. What we found has been heartening. Students who visit the writing lab have consistently higher GPAs across all four years of undergraduate education and during graduate school compared to students who do not visit the lab. These data hold true for nearly ten years, going back to the 2010–11 academic year. Additionally, when the data are filtered to only include underrepresented minority students, who are often placed in at-risk categories at Purdue, these patterns still hold true despite lower overall GPAs across all academic years ("Writing Lab"). While correlation does not equal causation, the data seem to show that usage of the writing lab has a genuine impact on student success.

And yet, there is so much more the lab could do. Being able to look at student numbers does not necessarily mean lab practices have changed. Consequently, it is up to the lab's administration and staff to use data actively to challenge our practices. But the lab cannot stop at the data, which may not reveal all the day-to-day problems inherent in writing center work and which may actually make it more difficult to understand how students with intersectional identities move through the lab. Therefore, it is important for the lab to consistently assess the assessment, making sure protocols are equitable and not static. And administrators and staff must create a public-facing mission and goals for the lab that hold them accountable. I have developed a set of recommendations not just for the Purdue Writing Lab but for any writing program that wants to better understand how to use large-scale assessment measures to improve the experience of marginalized students.

Recommendations for Writing Program Assessment

While big data research has problems and limitations, it can also illuminate the needs of specific student populations. Additionally, it reinforces the fact of these students' existence on campus. Writing programs, including writing centers but also first-year-writing programs, writing-across-the-curriculum programs, and other writing initiatives, have long been spaces for advocating for students in institutions that may otherwise ignore specific problems or types of at-risk behaviors. For students from marginalized populations, such as first-generation or poor students and students with various race, gender, sexuality, language, and disability identities, writing courses and tutoring services are often spaces to be seen and noticed, in part because the voices of students can be heard through their writing in those settings. However, these spaces also often ask students to disclose their identities in order to be heard, which puts the onus on students.

One of the benefits of having demographic data available, especially if it is anonymized, is that it can help writing program faculty and staff members see these students without asking them to take on the burden of self-disclosure. While partnering with other institutional offices can be tricky, and can have ethical complications, there are ways writing programs can partner with institutional research (IR) offices to help first-generation students better succeed in writing program spaces. Below, I describe four recommendations for making assessment partnerships useful, ethical, and student-focused.

Develop a collaborative partnership with your institutional research office.

Partnering with an IR office can be satisfying because it allows you to collect data that might not otherwise be available to you. IR consultants are educated in statistics and can perform the type of intricate analyses that most writing program administrators are not trained to do. It is important, though, not to ask IR consultants to do all the work of providing the data or doing the analysis themselves. Developing a true collaboration with an IR office, in which a writing program administrator works directly with a consultant, can allow the consultant to teach the administrator how to manage some statistical analyses on their own. At Purdue, for example, working with OIRAE has helped the writing lab director learn some basics of statistical work, which has since inspired the director and some graduate coordinators to learn *SPSS Statistics* and other statistical analysis programs.

Partnering with an IR office on assessment can also open paths for collaborative research projects that can be published through the institution. Because IR offices, especially at large or public universities, publish reports about specific topics, there is room to work with them on significant longitudinal research on writing and preparedness that can help both the writing program and institution better understand their students. The public nature of these reports can make the impact of a writing program visible to the wider campus, which increases the program's profile. Additionally, a writing program can demonstrate its commitment to research through these types of collaborative projects.

Of course, having a truly collaborative relationship with an IR office also means working on a two-way street, offering feedback to the office about its work. Writing programs should bring their spirit of student advocacy into their IR partnerships, pushing back on protocols that seem problematic or asking for new dimensions to data analysis that would better serve programs and students. As I argue above, one of the complications of working with institutional data is that they can rely too heavily on definitions of student identities that are problematic or unnuanced, and so writing programs that ask for specific information may signal to their IR partners that additional categories or ways of thinking about student experiences and data are necessary.

Use institutional data to complement local assessments.

Most assessments of writing programs, including writing centers, are meant to show how local interventions affect local populations. An assessment typically uses a combination of numbers—rubrics, evaluation scores, or usage numbers—and documentation to show improvement or the meeting of goals over time. Many scholars have written about how to do assessment well, so I will not go into that subject here; however, I think it is important to consider how we can use institutional data to complement our local assessment measures. The Purdue Writing Lab was able to connect student ID numbers from *WC Online* logins with the same ID numbers used to track student data across the larger university. This type of identification matching is relatively easy for a writing center that uses appointment software like *WC Online* or *TutorTrac*. It is much more difficult for centers that still take appointments by phone or through a system that does not use student log-in information that is common across all university profiles and programs.

Because writing courses enroll students differently from how writing centers schedule appointments, writing programs may need to approach statistical analysis and data collection in different ways. Writing programs that primarily do assessments of student writing may need to find a way to collect additional information as part of their assessment procedures, which might require an IRB protocol and additional labor, both of which can make this type of assessment difficult. However, as noted above, that additional labor may help administrators better understand how specific student populations are writing, including ways those students are improving or struggling. Often, student writing is assessed with no identifying student information specified for the assessors, which means all writing gets held to a standard defined by measures of success steeped in institutionalized white supremacy. Therefore, using anonymized but systematic information attached to student writing can provide an opportunity for programs to better understand how their assessment plays into problematic forms of standardization. This type of work can help us be better advocates for students who are often marginalized because of routinely blind assessment protocols that greatly disadvantage students who are already facing the uphill battle of being in spaces defined by white supremacy and socioeconomic privilege (Inoue).

Share assessments with the populations they most affect.

Writing programs that engage in assessment should make their assessment measures and data available to the populations who are directly affected by this work. Working with an IR office allows for the potential to publicly post reports and briefings about research and assessment. Additionally, writing programs that already make their annual reports and other documentation available online can easily add their assessment reports to their digital archives. The Purdue Writing Lab has done this with its assessment work, posting data in easy-to-read, visual formats (using *Tableau* software) on the Purdue Online Writing Lab website. Writing instructors who teach classes that are part of programmatic assessments might consider adding assessment information to the syllabus or discussing it in their classrooms. Helping students understand why an assessment is being done and what it measures, as well as the findings of that assessment, makes students a more active part of their own learning.

Making students active partners in their learning is especially important for first-generation and other marginalized student populations. Sharing assessment and research with the public can make marginalized students feel less alone while also demonstrating the program's commitment to working with those students (Denny and Towle). In the Purdue Writing Lab, we made a conscious effort to discuss openly the assessment work we did in tutor training courses, as well as in our regular lab tours for new students and in faculty committee meetings. We also shared this data with the tutors who conduct research in or about the lab. For example, as part of the required research study design project in our undergraduate tutor education course, students often use assessment data to support their work. This frequent and open sharing makes all the primary stakeholders in programmatic assessment visible to each other, as well as to the larger institution.

Make defining first-generation students one of the assessment protocols.

As discussed throughout this essay, one of the primary issues with focusing on first-generation students is the lack of a uniform definition of a first-generation student. Institutions and programs need to develop clear and reasonable boundaries for who it is they want to help through programs and services. I am an advocate for reclaiming the word *poor* to describe working-class first-generation students like me before I earned my doctorate. *Working-class*, *low-income*, and *lower socioeconomic status* are all terms that can serve us better than *first-generation* when we are talking about specific student needs and cultural experiences. As we found in the Purdue Writing Lab, the national poverty line is not a useful marker for who is and isn't disadvantaged, as students who fall above that line but are not comfortably middle-class still struggle with health care, food security, and finances and often are still the first in their families to attend college. For us in the lab, aligning assessment data with family income was more important for determining which students are disadvantaged, especially since we began to look intersectionally at the data. Another helpful data point was Pell Grant recipients, who, again, are usually students with less cultural capital than their peers (though, unfortunately, not all institutions grant access to financial aid data). These ways of looking at and interpreting the data were far more powerful than simply relying on generational status.

When writing programs do assessments, it is important for them to understand the unique demographics of their institutions. Perhaps you see and want to measure the ways students who are in a racial minority at your institution struggle with seeking out feedback for their writing. Or maybe you want to see how gender affects course outcomes. There are so many ways to understand and analyze data as they match your program's goals for assessment and writing. Pushing back against traditional definitions of who does or does not benefit from a writing class can open the eyes of the entire campus to students' needs. The point of using big data to complement localized assessment protocols is not just to show how students are doing but also to see and understand where programs need to improve. Reflective assessment should push back against handed-down definitions and boundaries for student populations and try to find new ways to make programs more equitable for all students.

Assessing the usage and success of writing programs, including writing centers, is central to the work administrators do every day. However, the commonness of this work means it can become dangerously routine, allowing our own assumptions or protocols to go unchallenged for years at a time. Partnering with an IR office or using available large data pools as part of assessment procedures can shake us out of our comfort zones and force us to confront ideas about our student populations. First-generation students, who are often poor, racial or ethnic minorities, and part of other vulnerable groups (e.g., undocumented and migrant students, students with disabilities, and LGBTQ+ students), are hard to categorize despite the insistence by scholars of and advocates for first-generation students that they need additional resources or special attention from their institutions. Often these students face a combination of racial prejudice, lack of cultural capital, and lack of material capital that affect their day-to-day lives and ability to succeed by traditional metrics. We need to follow the calls of scholars such as

Asao Inoue, in *Antiracist Writing Assessment Ecologies*, and Staci Perryman-Clark and Collin Lamont Craig, in *Black Perspectives in Writing Program Administration*, and challenge notions of what success means and how we assess it in our programs. While the use of IR partnerships and big data will not necessarily make our assessment practices more equitable, it can help us pay attention in our assessments to how experiences of identity affect students' ability to meet top-down learning outcomes.

At Purdue, looking at data related to family incomes, race and ethnicity, and residency made us realize that we were not seeing usage numbers that correlated with these marginalized student population numbers on campus. These gaps forced those of us in the Purdue Writing Lab to confront what we do and how we do it, a problem the lab is still trying to account for, without asking students to take on the burden of self-disclosure in its spaces. That said, the biggest issue the lab still faces is making its spaces safe enough for students to feel comfortable self-disclosing. How do we as writing program administrators and staff and faculty members make our spaces fit for all students and not make students fit our spaces? Big data cannot help us solve these problems, but it can help us understand the gaps that exist in the first place. Additionally, partnering successfully with an IR office can allow us to challenge our universities' racist, classist, and ableist understandings of what success and failure are. Strategic assessment protocols and partnerships can offer us new ways of seeing student populations that are often treated as invisible.

Note

1. O'Neill, for example, ties assessment to the narrative of Harvard University's first-year writing requirement in the 1870s.

Works Cited

Cataldi, Emily Forrest, et al. *First-Generation Students: College Access, Persistence, and Postbachelor's Outcome*. US Department of Education, National Center for Education Statistics, 2018, nces.ed.gov/pubs2018/2018421.pdf.

Collier, Peter J., and David L. Morgan. "'Is That Paper Really Due Today?': Differences in First-Generation and Traditional College Students' Understandings of Faculty Expectations." *Higher Education*, vol. 55, no. 4, 2008, pp. 425–46.

Crenshaw, Kimberlé. "Mapping the Margins: Intersectionality, Identity Politics, and Violence against Women of Color." *Stanford Law Review*, vol. 48, no. 6, 1991, pp. 1241–99.

Denny, Harry. *Facing the Center: Toward an Identity Politics of One-to-One Mentoring*. Utah State UP, 2010.

Denny, Harry, and Beth Towle. "Braving the Waters of Class: Performance, Intersectionality, and the Policing of Working Class Identities in Everyday Writing Centers." *The Peer Review*, vol. 1, no. 2, 2017, thepeerreview-iwca.org/issues/braver-spaces/braving-the-waters-of-class-performance-intersectionality-and-the-policing-of-working-class-identity-in-everyday-writing-centers/.

Denny, Harry, et al. "'Tell Me Exactly What It Was I Was Doing That Was So Bad': Understanding the Needs and Expectations of Working-Class Students in Writing Centers." *The Writing Center Journal*, vol. 37, no. 1, 2018, pp. 67–100.

Engle, Jennifer, and Vincent Tinto. *Moving beyond Access: College Success for Low-Income, First-Generation Students*. Pell Institute, 2008.

Greenfield, Laura, and Karen Rowan, editors. *Writing Centers and the New Racism: A Call for Sustainable Dialogue and Change*. Utah State UP, 2011.

Guerra, Juan C. *Language, Culture, Identity, and Citizenship in College Classrooms and Communities*. Routledge, 2016.

Harrington, Susanmarie. "What Is Assessment?" *A Rhetoric for Writing Program Administrators*, edited by Rita Malenczyk, Parlor Press, 2013, pp. 156–68.

Inoue, Asao B. *Antiracist Writing Assessment Ecologies: Teaching and Assessing Writing for a Socially Just Future*. WAC Clearinghouse, 2015, wac.colostate.edu/books/perspectives/inoue/.

Lerner, Neal. "Counting Beans and Making Beans Count." *Writing Lab Newsletter*, vol. 22, no. 1, 1997, pp. 1–3.

London, Howard B. "Transformations: Cultural Challenges Faced by First-Generation Students." *New Directions for Community Colleges*, vol. 80, 1992, pp. 5–11.

Lubrano, Alfred. *Limbo: Blue-Collar Roots, White-Collar Dreams*. Wiley, 2004.

O'Neill, Peggy. *Writing Assessment and the Disciplinarity of Composition*. 1998. U of Louisville, PhD dissertation.

Perryman-Clark, Staci M., and Collin Lamont Craig, editors. *Black Perspectives in Writing Program Administration: From the Margins to the Center*. National Council of Teachers of English, 2019.

Ramos-Sánchez, Lucila, and Laura Nichols. "Self-Efficacy of First-Generation and Non-First-Generation College Students: The Relationship with Academic Performance and College Adjustment." *Journal of College Counseling*, vol. 10, no. 1, 2007, pp. 6–18.

Salem, Lori. "Decisions . . . Decisions: Who Chooses to Use the Writing Center?" *The Writing Center Journal*, vol. 35, no. 2, 2016, pp. 147–71.

Schendel, Ellen, and William J. Macauley. *Building Writing Center Assessments That Matter*. Utah State UP, 2012.

Thompson, Isabelle. "Writing Center Assessment: Why and a Little How." *Writing Center Journal*, vol. 26, no. 1, 2006, pp. 33–61.

Ward, Lee, et al. *First-Generation College Students: Understanding and Improving the Experience from Recruitment to Commencement*. Jossey-Bass, 2012.

"Writing Lab Usage Data." *Purdue Online Writing Lab*, Purdue U, 2019, owl.purdue.edu/research/writing_lab_usage_data.html.

Zehner, Andy. "First-Generation Students at Purdue, 2011–2015." Purdue University, Office of Institutional Research, Assessment, and Effectiveness, 2016, www.purdue.edu/oirae/documents/White_Papers/First_Generation_Report_2.0.pdf.

Part Two

First-Generation Students in the First Year and Beyond

Dual Enrollment First-Year Writing for First-Generation Students

Casie Moreland

Dual enrollment (DE) programs and DE first-year writing (FYW) courses are increasingly popular today for economic and academic reasons. Most students that participate in DE courses will receive credit. DE FYW course completion also "decreases the time to completion of a college degree," which does, in many cases, result in tuition being waived, discounted, or reimbursed (Cassidy et al. 4). Students and parents, therefore, see DE as a cost-effective approach to FYW credit. DE programs also provide ways for institutions to make or save money (Anson 247). When the cost-benefit perspective is applied to DE FYW, it highlights what Kristine Hansen describes as the "composition marketplace," where FYW is viewed as a "market commodity" (1). And, according to Mary Kanny, DE FYW is one of many pieces in what is quickly becoming the "college completion landscape" (8).

In 2019, one-third of all high school students in the United States enrolled in DE programs (Shivji and Wilson). Additionally, at least forty-seven states in the United States have DE mandates to ensure that high schools and colleges partner to provide DE opportunities for students (Macdonald). And across the United States, there are recorded accounts of disparities in DE enrollment for first-generation students and students of color (Hugo; Hughes; Palaich et al.; Moreland and Miller; Moreland, "Chasing"). In a US Department of Education study, Nina Thomas and colleagues identify that of the eighty-two percent of public high schools with students enrolled in DE programs, ninety-one percent of these schools report less than six percent enrollment of students of color (9).

First-generation students are also disparately represented in DE courses. In a recent US Department of Education study, Azim Shivji and Sandra Wilson report that a mere twenty-six percent of students enrolled in DE courses were first-generation. Shalina Chatlani reports that "lower-income students of color and first-generation students are less likely to participate." In "The Triumph of Whiteness," Keith Miller and I argue that "because [of] the selective availability of DC [dual credit] courses . . . less affluent students . . . start climbing their professional ladders *later* than their affluent white counterparts. For that reason, these less affluent students are *more* disadvantaged than their previously 'tracked' parents were" (Moreland and Miller 192).

In Kristine Hansen and Christine Farris's collection, *College Credit for Writing in High School,* contributors explore ways that students can gain college credit for writing in high school—Advanced Placement, International Baccalaureate, Dual Credit, Concurrent Enrollment, and Early College. While Hansen and Farris "limit [their] focus . . . to just the ways in which high school students are offered instruction in college composition," the aim of their collection, they highlight, is to "bring fully onto the radar screen a picture of what we see happening across the nation as educational institutions and state governments pay growing heed to the businesses and private foundations urging integration of high school and college" ("Introduction" xx). The main areas of concern identified in the collection are student maturation levels, curriculum, assessment, teacher training, and program accreditation. Many of these areas of concern are also problems associated with traditional FYW courses on college campuses. However, the high school context, as Hansen and Farris assert, requires just as much, if not more of a focus from those in the field, as very little is known about DE. I have found that the issues in contemporary DE programs identified by contributors of *College Credit for Writing in High School* have connections to the historical origins of DE. For instance, the programs as they were originally designed seemed to have very little to do with first-generation and other historically underrepresented students.

Over the past few years I have sought to understand the misalignment between those who DE programs are marketed to and the students who actually enroll in those programs. Questions about access and enrollment cannot be answered without better understanding the history—who were the programs created for? Which students were to benefit? What can the history of DE tell us about DE FYW today?

In rhetoric and composition studies, knowledge of the history of the field is what led to its professionalization (Connors, "Writing"). Historical views of the field also allow those in the field to constantly improve pedagogies and methods to better prepare their increasingly diverse student populations (Martinez; S. Miller; Kennedy et al.; Lamos). The critical race theorists Michael Omi and Howard Winant explain that "by knowing something of how [racial formations that cause further marginalization of historically marginalized communities] evolved, we can perhaps better discern where [they are] heading" (61). This echoes Robert J. Connors, who explains that "we cannot learn what to do from history. All we can learn is what others have done, perhaps a little about what not to do, and, perhaps, a little more about who we are" ("Dreams" 32). The critical race scholar Derrick Bell also asserts that "[w]e simply cannot prepare realistically for our future without assessing honestly our past" (11). To better understand how to best serve first-generation students, this essay details connections between the history and present state of DE programs to highlight how DE FYW has the potential to influence the advancement of opportunity for first-generation student writers.

There has never been a formal treatment of the history of DE or DE FYW in historical narratives about rhetoric and composition studies. Previous composition-specific DE scholarship pointed to state mandates and legislation (e.g., California's legislation in 1976 identifying qualifications for college–high school partnerships, and Minnesota's decision in 1985 to grant funding for DE options) when referring to the origins of DE programs. However, Patricia Moody and Margaret Bonesteel have complicated the origins presented by education scholars, as in the work of Christine G. Mokher and Michael K. McLendon and of Lawrence B. Friedman and colleagues, with references to Syracuse University's Project Advance, which began in 1972. Even further back, Helen J. Estes's 1959 "College Level English in High School" and Shirley A. Radcliffe and Winslow R. Hatch's 1961 US Department of Education report *Advanced Standing: New Dimensions in Higher Education* place the origins of DE programs much earlier than the 1970s—in the 1950s in Connecticut.

While DE programs were created during the same time as Advanced Placement, DE is very different in context and delivery. In the 1950s, the College Entrance Exam Board adopted what was referred to as an advanced standing program at Kenyon College—the Kenyon Plan. This program allowed incoming students, upon completion of courses and tests, to bypass first-year courses. College English was one of the first courses offered in this setting. As institutions began participating in the College Entrance Exam Board's Advanced Placement programs, other institutions developed individual advanced standing programs that were detached from Advanced Placement "to meet the needs of their particular communities" (Radcliffe and Hatch 12). The sources by Estes and by Radcliffe and Hatch were essential to my piecing together the historical origins of DE FYW courses.[1] With my knowledge of DE's origins in the 1950s in Connecticut, I sought to piece together a previously undocumented history—a history that, not surprisingly, seemed to have little to do with first-generation students.

In this essay, I detail findings from archival research conducted at the University of Connecticut, home to the self-proclaimed longest-running DE program (and therefore DE writing courses) in the United States, to narrate the history of DE FYW with a focus on the potential of the programs for first-generation students. I first provide an overview of the basics of DE FYW. I then detail archival research findings pertaining to the original program articulations—which were designed to benefit so-called superior students; this design differs from programs today that promote access to higher education for all, or at least many more, students. Next, I discuss what the history of the programs can tell us about writing courses offered in DE contexts today. This move has the potential to benefit or—if not given attention—to further marginalize first-generation and other historically marginalized student populations. I argue that to best support first-generation students, more attention and research must be invested in these programs. I offer suggestions for research to determine how, locally, DE writing classes do or do not support student success.

First-Generation Dual Enrollment Writers

First-generation students are poised to be among the students who are most positively affected by DE options. In *Teaching College Writing to High School Students*, Erin Scott-Stewart details how first-generation students' participation in DE increases their rates of high school graduation and college entry, persistence, and graduation (14). Kanny explains that many students can benefit from DE programs, including first-generation students, who might benefit "to an even greater degree" (6). For first-generation students, the benefits of DE programs sometimes go beyond students' obtainment of college credit—these experiences also give students access to cultural capital. In "Lessons Learned about Dual Enrollment" Matt Reed details how in one donor-supported DE program for first-generation students, two-thirds of the students that began the program graduated high school with an associate's degree. Upon high school graduation, these students reported that they "think of themselves—accurately—as college students" ("Lessons"). Through DE programs, these students gained cultural capital that, before the development of first-year writing, had historically been exclusive to "men of 'taste'" (Ritter and Matsuda 4).

In traditional, or what Jill Ashby and Dominic Parrot call standard enrollment, options, such as FYW on a college campus, first-generation students have historically been at a greater risk of academic departure than their continuing-generation peers. Kanny points out that "[f]irst-generation students' relative risk of departure [from higher education] was 71 percent higher than that of second-generation students between the first and second years" (20). Brian An finds that DE students "were more likely to attain a degree than nonparticipants" and that for first-generation students "participation may increase college degree attainment" (13). An's work, which is based on a national sample, finds that students whose parents are college-educated are as likely to attain a college degree regardless of the students' participation in DE programs (8). An's study is consistent with that of Melinda Karp and colleagues, which finds that first-generation students who participated in DE programs experienced a stronger positive effect in their likelihood of completing both two- and four-year degrees than their continuing-generation peers (Kanny 31). First-generation students, then, stand to have higher completion rates than otherwise possible when DE programs are available to them.

Historical Articulations of Dual Enrollment Programs

While contemporary DE programs are articulated as a way for all students to access higher education, the historical articulations of the programs were quite different, which might add to the reasons for the current disparity in enrollment for first-generation students in such programs. According to the UConn Early College Experience, the University of Connecticut's Cooperative Program for Superior Students is the "longest-running" in the United States ("About"). As one of the first DE programs to develop, UConn's program can offer insights into other DE program developments as well as trends in FYW and DE during the 1950s.

Given the disparities in the representation of first-generation students and other historically underrepresented groups in higher education, the name of the program at UConn and its articulation—as a program for "superior" students—created a lot of questions for me. Estes, one of the first high school teachers to teach college-level English in high school for UConn, reports that "[t]he values of the College Level English course in high school duplicate those of any grouping of superior students" (334). As Kelly Ritter explains in "Before Mina Shaughnessy," sorting students in such a way that divides them based on their abilities as they "align—or misalign—with the values and objectives of the particular institution" is known as "*stratification.*" In reference to Ira Shor's argument in "Errors and Economics," Ritter explains that "university writing courses are mechanisms of not only academic/intellectual leveling but also social and cultural discrimination" (17). I argue that classifying some students as superior could have potentially negative implications for the students who were not chosen to participate. My original hypothesis and questions therefore focused on how the name of this program signaled that the program was for particular students—I wanted to know whether officials intentionally created the program to separate historically underrepresented students, such as students of color and first-generation students, from white affluent students as schools began to integrate after the 1954 Supreme Court ruling in *Brown v. Board of Education.*

Before traveling to UConn, I spoke to the manager of University Archives, who suggested I consult the digitized daily journal of Albert E. Waugh, who served as provost from 1950 to 1965. Waugh maintained a journal from at least 1924 to 1984 that included pertinent details about the development and implementation of the university's DE program. Because of my interest in the program's origins during the African American civil rights movements, I also researched how integration took place and materialized in Connecticut and at UConn to see if there was a connection between the development of UConn's DE program and *Brown v. Board of Education*. During this investigation, I found information about the 1996 ruling of *Sheff v. O'Neill*. As I found (and argue in Moreland, *Impossible Plan*), the DE program developed under the guise of white complacency, which has resulted in the advancement of academically and socially privileged (i.e, white, affluent) students and the further marginalization of students of color. The findings I detail in this essay are specific to the implications of DE program articulation and implementation for first-generation students.

Findings: Program Articulation

Educational institutions are always adapting to social and political changes. However, the adaptations taking place at UConn during the 1950s—during the development of its DE program—seem to have been completely focused on the aftermath of World War II and on the Cold War. In archived documents that concern the development of UConn's DE program, I found no reference to extremely significant social and political events such as the African American civil rights movements, *Brown v. Board of Education*, or integration.

It is also well-documented that in the context of the Cold War, UConn felt increased pressure to contribute to the needs of the workforce by training teachers—and experienced decreases in government funding. Because of the population boom after World War II, more teachers for primary and secondary schools were needed, as there was "a shortage of about 100,000 prepared teachers" in Connecticut (University of Connecticut Board 1). UConn sought to find ways to train these teachers—and in the process increase their enrollment and, it was hoped, retention. DE courses were one approach. During this time, UConn also revisited and revised its philosophy of education, which used seemingly elitist rhetoric focused on individual students. The articulation of the purpose of the DE program at UConn would employ the same rhetoric, outlined by Provost Waugh in his philosophy of education.

Almost immediately after becoming provost in 1951, Waugh created a program to allow students to gain college credit in high school—a program that would provide students a direct path to enrollment at UConn. In April 1952 Waugh conveyed interest in implementing a program "to admit a few bright youngsters who have not graduated from high school" ("Daily Journal: 1952"

122). He detailed two key components of the program: first, that "outstandingly good students" be admitted without "meeting our admission requirements," and second, that students could potentially enroll after three years of high school (145). The purpose of the program was not stated in this journal entry.

In 1953 Waugh released a statement on his educational philosophy, which employed the same rhetoric that would later be used to substantiate and implement DE programs elsewhere. In "Comments on the Basic Curriculum for the Freshman and Sophomore Years at the University of Connecticut," Waugh explains his vision for how his philosophy should influence the basic curriculum at UConn. Waugh begins the document in a seemingly progressive way:

> there is no one pattern of education which is equally desirable for everyone—that to some extent one's education should be adapted to the needs of his individual case—that while we all wish to turn out "educated" young men and women, there is no single certain road to education. It is my belief that this University should offer several (many?) kinds of education, and that we need not worry if we find that the aims and purposes and methods and requirements of our various schools and colleges differ to a considerable extent. (1)

Understandably, Waugh specifies that the curriculum at UConn should be "intellectual" and "reasonably advanced" and should require from students "work of college grade." However, throughout the document, the elitist and potentially marginalizing undercurrents of his philosophy become more apparent as Waugh uses social values and democracy to describe what he believes are two basic principles of any "sound" education for college-level freshmen and sophomores (2).

Waugh goes on to explain at length what his philosophy means in terms of "education for all." If "we want 'education for all'" he states, "we must plan for greatly increased difference in education." Education for all should not be done "by destroying the educational system for those of better intellect by removing 'verbal skills and intellectual interests,' but by providing other and different institutions for those whose abilities and interests are not such as to make college or universities profitable." Waugh then suggests that higher education is not recommended for every student:

> We only mislead ourselves and the general public when we pretend that everyone can profit by a college education, unless we alter radically the meaning of the phrase "college education." And if we bow to the public pressure which insists that our Johnny, too, must be given a college degree despite his lack of intellectual attainments merely because Johnny and his parents desire it and because he will be handicapped in competition with others who do have one,

> then we short-change the public in the same way that we do when we try to make everyone rich by starting the print presses and issuing fiat money. ("Comments" 2)

While Waugh seems to support each student's educational path, at the same time, he suggests that providing education for all runs the risk of depreciating the value of education. Waugh then explains that the university must "feel free" to make subjective decisions about which students will be admitted "in the interests of justice" ("Comments" 3). A subjective approach to admissions would leave all students at the mercy of those evaluating them, which could have been detrimental to students of color and first-generation students who have been underrepresented in higher education. As DE courses further developed at UConn, there was a focus on personalized education for students who progress at what the university would have called a superior rate to other students.

In the 1950s the University of Connecticut Board of Trustees released a statement titled "The Rising Tide of School and College Enrollments." In this statement, the Board of Trustees suggests that in response to the increased student population at UConn there should be "a critical review of 'entrance requirements and procedures.' There are some young people now in college who should not be there. It is hoped [by the Board of Trustees] that in the future, youth with low intellectual interests and aptitudes will not be admitted to college" (4). This statement also echoes the educational philosophy of Waugh—that only certain students should be able to access higher education. A focus on qualified students as investments would go on to become an integral aspect of the articulation of the developing DE program at UConn.

The university senate's Committee on Curricula and Courses approved Waugh's proposed program in 1953 (Waugh, "Daily Journal: 1953" 25). The program would keep the structure of its initial articulation and outline throughout its development. The Committee on Scholastic Standards and the Committee on Curricula and Courses agreed on the following program articulation:

> Every teacher and every faculty is forced to give particular attention to the programs of the weaker students who need and deserve special attention and care. Yet it is important that we should not lose sight of the fact that the most able and promising students also have unusual problems in our educational system. We believe that much can be accomplished, both for the individual gifted student and for society, by so organizing the educational system that such students can be given work which will challenge their abilities and retain their interest, and that they may progress in learning at a rate commensurate with their ability. We believe that the best students are better college risks at

> the end of two or three years of preparatory school than are average students after finishing the full preparatory course, and that such students should be given the opportunity, if they desire it, of beginning their college work as soon as they demonstrate clearly their ability to profit by the richer and more challenging opportunities available to them there. While any acceleration of the academic pace makes problems for the institution which allows it, we believe that the problems are not insurmountable, and that they do not warrant us enforcing the best minds to follow an average pace merely because uniformity is simple to administer. (University of Connecticut Committee)

The program, then, would seem to answer the problem of rising enrollment by privileging already advanced students. Clearly, the students that Waugh and the university senate consider to be qualified—students with the "best minds"—should have more opportunities than "weaker students."

Shortly after the DE program began, UConn issued a press release, which explains that "[t]he University of Connecticut has put into operation a twin program of enrichment and acceleration which will be a boon to superior high school students." The "superior student," the press release notes, will be able to "shorten his years of schooling" and will arrive "sooner at his graduate studies or the threshold of a career" (University of Connecticut News Coordinator's Office).

An accelerated time to degree was then, and is now, marketed as an incentive for students to participate in the programs. However, while more information is needed, it does not seem like Waugh's program was successful in accelerating time to degree in the first few years. In 1959, it was reported that of "those students receiving credit during the first year of the program (1955–56), five entered the University of Connecticut. They have completed two years at the University and all five are currently enrolled in their junior year at the institution" (*Report* 1). Based on these initial data, while students did complete some college in high school, these students were not accelerating at advanced rates, as three years after high school the students were college juniors, which is a standard goal for undergraduates.

A status study developed by Alexander Plante gives an overview of the initial year of the DE program. In its first year, 112 students were accepted into the program; seventy-six students received credit (1). College credit for writing in high school was given to at least fifty-two students in the program's FYW courses ("Instructor's Mid-Semester and Final Grade Report").

Estes, one of the original English teachers for the UConn Cooperative Program for Superior Students, who taught at Manchester High School,[2] published a 1959 article about the program, "College Level English in High School." She details that, among other things, the FYW courses were set up as a semester each of composition and of literature and that, "the high schools in the program [could] combine the two emphases [for both semesters] if they chose" (332–33). I found no evidence that using the UConn composition syllabus made the courses more rigorous than high school English. However, Estes details trends in pedagogy and course materials in what would later be rhetoric and composition studies and also how these trends in literature-based course materials were carried out in the first DE courses. Literature-based writing courses were typical in the 1950s and, while less common, are still found in traditional and DE FYW courses today—depending on the program and institution.

Historically, literature-based composition courses were intended for those classified as elite students. John Brereton explains: "Throughout the era 1875–1925, literary works prevailed in [such courses at] elite colleges (with the exception of Harvard), while [composition courses at] the least prestigious colleges concentrated more on grammar and mechanics drills. At Wisconsin in the 1920s, 65 percent of first-year students had some literature in their composition course, and the best students had all literature (Brereton 16)." It is important to keep in mind, too, that many of the problems with traditional FYW courses are present in contemporary DE FYW, such as suggestions to move away from literature-based composition courses. These moves away from literature-based courses, in many cases, take into consideration how focusing on students' subjectivities, language use, and the communities in which students live can support them as they develop their composing processes. The curriculum in the UConn DE program reflected this approach to teaching writing—to an extent. There was an option for students to take a half term of composition at UConn, which it was up to the participating high schools to offer.

Estes provides examples of the course design of the DE English class. She details the multiple units that are based on themes such as "The Hero and the Principle of Obligation," "Conventional and Romantic Values," and "The Search for Self-Realization." Students read texts such as Niccolò Machiavelli's *The Prince*, *Beowulf*, and Shakespeare's *Hamlet*. Throughout the course, students wrote an average of five hundred words per week and submitted a "resource paper" of at least two thousand words at the end of each semester (Estes 333). The resource paper required student's collection and analysis of primary and secondary sources. Although no details of the composition portion of the course are given, Estes notes that the program followed the College Entrance Exam Board's Advanced Placement program format to an extent as students completed a vocabulary, grammar, and punctuation review.

In 1959, more high school students took college-level English than any other course in UConn's DE program. In this year, 119 students enrolled in the first section of first-year English. The only courses whose enrollments came close to that for English were a history course, with fifty-seven students, and a math course, with forty-five students (University of Connecticut Cooperative Program). The most "typical" pattern of the majority of students was to use the cooperative courses "to rid themselves of freshman-sophomore requirements," and this was most apparent in English courses (*Report* 2, 3). While most students enrolled in English, not one of those students went on to major in English.

With the continuous rise in students taking college credit for writing today and the continuous decline in English majors in colleges across the United States, I cannot help but think there is a connection here: is it possible that when students take college-level writing in high school, they see writing and English studies as something to get out of the way rather than as a serious field of study? How might students' participation in high school English classes, where at times students can choose what kind of credit they will receive (high school, Advanced Placement, or college credit), influence their decision to major or not major in English?

For now, though, I keep thinking back to Hansen's argument that DE supports writing as a commodity in a marketplace: where students might have once seen value in learning more about writing, it really has become, to some students, something to get out of the way and not revisit. I wonder how those in English departments might appeal to these students in high school. With an idea so appealing—getting college writing out of the way for free—what might change their minds?

The Changing Horizon for First-Generation Writers: Decentering First-Year Writing for All

DE programs were created to give students that educators believed were superior an earlier start at higher education, and the reasons for doing so were largely economic. DE programs reflect how historically FYW courses were not intended to last and were created to (and still) serve a gatekeeping function for students seeking a college education (Yancey; Crowley; S. Miller; and T. Miller, among others). FYW courses were considered a response to what Robert Connors refers to as the "first literacy crisis" as more students gained access to institutions of higher education ("Rhetoric").

My historical research shows how programs that enable students to gain college credit for writing in high school were an almost instantaneous response to the FYW requirement that began in 1885. However, DE FYW is largely unaccounted for in the history of FYW and rhetoric and composition studies. Current practices in DE FYW raise more questions than answers about the quality of

DE programs, their degree of alignment with the course content of FYW, and their overall utility. Additionally, there are disconnects between the rhetorical dynamics of a DE program's goals and the actual personal and professional gains for students and instructors of FYW. This disjuncture exists because, as it turns out, receiving credit for DE courses while in high school does not always adequately prepare students enrolled in these courses for the writing and rhetorical demands of the university classroom.

While first-generation and other historically underrepresented students do have the most to gain from DE programs, they are also in a position to be most negatively influenced when access is not available. As Carmen Kynard, Deborah Brandt, Aja Martinez, and Paul Matsuda separately argue—literacy is power. Because writing instruction at the postsecondary level helps students become better critical thinkers, readers, and writers, students who do not receive this instruction are not adequately prepared for the demands of university-level coursework. Ensuring access for historically underrepresented student groups to high-quality writing courses (DE or otherwise) increases those students' access to higher education and is essential to the work of rhetoric and composition studies.

Research and scholarship pertaining to first-generation writers and DE FYW creates innumerous potentials for growth in the knowledge of DE first-generation writers. The work of Hansen and Farris, Katie McWain, Christine Denecker, and others has paved the way for efforts that provide high-quality instruction to students in this quickly growing sector of FYW. A Conference on College Composition and Communication task force and statement now exist for DE, along with the conference's standing group Dual Enrollment Collective, an active listserv, and a rising number of publications and dissertations devoted to this topic. Commissions of higher learning are also creating standards for DE courses and programs. For instance, the Higher Learning Commission has issued a new mandate that requires all DE instructors to have eighteen credit hours in the subject area they teach by 1 September 2022 (*Determining Qualified Faculty*). In 2018, the Southern Association of Colleges and Schools created a requirement that faculty members that teach DE courses must have "the same academic credentials and/or documented professional experience required by the institution of all of its faculty [members]" ("Dual Enrollment"). One main takeaway of these developments is that educational policymakers and administrators still have a lot of work to do to veer away from the elitist conceptions of DE evidenced at UConn. DE programs continue to pose challenges for first-generation and other historically underrepresented students who may not be able to take advantage of them.

Currently, millions of students participate in these programs; however, there are no data sources that report the number of DE students that have graduated from college. Karp and colleagues report that "[o]verall, it remains unclear whether dual enrollment participation increases students' likeliness to enter college, preparedness for college-level work, or attainment of a college degree" (14). For DE FYW to become more equitable, there must be more research on student success in writing beyond DE programs. One way to do this would be to track students. Currently, many programs give high school students college credit with no specification of their dual credit on their transcripts. Therefore, it is difficult to study these students' matriculation and retention rates, as the students are not disaggregated from other students. Equity for all students requires validity—which requires that data on DE students be separated, for research purposes, from those of other students. More data are essential for analysis of program equitability, and if data are not analyzed for equitability, the programs are, as I argue in "Chasing Transparency," in violation of students' civil rights (Moreland, "Chasing").

Transfer requirements should also be validated to ensure the equitability of DE FYW for students that have been historically underrepresented in higher education. At Ohio Northern University, all students are required to take FYW on the college campus, regardless of credit earned elsewhere—while the DE writing courses transfer as general education credits. State schools in Ohio must accept other state schools' FYW credits if they meet transfer articulation guidelines. How, then, might articulations of what counts as transferable credit better support first-generation students in DE writing classes?

FYW is changing its traditional form, model, space, and context. Tyler Branson explains that DE programs are "poised to fundamentally change how we research, teach, and administer college writing." Ashby and Parrot argue that a move toward equivalency is taking place—and where it is not, it must. The rapid growth of DE FYW has prompted efforts by members of rhetoric and composition studies to increase the visibility, awareness, and the potential impacts of the programs (Denecker; Frick and Blattner; Hansen and Farris, "Introduction"). Yet the growth in DE programs is something the majority of the field seems reluctant to acknowledge and has been slow to investigate systematically. It is clearly time to address this gap, especially where it concerns first-generation students.

For DE FYW to be more equitable for first-generation students, there must be conversations, collaborations, and participation in how these programs are developed, implemented, and assessed, and they must involve department heads, undergraduate studies directors, advisers, writing program directors, and faculty at institutions that offer and accept the credits. As FYW decenters its traditional form, research should account for the history of DE programs as well as expand the scope of what is studied for the future of the field and for the students, traditional and historically underrepresented, such as first-generation students, that take the courses that make our work possible.

Notes

1. A special thanks to Christine Denecker for recommending these articles to me. She stumbled on both articles years ago and had saved them just in case.

2. I verified, on UConn's 1955–56 course roster and grade reports, that Estes taught in UConn's DE program at Manchester High School.

Works Cited

"About Us." "UConn Early College Experience." *UConn*, ece.uconn.edu/about/about-us/. Accessed 10 Sept. 2019.

An, Brian. "The Impact of Dual Enrollment on College Degree Attainment: Do Low-SES Students Benefit?" *Educational Evaluation and Policy Analysis*, vol. 35, no. 1, 2013, pp. 1–19, https://doi.org/10.3102/0162373712461933.

Anson, Chris M. "Absentee Landlords or Owner-Tenants? Formulating Standards for Dual-Credit Composition Programs." Hansen and Farris, *College Credit*, pp. 245–71.

Ashby, Jill, and Dominic Parrot. "But It's (Not) the Same: A Data-Driven Look at Equivalency Bias in Dual Enrollment Composition." Denecker and Moreland.

Bell, Derrick. *Faces at the Bottom of the Well*. Basic Books, 1992.

Brandt, Deborah. *Literacy and Learning: Reflections on Writing, Reading, and Society*. Jossey-Bass, 2009.

Branson, Tyler. "College Composition at Midwest High: Field Notes from a Concurrent Enrollment Classroom." Denecker and Moreland.

Brereton, John C. *The Origins of Composition Studies in the American College, 1875–1925: A Documentary History*. U of Pittsburgh P, 1995.

Cassidy, Lauren, et al. "Dual Enrollment: Lessons Learned on School-Level Implementation." US Department of Education, Office of Elementary and Secondary Education, 2010, www2.ed.gov/programs/slcp/finaldual.pdf.

Chatlani, Shalina. "Dual Enrollment Is Increasing College-Going Behavior, but Only for Some Students." *K–12 Dive*, 27 Aug. 2018, www.educationdive.com/news/dual-enrollment-is-increasing-college-going-behavior-but-only-for-some-stu/530590/.

Connors, Robert J. "Dreams and Play: Historical Method and Methodology." *Methods and Methodology in Composition Research*, edited by Gesa Kirsch and Patricia A. Sullivan, Southern Illinois UP, 1992, pp. 15–36.

———. "Rhetoric in the Modern University: The Creation of the Underclass." *The Politics of Writing Instruction: Postsecondary*, edited by Richard H. Bullock and John Trimbur, Boyton/Cook, 1991, pp. 55–84.

———. "Writing the History of Our Discipline." *An Introduction to Composition Studies*, edited by Erika Lindemann and Gary Tate, Oxford UP, 1991, pp. 49–71.

Crowley, Sharon. *Composition in the University: Historical and Polemical Essays*. U of Pittsburgh P, 1998.

Denecker, Christine M. *Toward Seamless Transition? Dual Enrollment and the Composition Classroom*. 2007. Bowling Green State U, PhD dissertation.

Denecker, Christine, and Casie Moreland, editors. *The Dual Enrollment Kaleidoscope: Reconfiguring Perceptions of First-Year Writing and Composition Studies*. UP of Colorado / Utah State UP, forthcoming.

Determining Qualified Faculty through HLC's Criteria for Accreditation and Assumed Practices: Guidelines for Institutions and Peer Reviewers. Higher Learning Commission, 2020, download.hlcommission.org/FacultyGuidelines_2016_PB.pdf.

"Dual Enrollment: Policy Statement." Southern Association of Colleges and Schools, Commission on Colleges, 2018, sacscoc.org/app/uploads/2019/08/Dual-Enrollment.pdf.

Estes, Helen J. "College Level English in High School." *The English Journal*, vol. 48, no. 6, 1959, pp. 332–34.

Frick, Jane, and Nancy Blattner. "Reflections on the Missouri CWA Surveys, 1989–2001: A New Composition Delivery Paradigm." *College Composition and Communication*, vol. 53, no. 4, 2002, pp. 739–46.

Friedman, Lawrence B., et al. *Research Study of Texas Dual Credit Programs and Courses*. Texas Education Agency, 2011, www.air.org/sites/default/files/downloads/report/TX_Dual_Credit_Report_with_appendices_FINAL_ADA_Checked_031711_0.pdf.

Hansen, Kristine. "The Composition Marketplace: Shopping for Credit versus Learning to Write." Hansen and Farris, *College Credit*, pp. 1–39.

Hansen, Kristine, and Christine R. Farris, editors. *College Credit for Writing in High School: The "Taking Care of" Business*. National Council of Teachers of English, 2010.

———. "Introduction: The 'Taking Care of' Business." Hansen and Farris, *College Credit*, pp. xvii–xxxiii.

Hughes, Katherine L. "Dual Enrollment: Postsecondary/Secondary Partnerships to Prepare Students." *Journal of College Science Teaching*, vol. 39, no. 6, 2010, pp. 12–13.

Hugo, Esther B. "Dual Enrollment for Underrepresented Student Populations." *New Directions for Community Colleges*, vol. 113, 2001, pp. 67–72.

"Instructor's Mid-Semester and Final Grade Report." 1955–56. U of Connecticut Libraries, Archives and Special Collections at the Thomas J. Dodd Research Center, Special Request from Archives, University of Connecticut's Cooperative Program.

Kanny, Mary. *Forks in the Pathway? Mapping the Conditional Effects of Dual Enrollment by Gender, First-Generation Status, and Pre-college Academic Achievement on First-Year*

Student Engagement and Grades in College. 2014. PhD dissertation, U of California, Los Angeles. *eScholarship*, escholarship.org/uc/item/43q1t1bp.

Karp, Melinda Mechur, et al. *The Postsecondary Achievement of Participants in Dual Enrollment: An Analysis of Student Outcomes in Two States*. U of Minnesota, 2007, ccrc.tc.columbia.edu/media/k2/attachments/dual-enrollment-student-outcomes.pdf.

Kennedy, Tammie M., et al. "The Matter of Whiteness; or, Why Whiteness Studies Is Important to Rhetoric and Composition Studies." *Rhetoric Review*, vol. 24, no. 4, 2005, pp. 359–73.

Kynard, Carmen. *Vernacular Insurrections: Race, Black Protest, and the New Century in Composition-Literacies Studies*. State U of New York P, 2013.

Lamos, Steve. "Literacy Crisis and Color-Blindness: The Problematic Racial Dynamic of Mid-1970's Language and Literacy Instruction for 'High-Risk' Minority Students." *College Composition and Communication*, vol. 61, no. 2, 2009, pp. W125–48.

Macdonald, Heidi, et al. "Fifty-State Comparison: High School Graduation Requirements." *Education Commission of the States*, 2019, www.ecs.org/high-school-graduation-requirements/.

Martinez, Aja Y. "'The American Way': Resisting the Empire of Force and Color-Blind Racism." *College English*, vol. 71, no. 6, 2009. pp. 584–95.

Matsuda, Paul Kei. "The Myth of Linguistic Homogeneity in U.S. College Composition." *College English*, vol. 68, no. 6, 2006, pp. 637–51.

McWain, Katie. "Finding Freedom at the Composition Threshold: Learning from the Experiences of Dual Enrollment Teachers." *Teaching English in the Two-Year College*, vol. 45, no. 4, 2018, pp. 406–24.

Miller, Susan. *Textual Carnivals: The Politics of Composition*. Southern Illinois UP, 1991.

Miller, Thomas P. *The Evolution of College English: Literacy Studies from the Puritans to the Postmoderns*. U of Pittsburgh P, 2010.

Mokher, Christine G., and Michael K. McLendon. "Uniting Secondary and Postsecondary Education: An Event History Analysis of State Adoption of Dual Enrollment Policies." *American Journal of Education*, vol. 115, no. 2, 2009, pp. 249–77.

Moody, Patricia A., and Margaret D. Bonesteel. "Syracuse University Project Advance: A Model of Connection and Quality." Hansen and Farris, *College Credit*, pp. 227–44.

Moreland, Casie. "Chasing Transparency: Using Disparate Impact Analysis to Assess the (In)Accessibility of Dual Enrollment Composition." *Writing Assessment, Social Justice, and the Advancement of Opportunity*, edited by Mya Poe et al., WAC Clearinghouse / UP of Colorado, 2018, pp. 173–201, wac.colostate.edu/books/assessment/.

———. *The Impossible Plan: A History of Dual Enrollment in an Era of White Complacency*. State U of New York P, forthcoming.

Moreland, Casie, and Keith D. Miller. "The Triumph of Whiteness: Dual Credit Courses and Hierarchical Racism in Texas." *Rhetorics of Whiteness: Postracial Hauntings in Popular Culture, Social Media, and Education*, edited by Tammie M. Kennedy et al., Southern Illinois UP, 2016, pp. 182–94.

Omi, Michael, and Howard Winant. *Racial Formation in the United States: From the 1960s to the 1990s*. 2nd ed., Routledge, 1994.

Palaich, Robert, et al. "Financing Accelerated Learning Options: Understanding Who Benefits and Who Pays." *Accelerated Learning Options: Moving the Needle on Access and Success: A Study of State and Institutional Policies and Practices*. Western Interstate Commission for Higher Education, 2006, pp. 57–72.

Plante, Alexander. "Status Study of Cooperative Program for Superior High School Students—School Year 1955–56." U of Connecticut Libraries, Archives and Special Collections at the Thomas J. Dodd Research Center, University Senate Records, box 14, folder 852.

Radcliffe, Shirley A., and Winslow R. Hatch. *Advanced Standing: New Dimensions in Higher Education*. US Department of Health, Education, and Welfare, Office of Education, 1961.

Reed, Matt. "Lessons Learned about Dual Enrollment." *Inside Higher Ed*, 18 July 2018, www.insidehighered.com/blogs/confessions-community-college-dean/lessons-learned-about-dual-enrollment.

A Report on the Cooperative Program for Superior High School Students: April, 1959. Box 14, folder 852, University Senate Records, Archives and Special Collections at the Thomas J. Dodd Research Center, U of Connecticut Libraries.

Ritter, Kelly. "Before Mina Shaughnessy: Basic Writing at Yale, 1920–1960." *College Composition and Communication*, vol. 60, no. 1, 2008, pp. 12–45.

Ritter, Kelly, and Paul Kei Matsuda. *Exploring Composition Studies: Sites, Issues, and Perspectives*. Utah State UP, 2010.

Scott-Stewart, Erin Dena. *Teaching College Writing to High School Students: A Mixed Methods Investigation of Dual Enrollment Composition Students' Writing Curriculum and Writing Self-Efficacy*. 2018. PhD dissertation, Louisiana State University. LSU Digital Commons, digitalcommons.lsu.edu/gradschool_dissertations/4522.

Shivji, Azim, and Sandra Wilson. *Dual Enrollment: Participation and Characteristics*. US Department of Education, National Center for Education Statistics, 2019, nces.ed.gov/pubs2019/2019176.pdf.

Shor, Ira. "Errors and Economics: Inequality Breeds Remediation." *Mainstreaming Basic Writers*, edited by Gerry McNenny, Lawrence Erlbaum, 2001, pp. 29–54.

Thomas, Nina, et al. *Dual Credit and Exam-Based Courses in U.S. Public High Schools: 2010–11*. US Department of Education, National Center for Education Statistics, 2013, nces.ed.gov/pubs2013/2013001.pdf.

University of Connecticut Board of Trustees. "The Rising Tide of School and College Enrollments." 11 Nov. 1954. U of Connecticut Libraries, Archives and Special

Collections at the Thomas J. Dodd Research Center, President Jorgensen Records, box 10, folder 59.

University of Connecticut Committee on Scholastic Standards and Committee on Curricula and Courses. "Joint Meeting of Committees on Scholastic Standards and Curricula and Courses: February 5, 1953." U of Connecticut Libraries, Archives and Special Collections at the Thomas J. Dodd Research Center, University Senate Records, box 18, folder 1037.

University of Connecticut Cooperative Program. "School-Course Breakdown: 1959–1960." U of Connecticut Libraries, Archives and Special Collections at the Thomas J. Dodd Research Center, University Senate Records, box 14, folder 852.

University of Connecticut News Coordinator's Office. "U of C Plan Boon to Top Students in High Schools," 28 Oct. 1955, for release 6 Nov. U of Connecticut Libraries, Archives and Special Collections at the Thomas J. Dodd Research Center, Office of Public Information Collection, box 5, "HS Plan" folder. Press Release.

Waugh, Albert E. "Comments on the Basic Curriculum for the Freshman and Sophomore Years at the University of Connecticut." 1953. U of Connecticut Libraries, Archives and Special Collections at the Thomas J. Dodd Research Center, University Senate Records, box 18, folder 1037.

———. Daily Journal: 1952. U of Connecticut Libraries, Archives and Special Collections at the Thomas J. Dodd Research Center, Albert E. Waugh Papers, box 16.

———. Daily Journal: 1953. U of Connecticut Libraries, Archives and Special Collections at the Thomas J. Dodd Research Center, Albert E. Waugh Papers, boxes 16–17.

Yancey, Kathleen Blake. "Delivering College Composition: A Vocabulary for Discussion." *Delivering College Composition: The Fifth Canon*, edited by Yancey, Boynton/Cook, 2006, pp. 1–16.

Writing Transitions of First-Generation Writers in a Paired Retention Program and First-Year Writing Course

Christina Saidy

As colleges and universities work to improve retention rates for first-year students, they use metrics to assess which students are most at risk of not being retained and design programs to serve these students. This is especially true at non-elite institutions and large state schools that attract students because of lower cost, geographic location, and accessibility. First-generation students are typically included in this at-risk category based on perceived risks that may hinder their retention: lack of familial support, missing knowledge about navigating the university, and potential financial constraints. Given increased awareness of the risk factors for first-gen students, it is common for instructors to hear reminders about working with first-gen students at faculty meetings and curriculum-focused meetings. Comments such as "that student might be first-gen" often arise when instructors discuss struggling students. Programs such as study abroad, honors programs, and general education programs consider targeting first-gen students. Often, *first-gen* becomes a catch-all term intended to account for the perceived risk factors, most of which are seen as deficits, students face when they enter the university.

While potential risk factors may hinder students in their success, the concept of risk is more complex, so it is an important one to examine, especially for those who work and do research in first-year writing (FYW) programs serving a large number of first-gen students. Because I was a first-gen college student identified as being at risk in my undergraduate education, I am committed to understanding the ways first-gen students navigate entry into college and college writing. The research I describe in this essay comes from a paired retention program (Jump Start) and composition course. Using data from this paired course, I focus on two first-gen college students to deepen understanding of these students' writing transitions, explore what it means for students and writers to be at risk, and use this information to inform the work writing program administrators (WPAs), teaching faculty, and university-level administrators do to serve first-gen students in composition courses, FYW programs, and beyond.

Risk in Composition Studies

Much literature on higher education pedagogy focuses on serving at-risk and first-gen students. Organizations such as the Lumina Foundation and the Center for First-Generation Success support first-gen college students by documenting their challenges, encouraging research, and supporting initiatives. Reports such as *Moving beyond Access* (Engle and Tinto) focus on ways to provide access and success for first-gen, low-income students. Other research focuses on the college engagement of first-gen students (Pike and Kuh; Soria and Stebleton), their college adjustment (Gibbons et al.), the risk factors that prevent their adjustment (Pratt et al.), and the efficacy of summer bridge programs in retaining at-risk students (Kodama et al.). Although the research on risk and first-gen students is prevalent in fields like education, far less research on first-generation students exists in the field of rhetoric and composition.

However, the concept of risk is not new to FYW. Since the establishment of the entrance exam at Harvard University in 1874, the field of rhetoric and composition has documented efforts to assess the level of risk for incoming students. In writing programs, the question of risk is most pronounced at the moment of placement, when we often use numbers—such as test scores and grades—to decide how students fit. As Holly Hassel and Joanne Giordano note, approximately eighty percent of first-year writing placement decisions are made solely based on test scores ("Blurry Borders" 60). At the moment of placement, an at-risk designation influences students' course assignments and communicates how well those students fit in the university.

In his work on race and assessment in writing program administration, Asao Inoue discusses how basic writing courses, Stretch courses, and retention programs focusing on writing remediation disproportionately comprise students of color, especially because of the reliance on test scores for placement. Inoue suggests that placement and assessment are part of a "white racial habitus, a set of white dispositions, that serve the white status quo" (149). In my own work with a first-gen Chicana student transitioning into college, I show how placement practices, such as those described by Inoue and by Hassel and Giordano ("Transfer Institutions"), are problematic because the at-risk designation often affects students in ways the WPA might not even see. First-gen and underrepresented students are typically grouped into a homogenous at-risk category rather than seen complexly.

For years, first-gen and traditionally underrepresented students have been discussed in basic writing scholarship. Since Mina Shaughnessy's *Errors and Expectations*, which documents questions about at-risk writers after the advent of open admissions in the City University of New York system, scholarship in basic writing has worked to explore who basic writers are (Gray-Rosendale; Matsuda; Stenberg), what it means to be prepared for college writing (Adams; Bernstein), and how best to teach basic writers (Adler-Kassner and Harrington; Lalicker; Sternglass). While first-gen students are often grouped into basic writing research, they are not often the sole subjects of study.

This trend is also common in scholarship exploring English in the two-year college. This literature explores the challenges of nontraditional students, many of whom are first-gen, and in particular considers returning students and students who move through requirements slowly (Flores and Flores), questions of accountability that may limit access for nontraditional students (Toth et al.), and writing genres that acknowledge the experience nontraditional students may bring to the university (Aguiar). While first-gen students are generally represented in articles exploring diversity in two-year college scholarship, Holly Hassel notes, "We know that first-generation (and usually working-class or low-income) college students face challenges in acculturating to the expectations of postsecondary education, and yet very little work published in TETYC [*Teaching English in the Two-Year College*] addresses this reality" (349). While the literature reviewed here acknowledges the challenges facing at-risk student writers, it fails to distinguish between at-risk, first-gen, and underrepresented writers, instead using these terms interchangeably.

Transition to College Writing

The transition to college writing is a complex one for even the most prepared students since they must renegotiate their conceptions of writing to adjust to the college context through introductions to academic discourse communities, academic literacies, or both. For example, Elizabeth Chiseri-Strater observes that students may struggle to enter discourse communities because the concept of a discourse community is fraught: the term "implies either that there is one unified shared set of academic language norms that encompass the entire university, or that each discipline or department itself displays internal agreement" (143). Since discourse communities are often various, Jenn Fishman and colleagues note that even traditionally well-prepared student writers become "[f]rustrated with busywork as well as the struggle to become part of different disciplinary discourse communities" (231). This frustration is less rooted in writing experience, since Fishman and colleagues' participants report readily doing self-sponsored and out-of-school writing, and more rooted in the complexity of negotiating the entrance to discourse communities that have varying practices and expectations.

Negotiating multiple discourse communities often proves even more challenging for first-gen students. When writing in a new context, student writers might think about how they have learned to write before, the genres and forms in which they've composed, and the language used to describe writing. Research in composition has found that there can be gaps in this prior knowledge and that when there are no gaps, students struggle to connect prior knowledge in new contexts (Reiff and Bawarshi; Yancey and Morrison; Hannah and Saidy). These issues are not always because of a lack of prior writing experience. In fact, many writers come to college with experience writing in many genres (Hannah and Saidy). Rather, in college, first-year students are asked to compose in similar genres as in high school but with different rules. When this happens, they may default to standardized genres and forms used in high school, but these standardized forms are often not what is expected in college writing, and students may not know how to adapt. First-gen and traditionally underrepresented students may struggle to adapt since many of them come from lower-performing schools (Engle and Tinto) and might never have learned writing beyond formulas in high school (Wiley).

In one of the few studies in composition focusing solely on first-gen students, Ann M. Penrose contends that this gap between prior knowledge and expected knowledge "may represent a critical site of vulnerability" for first-gen students (457). Penrose notes that first-gen students seem more keenly aware of the differences between academic discourse and the discourse of their home communities and may feel like outsiders in the college community, which makes these differences more visible. Penrose argues that for faculty working with first-gen students, "[h]elping students see themselves as members of the academic community may be the most important challenge faced in the university at large and in writing classrooms in particular" (458). FYW programs committed to access for first-gen students can heed Penrose's call for pedagogical innovations.

Paired Courses

Since nearly all students take FYW in some form, FYW programs are often involved in institutional initiatives to pair courses and improve outcomes for student learners. Paired courses have a long history and varied approaches including interdisciplinary or writing-across-the-curriculum pairings (Clark and Fischbach; Hutchinson), formal learning communities (Shapiro and Levine; Wardle), and pairings to improve retention (Holmes and Busser). Ann C. Dean notes, "Coupling composition courses with courses in other disciplines so that students form a cohort or learning community increases student engagement, retention and learning" (65). Yet, through a case study of her own institution,

Dean shows that paired courses are challenging to establish and sustain and that they place burdens on FYW programs. Ashley Holmes and Cristine Busser describe a paired writing course for retention and discuss the challenges of top-down models originating from university initiatives rather than from the expertise of WPAs or writing instructors. While Holmes and Busser see the benefits for students in paired courses, they advocate for models that also take WPA and faculty expertise into consideration.

The Study

This study took place at a university I refer to as Southwestern State University (as per IRB requirements, all the names mentioned with regard to the study are pseudonyms). The university, located in a large metro area in the Southwest, is a large public research university with a mission of increasing access to college. The average high school GPA of incoming students in fall 2018 was 3.53, and their average ACT score was 24.9. The Southwestern State University faculty and administration are tasked with maintaining high retention rates for all students, and the one-year retention rate of the 2017 first-year class was 86.8%. In the 2018–19 academic year, the student population identified as White (49.1%), Hispanic or Latino (twenty-four percent), international (nine percent), Asian (7.4%), Black or African American (4.2%), two or more races (4.4%), unspecified (0.4%), American Indian or Alaskan Native (0.33%), and Native Hawaiian or Pacific Islander (0.2%). That same year, approximately forty percent of students identified as first-generation college students, which is close to the national average.

In response to the university focus on increasing retention rates, especially in nonselective colleges such as the one for liberal arts and sciences, that college created a retention program—Jump Start—for students the university identified as at risk of not being retained. This program, which is explicitly not a study skills or remediation program, introduces students to college-level work, connects them with faculty and peer mentors, and familiarizes them with the campus and its services in the two weeks prior to the start of the academic year. Students self-select into Jump Start, and the number of participants has increased each year. Jump Start is not the university's only program serving at-risk students, however. The provost's office operates an academic-year program and recruits students into a student success class, and a variety of other campus programs operate their own summer programs targeted toward students from particular demographic groups. Students may be recruited for and participate in more than one program.

Jump Start is unique because it is organized disciplinarily and because the content and structure of the two-week program is determined by the faculty members directing each program division by discipline. My research focuses on students enrolled in the Humanities Jump Start program, which I codirected with a fellow faculty member. Students in this program come from majors such as English, film and media studies, history, religious studies, philosophy, and modern languages. In the humanities program, the mornings are spent on academics—exploring the university through writing—and the afternoons are for guest speakers, exploring the campus and local area, and presentations by peer mentors.

After the first year of the program, I saw an opportunity to extend the Humanities Jump Start program by pairing the summer program with an FYW course in the fall semester. This pairing was motivated by my interest in writing transitions, my desire to build a supportive community for at-risk students beyond the summer program, questions about student placement, and personal experience as a student in a college retention program. In response, the codirectors created a section of the FYW course for the Jump Start students, which I taught. Because Jump Start seemed to have a positive impact on our retention efforts and because I had questions about our own writing placement procedures, we allowed students who would have traditionally placed into our Stretch writing course an opportunity to enroll instead in FYW if they completed Jump Start successfully and enrolled in the paired FYW course. The Stretch course extends FYW across two semesters and is for writers who score 18 and below on the ACT.

The FYW course for Jump Start students followed the departmental requirements for FYW courses in goals and objectives, requirements for student work, and the approved textbook. Since I designed the class for Jump Start students, I took Penrose's invitation to see our writing classes as places where students can navigate their space in the university, negotiate the language of the university, and build relationships. I designed course projects to facilitate this navigation. During Jump Start, students completed a photo essay in which they used photographs and text to communicate the significance of entering college at Southwestern State. In FYW, the students completed three major projects: a literacy narrative focused on students' experiences of literacy in their pasts, their sponsors of literacy (Brandt), and ways those experiences of literacy have shaped them; a local issues podcast that invited students to choose an issue from a local community (home or school) to discuss and make an argument about for a larger audience; and a research project on the college student experience. For the third assignment, students worked individually on their research papers and in clusters surrounding their connected research interests to share sources and create a collaborative video public service announcement.

This essay focuses on the paired course in the summer and fall of 2016. That year, twenty-one students participated in the program. Of those students, six identified as first-gen college students. Only four of the first-gen students participated in both Jump Start and the paired composition course because the other two had taken a dual-credit FYW course while in high school. In this essay, I focus on two of the students enrolled in the paired course. I employed a case study of just two students in order to move beyond simplified ideas of risk and to deeply understand the experiences and stories of the students in the paired course (Jehangir; Reid and Moore). I collected data from multiple sources: surveys before and after the Jump Start program, Jump Start coursework and reflections, surveys before and after the FYW course, FYW coursework, writing reflections, research memos, and semistructured interviews after the completion of the FYW course. I collected all data sources from the two students. As the participant descriptions illustrate, these students represent two ends of the spectrum in terms of their comfort with writing, and their cases reveal findings helpful to those working with first-gen students.

Participants

The first participant, Carlos, came to Jump Start from a small city approximately two hundred miles from the university. He identifies as Latino and reports that Spanish was his first language and is the language spoken at his home. He is a first-generation college student who qualified for Jump Start, despite his high school GPA of 3.29 and experience with community college classes while in high school, because of his low admissions score. For the purpose of this essay, at-risk status was determined based on our university's admissions score assigned to each student. The admissions score is primarily calculated based on SAT or ACT score and high school GPA, though there are small adjustments made for socioeconomic status and first-gen status. Because of his low test scores, Carlos also placed into the Stretch writing course but was permitted to enroll in the Jump Start section of FYW.

The second participant, Ana, a local student who identifies as Latina, had taken a year off between high school and college. Ana was forced to move out of her family home after high school and used the extra year to make money. When asked who most supports her in her academic goals, Ana said her friends provided the most support. Ana has a full-tuition scholarship, and Pell Grants pay for her housing. She is financially independent.

My Role

My role in this research is as what James P. Spradley refers to as a participant observer. Spradley notes that a participant observer is identified by dual purpose, explicit awareness, wide-angle lens, insider/outsider experience, introspection, and record keeping (53–58). I met all of these criteria, as I was a professor in both the Jump Start program and the instructor of record in the paired FYW course. I delivered direct instruction, participated in small group workshops, and met with students formally and informally throughout the semester. I acknowledge my subjectivity in this role. As a first-generation college student, I participated in a formal retention program in the summer prior to my first year of college and continued to be served by that program through tutoring services. Later I became an undergraduate writing and literature tutor in the academic year program and in the summer retention program. The people in the program constituted a community that offered me emotional and academic support, and the program's services provided academic support and mentoring.

In making decisions about how the Jump Start paired course would work, I considered many of the powerful learning experiences I had in my own retention program and tried to offer space for the Jump Start students to have their own experiences of community building, valuing of students' prior experience, and a supportive academic context. It would be impossible for me to be completely objective in this research. However, my subjectivity is important, as it motivates me in considering ways my research and teaching can more effectively serve first-gen and traditionally underrepresented and underserved students.

Carlos: A Story of Growth and Persistence

In Jump Start and early writing in FYW, Carlos responded to surveys and writing prompts that offered a lens of how he viewed himself as a writer. In these early assessments, Carlos rates his preparedness for college as a three on a five-point Likert scale. Even more interesting, Carlos responds to the statements "My high school teachers taught me what would be expected of me in college writing" and "My high school English class prepared me for college writing" with a one on the Likert scale. Carlos writes, "Throughout high school most of my English classes taught nearly the same material—basic grammar, punctuation, how to write short stories and journals." He explained, "In college I expect to be writing at new levels I would never imagine myself doing. I know that I'm not fully prepared for the class but I am up for the challenge to become a better writer." Carlos's early self-assessment reflects what we might expect from a struggling writer—limited writing instruction in high school and average to low confidence in writing. However, what stands out is his understanding that while he may not have been fully prepared for college writing, he was excited to grow as a writer, and he believed he could do so.

For Carlos, progress in FYW was slow and steady. He participated seriously in peer review workshops and spent time reading his peers' writing, providing thoughtful responses, and revising his work based on feedback he received. Early in the semester there was a disconnect between the feedback Carlos received in workshops, his intentions for his revisions, and his written work. For example, in the first project for the course, the literacy narrative, Carlos included a story about breaking his arm when he was six years old. In the workshop discussions, his group encouraged him to remove or revise the story because it was not about literacy. In the revision plan, Carlos planned to shorten that part and focus on "writing how it affected me in writing, learning, and life." Yet, when Carlos submitted the final draft, the story of the broken arm was still there, disconnected from his literacy. Carlos told me he had not removed the section because he was worried about length. In his reflection Carlos wrote, "The weakest thing about this piece from my perspective is the number of short sentences and fragments that I used. I tried to correct them and expand on a few, but I still feel that it needs some work." Carlos's struggle is a common one for developing writers who often report concerns about issues such as length and correctness rather than the quality of ideas.

Carlos's perceived writing deficits were evident in the reflective writing on the literacy narrative. Each paragraph of the reflection begins from a point of deficit. The paragraph beginnings are as follows: "Something I struggled with was . . . ," "Something I worked on but is still not quite right . . . ," and "The weakest thing about this piece from my perspective is. . . ." Yet Carlos persisted in his writing development throughout the semester. As the semester progressed, Carlos worried less about length and correctness and began focusing on the quality of ideas. He learned how to use his peers' writing shared in workshops as a model, and his writing improved tremendously. In his reflection on the final research project, Carlos begins his paragraphs with the following statements: "I did my best writing in this paper" and "This assignment helped me to realize there are classes here that could help me in my major." The one negative point—"One of the weakest parts of my paper is the conclusion"—focuses on a technical glitch, not the quality of the writing.

Ana: Writing Assignments as a Point of Connection to College

Ana, a creative writing major, came to FYW with confidence in her writing. On her presurvey she wrote, "Writing is my passion." She was one of the few students in Jump Start who felt prepared for college writing and reported writing in many contexts, including writing for school and for fun. In her literacy narrative in FYW, Ana wrote, "Writing is part of who I am, and without it, I'm like a jigsaw puzzle missing the last piece." Even in her writing confidence, Ana saw room for growth and development as a writer that would help her succeed in college and beyond. In her photo essay for Jump Start, entitled "Reaching," Ana captures this expectation for growth with the photo of a hand reaching, accompanied by the following statement: "Reaching is the only word suitable as to why I am here. I am reaching to become a stronger writer. Reaching to meet every goal that I've scrawled down on paper."

Ana's risk factors in coming to college were not academic. In high school, her grades had been quite good, but she was in a financially precarious position. This became apparent a third of the way through the semester when Ana came to class with what was clearly a case of pink eye. After class, Ana told me she knew she had pink eye, but she had no insurance and did not know what to do. I encouraged her to go to the student health clinic and explain that she had no health insurance but needed help. She did, and the clinic saw her for a nominal fee and provided her with free eye drops. Coincidentally, Ana's health issue occurred as the students were beginning their podcast assignments. Ana came to my office to ask if she could turn this experience into a podcast about health insurance and young people. She believed that most traditional students who had health insurance from their parents were uninformed about how insurance worked and that students like her, who could not afford insurance, had much information they could share with traditional students. The podcast assignment offered Ana an opportunity to make connections between her own experiences as a financially independent first-gen student and the experiences of other college students.

Ultimately, Ana used the assignments in FYW to explore her own place in the university. When the class was discussing the final research project on aspects of the college experience, Ana wrote on the question board: "Is college even worth the money?" This sparked a class discussion about loans and the cost of college. Ana's research question became "Is college worth it?" She and her research cluster shared sources on financial aid, loans, scholarships, and funding. In her paper, Ana explored topics such as types of student loans, reasonable debt, debt aversion, debt reduction strategies, and strategies for educating students about debt. In her paper, Ana writes:

> [D]ebt in some form is inevitable, and is necessary in order to obtain a higher education. But without financial literacy, students will encounter crippling debt. Students must first become aware of all their financial options, and inform themselves on the different types of aid available, then make a decision as to how much should be borrowed, factoring in their intended field of study.

When Ana reflected on her research paper, she wrote, "I feel that I kind of scratched the surface, but I'm still content with the end result." While Ana saw the potential for even more depth of content in her writing, she used the assignments in FYW in fundamental ways to understand the university and advocate for health insurance and for financial literacy among students, both of which were important to her as a financially independent first-gen student.

Carlos and Ana: Community and Belonging

Scholarship on first-gen college students indicates that building a sense of belonging and engagement is one of the greatest challenges these students face (Engle and Tinto; Penrose). Therefore, the paired course was designed to help students develop and sustain a supportive community of writers and learners. Carlos and Ana both formed meaningful relationships in the writing classroom that benefitted them personally and academically. Carlos drew heavily from the supportive Jump Start community in his writing development. In the paired course, students worked in writing groups to give and receive writing feedback. In these groups, Carlos used his peers' drafts as models, often employing stylistic elements he had seen in peers' writing and multimodal work. Early in the semester, Carlos's workshop letters were full of praise for his fellow students. He wrote to one student, "I wish I was talented at writing like you and the others. I loved your piece." In early peer review, Carlos used the opportunity to read solid examples of writing and relied on his peers for honest feedback to revise his writing substantively. While at first Carlos found it challenging to have his writing workshopped, he trusted the relationships he formed in Jump Start that helped him develop as a writer.

Ana came to the program with confidence as a writer, so her peers often asked her for ideas and help. For example, Ana's research question, "Is college worth the cost," sparked lively discussion and inspired other research projects, and Ana's feedback to peers in writing groups reflected both confidence and deep engagement with her peers' writing. For example, in a workshop letter to Carlos, Ana offered constructive suggestions such as, "[M]aybe ask a few people in your math class what they think of the class and attendance. This is definitely a local issue, so I think this would make your argument stronger," paired with supportive comments such as, "I know you started this the day of, but good job in creating something! I like your topic." Not only was Ana often a resource for others in the class, but she also took the advice of her colleagues seriously and used it to shape her own writing.

An added benefit of the paired course was that I was deeply integrated into the community of students. Carlos and Ana regularly attended office hours and asked me for advice about academic and personal issues, such as health and financial issues. It was in office hours that I learned that Carlos was struggling financially. He wanted to work, but his supportive mother worried that working the first semester would impede his success. It was also in office hours that Ana and I worked through her many writing ideas and narrowed big writing ideas into manageable writing topics. The relationships we built in office hours helped me to understand the challenges facing both Ana and Carlos and to respond both personally and pedagogically. This approach runs counter to the research on first-gen students that shows they are less likely to engage with faculty by attending office hours or asking professors for help when needed (Engle and Tinto; Soria and Stebleton). The purposeful pairing of these courses established a community in which the first-gen students regularly sought out the advice of faculty in ways similar to continuing-generation students. After the paired program, both Carlos and Ana kept in touch with me, contacted me for recommendation letters and advice, and returned to Jump Start as peer mentors in subsequent summers.

The Complexity of Risk

Often, the scholarship and university edicts regarding at-risk students, especially first-gen students, focus on the deficits of these students and the challenges they face in entering higher education. These deficits are tied to measurable data—test scores, high school grades, socioeconomic status, first-gen status—and are measured by attrition rates. However, this focus leads to a homogenous view of first-gen students and their perceived risks. As the examples of Carlos and Ana show, risk is complex, layered, situated, and locally constructed.

For Carlos, his risk came from his being a first-gen college student from a historically underrepresented and underserved ethnic group. Yet in many ways he had been well prepared to understand what college was going to be like—he had taken community college classes, had mentors in high school who helped him navigate the college application process, and had supportive parents. Carlos had experienced a limited approach to writing in high school that left him feeling underprepared for college writing, yet he was persistent and believed he could succeed in college writing.

For Ana, risk was measured by her high school grades, socioeconomic status, and first-gen status. Ana had little support outside of the university except from friends. But she was driven and persistent, and she saw herself as a writer. Because she understood her challenges in the paired course, she used the writing assignments to explore the issues that arose from those challenges, to situate herself as a learner at the university, and to excel. The case study of Carlos and Ana, although limited in scope, points to practices that can be beneficial to first-gen students in their transition to college, and college writing in particular.

Pedagogical Implications: Supporting First-Generation Writers in First-Year Writing

While Carlos and Ana were first-generation students and the focus of this study, first-gen students did not constitute the majority of the students enrolled in the section of FYW described in this study. This trend highlights a need to support first-gen students in *all* FYW courses for a successful transition to college writing.

For writing teachers, these cases illustrate the power of meaningful assignments in helping students bridge their home communities and cultures with the community and culture of the university. The photo essay assignment in Jump Start invited students to visually represent the university and their place in it. The personal narrative assignment asked students to consider their past literacy experiences and the ways those experiences shaped their college experiences. The podcast assignment invited students to explore a local community and advocate for a position within that community. Finally, the research project invited students to take what they had learned and explore the workings of the university. For the first-gen students, especially, this sequence valued their past literacy experiences while demystifying the university.

Further, this case study illustrates the importance of developing meaningful communities of writers in FYW. In the paired course, students worked in a variety of groups: heterogenous peer workshop groups, research clusters, and small groups focused on drafting. The heterogenous writing groups used for peer workshops brought together students with varied writing abilities. In these groups, struggling writers like Carlos learned from writers he perceived as stronger. But even confident writers like Ana learned to communicate about writing and take advice from real audiences. In the research clusters, students worked together to answer big questions, share sources, and compose a multimodal product to share. Students were not approaching large research questions about the structure of the university alone but were working together to deepen understanding.

Instead of being seen as deficient because they were labeled as at-risk or because they were first-gen students, Carlos and Ana were supported and challenged through the program curriculum. They were invited to explore topics and ideas of their choosing, which gave them the opportunity to use writing to negotiate their place in the university.

Programmatic Implications: The Potential for Paired Courses

While challenges abound in paired courses, especially courses requiring collaboration across disciplines or across the university, my study shows that paired courses do greatly benefit students, especially first-gen students. However, we should heed Vincent Tinto's warning about learning communities not being "magic bullets" for retention and success (6). Retention programs and learning communities that thoughtfully work to establish community and increase access provide a bridge for students. In this case, the paired course aligned with my research interests and personal experience and built on my expertise as a scholar and teacher. Further, the program aligned with the larger university mission, was funded, and was supported by the writing program. These combined elements led to a successful paired course.

Therefore, based on this research, I suggest that FYW programs committed to access for first-gen students explore two particular avenues for success: shaping programmatic missions and approaches to appreciate first-gen writers and their risks as complex, layered, situated, and beneficial, and not to take a deficit approach to risk; and exploring paired courses that build on faculty expertise and interests and build on programmatic missions focused on access for first-gen students. This second approach may include pairing courses with existing retention programs, as I did, or identifying the potential for paired courses in the existing structure of the writing program.

Areas for Further Research

This research reminds us that writing plays an integral role in the transition to college and the retention of first-gen students. The FYW class, often a student's smallest class, is an important site of influence for students entering college, especially students who have been traditionally underrepresented and underserved. Further research is needed on first-gen students in composition programs, as existing research is limited. Furthermore, it is important for programs to interrogate the ways risk for students is constructed locally and how its identification influences placement in FYW and attitudes about students and their abilities. As the case study of Carlos and Ana illustrates, while they were identified as at-risk, they actually showed great promise and persistence.

Works Cited

Adams, Peter Dow. "Basic Writing Reconsidered." *Journal of Basic Writing*, vol. 12, no. 1, 1993, pp. 22–36.

Adler-Kassner, Linda, and Susanmarie Harrington. *Basic Writing as a Political Act: Public Conversations about Writing and Literacies*. Hampton Press, 2002.

Aguiar, Christian. "'What Work Is': Writing about Work in First-Year Composition." *Teaching English in the Two-Year College*, vol. 46, no. 2, 2018, pp. 147–52.

Bernstein, Susan Naomi. "Teaching and Learning in Texas: Accountability Testing, Language, Race, and Place." *Journal of Basic Writing*, vol. 23, no. 1, 2004, pp. 4–24.

Brandt, Deborah. "Sponsors of Literacy." *College Composition and Communication*, vol. 49, no. 2, 1998, pp. 165–85.

Chiseri-Strater, Elizabeth. *Academic Literacies: The Public and Private Discourse of University Students*. Boynton, 1991.

Clark, Irene L., and Ronald Fischbach. "Writing and Learning in the Health Sciences: Rhetoric, Identity, Genre, and Performance." *The WAC Journal*, vol. 19, 2008, pp. 15–28.

Dean, Ann C. "Understanding Why Linked Courses Can Succeed with Students but Fail with Institutions." *WPA*, vol. 38, no. 1, 2014, pp. 65–87.

Engle, Jennifer, and Vincent Tinto. *Moving beyond Access: College Success for Low-Income, First-Generation Students*. Pell Institute, 2008.

Fishman, Jenn, et al. "Performing Writing, Performing Literacy." *College Composition and Communication*, vol. 57, no. 2, 2005, pp. 224–52.

Flores, Juan, and Becky Flores. "The Gradual Student." *Teaching English in the Two-Year College*, vol. 30, no. 3, 2003, pp. 239–47.

Gibbons, Melinda M., et al. "How First-Generation College Students Adjust to College." *Journal of College Student Retention*, vol. 20, no. 4, 2019, pp. 488–510.

Gray-Rosendale, Laura. "Back to The Future: Contextuality and the Construction of the Basic Writer's Identity in JBW 1999–2005." *Journal of Basic Writing*, vol. 25, no. 2, 2006, pp. 5–26.

Hannah, Mark A., and Christina Saidy. "Locating the Terms of Engagement: Shared Language Development in Secondary to Postsecondary Writing Transitions." *College Composition and Communication*, vol. 66, no. 1, 2014, pp. 120–44.

Hassel, Holly. "Research Gaps in Teaching English in the Two-Year College." *Teaching English in the Two-Year College*, vol. 40, no. 4, 2013, pp. 343–63.

Hassel, Holly, and Joanne Baird Giordano. "The Blurry Borders of College Writing: Remediation and the Assessment of Student Readiness." *College English*, vol. 78, no. 1, 2015, pp. 56–80.

———. "Transfer Institutions, Transfer of Knowledge: The Development of Rhetorical Adaptability and Underprepared Writers." *Teaching English in the Two-Year College*, vol. 37, no. 1, 2009, p. 24.

Holmes, Ashley J., and Cristine Busser. "Beyond Coordination: Building Collaborative Partnerships to Support Institutional-Level Initiatives in Writing Programs." *Retention, Persistence, and Writing Programs*, edited by Todd Ruecker et al., UP of Colorado, 2017, pp. 38–55.

Hutchinson, Mary Anne. "The Composition Teacher as Drudge: The Pitfalls and Perils of Linking across the Disciplines." Mar. 1993. Files.eric.ed.gov/fulltext/ED359553.pdf.

Inoue, Asao B. "Friday Plenary Address: Racism in Writing Programs and the CWPA." *WPA*, vol. 40, no. 1, 2016, pp. 134–55.

Jehangir, Rashné. "Stories as Knowledge: Bringing the Lived Experience of First-Generation College Students into the Academy." *Urban Education*, vol. 45, no. 4, 2010, pp. 533–53.

Kodama, Corinne M., et al. "Getting College Students Back on Track: A Summer Bridge Writing Program." *Journal of College Student Retention*, vol. 20, no. 3, 2018, pp. 350–68.

Lalicker, William B. "A Basic Introduction to Basic Writing Program Structures: A Baseline and Five Alternatives." *BWe: Basic Writing e-Journal*, vol. 1, no. 2, 1999.

Matsuda, Paul Kei. "Basic Writing and Second Language Writers: Toward an Inclusive Definition." *Journal of Basic Writing*, vol. 22, no. 2, 2003, pp. 67–89.

Penrose, Ann M. "Academic Literacy Perceptions and Performance: Comparing First-Generation and Continuing-Generation College Students." *Research in the Teaching of English*, vol. 36, no. 4, 2002, pp. 437–61.

Pike, Gary R., and George D. Kuh. "First- and Second-Generation College Students: A Comparison of Their Engagement and Intellectual Development." *The Journal of Higher Education*, vol. 76, no. 3, 2005, pp. 276–300.

Pratt, Ian S., et al. "Should I Stay or Should I Go? Retention in First-Generation College Students." *Journal of College Student Retention*, vol. 21, no. 1, 2019, pp. 105–18.

Reid, M. Jeanne, and James L. Moore III. "College Readiness and Academic Preparation for Postsecondary Education: Oral Histories of First-Generation Urban College Students." *Urban Education*, vol. 43, no. 2, 2008, pp. 240–61.

Reiff, Mary Jo, and Anis Bawarshi. "Tracing Discursive Resources: How Students Use Prior Genre Knowledge to Negotiate New Writing Contexts in First-Year Composition." *Written Communication*, vol. 28, no. 3, 2011, pp. 312–37.

Shapiro, Nancy S., and Jodi H. Levine. *Creating Learning Communities: A Practical Guide to Winning Support, Organizing for Change, and Implementing Programs*. Jossey-Bass, 1999.

Shaughnessy, Mina P. *Errors and Expectations: A Guide for the Teacher of Basic Writing*. Oxford UP, 1979.

Soria, Krista M., and Michael J. Stebleton. "First-Generation Students' Academic Engagement and Retention." *Teaching in Higher Education*, vol. 17, no. 6, 2012, pp. 673–85.

Spradley, James P. *Participant Observation*. Waveland Press, 2016.

Stenberg, Shari. "Learning to Change: The Development of a (Basic) Writer and Her Teacher." *Journal of Basic Writing*, vol. 21, no. 2, 2002, pp. 37–55.

Sternglass, Marilyn S. "The Changing Perception of the Role of Writing: From Basic Writing to Discipline Courses." *BWe: Basic Writing e-Journal*, vol. 2, no. 2, 2000.

Tinto, Vincent. "Learning Better Together: The Impact of Learning Communities on Student Success." *Higher Education Monograph Series*, vol. 1, no. 8, 2003, pp. 1–8.

Toth, Christie, et al. "A Dubious Method of Improving Educational Outcomes: Accountability and the Two-Year College." *Teaching English in the Two-Year College*, vol. 43, no. 4, 2016, pp. 391–410.

Wardle, Elizabeth A. "Can Cross-Disciplinary Links Help Us Teach 'Academic Discourse' in FYC?" *Across the Disciplines*, vol. 1, 2004. Wac.colostate.edu/docs/atd/articles/wardle2004.pdf.

Wiley, Mark. "The Popularity of Formulaic Writing (and Why We Need to Resist)." *The English Journal*, vol. 90, no. 1, 2000, pp. 61–67.

Yancey, Kathleen Blake, and Brian M. Morrison. "Coming to Terms: Vocabulary as a Means of Defining First-Year Composition." *What Is "College-Level" Writing?*, edited by Patrick Sullivan and Howard Tinburg, National Council of Teachers of English, 2006, pp. 267–80.

On a Path to Fitting In? Listening to First-Generation Students at a Branch Campus

Caitlin Larracey

Postsecondary institutions and the teacher-scholars who populate them invoke the metaphor of a pathway for students who transition from two- to four-year campuses. For four-year institutions, a pathway signifies an access route for students traditionally denied admission based on their perceived academic unpreparedness, institutions' structural or cultural limitations, or the financial inaccessibility of college. Flagship state universities, in particular, often deploy this metaphor in program names, such as Ka'ie'ie Degree Pathway Partnership at the University of Hawaii, Manoa ("Ka'ie'ie"), and LSU Pathway Program at Louisiana State University ("Options"), and in marketing language like this quotation from Ohio State University: "You'll find a path that leads to the very best version of yourself" ("Regional Campuses"). Such pathways claim to serve underrepresented and marginalized students, to offer a set curriculum to move students toward the bachelor's degree, and to reduce college costs. This metaphor is frequently employed on the websites of two-year branch campuses of four-year universities, where students can complete two years of coursework before moving to the main campus.

Branch campus pathways can be attractive options for first-generation college students, who are more likely to be place-bound—because of family or work obligations, socioeconomic need, or a preference to live near home—and are often classified as academically underprepared for selective four-year institutions (Ward et al.; Penrose; Engle and Tinto; Davis). Branch campuses, if they function as described, allow first-gen students to begin college closer to home and offer tailored curricula to support students' academic success, enculturating students to the institution through more manageable steps. Yet there is little writing studies scholarship that maps this path first-gen students take. To chart this territory, I look to branch campus students' first-year writing experiences on the two-year branch (City) of MidAtlantic University (MU), an R1 flagship state university.[1] This interview-based study of first-gen MU students includes those currently enrolled on the branch campus and those who have transitioned to the main campus (Main). Reading across the interviews, I argue that, though one former MU president said the university promises a "smooth, seamless educational path," students recognize several bumps—challenges and pitfalls that were unnamed and so unknown at the time of their application—as well as seams: nuanced differences in their apprehension of their academic preparation and positioning once they transitioned to Main. More specifically, these bumps and seams affect their student identity, their first-year writing experience, and the reality of accessing resources in "one university" (Bird 69).

The National Branch Campus Identity Crisis

In this essay, I focus attention on two-year domestic branch campuses of four-year colleges and universities in the United States—one kind of branch campus among many. Branch campuses and their influence in higher education are understudied. Part of the challenge in this research stems from varied definitions of what constitutes a branch and inconsistency in how branch campuses are "counted" nationally (Bird 65). Put succinctly, "No one knows how many branch campuses and off-campus centers are operated by colleges and universities in the United States" (Bebko and Huffman 49). The National Center for Education Statistics' Integrated Postsecondary Education Data System does not track all domestic branch campuses, as they often do not meet the criteria for required reporting, and not all branch campuses match the system's definition of "a campus or site of an educational institution that is not temporary, is located in a community beyond a reasonable commuting distance from its parent institution, and offers full programs of study, not just courses" ("Integrated Postsecondary Education Data System"). But even this definition of branch campuses does not match the federal definition, which adds that branches must have their "own faculty and administrative or supervisory organization; and . . . [their] own budgetary and hiring authority" ("34 CFR § 600.2"). Researchers who study branch campuses often put forward their own variations of these definitions and also note issues with the terms *main* and *branch* because they can imply dependency on the main campus (Schuman 5) as well as contradict university administrators' "one university" model (Bird 69).

Recognizing, then, the varied histories and purposes of these campuses as well as their potential impact, one near-unifying characteristic that two-year branch campuses share is a focus on access for nontraditional students (Fonseca and Bird). The rhetoric of domestic branch campuses is largely defined by the possibilities they suggest regarding opportunity for students, but the connections these campuses have to selective institutions can inhibit their ability to realize those possibilities, as seen in the challenges students describe below. Branches wrestle with "having a purpose and population different from that of the larger institution" (Caldwell and Cote 23), their relationship with the main campus (Schuman 5), and the main campus's unclear "institutional understanding[s]" of branch students' "unique needs" (Nicholson and Eva 509). Branches face an identity conflict, where they must support one set of students while contending with the institutional practices, procedures, and policies that prioritize another, often more privileged, set of students.

This conflicted campus identity presents a barrier for first-gen students already challenged to acclimate to an environment where they may feel out of place, and this barrier is reinforced in first-year writing courses designed for main campus students. According to Lee Ward and colleagues, four-year institutions with more "threatening" environments for first-gen students must help students integrate into college to reduce their frustration when they feel out of place and to increase their chances of persisting and succeeding (28); Ward and colleagues note specifically that the first year of college is a "cornerstone" and "foundation" for students' overall experience (31). Branch campuses' competing identities complicate students' acclimation, as students must learn the attitudes and behaviors a research university expects while attending a more open-access campus with another set of assumptions. Thus, the work of branch campuses rests on identity formation or reformation as students navigate paths between two-year branches and their corresponding four-year institutions.[2] First-year writing can guide this navigation, as Holly Hassel and Joanne Giordano argue: "Writing studies professionals are perhaps in the best position to stage an intervention to increase the academic success and retention of students whose only pathway to a college degree is through an open-access institution" (126). As writing studies teachers, administrators, and scholars, we can speculate about some of the pressures the branch campus composition classroom presents for first-gen students. But given the opportunity that these campuses hold, we need to know more about how students experience them.

Road versus Path: Profiling MidAtlantic University

As branch campuses vary in their histories, missions, sizes, student populations, and institutional connections (Bird 65), so too do their pathways. Thus, having a sense of where MU sees City students beginning and where they end up provides important context for understanding students' literacy stories. In the larger "pathways" initiative for in-state students described on MU's website, MU details the "academic roadmap" students should follow to increase their likelihood of admission to Main. This metaphorical roadmap illustrates that MU anticipates applicants who have followed a traditional route, which includes college prep, honors courses, and Advanced Placement courses, a cumulative GPA of at least 3.3, and competitive SAT, ACT, and any Advanced Placement or SAT Subject Test scores (not required but encouraged). Additionally, students must maneuver the tolls on this road: that is, the cost of entry into higher education, which can top thirty thousand dollars a year for in-state MU students. Yet this road is not always accessible for in-state students, leading them to attend City instead. City is one location of MU's Associate in Arts Program (AAP), founded in 2005 with the express goal of facilitating access for in-state students who are geographically distant from Main or are less academically prepared than traditionally admitted students. City AAP students, then, are frequently those in-state students either who have gotten lost along this road or who can't afford the tolls. The minimum GPA required for the AAP is 2.5, and the program costs less than eight thousand dollars per year. This admissions structure has predictable results, visible in the campuses' fall 2018 demographics for white students (seventy-one percent at Main, 56.4% at City), low-income students (7.7% at Main, 21.3% in the AAP), and first-gen students (thirteen percent at Main, thirty-five percent in the AAP).

Bringing these campus differences in line with branch campus scholarship, City shares some characteristics with one type of branch campus, which Phyllis Bebko and Dennis Huffman call the "Model C: Four-Year Public Branch" in their branch campus taxonomy. Such campuses are part of large institutions; their "facilities often are co-located with another institution," particularly a two-year college; and they have some student support services (56). MU, City, and Main resemble this model in some ways. However, although City is an urban campus, it is significantly smaller than Bebko and Huffman's model's description of 1,000–1,500 branch students, instead enrolling approximately 200–250 students per semester. City's location in the largest city in the state often matters for AAP students, many of whom are not city residents. The suburban-urban split between Main and City are embodied materially by the two campuses—Main is known for its resonances with suburban academia and its attendant resources and campus features of white columns and red brick pathways; City is half in an MU downtown center and half on 1.5 floors of a community college, and the two buildings are separated by four blocks. These material differences come with racialized and socioeconomic associations and assumptions about campus safety, security, and desirability; in interviews some City students embraced City's diversity and rejected Main as a predominately white institution, while others were uncomfortable with or disappointed by a campus experience different from what they imagined. While we don't know enough about branch campuses to say with certainty, it is likely that this configuration is atypical for branch campus students, as many apply into branches directly or aim to attend the campus located closest to them. As Main is just one town (fifteen miles) away from City, several AAP students live just as close to Main. When they pictured MU, they pictured Main.

For many of the students described above, who belong to groups that have historically been marginalized in higher education, the AAP is a viable path to a research university. Over seventy percent of students who enroll in the program complete it within three years, and of those students, the majority transition to Main. That students make this journey matters, as it illustrates the potential that branch campuses hold for underrepresented students. It also matters that we better understand what this journey looks like for students. MU claims that students experience the same journey whether they begin in the AAP or at Main—the AAP "just starts in a different location." But calling the AAP a "smooth, seamless educational path," as one former MU president claimed, erases the differences between the campuses and does a disservice to MU AAP students when it fails to recognize or affirm the identities and literacies that they bring to City.

Bumps and Seams: Students' Literacy Stories

When it comes to writing, the smooth, seamless path described by the former MU president presumes that City students utilize all available writing resources on the branch campus, at Main, and in the community college; communicate with faculty and advisers; and, critically, identify as MU students. But theoretical access to these resources and identities does not mean that students use them or find them to be useful, nor does theoretical access tell teacher-scholars what's missing as students move from City to Main. This essay privileges students' experiences with and understandings of this path, paying particular attention to where it isn't smooth and seamless.

In this section, I draw on semistructured interviews with six MU students, three who were enrolled in the AAP at the time of the interviews and three who had transitioned to and were in their second semester at Main, to understand their experiences of the first-year composition classroom on this pathway (see table 1).[3] All six students had taken first-year writing at City at least once and self-identified as first-gen.[4] What came to the forefront across students' stories about their admission, histories as writers, and relationship with Main were the bumps and seams along the supposedly smooth, seamless path. Some of these bumps and seams resonate with higher education scholarship, particularly transfer studies. Anne Gere and colleagues forward these terms in their study of University of Michigan transfer students, discussing the shocks and stigmas

Table 1. Student participants (listed in alphabetical order)

Name	Current campus	Gender	Race	Age
Aeon	Main	Male	White	21
Bob	Main	Male	White	21
Bri	City	Female	South Asian	19
Diej	City	Female	African American	20
Hannah	Main	Female	White	23
Rage	City	Male	White	22

associated with the transitions students undergo as they move between institutions ("Mutual Adjustments"). Where applicable, I note similarities between branch and transfer students' experiences. However, I want to honor the fact that City students are not transfer students in their own or the institution's thinking; therefore, I build on the metaphor of the smooth, seamless path as I illustrate their experiences. I treat a *bump* as an event students describe that interrupts the institutional narrative that the program offers the "best of both worlds" between community colleges and research universities. A *seam* is visible evidence of how the campuses have been stitched together; while MU refers to "one university" (Bird 69), the bumps students experience expose the seams between campus populations, resources, and climates. This thematic analysis demonstrates how singular events can define students' college experiences and how these definitions manifest in first-year writing and the campuses' distinct writing cultures.

Admittance Bump: "What Did I Do Wrong?"

The first bump that the students experienced occurred before they arrived on campus. In response to the question, "What drew you to the AAP?" during the first interview, Bri said, "I actually didn't know that it existed. When I applied to MU, this was the program that I got accepted into. And I'm just like, what is this? What did I do wrong?" Bri's response led me to ask later participants if they knew about the AAP prior to their admittance to MU. Students' responses showed that acceptance into the AAP was often the initial bump along their paths. The interviewed students came to the AAP through varied admission processes, and whether they were placed in the AAP or chose to apply to and attend City has had consequences for their student identities and sense of belonging. Students' responses to this line of questioning can be summarized as follows: Bri, Aeon, Rage, and Hannah applied to Main but were accepted to the AAP; for Bri and

Aeon, their acceptance was the first time they had heard of the program, and both of them felt hurt by the decision. In contrast, Rage knew about the AAP and saw it as a "back-up plan." Hannah was initially unaware of the program but pleased with the decision because of the AAP's small size. Bob and Diej were both accepted to Main but chose to enroll in the AAP: Bob for financial purposes and Diej because she was "a homebody." Additionally, both students had siblings who had attended or were attending City.

Bob and Diej did not describe negative feelings about the AAP, likely because of the information they had about it before they matriculated and the control they had through self-placement. Predictably, Bri and Aeon reported struggling with their student identity following their shock over their placement, and Aeon shared that this difficulty continued after he transitioned to Main. Hannah, despite her positive feelings about the AAP, talked at length about struggling with her MU student identity at Main. All six participants seem to fit the scholarly and institutional sketches of first-gen students who can benefit from pathway programs, as they are perhaps less prepared academically than their peers, nervous about attending a large university, or interested in saving money.

Admission into the AAP is sometimes seen as rejection from MU, solidifying student fears about whether they belong in college, which both Bri and Aeon discussed. Bri compared herself to other students, noting that she had a higher GPA than did some of her friends who were admitted to Main. MU told her, in contrast to institutional materials, that her placement had to do with enrollment constraints and her proximity to City. She recalled a friend of hers, however, wondering if her own admission to the AAP was due to her race, as the AAP matriculates a far greater percentage of Black and African American students than does Main, and the friend's remark raised the same question for Bri, who is South Asian. These comments illustrate that students question MU's characterization of the pathway for AAP students as the same as the path for any MU student, as for some AAP students this path begins with feelings of rejection over acceptance. This feeling of rejection can be typical for a transfer student. Gere and colleagues, drawing from higher education research (e.g., Jain et al. and Bahr et al.), define transfer stigma in part by "the assumption that transfer students are inherently less prepared or deserving of admission" ("Mutual Adjustments" 337). Branch campuses complicate this stigma, however, because students feel the stigma not only when transitioning between campuses but also when initially admitted to the branch campus. This perceived stigma emerges in several ways for students at MU, as they try to understand the City campus and program, engage in coursework, and transition to Main.

City students also have trouble explaining the AAP to family and friends, and this difficulty further unravels the MU student identity that they desire and that the university professes to cultivate. Unclear themselves on what the AAP program is, students struggle to explain it to their parents, especially since parents of first-gen students may be unfamiliar with higher education systems. Aeon argued that explaining the program was complicated by the AAP's use of a community college campus in addition to an MU-owned facility: "Whenever we try to tell our parents no, I go to MU . . . [They're like] 'Oh, you mean [the community college] State Tech?' And that sucks. Because you work as a student, and you want that recognition of, no I'm an MU student. But when you try to explain it to them, it's like, 'Oh, but you go to State Tech.'" Such conversations with parents alienate students from the larger institution and call into question the institutional discourse and students' efforts to self-identify. Bri and Aeon suggested that AAP students want to locate a sense of pride in being MU students. Students want this recognition from others, but their academic achievements are thrown into doubt by their admission to and study on the branch campus, which has a less legible structure and an association with a two-year college. Moreover, the bump created by admission to the AAP remains a feature of students' experiences, creating a distinctive seam when those students transfer to Main.

Admittance Seam: "We Just Carry Ourselves Differently"

This struggle to maintain an MU student identity can persist even after students transition to Main. What might have been just a rough patch in the road can become a more permanent divide between students and the institution. Contrasting those negative characterizations students used to describe their entry into the AAP are those positive associations that students build within the program. These optimistic assessments still lead students to separate themselves from other MU students, reframing their relationship with MU. Gere and colleagues note a similar experience of difficulty negotiating peer relationships among transfer students, pointing specifically to students' "[perception of] themselves as coming from a social background quite different from [that of] their new classmates" ("Mutual Adjustments" 350). Hannah and Aeon described a similar difficulty. In addition to having different backgrounds from those of Main students, they came to doubt MU's promise that they were the same as Main students—even though the branch campus students are always, technically, part of the university.

This reframing of students' relationship to the university, and the difficulty fitting in with Main peers, emerged in Hannah's remarks. Unlike many first-gen students, Hannah has had consistent exposure to the university because she lives nearby and because her mother works in the Main library. But despite her "memories of wandering around the library as a little kid," she welcomed MU's decision to admit her to City: "I know I would be like a fish out of water, even though I would be in my own hometown." At City, "I felt like I was more at my roots, because I saw people of all backgrounds there. Like poor folks, you know, diverse community. Because that's what I grew up with . . . I felt I could connect with people there." Hannah drew many of the differences between campuses along racial and socioeconomic lines, citing experiences of oppression at City in contrast to experiences of privilege at Main. Hannah stated, "A lot of the [City] students who were there with me, they were first-generation too. They had the same struggles as I did. Some of them had more struggles than I did," whereas at Main, "[there are a] bunch of rich folks walking around. Rich, privileged, a lot of white people." Hannah differentiated herself from the "tall, thin, pretty, white students who can go on vacation every summer" because of her experiences with poverty, with what she described as her more ambiguous appearance in terms of race (she stated that her family is white but that she and her mother are sometimes read as Black Americans), her self-described "fatness," her age (twenty-three), and her prior attainment of an associate's degree. She felt like she belonged at City, not on the main campus she grew up on. In these ways, Hannah's story valorizes the work of City.

Yet there is another chapter to Hannah's story. Hannah described that she didn't fully realize how much she would feel like a fish out of water at Main until she transitioned to that campus. Before that point, the connections she made at City had characterized her college experience. When I asked her if she felt ready when she transitioned to Main, Hannah reflected: "I was just thinking, it's going to be different because I feel like then *I'll be a real MU student*. But, what they don't tell you is you'll *never* quite feel like a real MU student. Whether you're on main campus or at City . . . I felt like I more so belonged there than I do here. It wasn't until after I got here that I realized that" (emphasis added). Hannah framed this separation negatively by expressing her longing for City and criticizing the university discourse that promised she would feel like she belonged to MU.

Aeon, who, unlike Hannah, was initially disappointed in MU's decision to place him in the AAP, shared her criticism of Main; he had attended a more racially diverse high school and felt that the AAP had a stronger "balance" of students. But beyond racial and socioeconomic differences, Aeon argued that Main and City students are simply not the same, saying, "We just carry ourselves differently," and he valued these differences. Yet his reflections also suggested that he had constructed a student identity around both difference and rejection. Toward the end of the interview, Aeon remarked that City students band together around an identity as "rejects": "We were placed there, rejected." In contrast, he describes efforts to fit in at Main as "conforming" to the university that didn't really want him and that suggested that he was "lucky" he even got the chance to attend through City, in another instance of Gere and colleagues' notion of "transfer stigma" ("Mutual Adjustments" 337). Hannah and Aeon came to question the institutional discourse surrounding their promised college experience. In doing so, they exerted "a counterforce in response to the regulating force of texts circulating within the institution" (Gere et al., "Interrogating" 258). Just because the university wills it (and writes it), does not mean it is so. That first bump students experience on their pathways through the university unearths the seam between the campuses.

MU recognizes this tension in AAP students' identity, as the university's periodic review lists the goal to "strengthen the MU identity of AAP faculty, staff and students." But the duality within students' stories above—where students arrive at City longing for that MU identity but get to Main feeling cut off from it or rejecting it themselves—shows that strengthening that identity is a complex task. These questions of identity can matter more for first-gen students who may come to distrust the institution and may not have external resources to navigate it successfully. Ward and colleagues explain that first-gen students often struggle with role conflict and ambiguity and need to work harder to learn the behaviors, attitudes, and goals expected of college students. The researchers write, "What works on one campus may be inappropriate or ineffective at another campus, which can be a tremendous source of frustration" (59). It is important for universities with branch campuses to consider not only how students might adapt to fit in but also how the institution can adapt, what Gere and colleagues, working again from Peter Bahr and colleagues and Dimpal Jain and colleagues, discuss as transfer receptivity, which "acknowledges that the challenges some transfer students face are a function of the cultures, structures, and resources at the receiving institution" ("Mutual Adjustments" 337). When they start at City, many students already struggle to reconcile their desired identity with their placement. For branch campus students, this reconciliation is layered and fraught, for the distinct qualities of each campus mean that coming to identify with one campus might signify rejecting the other.

First-Year Writing Bump: "I Had Not One but Two English 110 Classes"

Many City students bring these conflicted feelings to first-year writing, which takes place in their first semester. The assumptions about students built into first-year writing courses can help affirm students' identities or ignore them. While AAP faculty members adapt the first-year writing course at MU according to their own teaching expectations, the course overall was designed by faculty and administrators at Main, and the goals and practices built into the course are intended for Main students with their average high school GPA of 3.71, median family income of $140,000 per year, and residential student experience. City faculty and administrators have little input on the curriculum and limited access to Main's writing program administrators (WPAs). Pass rates for the course reveal significant differences: for fall 2016, 2017, and 2018, the pass rate at Main hovered around ninety-three percent, whereas City's pass rate was approximately seventy-six percent. In individual classes, according to writing administrators on both campuses, the City pass rate might only reach sixty percent. Interview participants experienced the course in distinct ways, demonstrating varied relationships to writing. As might be expected in a self-selected study of this sort, several participants expressed high confidence and interest in writing: Diej and Hannah identified themselves as creative writers, Aeon wrote a novel in high school, and Bob felt highly prepared to write based on his experiences doing Advanced Placement coursework. Still, variations in faculty pedagogy and students' misunderstandings about the function of the course affected students' success and satisfaction with first-year writing.

The six students gave markedly different descriptions of the focus, teaching style, and difficulty level of first-year writing and had varied results in their sections of the course, leading two to take first-year writing twice. This fail rate correlated with the larger context of first-year writing at City. The two students that retook the course, Hannah and Bri, noted that they succeeded in all their other courses that semester. Bri withdrew from the course primarily because of her own misperceptions around it—she thought it would be easy. She assumed a lower difficulty in part because she was in the AAP—the program for underprepared students (and she didn't see herself as underprepared). Main campus friends reinforced this perception: "They always make me feel like I have it easier because I'm here, but mostly it's kind of like, I'm actually struggling." Bri talked about the course as being all about "rhetoric," whereas her City friends took sections that were grounded in reading novels, a more familiar activity. She retook the class with the same professor, though she tried to avoid doing so, and found the work the second time more manageable because of her familiarity with the class. She questioned, however, if she "would have been a different writer" if she had taken another section, and she argued that the varied approaches to the first-year writing course were "confusing" for students.

If Bri's experience can be considered common for students who do not initially succeed in first-year writing, Hannah's experience offers an extreme example of how faculty can shape student success. Hannah remarked that she had an "interesting" experience with English 110, the first-year writing course, because "I had not one but two English 110 classes." But Hannah did not take the class twice because she failed to pass it the first time. Rather, she thought she had failed the first time based on her sense that her professor "didn't care if we passed or not." Although she had actually achieved the C minus required for the course, when she reregistered for the class "it's not like MU said, hey you already passed this class. They [her academic adviser] said, you already took this class, but they didn't stop me from adding it again." While her repetition of the course likely extended her time to degree and added additional cost, Hannah reflected positively on retaking the course. She remembered her first professor saying, "I laugh when my students fail," which likely heightened students' anxiety about the course, but she described her second instructor as caring and helpful. She concluded, "Even though I didn't fail my previous class, I was actually able to succeed in my second class," whereas in her first semester she had "felt like no matter what I was wrong." It was only her misperception that she'd failed that led Hannah to rebuild her writing confidence at City and her identity as a capable student and writer.

Students do not always know where to turn to for writing guidance, despite MU's assurances that they have access to both the university's main campus and community college resources. While Main resources are always theoretically available for students, it is not always possible for students to use them. Some students live close to Main but still report feeling uncomfortable navigating the campus. They often rely on resources of their own design, such as friends who are English majors, older siblings, and parents. Rage, who saw his writing abilities as neither great nor terrible but described having a strong work ethic to improve his writing through professor and peer feedback, talked about how he frequently didn't have time to use Main's writing resources because of his job and that he didn't realize until his last semester that City had a writing tutor who offered limited hours each week. Students who did use City's writing tutor described that experience positively and suggested that all City students should take advantage of that resource, while noting that it wasn't always possible to match their schedule with available appointments. Few of the students reported feeling comfortable with seeking out institutional resources; they were resourceful on their own and worked hard to manage their various responsibilities, but they could have benefited from more consistent use of campus resources. There are, of course, many pressures on students that can prevent them from success in first-year writing, several of which need to be addressed through student support services and not through academic resources. Writing studies scholars and program administrators, however, can address many of the barriers that are inadvertently or deliberately placed in front of students by gaining more knowledge about the first-year writing course and adopting a more tailored approach to the students taking it.

First-Year Writing Seam: "Is This for Me?"

Until she retook first-year writing, Hannah felt actively excluded from college writing despite her aspirations to be a writer. But it was Bob, a student who expressed a strong confidence in his writing and stated his sense of belonging as an MU student after choosing the AAP, who actually asked the question "Is this for me?" He asked this question both when he got his first-year writing syllabus at City and again when he transitioned to Main and saw that he would need to write a twenty-page paper for an upper-level history course. Bob ultimately answered that question with a resounding yes. Though he noted that he saw many students withdraw that first semester at City because "college just wasn't for them at that time," he described having a highly positive experience in first-year writing. He carried this sense of what he saw as a "family" working together in his first-year writing class to Main, where he described overcoming his initial fears about writing requirements by outlining, drafting, and staying on top of his work as he had learned to do in first-year writing. Alongside Bri and Hannah's stories, Bob's interview demonstrates that student identity in first-year writing varies based on course content, teaching practices, and students' expectations and that, perhaps most important to student success rates, student identity isn't consistent across the branch.

Student experiences aren't always as extreme as Hannah's story of what she saw as a cruel faculty member; rather, they can emerge out of individuals' attempts to adapt the course for the most academically underprepared in the room. Aeon came into first-year writing with a different mindset, for instance, than Bri (who thought her classes would be easy). He was concerned with being successful in college, especially following what he perceived as a rejection from MU Main, something he ascribed to his own lack of effort and inadequate academic performance in the first half of his high school career:

> I'm like, I gotta get ready for this. I'm not gonna blow this whole college thing. Because I was worried about that. I was like, I don't want to blow this. Because my sister tried to do college. She blew it. So I can't mess this up. So I walked in thinking it was first day analysis stuff. Where is this book [a summer reading book] that we had? I honestly felt that—I got worse? Not worse. Maybe I worded that wrong. I felt I was so overprepared that it ended up hurting me. Like, we ended up doing basic grammar stuff, things that everyone should know. And maybe that's what E110 is, like make sure that you know this kind of stuff. It's basics. But I don't know. That's how I felt.

If we apply Bob's question "Is this for me?" to students such as Aeon, we can say that first-year writing is not always for them, for reasons as varied as the students themselves. Students do not always feel as though they fit in their courses. Sometimes this is because of hostile interactions or academic difficulties, but not always. For Aeon, first-year writing was too easy. Despite Aeon's tongue-in-cheek summary of the course—"Here's the thing about E110. It was awfully forgettable"—his larger narrative demonstrates the pressure students bring to bear on themselves in first-year writing. It's not only about writing in that one class but also about their commitment to college (Aeon), their major or their career goals (Hannah), or their understanding of themselves as students (Bri and Bob). It becomes even more important, then, that students succeed and feel supported in the class. And, thus, it becomes more problematic that the course design is determined at Main and that there are few writing program connections across City and Main to support course development. Students experience many different kinds of bumps in first-year writing, some that are easily addressed and some that create more lasting damage, leading students to have doubts about belonging or about their capabilities that potentially unravel the institution's claim that this pathway represents the best route to the university for these students. Bri commented on AAP coursework in general: "Maybe I'm doing better with my work [because I'm here and not at Main], but is this the work I need to be doing?"

Bri reflected that her inability to use the writing resources at either City or Main raised her doubts about fitting into MU, and in some ways she connected her identity as a City student to her resource use. She said that the AAP "feels like high school," where you "do your 9–5" at school and then work or help out at home: "When you're here it's a different mindset. When you're on [Main] campus it's like oh I'm in school, it's all about school, I always make time for school." City's structure shaped her behaviors, distancing her not only from academic resources but also from the social and cultural college world. But perhaps the mindset Bri describes is unsurprising; after all, students are on a path. They are not at their destination but are seeking to reach it. The seams this bump exposes, then, may be that AAP students' use of resources follows those resources' inaccessibility—which is the institution's responsibility—and that the mindset of City students, as Bri described it, is a direct result of their external obligations and MU's discourse that figures City students as not really there.

Road Work Ahead

Considered together, the interviews with Aeon, Bob, Bri, Diej, Hannah, and Rage move us toward understanding the needs of first-gen students whose pathways through higher education begin on a two-year branch campus. Though they share many characteristics with first-gen students more broadly, their placement on a branch campus creates an institutionally specific set of pressures on their identity and mindset and influences how they experience composition instruction. Writing faculty and administrators are in the position to study and recognize how students' identities intersect with composition and college. We can gain much through the study of branch campus student identity and writing through campus-specific and comparative writing assessments, research, pedagogical development, and cross-campus advocacy efforts to better support branch campus students. This essay shows that branch campus students overlap with transfer students more than institutions indicate, and following Gere and colleagues' work on transfer students, there are "three levels" at which teacher-scholars in writing studies can support branch campus students: "as researchers operating on the national scene, as researchers and writing program administrators within our own institutions, and as instructors in our classrooms" ("Mutual Adjustments" 353).

At the national and potentially international level, this essay shows the need for branch campuses to be explicitly recognized in writing studies research. Broadly speaking, we need more research in nearly all aspects of writing on branch campuses:

Institutional context: We must learn more about branch campuses' histories, missions, and organizations, especially relative to access initiatives.

Administration: Branch campus researchers frequently mention inequitable access to institutional power (e.g., curricular control) in instructors' syllabi and assignments, in access to writing resources, and in the ability to reach external supports like library services, tutoring groups, or robust writing center resources.

Student experience: This essay addresses a small number of first-gen students' experiences. This research could be enriched and complicated by surveys, longitudinal studies, and classroom observations that consider how students identify with branch and main campus institutions and how other facets of their identity intertwine with their campus location or locations.

Student writing: Further research should also examine branch students' writing in the context of whether the branch campus offers a two- or four-year degree and whether students move to the main campus.

Perhaps most significantly, for readers whose institutions do not have branch campuses, this research emphasizes the complexity of writing as it pertains to sites of writing. These sites do not have to be as conceptually far apart as a two-year college and an R1 university. Gere's recent collection comparing the writing development of students who minor in writing with the development of those who don't, as measured across their time in college, illustrates "the variability of writerly development as shaped by shifting contexts and resources" ("Introduction" 249). Students programmatically separated from a main campus student body may also experience writing in significantly disparate ways. This strain of research, like Gere's work and this essay, thus calls for even closer attention to students' institutional contexts, whether they transfer, matriculate through initiatives like Upward Bound, are in honors programs, or participate across a combination of programs, campuses, and institutions.

In the absence of larger national research, writing program faculty and WPAs across campuses can still work locally to support branch campus students. Gere and colleagues' concept of "mutual adjustment" is particularly applicable here: "Instead of the one-directional expectation that transfer students adapt to our institutional environment, we recognize that the university also has a responsibility to make research-based adjustments to become more receptive to transfer students" ("Mutual Adjustment" 336). MU's AAP is, in many ways, a placement program, and the university expects that this program will adjust students to the university's expectations. But for branch campus students, mutual adjustment requires that the institution also recognize the changes it must make to provide promised access. WPAs and faculty are in a unique position to advocate for this adjustment. First, WPAs and faculty need to dismantle assumptions that all the students in the program or classroom have taken the same path to get there. For WPAs on main campuses, this action might lead them to cooperate with institutional research offices to get a local count of how many students come to the main campus from any university branch campuses. WPAs can also cooperate with branch campus administrators and faculty—particularly when branch campuses do not have an institutionally recognized WPA—to build sustained and cooperative relationships that acknowledge branch campus faculty's expertise while also extending additional writing resources and assessment protocols to the branches. It is likewise important, because of writing courses' role in acclimating students to institutional contexts and expectations, for writing faculty members on the branch campus to recognize the unique challenges their students might face when coming to the branch and transitioning to the main campus. First-year writing courses provide an opportunity for students to engage in explicit discussion of, and writing about, student identity. Branch campus students can get many conflicted messages about their identities; acknowledging those messages through in-class writing, discussion, analysis of institutional materials, and other activities can support students in creating their own vocabulary about who they are and what they hope to accomplish.

Taken together, these suggestions emphasize that the pathways offered by branch campuses need not be another stressor for first-gen students trying to reach their personal, academic, and professional goals. As the title of this collection suggests, there is more to their experiences and their potential than simply fitting in. We need to be sure that in trying to provide pathways to the university, we are not actually getting in students' way.

Notes

1. MidAtlantic University and City are pseudonyms used to preserve the anonymity of participants.

2. The work of the branch campus is similar to the work of the composition classroom as described by writing studies scholars in their historical approaches to first-year writing across different contexts. See Ritter; Crowley; Miller.

3. This study received IRB approval, and the participants chose their pseudonyms. Interviews lasted thirty to sixty minutes, and students received a ten-dollar gift card for their participation, an amount that exceeds the state's minimum hourly wage. I'd like to thank the students for their generosity, good humor, and time.

4. For this study I used the following definition, which I shared with the student participants: "A first-generation college student is one where neither of their parents has received a bachelor's degree (they might have an associate's or attended some college at any level)."

Work's Cited

Bahr, Peter Riley, et al. "A Review and Critique of the Literature on Community College Students' Transition Processes and Outcomes in Four-Year Institutions." *Higher Education: Handbook of Theory and Research*, edited by Michael Paulsen, Springer, 2013, pp. 459–511.

Bebko, Phyllis, and Dennis Huffman. "Developing a Typology of Branch Campuses: Findings from the NABCA Campus and Center Administrator Survey." *Metropolitan Universities*, vol. 22, no. 1, 2011, pp. 48–64.

Bird, Charles P. "A Perspective on the Future of Branch Campuses." *Metropolitan Universities*, vol. 22, no. 1, 2011, pp. 65–78.

Caldwell, Corrinne A., and Lawrence S. Cote. "Accreditation and Two-Year Branch Campuses." *New Directions for Community Colleges*, no. 83, 1993, pp. 17–25.

Crowley, Sharon. *Composition in the University: Historical and Polemical Essays*. U of Pittsburgh P, 1998.

Davis, Jeff. *The First-Generation Student Experience: Implications for Campus Practice, and Strategies for Improving Persistence and Success.* Stylus, 2010.

Engle, Jennifer, and Vincent Tinto. *Moving beyond Access: College Success for Low-Income, First-Generation Students.* Pell Institute, 2008, files.eric.ed.gov/fulltext/ED504448.pdf.

Fonseca, James W., and Charles P. Bird. "Under the Radar: Branch Campuses Take Off." *University Business*, 1 Oct. 2007, dev-new.universitybusiness.com:8080/article/under-radar-branch-campuses-take. Accessed 22 Aug. 2018.

Gere, Anne Ruggles, editor. *Developing Writers in Higher Education: A Longitudinal Study.* U of Michigan P, 2019.

———. "Introduction to Section Five." *Developing Writers in Higher Education: A Longitudinal Study*, edited by Gere, U of Michigan P, 2019, pp. 247–54.

Gere, Anne Ruggles, et al. "Interrogating Disciplines/Disciplinarity in WAC/WID: An Institutional Study." *College Composition and Communication*, vol. 67, no. 2, 2015, pp. 243–66.

Gere, Anne Ruggles, et al. "Mutual Adjustments: Learning from and Responding to Transfer Student Writers." *College English*, vol. 79, no. 4, 2017, pp. 333–57.

Hassel, Holly, and Joanne Baird Giordano. "Occupy Writing Studies: Rethinking College Composition for the Needs of the Teaching Majority." *College Composition and Communication*, vol. 65, no. 1, 2013, pp. 117–39.

"Integrated Postsecondary Education Data System (IPEDS)." *National Center for Education Statistics*, US Department of Education, nces.ed.gov/statprog/handbook/ipeds.asp.

Jain, Dimpal, et al. "Critical Race Theory and the Transfer Function: Introducing a Transfer Receptive Culture." *Community College Journal of Research and Practice*, vol. 35, no. 3, 2011, pp. 252–66.

"Ka'ie'ie (Degree Pathway Partnership)." *University of Hawai'i Community Colleges*, 2018, uhcc.hawaii.edu/kaieie/.

Miller, Susan. *Textual Carnivals: The Politics of Composition.* Southern Illinois UP, 1991.

Nicholson, Heather, and Nicole Eva. "Information Literacy Instruction for Satellite University Students." *Reference Services Review*, vol. 39, no. 3, 2011, pp. 497–513.

"Options to Transfer to LSU." *Louisiana State University*, 2018, www.lsu.edu/admissions/apply/options-to-transfer.php.

Penrose, Ann M. "Academic Literacy Perceptions and Performance: Comparing First-Generation and Continuing-Generation College Students." *Research in the Teaching of English*, vol. 36, no. 4, 2002, pp. 437–61.

"Regional Campuses." *Ohio State University*, 2022, undergrad.osu.edu/regional-campuses.

Ritter, Kelly. *Before Shaughnessy: Basic Writing at Yale and Harvard, 1920–1960.* Southern Illinois UP, 2009.

Schuman, Samuel. "Introduction: The University of Minnesota's Main(e) Campus." *Leading America's Branch Campuses*, edited by Schuman, Rowan and Littlefield, 2009, pp. 1–14.

"34 CFR § 600.2—Definitions." *Legal Information Institute*, www.law.cornell.edu/cfr/text/34/600.2.

Ward, Lee, et al. *First-Generation College Students: Understanding and Improving the Experience from Recruitment to Commencement*. Jossey-Bass, 2012.

Bridging Literacies: First-Generation Transfer Students in a Writing Studies Major

Christie Toth, Cristina Guerrero Perez, Kathryn Henderson, Jose Loeri, Joseph Andrew Moss, Jacque Thetsombandith, Adilene Tolentino, and Clint Gardner

In summer 2019, a team of seven first-generation transfer students from Salt Lake Community College (SLCC) collaborated with Christie Toth, a University of Utah faculty member, to compose what we call a *collective autoethnography*. All student coauthors were participants in Writing Studies Scholars, a bridge program for SLCC students transferring into the university's writing and rhetoric studies (WRS) major. Our collective approach adapts the autoethnographic method A. Suresh Canagarajah, following the methodologist Caroline S. Ellis, calls the "interactive interview," in which coresearchers develop mutual interview questions and construct a narrative in the form of a written dialogue (119). We expanded this method into a polylogue. We developed a set of questions for ourselves, responded to those questions in writing individually, discussed our responses, revised collaboratively over seven face-to-face meetings, and invited Clint Gardner, program manager of SLCC's College Writing and Reading Centers and coteacher in our 2018 summer bridge course, to incorporate his written response. According to Canagarajah, autoethnography is often motivated by a desire for social change (115), and our collective autoethnography was crafted in that spirit. Together, we sought to reflect critically on first-gen experiences in Writing Studies Scholars and to arrive at insights that could improve the program for future students.

Here is what we learned: First-gen students often benefit from a strong and supportive community of peers, faculty, and advisers at their educational institutions. Our 2018 summer bridge course, Writing across Locations, succeeded in fostering community among the students who contributed to this essay, and that community helped encourage them to transfer to the university and persist through initial challenges. However, Writing Studies Scholars is not yet succeeding in sustaining posttransfer community for all students. The university remains alienating for some first-gen students because of attendance costs, the predominantly White and comparatively affluent culture of the students and faculty, and campus opportunities that are typically structured for so-called traditional middle-class students. In response to these collaborative insights, we are making changes to Writing Studies Scholars to better sustain community in the coming years.

Introductions

Joseph Andrew Moss: I am a twenty-two-year-old African American cis man and a transfer student who started at the University of Utah in fall 2019. I'm majoring in WRS and communication (with an emphasis on journalism) with a minor in creative writing. Without telling the whole story, my biological father and mother weren't always in my life, so at times I didn't have my parents around, and at times it felt like I didn't have any at all. Not to disrespect my grandparents who raised me, but I knew they weren't my parents. They didn't look like me. So you can check that box on top of all the other ones I already had for being a young Black child in a majority White state that wasn't created for me since I'm also not of the majority religion. You could say that from the jump I was an outsider, and even at such a young age I understood there wouldn't be any help from the inside group.

Jose Loeri: I'm a twenty-one-year-old Latino cis man born in the United States. My dad never went to college, and my mom went to college on and off for a long time. She got her associate's degree a year after I got mine. I'm currently a junior at the university, majoring in WRS and linguistics and working toward getting a TESOL certificate. I got my associate's degree at SLCC, where I still work at the Student Writing and Reading Center (SWRC).

Cristina Guerrero Perez: I am a twenty-one-year-old first-generation DACA transfer student. I obtained an associate's degree, and I am furthering my education by moving on to a bachelor's degree. When I was born my parents made the decision to move their family across borders so their children could have many opportunities. I come from a family of seven: my parents and five children. I am the youngest. In their own unique ways, my siblings are successful—we all chose different paths. I am the only one pursuing a college degree and attempting a different lifestyle. Because of this, I don't always have support, and I also don't have guidance or help. I learned my own way around higher education, from the language to time management to logistics. There were many times I wanted to quit, but I haven't yet, and I hope I never do because I want to be able to support others like me.

Jacque Thetsombandith: I'm a twenty-one-year-old Asian American student attending the university. I am double majoring in chemistry and WRS. I grew up in a primarily Laotian-speaking household. I am the oldest child with two younger siblings, ages twenty and eighteen. My parents came to the United States in the 1990s. They attended SLCC for ESL classes because they needed to improve their English to apply for decent jobs. I got my associate's degree at SLCC and transferred to the university in 2018. I was filling a role that parents typically have for my siblings. They came to me about their college prospects. Yet throughout college, they also filled that same role for me. We became each other's connection.

Adilene Tolentino: I am a twenty-one-year-old Chicana, meaning I am of Mexican descent, born in the United States, divided between two cultures and opposing identities. Ever since I learned how to speak and read in English, I've been a translator for my parents. I was an adult before I was of legal age. Being Mexican American is exhausting and anxiety-inducing, because as part of a minority population, I have to work twice as hard. But it also means I get to create my own path. I received my associate's degree in English from SLCC and transferred to the university. I majored in WRS and graduated in fall 2019. Even though my parents didn't have any experience with higher education, they worked tirelessly to help me acquire everything I needed to succeed and infused a strong work ethic in me. Even though, three years later, I still need to explain to my parents what I majored in, the truth is, they have their eyes and hopes on me.

Katie Henderson: I'm a forty-year-old English-speaking White cis woman born in the United States. I'm a mother and a wife and was a mortgage professional for twenty years. I'm double majoring in WRS and anthropology. I grew up military, the oldest of four children. My father enlisted in the navy at nineteen and trained in information technology. My mother went to vocational school and certified as a medical assistant. When I first decided to go to college after high school, I started at a local state college because it was inexpensive and had open admissions. By age twenty, I had a family and a career, so I ended up in and out of school more than once. I'd always hoped to finish a bachelor's degree and possibly even go on to graduate school, but doing so seemed unrealistic given the challenges of a full-time career and family. When I decided to go back two years ago, I was trying to encourage my daughter, a recent high school graduate who'd had a bad first experience with college, to give school another chance. I figured the best way to advocate for her was to navigate the process myself, so we enrolled together at SLCC.

Clint Gardner: I am a fifty-four-year-old White cis man born in the United States. I grew up on a farm in a predominantly English-speaking community. I am also a first-generation college student, but I was not a transfer student. For approximately thirty years, I have managed the College Writing and Reading Centers at SLCC. I see the writing center not only as a place of student learning and support but also as a place that can address issues of oppression and exclusion that may go unnoticed in the traditional classroom and as a place that can engage students—as peer consultants—in new learning opportunities by having them take part in planning and developing the center's overall mission. I bring this orientation to my collaborations with university faculty and SLCC-U transfer students.

Christie Toth: I am a thirty-seven-year-old White cis woman born in the United States. Unlike my coauthors, I am continuing-gen and did not transfer from a community college. I grew up in predominantly English-speaking US military communities, mostly overseas. When I graduated from high school, my parents expected me to go to college, had some knowledge of the application process, and were able and willing to pay for much of my undergraduate degree. For a decade and a half, however, I have taught first-gen students at a range of two- and four-year institutions. In fall 2019, I entered my sixth year in WRS, where I have been working with SLCC faculty and students to develop Writing Studies Scholars. My educational trajectory, cultural and linguistic background, and embodied experiences and privileges as a middle-class White woman are different from those of my coauthors, so I try to listen carefully to the perspectives they relate, particularly when those perspectives challenge my assumptions about what we are building together.

Challenges and Resources for First-Generation Students

Community college transfer students have been largely invisible in writing studies (for exceptions, see Mathison; Goldblatt; Alexander; Gere et al.), a phenomenon that reflects the pervasive university-centrism of the discipline (Hassel and Giordano; Rodrigo and Miller-Cochran; Toth et al.; Toth). That university-centrism obscures the writing experiences of a large group of first-gen students. Forty-one percent of US undergraduate students are enrolled in open-admissions community colleges, and twenty-nine percent of those students are in the first generation of their family to attend college (*AACC Fast Facts*). That last percentage is considerably higher at some institutions, including SLCC, where fifty-six percent of students are first-gen ("About SLCC"). Community colleges enroll a disproportionate share of students from many groups underrepresented in US postsecondary education:

White people constitute seventy-seven percent of the US population but forty-six percent of community college students.

Fifty-six percent of Native American college students, fifty-two percent of Latinx college students, forty-two percent of Black or African American college students, and thirty-nine percent of Asian and Pacific Islander college students attend two-year institutions.

Fifty-six percent of community college students are women.
Forty-six percent are older than twenty-two.
Fifteen percent are single parents.
Twelve percent have documented disabilities.
Five percent are veterans.
Nine percent are not US citizens (*AACC Fast Facts*), and community colleges are the primary point of access to postsecondary education for undocumented and DACA students (Perez).

Community college transfer is an important pathway for first-gen students seeking a bachelor's degree, and their first-gen status intersects with many other identities, experiences, and material factors that influence their educational trajectories. Nationally, transfer rates are low and inequitable. While eighty-one percent of entering community college students say they aspire to earn a bachelor's degree, only twenty-five percent transfer to a four-year institution within five years (Jenkins and Fink 1), and just sixteen percent ultimately earn a bachelor's degree (Shapiro et al., *Completing College* [Signature Report No. 12] 5). There are also racial disparities in transfer rates: eleven percent of Latinx students and nine percent of Black students who begin at two-year colleges eventually complete bachelor's degrees, compared to nineteen percent of White students and twenty-three percent of Asian-heritage students (Shapiro et al., *Completing College* [Signature Report No. 12b] 17). Following the insights of critical higher education scholars (e.g., Jain et al.), we believe two- and four-year institutions have a shared responsibility to support community college transfer students and should make explicit commitments to addressing race- and class-based transfer gaps (see Toth). Fulfilling that responsibility requires working to understand the challenges first-gen transfer students face and valuing the resources they bring.

Jacque: After graduating high school in 2016, I had an important decision to make: which college should I attend? Unfortunately, I was alone in this decision-making process. I remember walking into my parents' room with my laptop. There were multiple tabs opened to different colleges. I asked them which one I should attend. They told me: "Whichever one works for you." SLCC seemed like the perfect choice for me because class size at the school typically did not exceed thirty students. My parents knew right from the start how important education would be for me and my siblings, so they worked weekends and overtime to start saving toward our college funds. My parents have such high expectations, and for good reason: they don't want their kids to live a life of struggle like they did. Regardless, such expectations make things more complicated for us.

Adi: I've always known I'd attend college. I didn't know what to expect or how I would do it, but I knew I would. I've always been an overachieving honor student, and I knew I wanted more than just a high school diploma. After applying for scholarships for four consecutive years, I earned a full ride to SLCC. But I never had anyone to guide me or teach me what I had to know to get through college. I was learning and teaching myself as I went. I struggled with college readiness, financial challenges, lack of self-esteem, adjusting to college, and racial disparities on campus. I was unfamiliar with the rigor and expectations of the college curriculum, but I was also unable to ask my family for help. I had to rely on school personnel and peers for guidance and information. It seems as though everyone is counting on me to be perfect—they've placed all of their bets on my success. Being a first-gen student has been a challenge, but it's a challenge I now recognize as a blessing. I ingrained the value of academic achievement in my younger siblings and modeled strong academic behaviors that will encourage them to pursue scholastic endeavors.

Katie: My parents wanted me and my siblings to go to college, but there wasn't really money or a plan to make it happen. I got decent grades in high school, but I never applied for scholarships or filled out any college applications; I had no idea how any of that worked. Instead, I pursued a career and took classes when I could, always hoping I'd eventually finish a degree.

Jose: I've found being first-gen somewhat challenging. Even though my mom had been going to college on and off, I didn't have any help to find what I needed in college. I remember my parents telling me to go but not really giving me any direction on how to do so: how to find the funds, what classes to take, who to talk to, etc. I think this experience makes being a first-gen student unique. My parents didn't have the same connections or knowledge as traditional students, making my transfer to the University of Utah much harder. However, I think my experiences being first-gen helped me understand more readily the power dynamic of the discourses at the university. Who makes the rules? And how do the rules keep me out of certain spaces and places?

Cristina: Being a first-generation college student is exhausting. We don't come from generations of degrees. Everything we do in college is a first experience for everyone in our families. No connections and no guidance. Apart from school, first-gen students deal with familial expectations, bills, work, and the -ships (fellowship, internships). I was expected to do certain house obligations as a daughter living with my family, I was expected by my professors to do my homework and readings every night, I was expected by my managers to work eight- or nine-hour shifts five times a week, and I expected myself to stay calm and breathe even when I hated the life I was living. I always hear, "If college were easy, everyone would do it." Some challenges are more difficult for some people. Not everyone qualifies for financial aid or student loans, not everyone has support from their family, not everyone has peers they can fall back on, and not everyone sticks around to graduate. At some point, the cons can outweigh the pros.

Joseph: Some of the experiences I have daily as a POC (Person of Color) are the same as the ones I have as a first-gen student. There's always a looming sense that "you aren't welcome here. Why are you here? Who let you in?" It's like I've been playing a video game with only half the controller, or a game of Uno but I have to find a way to get rid of half the deck versus the regular seven cards everyone else gets. Not only do I need to overcome the disadvantages I face, I need to go beyond them to succeed. There isn't room to screw up. Don't get me wrong; there are places I can turn to for help. However, most of the places and spaces that are meant to help seem to be anything but. There's always a gatekeeper in those spaces waiting to strike you down whenever you attempt to go in their space, and there is no guide or mentor to walk you through this confusing and stressful time. It feels like I'm walking through an endless void hoping one day I'll find my Obi-Wan Kenobi to guide me.

Reflections on the Summer Bridge Course

Since spring 2015, the Department of Writing and Rhetoric Studies has been working with SLCC faculty and student colleagues to better support transfer students. These efforts led to the establishment of the Writing Studies Scholars program in 2017. Writing Studies Scholars aims to connect with prospective WRS majors at SLCC, help them navigate the transfer process, and support their efforts to achieve their personal, academic, professional, and community goals at the University of Utah. The program is funded by grants from several local foundations, as well as individual donations from faculty members, WRS alumni, and other community members. The entry point is the summer bridge course, Writing across Locations, which is offered for free to any SLCC students considering transferring to the university. Participants who transfer and declare a WRS major receive a two-thousand-dollar transition scholarship during their first semester. Throughout their time at the university, participants in Writing Studies Scholars also have access to a parking pass subsidy, dedicated advising, faculty mentorship, professional development opportunities, peer-led social events, and assistance finding additional scholarships and campus resources. In the first three years of the program, sixty-eight percent of the fifty-four students who took the summer bridge course transferred, and another twenty percent planned to transfer within the coming year. To date, two-thirds of the participants have been first-gen (see Toth et al.; Toth).

Each summer, the bridge course is cotaught by Christie, an SLCC faculty colleague, and an in-class transfer mentor who is a senior (i.e., already-transferred) participant in Writing Studies Scholars.[1] In the course, we construct what writing studies is by reading scholarship by writing faculty members and students at SLCC and at the university. Those authors—several of whom were first-gen students themselves—visit the class as guest speakers, and students have the opportunity to ask them questions about their research as well as their personal and educational trajectories. Our goals are to introduce students to major themes and disciplinary discourses in writing studies; humanize scholarly writing and enable students to see how personal experiences, embodiment, and community commitments can fuel academic work; and provide students with an opportunity to connect with faculty members who will be their professors and prospective mentors.

Alongside readings, students complete three projects, each of which goes through multiple rounds of revision based on peer and instructor feedback. These projects are informed by the resource-based, antideficit approaches advocated by theorists of transfer-receptive culture (e.g., Jain et al.) and of culturally sustaining pedagogies (e.g., Paris and Alim), as well as by the approaches of many scholars in writing studies who advance antiracist, decolonial, translingual, and community writing pedagogies. The first project is a literacy narrative that students compose out of their own experiences as readers, writers, and language users. The second is an autoethnography in which students put their community-based language and literacy experiences in conversation with scholarship in writing and rhetoric studies. The final project invites students to remediate their autoethnographies into a multimodal composition. There are two overriding goals for this sequence: to recognize transfer students' experiences and community knowledge as valuable resources that can contribute to writing studies, and for students to get to know one another through peer workshopping and other collaborative work, which helps them build a supportive community. Throughout the summer, students can also get peer feedback from senior participants in the program at the drop-in writing studio, developed through Claudia Sauz Mendoza's leadership in 2018.

Clint: When Christie asked me to coteach the bridge course, I was hesitant. I asked myself what I could contribute to such a class, being that my primary focus—on writing center pedagogy—may not necessarily fit well. I understood that holding a course on our campus would ease the transfer burden by enabling students to take an upper-division course in a familiar setting, but prior to coteaching the course, I saw it as simply another writing class. I didn't realize the social justice element of the course and the support it offered students. Nor did I realize how the course would encourage students to understand that their own identities were valued and would help them develop connections with fellow students and supportive faculty members. Claudia's writing studio work was a particular inspiration in that, for the first time, I could see how a flexible and mobile approach to writing center work would allow better access for students.

Cristina: One day while walking out of class, I saw Christie and a few of her students tabling for a free bridge course being offered at SLCC for university credit. I signed up, no questions asked. The bridge course motivated me to continue and helped me realize that there are opportunities being offered at SLCC. The WRS major was something I was searching for but had never heard of until that day. The course readings were written by people within the WRS department. We were introduced to various styles of writing, but the readings also introduced new kinds of identities to the conversation that are usually never mentioned in school. It was very refreshing to know I can write personal material in courses for the major. The class taught me to learn from other writers to improve my writing. I always pour myself into my writing because I want to feel passionate over what I'm creating. I want to care about the work, not only do it for a grade. In my previous courses, none of that was allowed, so my passion was all bottled up. The assignments in the bridge course allowed me to explore those trajectories.

Jacque: I took the bridge course after being introduced to the course in my Writing as Social Justice class, taught by Andrea Malouf. I was interested because I lived much closer to SLCC than to the university. Our first major project was an autoethnography. I couldn't quite understand the assignment initially because some of my other professors dissuaded students from using the first person in writing assignments, and it seemed to me that the word *I* was taboo. I decided to write about my volunteer work for the American Red Cross and how volunteering has not only affected my life but also my writing. My first draft looked more like a traditional academic paper, as I was not used to writing this way. The peer reviews also differed from reviews in my other classes. My paper was not littered with red marks indicating my grammar or spelling mistakes. In this class, everyone focused on the content of the paper. I knew then that grammar and spelling did not have to make my entire paper. The students had their own voices in their writing. But I rarely used mine. I had to dig deeper. Where was my voice?

Joseph: For me, finding the bridge course was like finding my Obi-Wan Kenobi, my guide. To this day I think it was a complete fluke that I received an email about the course. An upper-level class that I don't have to pay for and that I could also gain a scholarship from once I'm finally at the university? Taking the class was an absolute no-brainer. However, once the class started it seemed to be the reality check I needed. The workload, reading load, the number of weeks of class, and everything else about the class were not only new but also challenging on a level I hadn't experienced before. Somehow the class wasn't stressful—though there were times I worried about assignments and stayed up until ungodly hours to finish them. I'd go as far as saying it was enjoyable. On top of that, I even somehow started bonding with my peers. After the summer ended, I was hopeful I could continue on with these people and find more peers I could enjoy my classes with, even if we ended up sweating about how our classes were gonna go.

Jose: Once I got my associate's degree I was going to stop going to school. I didn't know what additional classes I wanted to get into, let alone how to pay for them. But this bridge class changed things. My adviser directed me to it, and it gave me so many opportunities. I could receive a scholarship for two thousand dollars during my first semester at the university. I was worried about funds, but after doing some math, it seemed as though going to the university was viable. In the bridge class I was writing about things I cared about. I was able to get a job through the class, too. I worked at a call center, but this class opened the door to my working at SLCC's SWRC. Clint, the program manager, let us know that he was hiring, and I jumped on board. I love writing as well as peer review, so the job was perfect for me. I've never felt so invested in a class.

Katie: While enrolled at SLCC, I happened to see an email about an upper-level university writing course offered for free on the SLCC campus. Scholarship money and a paid parking pass would be given to students who transferred to the university, and they would also have opportunities to meet advisers, staff, and faculty members from the university's WRS department and to learn about campus resources. So I signed up. In the bridge course, we learned about ourselves as students, people, and writers. Throughout the semester, I'd written about the challenges and frustrations I'd had trying to get a college education. For my remediation project, I took an old writing handbook and pulled it apart, and then I rebound the covers, selecting pages from the original book and blank pages to make a journal I could use throughout the remainder of my undergrad experience. I added artifacts related to my personal life and my relationship with language and education. The journal was a reminder to myself of my commitment to my education and my hopes for my future, and it was empowering. The bridge course gave me a feel for the requirements of upper-level coursework and discussion, and I started to have confidence that I had what it took to transfer to the university. More than that, the course gave me a glimpse into an academic community I was excited about, and I began to imagine the possibility that I might have something to contribute to the ongoing conversation within that community. The most exciting thing I got out of the course was the realization of what could be. But the most important thing I got out of the class was the knowledge and support to feel like I could make it happen.

Adi: At SLCC, I was introduced to the Access U program. Coordinators of this program introduced me to the WRS department and encouraged me to take the bridge course. I'm glad I did, because this class had an immense impact on my experience at the university. The bridge course was the first upper-division course I took, and I was anxious. As I walked into this class, it was not what I had expected. I was not intimidated. I was in a safe space. Because it was a relatively small class, I got to interact and engage with everyone. I wasn't reluctant to ask questions or speak openly. We also got the golden opportunity to meet department faculty members. It was substantial having them come in and discuss what classes they taught and the distinct subject matters they explored. It was a significant advantage meeting everyone from the department before we transferred because it was a start to building a strong rapport.

Christie: As we drafted this essay, I listened for features of the bridge course that my coauthors appreciated. Clearly, material conditions mattered: the fact that the course was free and provided access to scholarship funding was an important draw, and the accommodation of students' out-of-school responsibilities helped students stay. Several appreciated the opportunity to make connections with university faculty and campus resources, and valuing students' full range of identities and knowledge seems to have fueled their engagement in the course and their enthusiasm for further study. Perhaps most important, students appreciated the sense of community in the class. They enjoyed the small-group discussions, sharing their work in progress with peers, learning from their classmates' projects, and becoming invested in one another's success. For many, this kind of writing community provided motivation to transfer to the university and gave them hope that WRS offered a place where they could belong. I want our department to be that place, but, as my coauthors showed me, the university still presents many barriers to students' belonging.

Reflections on Transfer Experiences

SLCC serves more than sixty thousand students across ten campuses in the Salt Lake Valley ("About SLCC"). However, its class sizes are small, its campuses are accessible to working-class communities on the west side of the valley, and its annual full-time tuition is less than half that at the University of Utah. The university is predominantly a commuter campus enrolling around 25,000 undergraduates, but it is also the state's flagship research university, located in the affluent and predominantly White neighborhoods in the foothills east of downtown. The university joined the Pacific-12 Conference in 2011 and the Association of American Universities in 2019, and it enrolls an increasing number of residential, out-of-state, and international students. While about two-thirds of the student body at both SLCC and the university is White, SLCC enrolls significantly more Latinx, Black, Native American, and Pacific Islander students than the university, and its students are, on average, older, more likely to receive Pell Grants, and more likely to be women. Until recently, transfer students made up nearly forty percent of the university's undergraduates, the majority from

SLCC, but over the last decade the number of SLCC transfer students enrolling each year has declined from almost 1,400 to fewer than 850 (Toth).

For these reasons, the university can be an alienating place for some first-gen transfer students. While Writing Studies Scholars helps facilitate the transfer of students, our work together on this essay revealed that the program is not yet sustaining community well enough to counter the challenges some transfer students face in the university's predominantly White, presumptively middle-class environment.

Joseph: Transferring was maybe one of the worst experiences I've gone through, not only academically, but also in terms of the bureaucracy. To start off, there is no easy way to find information on the transfer process. Most of us assume that we just have to tell someone in the administration we are going to whatever institution we plan on attending and that everything ends up working out. Unfortunately, that isn't the case. I waited a month, if not more, for a response to my application to transfer to the university, then got denied. After getting denied, if you aren't defeated, you can appeal the admissions decision. But if you don't have two or more people to write letters convincing the admissions office you should be let in, you don't get in. No more higher education for you. Luckily for me, the people I've met from taking the bridge course were able to help me appeal and get in. However, this isn't the case for all students. If I hadn't taken the bridge course, I might not be a student at the university.

Jacque: Luckily, my transfer to the university was smooth. In the bridge course, I met the transfer adviser Paul Fisk, who connected me with all sorts of resources, including the Asian American Student Association. Growing up as an Asian American was difficult because of prejudice and my desire to fit in. The Asian American Student Association has helped me to dig deep into my roots and flourish in my cultural identity. I was also introduced to scholarships to apply for, and I could ask for letters of recommendation from the connections I made through the bridge course. Money is a concern to families of many first-gen students. In 2019, I received the Utah Asian Charitable Foundation scholarship Paul told me to apply for, and that one-thousand-dollar award was no joke. A huge burden was lifted off my parents, who were already struggling with medical bills. Transfer students must seek out these resources on their own unless they are lucky enough to have those connections.

Cristina: My transfer from SLCC to the university was smooth because I took the bridge course. It allowed me to meet people in the department I was heading into and to share courses with the same students. I had a lot of fear: fear of not being able to continue financially, of not knowing who was available to assist me, and of not fitting into the community. If I hadn't taken the class, I would've started out not knowing anyone at the university, being intimidated by the professors, and possibly, because of fear, neglecting the chance I had to continue toward my goal. I strongly believe your environment affects how you learn. The bridge course provided many resources and assistance, but it did not fix everything. I noticed that the university prides itself on being involved with its students and the community, but the community is specific to a certain group of people, traditional students who are from particular backgrounds and are accustomed to privileges not everyone shares. It's a community with boundaries and areas of neglect that should be addressed but will only be fixed if all its members put in their part.

Jose: I experienced many good things during my transfer to the university, but I definitely saw a class difference. I remember sitting down in Introduction to Linguistics on my first day and hearing three White guys to my left talking when one of their friends walked up and said, "How was your trip to Alaska?" to which one of the guys responded, "It was awesome! I'm so glad my dad was able to pay for all three of us to go!" I just remember being flabbergasted at that statement, and I immediately felt out of place: I am constantly worried about money, and these guys obviously don't have those worries. For a couple of months, I felt resentment toward those who had money: I felt alienated, frustrated, and annoyed that others were able to access the university so easily when I constantly struggled. This feeling changed when I actually got to talk to some of my classmates. Many of them were nice, and you can't control where you're born. But I don't think I would have felt as comfortable at the university without the bridge class because I would not have had a community that understood me.

Adi: One of the challenges to being a transfer student is that it isolates you to an extent. As a transfer student, you go through a lot of transitions in a short span of time. Before transfer, I was afraid I'd fail. I was aware of the statistics about transfer students, and I didn't want to be another statistic. In the bridge course, we established a comfortable community. Unfortunately, this community didn't transfer to the university with me. Coming from a different cultural background and having different levels of college preparation from other students is a reason for limited communication and interactions. It also includes absence of interests, experiences, and resources. These differences can contribute to low levels of academic self-esteem and difficulty adjusting. Being a transfer student has given me the chance to experience how different two colleges can be. Location, size, and culture go into this, and their impact on my experience wasn't something I fully realized until I had been in both spaces.

Katie: Before transferring from SLCC to the University of Utah, I felt supported and excited to become part of the WRS department. Once I'd made the move, I found I missed the sense of community that I'd felt in the bridge course at SLCC. SLCC was a smaller, more diverse campus, and a lot of the students there seemed to face challenges similar to mine. The university is big: big campus, big classes, big expectations and competition for resources. The kids going there—and most of them are kids—are smart, ambitious, and acclimated to a high level of educational rigor. A lot of them seem to come from money, or at least from continuing-gen families. By comparison, I've struggled to find the time and resources to give one hundred percent in my classes, and I know I've missed out on numerous out-of-class opportunities. I tend to be an overachiever, so it's been difficult for me to accept that I can only give so much at school while working and taking care of my family.

There seems to be a lot of potential for the university to help students coming from nontraditional backgrounds make the transition into a welcoming, supportive learning environment that will value and expand on their skills, life experience, and community- and culture-specific knowledge. Many nontraditional students have worked hard, invested a lot, and made numerous sacrifices to be there. It only makes sense to take full advantage of that dedication and excitement and explore what those students can bring to the university.

Clint: After a year of reflection on the interactions with my faculty and student colleagues in the bridge course, I now see writing centers in a different way. Claudia's work brought home the problems that writing centers situated in fixed places present (see Castillo et al.). Writing centers can unwittingly present barriers that are unseen by White directors and staff but are often clearly evident to people of color. This is as true of writing centers in community colleges as it is in four-year institutions. While Joseph may not be describing writing centers when he writes about gatekeeping, I believe writing centers can and do replicate oppressive conditions that keep out students of color. Listening to the students gave me deeper insight into how writing centers are situated institutionally. Often students of color and first-gen students come to writing centers seeking support and allies, but the nature of our staffing decisions as well as adherence to policies and procedures can alienate them (see Greenfield).

Collaborating with my colleagues from the university has helped broaden my perspective of transfer, and together we are improving the work we do with students. I was fortunate enough to be able to hire Jose and Joseph to work in the SWRC. From our conversations, I don't think either of them would have even thought of applying for writing center positions before taking the bridge course. Their presence and the perspectives they bring have allowed the SWRC to grow. Joe and Jose also act as allies, informants, and accomplices for their fellow transfer students. I've witnessed them discussing what it is like at the university with students. Following Claudia's advice, I've also begun to find ways to decenter our consultations (Castillo et al. 106) by having consultants work in various spaces around campus that are more accommodating to students of color and first-gen students. Such work wouldn't have been possible without the insights that came from this interinstitutional partnership.

Christie: The bridge course succeeded in creating a strong sense of community that motivated my student coauthors to transfer, but that community did not necessarily carry over to the university in the ways that they'd imagined (and that Clint and I had hoped). Joseph found the relationships he gained through the bridge course essential for navigating the bureaucratic barriers of transfer, and Jacque built on connections he made in the course to find material support and community beyond the WRS department. Although Jose found the dominant class culture at the university alienating, he was able to sustain a sense of community, in part through his continued work at SLCC's SWRC. The Writing Studies Scholars program helped alleviate Cristina's financial fears and provided a support network, but she still experienced the university as exclusionary. Likewise, although Adi and Katie were academically successful after transferring, both describe persistent feelings of isolation at the university. As Clint suggests, faculty and staff must listen carefully to first-gen students, particularly first-gen students of color, when they tell us these educational spaces are not yet working for them. The range of transfer experiences my coauthors describe makes it clear we must find ways for all the participants in Writing Studies Scholars to sustain community after transferring.

Next Steps

Given these findings, we have undertaken several changes to better sustain the Writing Studies Scholars community after participants in the program transfer to the University of Utah. First, we are expanding our social media presence so participants have more opportunities to connect with one another digitally. Second, we have increased the number of student get-togethers from once a semester to once a month. We now hold these monthly events at different times and days of the week to make them more accessible to students with varying schedules and out-of-school commitments. Third, because working in writing centers, coteaching courses, and participating in scholarly projects like this essay help sustain community, we are working to create more flexible, team-based, paid cocurricular opportunities that accommodate participants' coursework, out-of-school responsibilities, and material constraints.

Cristina came up with our most effective new initiative for sustaining community: forming one-credit study groups that provide additional structure for maintaining social connections and sharing resources. This initiative is an adaptation of the writing studio that Claudia piloted with Joseph and Kelly Corbray in 2018 (Castillo et al.). Each semester, we provide all interested participants in Writing Studies Scholars with an additional scholarship to cover this credit. Students form groups with peers who commit to meeting at least three hours a week, and participants must attend at least twelve study sessions, meet with Christie for a midterm check-in, and submit end-of-semester reflections to earn their credit. The response has been overwhelmingly positive—participants are sharing resources and information, helping one another with coursework, and supporting one another emotionally while carving out dedicated space and time for their studies. They have also formed an active group chat as another way of staying connected. Some students have opted to participate in multiple study groups or to attend different groups each week, and some have started bringing friends who are not in Writing Studies Scholars. The study group initiative seems to be helping first-gen students find a crew that supports their sense of belonging at the university, and we plan to make it a permanent part of Writing Studies Scholars going forward.

In this essay, we focus on our local experiences, but we believe our insights can contribute to the broader national conversation about first-gen students and writing studies. First-gen status intersects with community college transfer status and many other aspects of students' backgrounds, identities, languaging, and material conditions to shape students' educational experiences. Finding a sense of belonging can be particularly difficult for first-gen transfer students at institutions like the University of Utah, where students are predominantly White, of traditional college-going age, and middle-class. The successes of the summer bridge course demonstrate that, if we embrace an antideficit, asset-based orientation that values students' diverse intellectual and rhetorical resources, accommodates their material circumstances, and emphasizes collaboration and community building, writing studies can play an important role in encouraging first-gen community college students to transfer while countering inequitable transfer gaps.

However, it is not enough to provide a summer bridge course or scholarships. We must also put consistent effort into sustaining community for students after they transfer. Approaches to sustaining community cannot be one-size-fits-all, given the diverse backgrounds and interests of first-gen transfer students, the many demands on their time and energies, and the material constraints under which they are often pursuing their education. Rather, programs should create flexible opportunities that connect students with resources while encouraging them to develop relationships with peers, faculty, and staff. As Jose's and Joseph's SWRC experiences suggest, these opportunities can include continued engagement with community colleges. Transferring to the university doesn't have to mean leaving behind the relationships and support systems at prior institutions, where students might maintain meaningful connections with mentors and not-yet-transferred peers.

Finally, we believe this essay demonstrates the importance of collaborating with first-gen transfer students to learn about how programs are working and determine how they can improve. Students are the experts regarding their own experiences, and they are best equipped to tell faculty what's missing and what changes will address their needs and desires. Working together to understand students' experiences and make change accordingly has provided opportunities to strengthen our interinstitutional community. Writing together has helped us to see new commonalities and differences across student experiences and to reestablish bonds forged in the bridge course. We will carry those connections forward as we seek to sustain community for future cohorts of Writing Studies Scholars.

Note

1. The initial curriculum for the bridge course was developed in 2017 by Christie, the SLCC coteacher Andrea Malouf, and a team of seven transfer student researchers who were all first-gen: Nic Contreras, Kelly Corbray, Cassie Goff, Nathan Lacy, Westin Porter, Sandra Salazar-Hernandez, and Claudia Sauz Mendoza. The course has been improved each year through collaborations with the SLCC coteachers Clint Gardner in 2018 and Bernice Olivas in 2019, as well as with the first-gen coteachers Charissa Che, Joanne Castillo, and Cristina Guerrero Perez.

Works Cited

AACC Fast Facts 2019. American Association of Community Colleges, www.aacc.nche .edu/research-trends/fast-facts/aacc-2019-fact-sheet/.

"About SLCC." *Salt Lake Community College*, www.slcc.edu/about/index.aspx.

Alexander, Jonathan. "Queered Writing Assessment." *College English*, vol. 79, no. 2, 2016, pp. 202–05.

Canagarajah, A. Suresh. "Autoethnography in the Study of Multilingual Writers." *Writing Studies Research in Practice: Methods and Methodologies*, edited by Lee Nickoson and Mary P. Sheridan, Southern Illinois UP, 2012, pp. 113–24.

Castillo, Joanne Rose Andres, et al. "'Work' as Taking and Making Place." *Journal of College Literacy and Learning*, vol. 45, 2019, pp. 104–06.

Ellis, Carolyn S. *The Ethnographic I: A Methodological Novel about Autoethnography*. Altamira, 2004.

Gere, Anne Ruggles, et al. "Mutual Adjustments: Learning from and Responding to Transfer Student Writers." *College English*, vol. 79, no. 4, 2017, pp. 333–57.

Goldblatt, Eli. Because *We Live Here: Sponsoring Literacy beyond the College Curriculum.* Hampton Press, 2007.

Greenfield, Laura. *Radical Writing Center Praxis: A Paradigm for Ethical Political Engagement.* UP of Colorado, 2019.

Hassel, Holly, and Joanne Baird Giordano. "Occupy Writing Studies: Rethinking College Composition for the Needs of the Teaching Majority." *College Composition and Communication*, vol. 65, no. 1, 2013, pp. 117–39.

Jain, Dimpal, et al. "Critical Race Theory and the Transfer Function: Introducing a Transfer Receptive Culture." *Community College Journal of Research and Practice*, vol. 35, no. 3, 2011, pp. 252–66.

Jenkins, Paul Davis, and John Fink. *What We Know about Transfer.* Community College Research Center, 2015.

Mathison, Maureen. "Make Rhetoric Explicit: Demystifying Disciplinary Discourse for Transfer Students." *Teaching/Writing in the Late Age of Print*, edited by Jeffrey Galin et al., Hampton Press, 2003, pp. 53–62.

Paris, Django, and H. Samy Alim. "What Are We Seeking to Sustain through Culturally Sustaining Pedagogy? A Loving Critique Forward." *Harvard Educational Review*, vol. 84, no. 1, 2014, pp. 85–100.

Perez, William. *Americans by Heart: Undocumented Latino Students and the Promise of Higher Education.* E-book ed., Teachers College Press, 2015.

Rodrigo, Rochelle, and Susan Miller-Cochran. "Acknowledging Disciplinary Contributions: On the Importance of Community College Scholarship to Rhetoric and Composition." *Composition, Rhetoric, and Disciplinarity*, edited by Rita Malenczyk et al., Utah State UP, 2018, pp. 53–69.

Shapiro, Doug, et al. *Completing College: A National View of Student Attainment Rates by Race and Ethnicity—Fall 2010 Cohort.* National Student Clearinghouse Research Center, Apr. 2017. Signature Report No. 12b.

Shapiro, Doug, et al. *Completing College: A National View of Student Attainment Rates—Fall 2010 Cohort.* National Student Clearinghouse Research Center, Nov. 2016. Signature Report No. 12.

Toth, Christie. *Transfer in an Urban Writing Ecology: Reimagining Community College–University Relations in Composition Studies.* Southern Illinois UP, forthcoming.

Toth, Christie, et al. "Two-Year College Teacher-Scholar-Activism: Reconstructing the Disciplinary Matrix of Writing Studies." *College Composition and Communication*, vol. 71, no. 1, 2019, pp. 86–116.

First-Generation Students at a Historically Black University Talk about "Proper English"

Shurli Makmillen

> I can agree that in society when speaking "proper English" over black vernacular it can be more beneficial when trying to secure a job, but at the end of the day who is to be the judge of what is "proper" and "improper" English?
>
> —Student paper

Propriety when it comes to writing is often a highly valued attainment for first-year students at historically Black colleges and universities (HBCUs), and it can be linked to other forms of social practice—including politeness and respect. Indeed, the value of so-called proper English is a foregone conclusion, such that to suggest alternative values related to language and writing can render one incoherent. Evidence suggests that critical pedagogies that prioritize other aspects of literacy, such as language rights or the validity of African American vernaculars, have been slower to take hold at HBCUs, which tend to favor a current-traditional approach (Redd 5). Amongst sociolinguists and critical pedagogues, however, the deconstruction of ideologies of Standard English, of correctness, and of proper English has long been underway, and various models for enhancing this critical language awareness in writing classrooms have come to the fore (Young et al.; Inoue; Alim, "Critical Language Awareness" and "Critical Hip-Hop Language Pedagogies"; Alim and Smitherman), some designed in particular for HBCUs (Green; Taylor; Stone and Stewart). These are the models I draw on for teaching first-year composition at the HBCU Claflin University.

Like many regional HBCUs in the South, Claflin University enrolls a large portion of in-state students, often from small-town or rural South Carolina, who are looking for an educational experience closer to home. Ninety-four percent of Claflin's students are African American, and seventy-seven percent are Pell Grant recipients (*Fact Book*); additionally, according to one recent report, approximately forty percent are "first-generation students from families with limited financial means and who are eligible for federal student aid" (Valbrun). Despite some homogeneity in terms of geography, students evince a variety of linguistic backgrounds. In her study, "Sounding Black: Labeling and Perceptions of African American Voices on Southern Campuses," Tracey Weldon lists the labels that circulate among students in South Carolina, and notes "country," "ghetto," "Geechee," and "proper" as the most salient (176). Speaking "proper" was often associated with not sounding Black and could be viewed negatively as evidence of students not "embrac[ing] their African American heritage and culture" (177).

In the study I report on here, which shifts the focus from oral to written performances, the term *proper* carries a more ambiguous valence, reflecting "push-pull" dynamics first described by Geneva Smitherman, to "highlight the ways that Black linguistic and cultural attributes are, at times, celebrated as creative and innovative, and at other times admonished" (Green 154). In the context of my writing class, students are being *pushed* toward seeing their language use as a social justice issue—through readings, class discussions, and assignments that address the topics of language, race, and power; they are also being *pulled* back in toward the proper English that has been an educational and, for many of them, a family value all their lives.

Adopting Fairclough's concept of "critical language awareness" (2), I fashioned an approach to first-year writing that challenges students to hold the idea of proper language use up for scrutiny. I then sought an empirical means of observing the results of that scrutiny that took me beyond anecdote. My method of linguistic analysis highlights students' negotiations between the racialized language ideologies they are learning about and the perceived need for Standard English in both their academic and working lives. Specifically, I draw data from the writing of twenty-four first-year students, as well as from interviews with four of the twenty-four students who are first-generation students of color, two of whom are from immigrant communities in the United States. My analysis of forty-seven papers by these students focuses on their use of the term *proper* adjectively and adverbially to describe speech and writing over the course of one semester. This analysis is followed by more detailed accounts from the discourse-based interviews.

Though HBCUs educate only sixteen percent of Black students in the United States (Cole 358), they are responsible for graduating approximately one quarter of Black students, affirming their value in addressing educational inequalities nationally. However, , Victor B. Saenz and colleagues point out that graduation rates for African American students are decreasing and that the rate of enrollment of first-gen Black students is decreasing even more, suggesting the need for more research on this population in particular. Other research explores multiple factors affecting first-gen student experiences and academic outcomes and includes quantitative (e.g. Kim and Sax; Longmire-Avital and Miller-Dyce) and qualitative (Bollig; Lehmann) studies. Young Kim and Linda Sax looked at the effects of student-faculty interaction and found that although such interactions generally improved the performance of all students in a variety of ways, they did not improve GPAs for first-gen students, who were also less likely to interact with faculty in class or communicate over email. Their study was conducted over large populations where African American students are in a minority, whereas Buffie Longmire-Avital and Cherrel Miller-Dyce report on how HBCU research can, in a sense, control for race such that factors like first-gen status can be empirically isolated. Using parental education as an indicator of first-generation status, Longmire-Avital and Miller-Dyce found that objectively measured "parental occupational prestige" and subjectively "perceived family SES" (socioeconomic status) were the only statistically significant differences between first-gen and non-first-gen groups (among a variety of other differences, including measures of self-esteem, GPA, and hours worked per week). The results of their study of 134 HBCU students suggested to them that "being [first-gen] may have been a very salient experience" for students (381).

But researchers also recommend caution, as the category of first-gen students gains rhetorical salience for administrators and students both. As the essay by William DeGenaro and Michael MacDonald in this volume warns, when the category is used in administrative circles to produce a logic of aid, slippages in the category's meaning can lead to the framing of first-gen students' traits as deficits. Chase Bollig worries about the rigidity of such identity claims for and about students, preferring the notion of "positionality" to reflect their shifting "identification[s]" as they negotiate university culture (35)—sometimes wanting to play up, and sometimes strategically playing down various elements of their backgrounds. He also suggests that geographic location, race, and language can be more salient signifiers than class or first-generation status.

Following Bollig, who also suggests that any further exploration of the category of first-generation students would usefully consider its inflections with race and language, this chapter gives space to student perspectives on the relationship between language and power in their first-year essays at an HBCU. As I demonstrate below, the category of first-generation students did prove to be a slippery target in my research, such that I conclude that hometown origin often resonated more for African American students—often with the signifier "country"—as a marker of language use and rural upbringings, in ways that seemed to stand in for socioeconomic or first-gen status. For those students whose positionality is rooted in locations outside the United States, family immigrant status or accented language functioned similarly.

Historically Black Colleges and Universities

The history of HBCUs is rooted in the histories of slavery and emancipation, the Civil War, and the Civil Rights Movement and has been thoroughly attended to by a variety of scholars, from the institutional origins of these colleges in the years immediately following the Civil War (Du Bois; Cole 356–58), to the milestone court cases of the twentieth century that further changed the landscape of Black education in the South (Allen et al.; Bennet). Some of these court cases involved considerations of African American Vernacular English, which both resulted from and led to contentious debates about whether this vernacular was indeed a language and whether its use should be validated in educational contexts (Bennet; Alim "Critical Language Awareness; Lippi-Green).

Another early tension regarding the mission of HBCUs was between a focus on vocational training and one on the liberal arts. Northern philanthropists (mostly white) who funded many HBCUs were thought to believe that the liberal arts were "too challenging" for African American students or would create discontent as they became more aware of their own racial oppression (Allen et al. 267). Job training superseded a liberal education in many HBCUs, and in 1903 W. E. B. Du Bois wrote about the "lowering of ideals" that this focus on vocational training represented.

Du Bois would see a parallel, I believe, in the current focus on job readiness that has infiltrated higher education in general and that for African American students implies a focus on both literacy skills (Alim and Smitherman) and training in technology (Banks). Adam Banks suggests that access to technology alone can do little to ameliorate systemic "exclusions" in job markets for African American students, exclusions in which Black English is implicated (12). Ideologies of language, I would argue, intersect with such instrumental approaches toward a university education, in that proper English is seen as a prerequisite for succeeding on the job—or, in particular, in the job interview—and that cleaning up student language is posited as the responsibility of the writing instructor.

Language Policies and Policing Language

Sociolinguistic knowledge about language varieties now explicates the real relationship between language variety and racism, including the types of discrimination that can happen in the workplace (Young et al.; Alim and Smitherman). Despite the linguistic research on Black English that demonstrates its complex conventions and rhetorical patterns, in the larger context of race, language, and power, Eurocentric language norms continue to determine what is "standard," "official," "normal, "appropriate," and even "respectful" (Alim and Smitherman 171; see also Alim, "Critical Hip-Hop Language Pedagogies" 165). This slippage between propriety in behavior and that in speech and writing, and the intersections of propriety with both race and socioeconomic status, have implications for our considerations of first-gen students when those students are African American.

The performance and reception of vernacular languages in the South, as elsewhere, reflect a complex interplay of demographics, economics, and culture, as well as uneven histories of desegregation (Kohn). As previously mentioned, in college students' reactions to "sounding black," "proper" is a "label that circulates widely within the African American speech community" (Weldon 177). Interestingly, both *appropriate* and *proper* have their roots in Middle English, from the Old French *propre*, and back to the Latin *proprius*, which, according to the *Oxford English Dictionary*, means "one's own, . . . special" ("Proper"). There is some irony here, given that the proper English that is the purported goal for African American students in first-year writing courses may be a language variety that is far from their own.

In contrast, "Students' Right to Their Own Language," a policy statement by the Conference on College Composition and Communication in 1974, seeks to "affirm the students' right to their own patterns and varieties of language—the dialects of their nurture or whatever dialects in which they find their own identity and style." Stacey Perryman-Clark and colleagues write that this policy is designed to respect the rights and identities of African American students, "embracing, affirming, valuing, and bearing witness to who they are, have been, and shall become" (15). This policy is at the forefront as I design my first-year courses.

My own background as a first-generation academic and my positionality as a white woman and relative newcomer to the United States inform my teaching and this study. Having been at an HBCU for over four years now, I see myself as teaching from a critical language perspective, working to engage students in the analysis and appreciation of the linguistic practices they engage in—with facility and prowess—both inside and outside of school. However, to repeat a point made recently to white compositionists by Asao Inoue in his 2019 Conference on College Composition and Communication address, "racism and white language supremacy" are perpetuated "not just through your words and actions but through your body . . . in your classrooms, despite your better intentions" (357). To best support my students and colleagues in the South, I seek out a balance between attending to the perspectives about writing that currently hold currency at my institution and implementing some of the emancipatory writing pedagogies coming from twenty-first-century scholarship in Black composition studies. Faye Spencer-Maor and Robert E. Randolph describe this as a "struggle to reconcile traditionally entrenched attitudes and approaches, often fueled by the mission to teach students 'correct' ways of speaking and being, with [HBCUs'] liberating and unique potential to provide students with grounds for innovation and exploration" (179). Like my colleagues on campus, I work to counter the "ideology that views students at HBCUs as deficient" and see fostering the emancipatory potential of education as part of the historical mission of HBCUs. And like my campus colleagues, I want to equip students for upward mobility in contexts of unresolved systemic and racially motivated wealth inequality. For me, writing pedagogies that are "innovative and responsive to contemporary demands" play an important role (Spencer-Maor and Randolph 181), including understanding code-meshing as a legitimate rhetorical option in students' academic work (Young et al.).

Indeed, when wandering around my campus, I am struck by how my institution is a scene for what Spencer-Maor and Randolph call "innovation and exploration" in language use that is typical of HBCUs (179). In ways that would not happen at predominantly white institutions, students are "mak[ing] meaning within a Black rhetorical world" (Gilyard and Banks 56). HBCUs are unique in higher education for what they provide, as glocalized speech communities (Alim, "Translocal Style Communities") within which African American students can freely perform their ongoing and shifting positionalities. And they can bring these positionalities effectively and creatively to their academic work.

Theoretical Framing

To understand the pragmatic inferences associated with the term *proper* when applied to language in the teaching of writing, it helps to consider the history of language standardization as a function of class and geography. British schooling of the nineteenth century focused heavily on the eradication of dialectal variety through prescriptivism, which in turn gave rise to a class of grammar experts purportedly "concerned with clarity, effectiveness, morality, and honesty in the public use of the standard language" (Milroy and Milroy 38). In France, a similar move toward a state-mandated national common language, equipped with a program to eliminate natural variation in regional dialects, revealed to the French sociologist Pierre Bourdieu a class consciousness that was rooted in language use and that structured education. Economic metaphors reigned in this time to describe the language competencies of individuals and groups, and Bourdieu paved the way for asking questions about social and economic access to this language competence, introducing the term "linguistic capital"—that which a competent speaker of the legitimate, standardized language possesses—to signify how this competence is accumulated, including through the "legal sanction of academic qualification" (45). This linguistic marketplace is a unified system in which languages and dialects are ranked and in which linguistic capital, like all commodities, derives its value from its scarcity.

Thus we can draw from Bourdieu to note how educational institutions cooperate in maintaining this status quo by delivering previously ranked speakers to the labor market. Linguistic capital names what many students—especially speakers of devalued languages and dialects—often do not have, and what they and their teachers are taught to value as an educational product, which can be usefully exchanged for other types of capital (social, cultural, or economic) in the marketplace.[1] In the current climate of neoliberal reforms that streamline statistical bases for the evaluation of teaching and learning (Ball), linguistic capital also lends itself easily to measurement in writing classrooms, according to the degree to which language use deviates from the standard. In the face of such forces, a critical language awareness approach is designed not just to help students build linguistic knowledge and appreciation of language as situated and social but also to bring awareness to how episodes of discrimination based on language (such as linguistic profiling) are a substitute and disguise for other kinds of discrimination—namely racial and class.

Discourses of Propriety in Student Essays

The data for this IRB-approved study come from two assignments in a first-semester writing course. In the first assignment, students reflect on their own histories of language use and put that experience in the context of secondary material, including Barbara Mellix's "From Outside, In," documenting the author's linguistic journey from small-town South Carolina to a PhD program in English, and Jamila Lyiscott's TED Talk "Three Ways to Speak English," in which Lyiscott defends her multifaceted linguistic prowess as legitimate in both academic and workplace contexts. After writing the first assignment, students were required to read Rosina Lippi-Green's "What We Talk about When We Talk About Ebonics," and their final paper included an option of continuing the conversation about language, race, and power begun in their first paper. The resulting essays were formed into two corpora, consisting of essays from, respectively, the beginning and the end of the term, and I analyzed and categorized instances of the keywords *proper, properly, improper,* and *improperly.* The use of quotation marks around these terms was then quantified (Barber; Gutzmann and Stei). Instances of *proper* were coded using a recursive method for generating categories, and the linguistic term *markedness* was used to cover the ways these keywords could vary from a usual inference, replacing the less nuanced category scare quotes.

From a linguistic perspective, Daniel Gutzmann and Erik Stei point out that we interpret quotation marks in a two-stage process: the first stage is to identify that something is being indicated, and the second stage is to work at the pragmatic inferences. This second stage in cognitive processing is highly contextual, as readers (and listeners for air quotes) draw on presumptions of shared background knowledge to interpret meaning. Put another way, quotation marks can be thought of as producing a "blocking effect" (Gutzmann and Stei 2653) whereby the standard use of a term is foreclosed. Thus, at the first stage, all uses of quotation marks have a uniform significance; it is after we take note that we need to take note, that other-than-usual inferences are made and meaning finally takes shape.

When associated with linguistic performance, problematic assumptions attached to the word *proper* are kept at a distance by enclosing *proper* in quotation marks. For example, Mellix writes about growing up in rural South Carolina and being visited by city relatives from the North:

> Then there were the "others," the "proper" blacks, transplanted relatives and one-time friends who came home from the city for weddings, funerals, and vacations. And the whites. To these we spoke standard English. "Ain't?" my mother would yell at me when I used the term in the presence of "others." "You *know* better than that." And l would hang my head in shame and say the "proper" word. (259)

Mellix's use of "proper" would fit into the category of scare quotes, also called "modalizing quotes" in the literature (Gutzman and Stei 2650). And in a straightforward way, Mellix models their use for students. Additionally, she models taking a critical stance; for example, when describing her experience adopting a language style in academia that differed from that of her home community, she characterizes this process as "a certain kind of highbrow violence" (266). Using terms from Basil Bernstein to understand the plight of working-class students in universities, Mellix's account reflects the "alienation" and "estrangement" she felt (qtd. in Lehmann 531), in ways that also resonate with what Bourdieu calls "symbolic violence" (210).

The narrative essay in my writing course was a chance for students to share their own encounters with different language registers—as writers, speakers, readers, or listeners—after reviewing the secondary material by Mellix and Lyiscott. My overall goals for the assignment included that students would practice reporting expressions, summarizing and paraphrasing, and quoting directly. And we did talk in class about the use of scare quotes, as illustrated for them by Mellix's use of *proper.*

All of the instances of quotation marks around the term *proper* in my data indicate some form of blocking or distancing from the ideological assumptions of the term as previously discussed. But as I passed through the examples, I soon realized that other ways of marking the term *proper* were evident without the use of quotation marks. This happens through what can be called, following Bakhtin, "double-voicedness," wherein a "new semantic intention" is inserted "into a discourse which already has, and which retains, an intention of its own" (189). This double voicedness happens either through the term being questioned (e.g., "What is proper English?") or through the term being inflected with the perspective of another speaker (e.g., "Her mother highly encouraged her to speak proper English in the household as well"). In both cases, the writers have removed themselves from the pragmatic intentions of the term *proper* on its own.

To sum up, here are the categories emerging from the data on a continuum of increased markedness:

Unmarked: "Everybody was speaking more slang than proper use."

Double-voiced: "Her mother highly encouraged her to speak proper English in the household as well."

Marked: "For my family speaking 'proper English' was imperative, they had many barriers and stereotypes in society to break with being both black and Hispanic."

In table 1, I present the total combined frequencies of all instances of *proper, properly, improper,* and *improperly* in the twenty-four first and twenty-three last essays (assignments 1 and 2 in the table) submitted by students in the course. Students had the option of continuing to work on the topic of language, race, and power for the last assignment, but not many students did, hence the reduced number of instances of the term (twenty-four). Table 2 presents degrees of markedness, as per the definitions above, and the frequency with which students marked the terms in their first and last papers, to form the basis of a comparison. While not conclusive, given the small corpus size (52,000 words), these quantitative data do suggest a decline in markedness of the term *proper* over the course of the semester (31.5% of instances are unmarked in the first essay, whereas over half the instances are unmarked in the last essay), suggesting that students who took on the task of writing about language for the last essay were

Table 1. Frequency of *proper, properly, improper,* and *improperly* in student essays

	Assignment 1	Assignment 2	Total
Number of essays	24	23	47
Combined word count of essays	19,731	32,241	51,972
Combined frequency of *proper, properly, improper,* and *improperly*	95	24	119

Table 2. Degrees of markedness and frequency of *proper, properly, improper,* and *improperly* in student essays[a]

Markedness	Assignment 1	Assignment 2
Unmarked	30 (31.5%)	14 (58.5%)
Double-voiced	17 (18%)	1 (4%)
Marked	35 (36.5%)	8 (33.5%)
Other	13 (14%)	1 (4%)

a. Shown as the instances of the four terms in the essays for each assignment (and the percentage of total instances of the four terms in those essays).

less likely to critically engage with the term and more likely to use it for its face-value assumption that proper English is an unproblematic good. This decline could be explained by the time that had elapsed since the intense focus on language ideology at the beginning of the term, where the use of quotation marks was covered in detail. But also, in some essays the student writers move back and forth between marking and not marking the term *proper,* a topic to which I return below.

The category of double voicedness seems to be validated by the data as a useful addition to the focus on quotation marks, and double-voiced instances of *proper* in the essays often reveal that the inflection—or secondary "intention," to use Bakhtin's term (189)—comes either when the writer questions the notion ("They both have the same views on the English debate, what is proper English?") or when the inflection is from someone else such as a parent or teacher, most often a female speaker ("All of my teachers strongly instructed me to always use proper English or you won't get far in life"). Here, the double voicedness is further indicated by the use of the second person. As do many good writers, Mellix artfully weaves together various voices throughout her sentences, giving phrases a double voice and using free indirect discourse, as evident when she also occasionally inflects her use of the term *proper* with other voices: "by then I knew the implied rules that accompanied all writing assignments. Writing was an occasion for proper English. I was not to write in the way we spoke to one another" (261). Seeing this same strategy in student writing speaks to students' rhetorical skills.

As with many of the double-voiced inflections surrounding the term *proper* in student essays, female speakers are often mentioned in relation to language training in the home: "When I was growing up I was taught by my mother that one's perception of the world is massively based on the language spoken at home." In one case a teacher is mentioned: "I was at school one day when I saw one of my teachers cursing her son because he was talking 'inappropriately.' He was just simply speaking the same way I was and I just couldn't understand what she meant by speaking inappropriately. He said, 'Mi nuh know,' and she kept saying that he shouldn't say that, he should say, 'I don't know.'" This writer is an international student from the Caribbean, and in her essay she expands on her account to reflect on her growing awareness of the relationship between linguistic and other forms of capital: "A few of my classmates spoke that proper English, and I realized that the teachers favoured them the most. They were the students that [were] most likely [to] be picked to attend school trips and get positions such as class representatives. Due to the level of praise that they got, I was eager to learn the language just to gain the benefits."

In their essays, numerous students discuss being described as "talking white," which they take on as a point of pride: "because I've had the proper training from teachers," and "[I am] a serious writer and reader in front of my teachers." Interestingly, this same student reports on being told "'you talk country' due to . . . being from [the] South," continuing that he "was ashamed to say certain words."

Over the two assignments, thirty-seven percent of uses of *proper* are unmarked, indicating that for a good number of students, the accrual of linguistic capital in the form of standardized English was an unproblematic goal or attainment: "I personally struggle with speaking proper when my family from Baltimore come down." In some cases, there is evidence that students were working through the problems language posed, using writing to come to an understanding of a given topic. This is evident in the following student's description of talking to her daughter back in the Caribbean on the phone:

> My daughter was born in a household with persons who speak only Patois. . . . She can formulate many sentences, but they are in Patois. We spoke on the phone a few days ago, and I was shocked by what I heard . . . she said "Mi waa talk to him." . . . I want her to also learn how to speak proper English because it is good to be articulate. The only time she talked proper was watching cartoons and repeating what was said. She is an adaptable communicator, knowing when each style is appropriate.

The writer moves quickly from "shock" and concern about her child's use of Patois, to confidence in her daughter's ability to code switch. Her comments also reflect the scholar and spoken word artist Lyiscott's "Three Ways to Speak English," whose refrain to professors and potential employers in the face of criticism for Lyiscott's language use is "I am articulate!" The passage by this student writer includes unmarked uses of *proper* but ends on a note of an emerging rhetorical awareness.

In sum, markedness seems to be a potential measure of how students negotiate the borders of the language-aware community that their first-year writing course asks them to join and participate in. Given that their understanding of Standard English as proper English likely comes from previous mentors, teachers, and family members, they may not feel or write as though they are full members of their university community in this first-semester course. Nonetheless, noting students' uses of the term *proper* can be an entry point for addressing standard language ideologies in first-year classrooms, not just for those students who are linguistically marginalized, but also for those mainstream students whose linguistic capital can come at a cost to others.

The Salience of Place

In his study, Bollig found a "geography of class difference" for first-generation students, showing "how place itself serves as a class marker" (31). My students also wrote about their hometowns in the South in ways that rendered them as signifiers of linguistic marginalization, often attached to the term *country* used with quotation marks: "One last common term I would hear was 'you talk country' due to me being from South." "Before I came to college I never really [knew] how 'country' I was." And one African American student related their language use to their Gullah Geechee heritage: "I would listen to my geechee aunts and uncles gossip and pick up on their sayings. For example, if someone didn't present themselves well, my family would say that they were 'buss up.' This was a part of our family's culture, our own personal language. I however, didn't see it as normal and I didn't want to use it. I had the internal conflict of wanting to learn the language, yet I wanted to hide it from my friends." Mellix describes a similar conflict when she speaks of mastering academic English at the same time as feeling "separate from the language—as if it did not and could not belong to me. I couldn't think and feel genuinely in that language" (264).

It is not new in the literature to make connections between language and identity in academic contexts, but doing so was new for these students. Their accounts demonstrate their linguistic transition as a double-edged sword, with the accrual of linguistic capital on the one edge and the potential symbolic violence of alienation from self, community, and family on the other. Young describes such inter- and intrapersonal conflicts as potential side effects of pedagogies that promote code-switching (3), which gained so much currency in educational circles as a concession made in US K–12 and college settings to the Conference on College Composition and Communication's policy statement "Students' Right to Their Own Language."

Reflections on Language and Immigrant Status

The second stage of this project involved discourse-based follow-up interviews with four of the student participants, who were first-gen students by then in their second year of college. Following Lee Odell and colleagues, the interviews were semistructured, and in each interview I and the student read over their original papers, and the student was encouraged to reflect on whatever came to mind about the content. I interjected with questions, especially about whether the student had taken from the class any new understandings about language and whether those understandings had shifted the student's talk about and practice of writing.

One of the students interviewed, Maria, was the daughter of Spanish-speaking immigrants. As we read over her first paper during the interview, I was taken by her mention of a gut reaction: "As I learned the alphabet along with my peers, I remember my five-year-old gut telling me that the language I spoke at home and the language I learned in school were very different." I interjected to ask if this issue still came up for her since taking the first-semester writing course. She responded, "Yeah, you know how recently there have been so many incidents where people are calling the police or getting mad at people for speaking a different language in public. So that resonates within me because it's almost as if that could happen to me, very easily. Or that could happen to my mom or my dad. It resonates very personally."

Maria was one of the few that took up the topic of language, race, and power for the final paper, for which she drew on linguistic research about Spanglish. In the paper, she once again comments on the current political climate in the United States: "Spanglish is a language that combines both Spanish and English. It is often viewed as 'improper' or a random slew of words from both languages. This plays into the invalidation of identity within many Mexican-American and other Hispanic groups. This identity issue manifests itself into a sense of feeling that one is neither from America or the Spanish speaking country they identify themselves with." I asked Maria if this feeling had become heightened since the first-semester course. She replied, "Definitely. I think that in this very political and very divisive climate that we're living in this issue is heightened. Especially with the way that this country treats people who are foreign. So it's definitely heightened and it's an issue that's become heightened in the last few years and since a year ago."

Maria's concern about people reacting negatively to Spanish-speaking immigrants like her parents for not speaking English constitutes an added factor of linguistic self-consciousness seemingly not considered in the literature before. As I was writing this essay in August 2019, news emerged of a shooter gunning down fifty shoppers in a Walmart in El Paso, Texas. Reports were quick to explain that the shooter claimed to be "acting in response to 'the Hispanic invasion of Texas'" (Corchado et al.). The astute words of Maria resonate for me, as no doubt this news resonated for her and her family. While English is "valorized . . . as the language of power and success" (García et al. 174), to be able to speak it, and maybe to speak it without an accent, is, to her, about more than academic success and social mobility; it concerns her and her family's safety and perhaps existence in the United States.

A Cautionary Tale about Terminology

Bollig notes that *first-generation* can be an empowering identification for students but can also be a category that "obscures intersectional marginalization" (27). As a "constitutive rhetoric," it is one that needs a corrective in the form of "students' own rhetorics of difference" that shape students' experiences on campus (Bollig 23). Curious to find out about rhetorics my interviewees might adopt, I asked questions about first-gen and working-class labels. For example, in response to an email asking "Which of the following categories would you use to describe yourself as a student, and why?" Maria reported that she felt that she fit into both "first-generation" and "working-class" categories, although the "first-generation" category was the only one she had ever thought to use to describe herself. Like respondents in Wolfgang Lehmann's study of Canadian students, Maria associated the term *working-class* with her parents, who "have jobs and work really hard to help support me through college." When asked for clarification, she commented interestingly on the term itself: "I think that *class* today has sort of been separated into the 'top one percent' and then the rest of 'us.'" This distinction between the "top one percent" and "the rest of 'us'" could obfuscate some of the real disparities between middle- and low-income students, suggesting a reason to further explore class constructions among undergraduate students.

There was also some confusion among interviewees about the category of first-generation students. When asked if she was first-generation, another student responded, "I would not consider myself a first-generation student for the simple fact that my sister attended and graduated from Francis Marion. I will give that question a no." There is a logic to this response, that younger members of families could consider older siblings as part of a different generation, who grew up with cultural markers from a different era. Additionally, a student whose older siblings gained degrees or professional jobs might begin college with higher levels of cultural capital. Again, we need to be aware that fixed identity categories "prior to rhetorical encounters with others" can leave out the degree to which those categories can be "displaced, devalued, or minimized for rhetorical effect" (Bollig 33).

This essay has shown how students of color at an HBCU position themselves in relation to proper English, revealing the salience of geography, family attitudes that link education to propriety in behavior and language, and, for two students of color from immigrant communities, the salience of other languages (Patois and Spanish) spoken in the home. These aspects of positionality outshone any particular consciousness the students had of their first-generation or working-class status, as understood in the literature. A focus on language, race, and power in the course content, and the resulting opportunity to consider students' critical language awareness in their academic writing, reveals students' dexterity in voicing the perspectives of others through written linguistic repertoires, but also some tensions between the push of resistance and the pull of compliance to dominant discourses about language, a tension instructors can also feel.

As for treating first-gen students as a research category, we need to be wary. As others have noted, the category can be used by universities to support funding lines and institutional aggrandizement. It can also feed into a crisis rhetoric with links to perceptions of the declining literacy of underprepared students, reinforcing the deficit model discussed above. Philanthropy often steps in to meet these perceived crises, but philanthropy can come with strings attached, for example, in the required reporting of measurable outcomes or the adoption of particular technological solutions—both of which, in my experience, can come entangled with ideologies of correctness and of standard language mastery.

I did not clarify the meaning of terms like *first-gen* for my research participants at the beginning of this study because their face-value understandings were of interest. Still, there could be benefits to explicating in more detail the options students have to describe their positionality, because relying on terms used by news media or in university administrative frameworks can oversimplify the divisions between student populations and deprive students of a vocabulary to articulate experiences of financial or other hardships.

Including a critical language awareness component in writing classes can enhance and radicalize this process of self-articulation and develop an awareness in students of the systems of oppression that can constrain their success in contexts of increasing wealth disparity and diminished opportunities for upward mobility (Greenstone et al.). But those who teach writing also need some grounding in language policy and politics, identified by Elaine Richardson as a "clear need" in her report on the awareness and practice of language diversity in teaching by members of the Conference on College Composition and Communication and the National Council of Teachers of English (62).

In sum, this essay illustrates how, for students of color in first-year writing courses, positionalities that attach their language use to a wide variety of demographic factors may temper the salience of the label *first-generation* in this context. How they position themselves in relation to what they often describe as proper English reveals their growing critical language awareness and their rhetorical skills in using resources such as double voicedness; it also reveals the ultimate pull of normalizing discourses that idealize accruing much-needed educational capital through standard language use.

Notes

I thank Amori Washington for her insightful research assistantship and the Claflin students whose words are represented here.

1. While the notion of social capital has entered the vernacular as a common good, for the purposes of this paper, following Bourdieu, I will retain the critique attached to all forms of capital as a way to highlight structural inequalities within late capitalism that shape instructors' and students' lives.

Works Cited

Alim, H. Samy. "Critical Hip-Hop Language Pedagogies: Combat, Consciousness, and the Cultural Politics of Communication." *Journal of Language, Identity, and Education*, vol. 6, no. 2, 2007, pp. 161–76.

———. "Critical Language Awareness in the United States: Revisiting Issues and Revising Pedagogies in a Resegregated Society." *Educational Researcher*, vol. 34, no. 7, 2005, pp. 24–31.

———. "Translocal Style Communities: Hip Hop Youth as Cultural Theorists of Style, Language, and Globalization." *Pragmatics*, vol. 19, no. 1, 2009, pp. 103–27.

Alim, H. Samy, and Geneva Smitherman. *Articulate While Black: Barack Obama, Language, and Race in the U.S.* Oxford UP, 2012.

Allen, Walter R., et al. "Historically Black Colleges and Universities: Honoring the Past, Engaging the Present, Touching the Future." *The Journal of Negro Education*, vol. 76, no. 3, 2007, pp. 263–80.

Bakhtin, Mikhail M. *Problems of Dostoevsky's Poetics*. Edited and translated by Caryl Emerson, U of Minnesota P, 1984.

Ball, Stephen J. "The Teacher's Soul and the Terrors of Performativity." *Journal of Education Policy*, vol. 18, no. 2, pp. 215–28.

Banks, Adam J. *Race, Rhetoric, and Technology: Searching for Higher Ground*. Lawrence Erlbaum Associates, 2005.

Barber, Marjorie. *Quotation Marks*. Routledge, 2002.

Bennet, James. "Administration Rejects Black English as a Second Language." *The New York Times*, 25 Dec. 1996, p. A22.

Bollig, Chase. "'People Like Us': Theorizing First-Generation College as a Marker of Difference." *Literacy in Composition Studies*, vol. 7, no. 1, 2019, pp. 22–43.

Bourdieu, Pierre. *Language and Symbolic Power*, edited by John B. Thompson, translated by Gino Raymond and Matthew Adamson, Polity Press, 1991.

Cole, Wade M. "Accrediting Culture: An Analysis of Tribal and Historically Black College Curricula." *Sociology of Education*, vol. 79, no. 4, 2006, pp. 355–87.

Conference on College Composition and Communication. "Students' Right to Their Own Language." 1974. National Council of Teachers of English, cdn.ncte.org/nctefiles/groups/cccc/newsrtol.pdf.

Corchado, Alfredo, et al. "Massacre Suspect with Collin County Ties Charged with Capital Murder after Twenty-One Slain at El Paso Walmart." *The Dallas Morning News*, 4 Aug. 2019, www.dallasnews.com/news/texas/2019/08/04/massacre-suspect-with-collin-county-ties-charged-with-capital-murder-after-21-slain-at-el-paso-walmart/.

Du Bois, W. E. B. *The Souls of Black Folk*. *Project Gutenberg*, 2008.

Fact Book 2018–19. Claflin University, Office of Institutional Research, www.claflin.edu/docs/default-source/planning-assessment/fact-book/2018-19-fact-book-chart-packr1.pdf?sfvrsn=6e463e0e_6.

Fairclough, Norman. Introduction. *Critical Language Awareness*, edited by Fairclough, Routledge, 2013, pp. 1–30.

García, Ofelia, et al. "Educating International and Immigrant Students in US Higher Education: Opportunities and Challenges." *English-Medium Instruction at Universities: Global Challenges*, edited by Aintzane Doiz et al., Multilingual Matters, 2012, pp. 174–95.

Gilyard, Keith, and Adam J. Banks. *On African-American Rhetoric*. Routledge, 2018.

Green, Jr., David F. "Expanding the Dialogue on Writing Assessment at HBCUs: Foundational Assessment Concepts and Legacies of Historically Black Colleges and Universities." *College English*, vol. 79, no. 2, 2016, pp. 152–73.

Greenstone, Michael, et al. *Thirteen Economic Facts about Social Mobility and the Role of Education*. Hamilton Project, 2013, www.brookings.edu/wp-content/uploads/2016/06/THP_13EconFacts_FINAL.pdf.

Gutzmann, Daniel, and Erik Stei. "How Quotation Marks What People Do with Words." *Journal of Pragmatics*, vol. 43, 2011, pp. 2650–63.

Inoue, Asao B. "2019 CCCC Chair's Address: How Do We Language So People Stop Killing Each Other; or, What Do We Do About White Language Supremacy?" *College Composition and Communication*, vol. 71, no. 2, 2019, pp. 352–69.

Kim, Young K., and Linda J. Sax. "Student-Faculty Interaction in Research Universities: Differences by Student Gender, Race, Social Class, and First-Generation Status." *Research in Higher Education*, vol. 50, 2009, pp. 437–59.

Kohn, Mary. "(De)segregation: The Impact of De Facto and De Jure Segregation on African American English in the New South." *Language Variety in the New South: Contemporary Perspectives on Change and Variation*, edited by Jeffrey Reaser et al., U of North Carolina P, 2018, pp. 223–40.

Lehmann, Wolfgang. "Working-Class Students, Habitus, and the Development of Student Roles: A Canadian Case Study." *British Journal of Sociology of Education*, vol. 33, no. 4, 2012, pp. 527–46, https://doi.org/10.1080/01425692.2012.668834.

Lippi-Green, Rosina. "What We Talk about When We Talk about Ebonics: Why Definitions Matter." *The Black Scholar*, vol. 27, no. 2, 1997, pp. 7–12.

Longmire-Avital, Buffie, and Cherrel Miller-Dyce. "Factors Related to Perceived Status in the Campus Community for First Generation Students at an HBCU." *College Student Journal*, vol. 49, no. 3, 2015, pp. 375–86.

Lyiscott, Jamila. "Three Ways to Speak English." *TED*, 2014, www.ted.com/talks/jamila_lyiscott_3_ways_to_speak_english?language=en.

Mellix, Barbara. "From Outside, In." *The Georgia Review*, vol. 41, no. 2, 1987, pp. 258–67.

Milroy, James, and Lesley Milroy. *Authority in Language: Investigating Language Prescription and Standardisation*. Routledge, 1985.

Odell, Lee, et al. "The Discourse-Based Interview: A Procedure for Exploring the Tacit Knowledge of Writers in Nonacademic Settings." *Research on Writing: Principles and Methods*, edited by Peter Mosenthal et al., Longman, 1983, pp. 220–36.

Perryman-Clark, Staci, et al., editors. "Introduction: Understanding the Complexities Associated with What It Means to Have the Right to Your Own Language." *Students' Right to Their Own Language: A Critical Sourcebook*, Bedford / St. Martin's, 2014, pp. 1–16

"Proper, *Adj.*, *N.*, and *Adv.*" *Oxford English Dictionary*, Oxford UP, 2021, www.oed.com/view/Entry/152660?rskey=b7fGmu&result=1&isAdvanced=falseeid.

Redd, Teresa. "Keepin' It Real: Delivering Composition at an HBCU." *Delivering College Composition: The Fifth Canon*, edited by Kathleen Blake Yancey, Boynton Cook, 2006, pp. 72–88.

Richardson, Elaine. "Race, Class(es), Gender, and Age: The Making of Knowledge about Language Diversity." *Language Diversity in the Classroom: From Intention to Practice*, edited by Geneva Smitherman and Victor Villanueva, Southern Illinois UP, 2003, pp. 40–66.

Saenz, Victor B., et al. *First in My Family: A Profile of First-Generation College Students at Four-Year Institutions since 1971*. Higher Education Research Institute, 2007.

Smitherman, Geneva. *Word from the Mother: Language and African Americans.* Routledge, 2006.

Spencer-Maor, Faye, and Robert E. Randolph, Jr. "Shifting the Talk: Writing Studies, Rhetoric, and Feminism at HBCUs." *Composition Studies*, vol. 44, no. 2, 2016, pp. 179–82.

Stone, Brian J., and Shawanda Stewart. "HBCUs and Writing Programs: Critical Hip Hop Language Pedagogy and First-Year Student Success." *Composition Studies*, vol. 44, no. 2, 2016, pp. 183–86.

Taylor, Hill. "Black Spaces: Examining the Writing Major at an Urban HBCU." *Composition Studies*, vol. 35, no. 1, 2007, pp. 99–112.

Valbrun, Marjorie. "The Secret's Out." *Claflin University*, 01 Oct. 2019, www.claflin.edu/news-events/news/2019/10/01/the-secret-s-out.

Weldon, Tracey L. "Sounding Black: Labeling and Perceptions of African American Voices on Southern College Campuses." *Language Variety in the New South: Contemporary Perspectives on Change and Variation*, edited by Jeffrey Reaser et al., U of North Carolina P, 2018, pp. 175–202.

Young, Vershawn Ashanti, et al. *Other People's English: Code-Meshing, Code-Switching, and African American Literacy.* Teachers College Press, 2014.

Part Three

Writing Contexts for First-Generation Students, Teachers, and Administrators

Writing Transfer Strategies of First-Generation College Students: Negotiation as a Metaphor for Adaptive Transfer

Neil Baird and Bradley Dilger

> I'm the first in my family to go to college. When my dad says, "You're going to be my first kid to graduate," I could get a degree with a 2.0 and not be in any organizations on campus and still please my family. That's all they wanted. Well, that's not okay with me. There's no room for error or failure. I will do anything and everything I can to make sure I'm on top. I just want to be on top of the world. If I'm writing a paper, you aren't going to get a bad paper from me.
>
> —Nicholas, double major in communication and in recreation, parks, and tourism

How do first-generation students understand the relationships between academic cultures and the writing that shapes them? We begin with Nicholas, a participant in our longitudinal study of writing transfer in the major, to offer a concrete example of the complex interchanges between writing and identity that occur when students attempt to transfer previously acquired writing skills to college contexts.[1] Nicholas hoped to become an event planner and had begun leveraging student organization experiences in her communication and recreation, parks, and tourism administration coursework. A mixed-race woman from a small Midwestern city, Nicholas chose to be referred to in our study by a male pseudonym to honor a family member—but also because she saw in herself personal characteristics traditionally identified as masculine and as representative of success: competitiveness, leadership, and directness. Nicholas presented many attributes examined in scholarship about first-generation students: pressure from family, drive to succeed, and fear of failure. As she learned to write in her majors, difficult engagements with authority figures and tense interactions with peers highlighted the importance of the interpersonal dimensions of writing transfer.

In a course focusing on student leadership in sororities and fraternities, Nicholas and several fellow students were required to propose a group writing project benefiting these organizations at Western Illinois University (WIU), our regional state comprehensive university. Nicholas wanted to educate sororities and fraternities about the dangers of hazing, but other students wanted to show how social media could inform the members of these organizations about events—a topic she frowned on. "There are already pages like that," Nicholas explained, "and students can't be in charge of a social media site with Western's name on it." Nicholas thus called on her prior knowledge, shared it with her group, and suggested its relevance for the writing project. But when her classmates disagreed, rather than persist in negotiating with them, Nicholas fell silent, allowing their idea to go forward.

The social media proposal failed, earning a grade of sixty-three percent. At this point, Nicholas seized control of the project, approaching her instructors in office hours and requesting a rewrite, even though they had said that would not be allowed. Faced with a failure she "had no room for," Nicholas worked alone. She not only successfully negotiated a rewrite but also persuaded her instructors to provide a rubric to guide revision. Adopting a leadership role in her group offered an approach to negotiation that Nicholas was happier with, not to mention a better grade of eighty-two percent: "It was easier the second time around. I didn't have to stress myself out or prove my points. They were more than willing to listen to my ideas, and they were more than willing to let me take the lead. At the end, everyone thanked me and was so happy that we got a way better grade." Here Nicholas exhibits a typically first-generation perspective, identifying success with good grades, though she shouldered the work of meeting with her teachers and writing the new proposal. "Whatever you need me to do to get an A, I will," she explained. This solo approach clashed with Nicholas's description of her field as "collaborative," not focused on one individual but "about the bigger group itself." Unlike many of our other participants, Nicholas accurately perceived the disciplinary identities of her field. Yet faced with a high-pressure situation, she reverted to strategies she learned in high school.

In the experiences of Nicholas and other participants, we repeatedly saw the critical role of interpersonal interactions in writing transfer, which we define as the adaptation of writing-related skills, experience, and knowledge for use in new contexts.[2] Transfer research seeks to understand how and why individuals call on prior knowledge when writing—even when, as we suggest for Nicholas, that knowledge is not always well-adapted to the situation. Nicholas used the experience and knowledge she gained as a student organization leader, benefiting herself and her group, but at a high cost of effort, given her preference for negotiating with her instructors instead of with her peers. Our student participant Scarlet, who had one parent with an associate's degree, performed well when leading a group project but struggled to confront a professor whose course design prevented her from drawing on work experiences she deeply valued. On the other hand, personality benefited the continuing-generation student Steve, who used his charm and exceptional preparation to persuade teachers and students of the value of methods he had learned in previously completed undergraduate research projects.

In this essay, we suggest that the metaphor of *negotiation* accurately describes writing transfer for first-generation students by acknowledging how their contextual knowledge differs from that of continuing-generation students. The metaphor of negotiation highlights the interpersonal dimensions of writing transfer, particularly the power dynamics involved. It highlights the possibility of both gains and losses raised by adapting prior knowledge. Finally, negotiation explicitly affirms connections between identity negotiation and learning to write, as demonstrated by scholarship on writing in the disciplines. We describe why a better understanding of the role that negotiation plays in writing transfer can help instructors better serve first-generation students, and perhaps all writers, then we offer implications intended for writing program administrators, transfer scholars, and other advocates for first-generation students, broadly conceived.

Negotiation as a Metaphor for Adaptive Transfer

The study of writing transfer should be of vital importance to all writing research, since writers rarely begin from scratch but draw on learning from other contexts. Thus, all research questions concerning writing transfer ask how writers adapt knowledge between contexts of writing. For example, elementary education major Billie wrote lesson plans rich in reflection and detail for her professors, but quickly recognized that this approach would not work in student teaching, given time pressures. A literal conceptualization of *transfer* denotes transportation and connotes application: simply deploying writing-related knowledge developed in one context in a second context without alteration. But transfer scholars now generally agree these simple metaphors can be misleading and, as King Beach shows, favor the carefully planned and staged "lateral transitions" of traditional academic environments (108, 114). Michael-John DePalma and Jeffrey Ringer suggest the framework of "adaptive transfer" to better represent the often messy work of transfer (135), especially for studies like ours that engage workplaces, multiple classrooms, and other scenes of writing.[3] Transfer is challenging: our participants described struggling to learn both when to attempt transfer and how to execute it.

Even though most scholars now agree that transfer is adaptive, there are many approaches to describing those adaptations, and each highlights a slightly different type of transfer. For example, Elizabeth Wardle discusses "transformation" and "creative repurposing," focusing on writers' mindfully adapting prior knowledge ("Creative Repurposing"). Beach prefers "generalization," a reflection of his focus on the dynamic nature of the social relationships that shape learning (112). Stuart Blythe has suggested researchers "must pay more attention to ways that subjects adapt from one situation to another" (52). We oblige by exploring how the metaphor of negotiation engages interpersonal dimensions of transfer present neither in transportation and application metaphors nor in many of the adaptive metaphors suggested as their replacements. While some scholars have touched on the role of negotiation in transfer (Donahue; Reiff and Bawarshi; Dyson), to date, there has been no in-depth investigation of transfer as negotiation. In addition to issues of power and authority, and connections between writing and identity, negotiation affords discussion of students' dispositions, which many scholars agree can balance consideration of individual and contextual influences on transfer. Each of these three concepts—dispositions, power and authority, and identity—merits separate discussion.

As Blythe observes (56), dispositions became important to studying transfer thanks largely to the work of Dana Lynn Driscoll and Jennifer Wells, who synthesized early transfer scholarship with educational psychology. According to them, dispositions "are not intellectual traits like knowledge, skills, or aptitude, but rather determine how those intellectual traits are used or applied." For example, in our study, the zoology major Alison was well-organized and well-prepared given her high school and community college education, but her lack of self-efficacy hindered her success. Like many arenas of educational research, studies of transfer engage both individual-level concerns (how habits of mind shape writers' decision-making) and contextual influences (the influence of authority figures or resources available to support learning). Reviewing the literature in the light of their study data, Driscoll and Wells suggest four dispositions important for transfer:

Value: When motivation is shaped primarily by the short- or long-term value expected to be gained from a task or educational experience.

Self-efficacy: The capacity of individuals to trust their own abilities, influencing their confidence in asking for help when needed.

Attribution: How learners assign causality to educational successes and failures, taking responsibility as needed or shifting blame to other individuals or contexts.

Self-regulation: The ability of learners to establish goals, evaluate their progress, and adjust their work constructively.

These dispositions, especially self-efficacy and self-regulation, are well-represented in scholarship about first-generation students and in many scholars' approaches to studying transfer, including our own studies of science writing and internships (Baird and Dilger, "Dispositions" and "How Students"). There we show how science laboratories and internships, respectively, were perceived differently by different participants, largely because of their very different dispositions. But exactly how to consider dispositions remains a challenge, even though researchers have the luxury of reflection over time unavailable to writers working in the moment. Driscoll and Wells use the approach suggested by David Slomp: Urie Bronfenbrenner and Pamela Morris's bioecological model of human development, which considers if dispositions are developmentally "generative" or "disruptive" to individuals' interactions with their environments (Bronfenbrenner and Morris, 810). Bronfenbrenner and Morris acknowledge that this influence can be context- and time-sensitive (817, 820). Recent work in educational psychology suggests a more complex model of dispositions that also considers the level of support perceived by students in the learning environment (Ambrose et al. 80).

Negotiation also highlights how power and authority shape writing, long a concern for writing scholars, starting with early compositionists like Peter Elbow, who questioned the power of teacherly authority and positioned writing as a means for empowerment. In scholarship focused on transfer, Wardle has shown how negotiations of authority and identity influenced the writing transfer strategies of a recent college graduate adapting to a new workplace, including extensive conflicts ("Identity"). Our interviews with our study participants followed suit: like Nicholas's story, their stories of writing were often about interchanges with other people, some friendly, some not, that usually shaped their decision-making about the value of their prior knowledge. With those stories in mind, we have followed the lead of other transfer scholars by turning to psychology for models to help us explore negotiation in depth.

Building on the dual concern model developed by Dean Pruitt and Peter Carnevale, Carsten de Dreu maps negotiation styles based on approaches to social situations, drawing two axes based on concern for others and concern for self. This model has been represented with other language (Cai and Fink 69), so we have synthesized the work of several researchers in table 1. The dual concern model offers language for discussing writing situations where relationships or engagement with others, real or imagined, is formative: What attitudes shape interactions? How do writers approach other people shaping writing situations

Table 1. Dual concern model for negotiation

		Concern for relationship or others (empathy, cooperation)	
		Low	High
Concern for self or outcome (assertiveness)	High	Forcing (competition, domination)	Problem-solving (collaboration, integration)
	Low	Avoiding (avoidance)	Yielding (accommodation, obligation)

Source: Adapted from de Dreu 470.

with direct or indirect feedback? We call this phenomenon *external negotiation* to highlight interchanges between writers that involve discussion of their internalized prior knowledge or their understanding of contexts. Such negotiation often takes place in public, as writing or conversation. On the other hand, writers also "negotiate between the resources of their previous writing experiences and the expectations of new academic contexts," as Mary Jo Reiff and Anis Bawarshi put it, as they weigh their options in moments of composition (313). While this *internal negotiation* does not directly involve others, our participants often described imagining what teachers or coworkers would think as they made writing choices. Sometimes this took the classic form of "thinking about what my teacher wants," but participants also described the influence of coworkers, parents, and nonhuman agents such as written procedures.

Finally, as Roz Ivanič has suggested, writing is deeply connected to identity, and writing researchers such as Wardle describe learning to write as a process of identity negotiation ("Identity"). That is, to use Anne Beaufort's model for the knowledge domains of writing, researchers recognize that learning the "subject matter knowledge, genre knowledge, rhetorical knowledge, and writing process knowledge" of a given field shapes writers' acclimation to discourse communities (18–19). Two elements are especially critical here. First, Ivanič underscores the role of power. That role becomes critical when we consider negative transfer, which we define as the unsuccessful adaptation of prior knowledge in a context where it is not valued. In our study, negative transfer occurred most frequently when instructors imposed hard-and-fast rules about writing—often simply asserting that what students valued in writing was incorrect or irrelevant. As Rebecca Nowacek writes, "In a classroom, it is the instructor who has the power to decide whether to recognize and whether to reward or punish a given instance of transfer" (37), and students simply cannot negotiate for the value of their prior knowledge. This situation can be demoralizing. Study participants such as Billie, Jordan, Karina, Lenore, and Scarlet were frustrated by their lack of control of their own writing. Second, writers often become aware of their identity negotiation at times of crisis. Other scholars have also examined these "critical incidents" with regard to transfer, pointing out their lasting impacts, sometimes positive, as writers recall their successes and draw general inferences from them (Yancey et al. 5). Indeed, sometimes catastrophic failures can lead to long-term successes, when writers reevaluate prior decisions based on feedback from others. In "Dispositions in Natural Science Laboratories," we describe this outcome for our student participant Elbow: getting a twenty-six percent on his first lab report pushed him to read scientific journals to better understand his professor's expectations—and eventually, to earn an A in the course (Baird and Dilger, "Dispositions"). In these important moments, the ability or inability of writers to successfully enact transfer can have lasting impacts on their identities and the consequences of their successes or failures.

Gathering and Analyzing Data in Our Institutional Context

This essay and our other articles (Baird and Dilger, "Dispositions" and "How Students") draw from data collected from a longitudinal study of writing transfer in the major at WIU, a regional state comprehensive university enrolling about ten thousand students when data collection concluded in spring 2014. Our guiding research question was, "What are the classroom practices, curricular elements, habits of mind, and cultural forces that influence writing transfer for students writing in the major?" Our key participants were sixteen students recruited from courses satisfying WIU's requirement for writing instruction in the disciplines, completed in students' junior or senior years. For at least one academic year, we interviewed these students regularly, collected writing samples from them, and learned much about their writing for school, work, and other contexts. We also interviewed fifteen of their writing-instruction-in-the-disciplines instructors in order to fully understand the environments intended for the teaching of disciplinary writing. When possible, we continued interviewing students after this first year, whether they remained at the university or moved into the workplace.

Our study complements existing writing transfer scholarship in several ways. By focusing on writing in the major, we build on the considerable research targeting first-year writing and engage disciplinary genres not usually considered in those courses, such as lab reports, research posters, and white papers. When our study began in fall 2010, few scholars were using longitudinal designs, limiting researchers' ability to see writing transfer that transcended a semester of coursework. Since then, we're glad to see that more studies are examining transfer over time (e.g., Downs and Schlenz). Perhaps most important, our institutional context engages a student population far different from those of the flagship research universities where much writing research is sited (Moore). First-generation students made up forty percent of WIU's population during our data collection period. Among our participants, that number is even higher: only four of the fourteen participants who shared information about their parents' education with us fit the traditional continuing-generation definition of having one or more parents who earned a college degree. Five of the fourteen were the first in their families to earn a college degree.

The strong presence of community college transfer on WIU's campus leads us to consider our students' continuing- or first-generation status beyond the binary terms of traditional definitions. Seven of our sixteen participants earned associate's degrees before matriculation; only two took all their courses at WIU.

As a result, the academic culture at WIU is diverse; the preparation, age, and available free time of students and the support resources available to them vary widely. Following Eric Dubow and colleagues, we developed a point system to rank the education of our participants, separating them into five types. For much of the analysis in this essay, we use the traditional definition of first-generation students. However, interview data allow us to note when participants' engagement with community colleges, directly or through family, provides insights that complicate the use of the bachelor's degree as the sole mark of continuing-generation status (table 2).

As noted earlier, our data collection was driven by interviews. We interviewed participants multiple times, building literacy histories that documented how first-year writing, writing at work, personal writing, and writing for student organizations or other contexts interacted. Discourse-based interviews, in particular, were extremely important for us. In these interviews, we extensively discussed participants' writing and asked questions about specific writing choices they made, shedding light on their tacit writing knowledge and motivations for transfer (Odell et al.). We concluded the first year of the study by offering participants a written summary of findings related to their participation and by inviting them to engage in joint decision-making about our portrait of their successes and challenges. All interviews were transcribed; documents provided by participants were scanned for secure storage if they had not already been shared digitally. Identifying information was redacted or replaced with pseudonyms, which were self-selected by students and, for faculty, were assigned using a random name generator.

For this essay, we consider only the fourteen participants who identified their parents' education and only each participants' first study year. Doing so reduces the size of our data set but makes it more uniform, given that our sequence of interviews began the same way for thirteen of these fourteen participants: literacy history interviews followed by discourse-based interviews and a member check. (One participant included here, Alex, withdrew from the university after one semester, so his data are incomplete.) We do not consider faculty interviews directly here, though they helped with triangulation. Our data set, then, centers on ninety-eight interviews, most about an hour long, with fourteen participants.

Prior analysis offered us familiarity with participants' transfer strategies, suggesting the metaphor of negotiation and exposing significant differences between participants that merited systematic exploration. With that in mind, we asked what the metaphor of *negotiation* reveals about the writing transfer strategies of first- and continuing-generation writers. To explore this question, we coded interview data using the frameworks introduced above. This process involves assigning identifying codes to segments of writing where we observe certain behaviors. For example, a conversation with a coworker about the time

Table 2. Student participant data

Student's pseudonym	Student's major	First parent or guardian	Second parent or guardian	Summary of parents' or guardians' education
Hazel	Anthropology	Graduate degree	Bachelor's degree	At least one parent earned a four-year degree[a]
Mitchell	Music	Graduate degree	Bachelor's degree	
Ford	Law enforcement	Bachelor's degree	Associate's degree	
Steve	Biochemistry	Bachelor's degree	High school diploma	
Lenore	Psychology	Associate's degree	Associate's degree	Both parents have some college; at least one has an associate's degree
Billie	Elementary education	Associate's degree	Some college	
Sophia	Early childhood education	Associate's degree and professional school	High school diploma	One parent has an associate's degree
Alison	Zoology	Associate's degree	High school diploma	
Scarlet	Journalism / instructional design	Associate's degree	High school diploma	
Alex	Forensic chemistry	Some college	Some high school	One parent attended college but did not earn a degree
Nicholas	Communications / recreation and parks administration	Some college	Some high school	
Karina	Forensic chemistry	High school diploma	High school diploma	Neither parent had any exposure to college[b]
Jordan	English (was English education)	High school diploma	High school diploma	
Elbow	Forensic chemistry	High school diploma	Some high school	
Blake	Economics	Unknown	Unknown	No data
Jenna	Sociology / political science	Unknown	Unknown	

a. These four students meet the traditional definition of a continuing-generation student.
b. These three students meet the traditional definition of a first-generation student.

management needed to write a quarterly report might be coded "external negotiation" and "disposition: self-regulation (generative)." Using the qualitative analysis software *NVivo*, we focused on dispositions and negotiation but also coded for other factors suggested by scholarship on identity negotiation.

Our primary disposition codes were attribution, self-efficacy, self-regulation, and value, the four dispositions named by Driscoll and Wells above.

Each disposition code was marked as disruptive or generative. We also coded for instances of negotiation, using the four negotiation styles of avoiding, forcing, problem-solving, and yielding identified in the dual concern model, and marking each negotiation code as internal, external, or identity negotiation. We also coded environmental factors affecting negotiation, as suggested by the research we summarize above (Ambrose et al.; Ivanič). Finally, we noted when the behavior of participants seemed to be influenced by their first- or continuing-generation status. After completing the coding for each participant, we wrote reflective memos summarizing trends and identifying issues to discuss, using Johnny Saldaña's approach to help us resolve differences in our interpretations of study data.

Data analysis was supported by *NVivo*, which we used to count the frequency of codes, creating a disposition and negotiation profile for each participant. We then created "continuing-generation" disposition and negotiation profiles for the four students who satisfy the traditional definition of continuing-generation students (Ford, Hazel, Mitchell, and Steve), an "associate's-generation" profile for the five students whose parents or guardians have associate's degrees (Alison, Billie, Lenore, Scarlet, and Sophia), and a "first-generation" profile for the five students whose parents had no college degrees among them (Alex, Elbow, Jordan, Karina, and Nicholas). We exported code frequency data from *NVivo* and used *Microsoft Excel* to create radar charts to overlay the profiles, illuminating differences between then visually and helping us compare the frequency of negotiation and environmental factors. Finally, we used *NVivo*'s data matrix tool to explore possible relationships between dispositions, negotiation styles, and environmental factors.

The Impact of Dispositions on Writing Transfer

Calling for future research on dispositions, Driscoll and Wells ask, "Are there certain 'key' or 'critical' dispositions for learning to write and transfer that can be generalized beyond individual students?" We anticipated that value and self-efficacy would emerge as critical dispositions, but in our study self-regulation received the second highest frequency of codes, suggesting its importance for writing transfer (fig. 1). Even so, value occurred more frequently for our first-generation participants than for our other two participant categories. For example, the first-generation background of Jordan, an English education major, shaped her engagement with a series of close reading assignments in a core English course taught by Douglas Edge. Jordan voiced a strong dislike of Edge's assignments and multiple revision requests. Explaining her orientation to error, Jordan referred to her father's long military career, noting that she had "been raised to be disciplined" and that if she was going to do something, she would

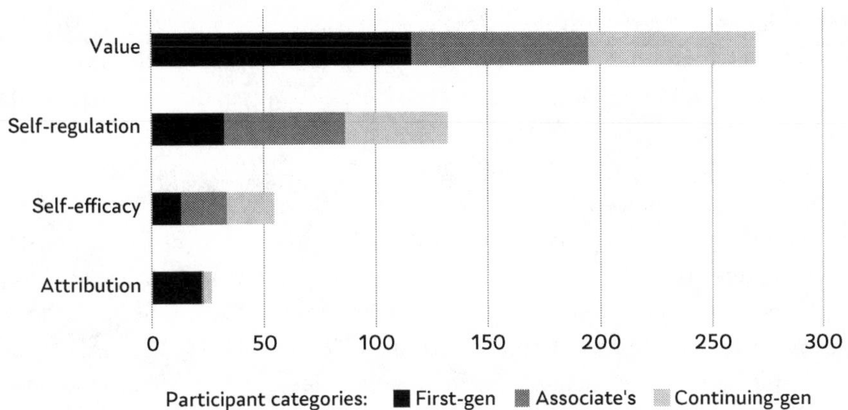

Figure 1. Disposition code frequency by participant category.

"do it right the first time." For Jordan, disruptive value and disruptive self-regulation reinforce each other to frustrate transfer.

In contrast to Jordan's experience, the first-generation background of Elbow, a forensic chemistry major, positioned him to find value in almost all of his learning experiences. Explaining that he had to go to college "whether I like it or not," Elbow described his working-class father, who was "wasting away" because of the physical labor required in his work as a cabinet maker. The sacrifices of Elbow's parents pushed Elbow to find value in his education, even in difficult situations, as when Elbow's instructor, the new faculty member Matthew Orrick, assigned lab reports resembling those found in professional journals. Rather than be consumed by frustration, as Jordan was, Elbow found that his generative sense of value allowed him to engage this new way of writing, not resenting the work required to adapt the conventions of the fill-in-the-blank report style he already knew.

The repeated presence of value and self-efficacy in our participants' stories confirms the need for further study. What we did not see in participants' stories also suggests future work. We expected that the interpersonal work of negotiation would manifest in the blame or causality of attribution, but few participants demonstrated that behavior. However, when we analyzed which disposition codes overlapped with those for external factors like genre, instructor identity, and student identity, we realized that self-efficacy affected our participants' relationships with faculty and other students. That is, the beliefs our participants held about their capabilities as writers shaped their relationships with authority more than their perceptions of control did. Unlike Elbow, his classmate Karina, a forensic chemistry major with a strong sense of self-efficacy, responded to Orrick by challenging him. Though Orrick told students to start their lab reports early because they could not be written quickly, Karina wrote hers the night before to "prove him wrong." As we argue below, environment influenced the way our participants negotiated prior knowledge, but perceptions of the environment were even more important. That is, dispositions shaped how participants interpreted contexts, which in turn profoundly influenced transfer.

Issues of self-efficacy were rarely mentioned by our first-generation participants, as figure 1 suggests, but disruptive self-efficacy was a powerful influence for several continuing-generation participants. Mitchell and Hazel, for example, overestimated their capabilities as writers, embracing writing processes disruptive to their long-term success. Mitchell, a music therapy major, often expressed pride in pulling all-nighters to pass writing assignments with a C. Though scholarship indicates that continuing-generation students often enter college with self-efficacy that allows them to succeed, our continuing-generation participants put pressure on this assumption: in our study, high self-efficacy can result in students overestimating their capabilities, especially as writers.

Our three categories of participants also differed in code frequency for attribution (external), self-regulation (generative), and self-regulation (disruptive). Figure 2 compares first-generation, associate's, and continuing-generation students, showing their considerably different disposition profiles. First-generation participants exhibited frequent attribution (external) codes. That is, more than our other participant categories, first-generation participants tended to look

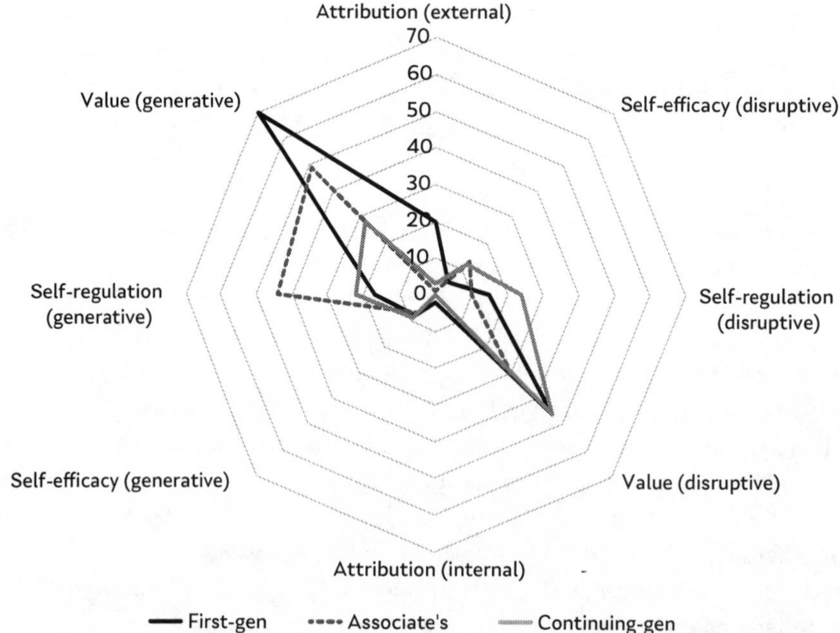

Figure 2. Disposition profiles for three categories of participants.

outside themselves, especially at their instructors, when experiencing setbacks. Participants whose parents or guardians have associate's degrees demonstrated more effective self-regulation strategies, yet our continuing-generation participants reported the most ineffective self-regulation strategies. As we argue below, these findings suggest not only pedagogical implications for each participant category but also the need to explore the contexts of community colleges and how having a parent or guardian with an associate's degree affects the performance of students.

The Impact of Negotiation on Writing Transfer

Extreme manifestations of dispositions led to particular negotiation styles. As an example, consider figure 3, which visualizes the disposition profile for Jordan alongside her negotiation profile, with sharp peaks showing how her behavior oscillated between extremes. Above, we describe Jordan's frustration with the close reading assignments in Edge's course. Jordan often struggled when required to perform academic work she did not understand or value. She was desperate for an A, as were many of our first-generation participants, and her primary negotiation style became *yielding*. That is, she offered her instructor the close reading he wanted, even though she didn't agree with the interpretation he offered when she visited office hours. To Jordan, Edge's interpretation of Blue Beard as a vampire was "stupid" but met the criteria of "ambition" Edge required for an A grade. Thus, she explained, "[I]f that's ambition to him, then darn it, I'm going to attempt to be ambitious." As a result, Jordan yielded to authority, voicing Edge's "stupid" interpretation and failing to adapt her prior knowledge by developing her own "ambitious" close reading.

Table 3 highlights other ways extreme dispositions resulted in particular negotiation styles. Hazel, an anthropology major and continuing-generation participant, manifested extremes in self-regulation (disruptive) and value (disruptive)

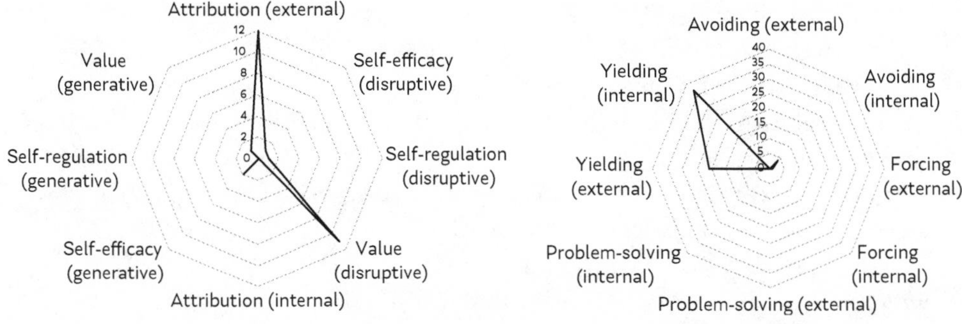

Figure 3. Jordan's disposition profile (left) and negotiation profile (right).

Table 3. Extreme dispositions and negotiation styles

Participant	Primary disposition	Secondary disposition	Negotiation style
Jordan	Attribution (external)	Value (disruptive)	Yielding
Hazel	Self-regulation (disruptive)	Value (disruptive)	Forcing
Lenore	Self-efficacy (disruptive)	Self-regulation (disruptive)	Avoiding
Steve	Value (generative)	Self-regulation (generative)	Problem-solving

that led to a primary negotiation style of *forcing*. For example, in the newsletter she wrote for her department, Hazel ignored her faculty supervisor's feedback because it conflicted with the importance she placed on creativity, a value learned from her engagement with fan fiction. Hazel forced creativity onto the conventions of a newsletter, using gaudy colors, fonts, and clip art, despite negative feedback from her faculty supervisor, who called the newsletter "unprofessional" and did not enthusiastically share it with other instructors as Hazel expected.

Lenore, a participant majoring in psychology and minoring in philosophy, whose parents both held associate's degrees, manifested extremes in self-efficacy (disruptive) and self-regulation (disruptive), especially in moments requiring her to engage in agonistic argument. These two dispositions led her to the negotiation style of *avoiding*, in which she took a scorched-earth approach by withdrawing, never to return, in order to avoid conflict. For example, she significantly reduced her engagement with her philosophy minor after a philosophy professor leveled a false accusation of plagiarism against her. In contrast to other participants, the continuing-generation participant Steve manifested powerfully generative dispositions that allowed him to adapt prior writing knowledge. Steve valued his major of biochemistry to the point of putting down other sciences, describing them as "soft." He displayed positive self-regulation strategies that led to his success as a student and also after graduation, when he adapted his chemistry and writing knowledge to successfully interview as a paint chemist for his first professional position.

But not all instances of responding to authority through yielding, forcing, or avoiding led to frustrated transfer. Like Jordan, Elbow *yielded* both externally and internally, though his dispositions were more often generative. Also, rather than pointing to a secondary extreme disposition, like those of the participants in table 3, Elbow's disposition profile suggests that several other dispositions, to lesser degrees, were important to his identity. Viewing his instructor, Orrick, as a disciplinary authority, Elbow yielded, writing the lab reports Orrick wanted. But even in yielding, Elbow learned new writing knowledge (in the form of disciplinary conventions) related to lab reports and adapted prior knowledge (about fill-in-the-blank lab reports) to much success.

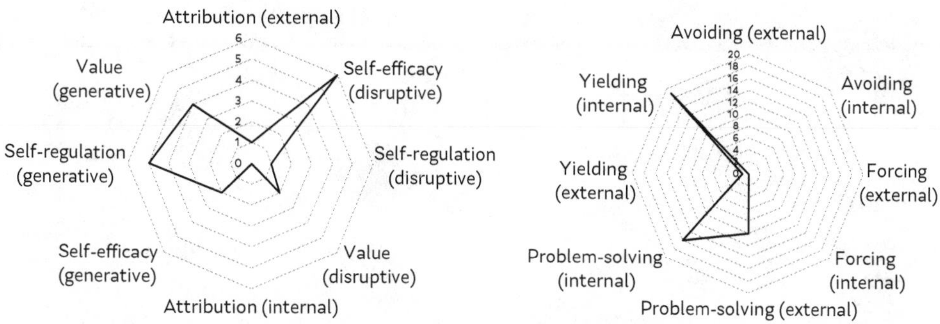

Figure 4. Sophia's disposition profile (left) and negotiation profile (right).

Dispositions and perception of environment both affected negotiation. In figure 4, Sophia's disposition profile suggests she valued her work in early childhood education and effectively self-regulated it, though she doubted her capabilities, especially as a writer. Sophia exhibited *yielding* (internal) and *problem-solving* (internal) negotiation styles because of her perceptions of power and authority in two environments. In the contexts of education courses, her writing in the disciplines course, and her block teaching as a student teacher, Sophia yielded by closely following the provided curriculum even though she recognized that it served her students poorly. But in extracurricular writing contexts, creating activities and newsletters for summer camp, Sophia demonstrated both internal and external negotiation for problem-solving. As a camp leader, she perceived herself as a colleague rather than a student, and this more confident relationship to authority provided her the agency to draw on prior knowledge (the aforementioned scripted curricula), modify these lessons, and adapt a problem-solving approach.

Differentiating between external and internal negotiation revealed how participants interacted differently with external audiences and their internal prior knowledge. Consider Nicholas, the participant whose experience opens this essay: she *avoided* negotiating with her peers, but successfully *problem-solved* with her instructors, even *forcing* them to construct a rubric on the fly for assessing her group paper. Nicholas then deployed this rubric to *yield* to her instructors but *force* her ideas on her group as she rewrote their paper, which netted a better grade, as seen in her instructors' summative feedback (fig. 5). Coding for external and internal negotiation helped us understand how Nicholas sacrificed deep engagement with collaborative writing, an important value in her major, to earn a good grade.

Finally, as suggested by figure 6, our three categories of participants differed in negotiation styles. First-generation participants exhibited more yielding. Participants whose parents had associate's degrees demonstrated more problem-solving, and continuing-generation participants manifested more forcing. These

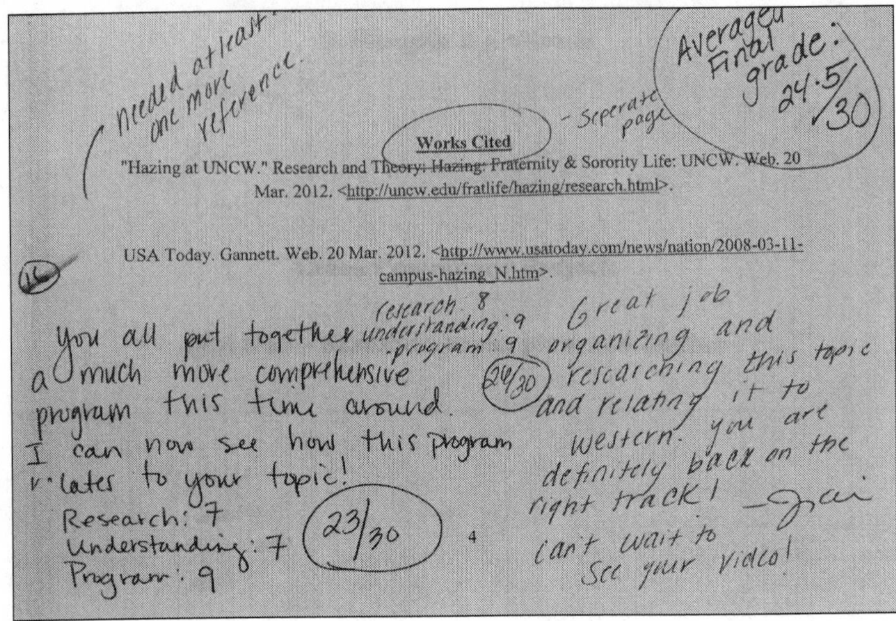

needed at least one more reference.

Averaged Final grade: 24.5/30

Works Cited — Seperate page

"Hazing at UNCW." Research and ~~Theory: Hazing:~~ Fraternity & Sorority Life: UNCW. ~~Web.~~ 20 Mar. 2012. <http://uncw.edu/fratlife/hazing/research.html>.

USA Today. Gannett. Web. 20 Mar. 2012. <http://www.usatoday.com/news/nation/2008-03-11-campus-hazing_N.htm>.

You all put together a much more comprehensive program this time around. I can now see how this program relates to your topic!
Research: 7
Understanding: 7
Program: 9
23/30

research: 8
understanding: 9
program: 9
24/30

Great job organizing and researching this topic and relating it to western. You are definitely back on the right track! can't wait to see your video!

4

Figure 5. Summative feedback on Nicholas's community project.

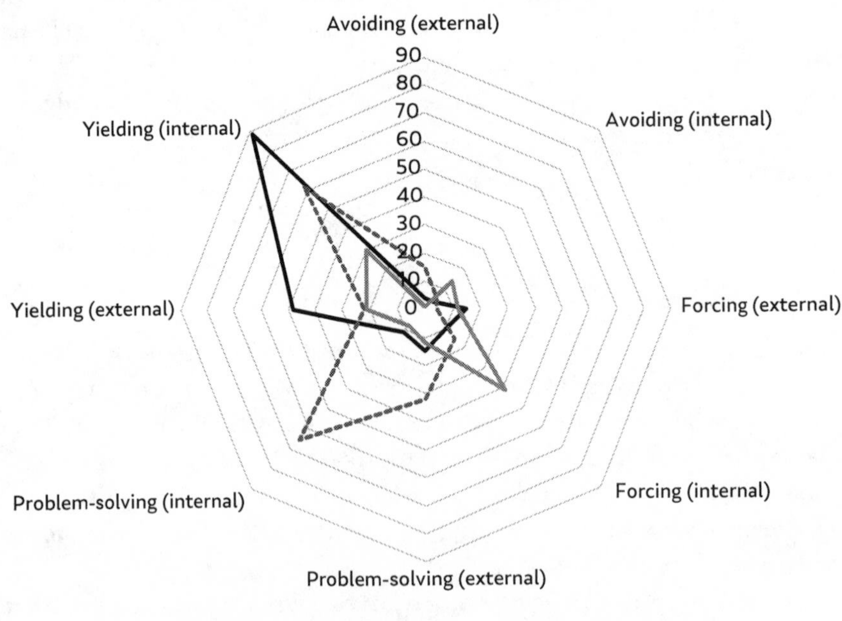

Figure 6. Negotiation profiles for the three categories of participants.

findings confirm the value of traditional definitions of first- and continuing-generation students but underscore the need to explore the contexts of community colleges and their impacts on students' negotiation styles—especially for institutions with large numbers of community college transfers. That is, how do students familiar with the academic contexts that generate associate's degrees understand the role of negotiation in school, compared to students acclimated to four-year institutions or those without any academic acculturation?

Toward Strategic Identification

Our analysis revealed a pattern that will require more research and that suggests the necessity of thinking beyond the single academic year of data represented here. Across our participant pool, participants more successful at transfer as adaptation demonstrated a larger number of dispositions and more diverse negotiation styles. In contrast, participants who exhibited only one or two disposition and negotiation patterns, like those in table 3, experienced more cases of frustrated transfer. For example, consider figure 7, which reflects Scarlet's disposition and negotiation profiles. Out of all our participants, Scarlet most effectively adapted her prior writing knowledge. As a double major, Scarlet adeptly moved between two worlds with radically different ways of thinking and writing. In our first interview, she described the "need to change my environment," writing for instructional design in the campus lab and for journalism in her bedroom so that she did not "forget what class I'm writing in."

Scarlet's disposition profile exhibited both more dispositions and more negotiation styles than others who experienced issues of frustrated transfer. But the high frequency of disruptive value apparent here is an anomaly that is related to Scarlet's difficulty in a particular class and that almost never resurfaced for the participant after the first year of our study. Driscoll and Roger Powell

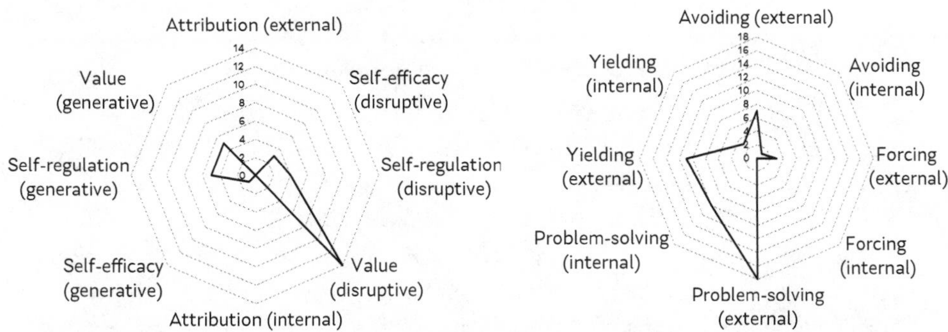

Figure 7. Scarlet's disposition profile (left) and negotiation profile (right).

make a distinction that applies to Scarlet and other participants: dispositions can be temporary "states" or persistent "traits." In contrast to Jordan, whose disruptive dispositions persisted over time and were part of her identity, Scarlet had a disposition profile that suggested her dispositions were temporary and context-bound.

In terms of negotiation styles, Scarlet exhibited a strong problem-solving style; however, she also yielded, avoided, and, at certain key moments, forced. Her negotiation profile also changed across environments. When she did the required professional writing for her major, yielding dominated because those genres were new to her; however, in journalism, where she felt more comfortable and empowered, her negotiation styles were highly varied and included yielding, avoiding, problem-solving, and forcing—all of which speak to her ability to internally negotiate, think through the feedback given by authority figures, then generalize given her writing goals.

In a previous article (Baird and Dilger, "How Students"), we forwarded the concept of strategic identification. We believe understanding transfer as negotiation is offering us a clearer understanding of this concept—though only with data that afford analysis of transfer over time. Our participants who were most successful at adaptive transfer could identify as professionals in their field (i.e., Scarlet as a journalist, or Sophia as an elementary school teacher). Persistently negative dispositions (traits) seldom frustrated their identification; dispositions are context-bound and flexible. As participants began to take on these identities, they developed agency that allowed them to negotiate with authority in strategic ways. They argued for the value of their prior knowledge, successfully mobilized that knowledge in their writing, and leveraged writing to take up professional identities. Learning how to encourage this persistence is important given that negotiation styles such as yielding and avoiding discourage the long-term engagement necessary for writers to realize how learning to write can shape their development of professional identities.

Implications

The small size of our study means we cannot offer concrete conclusions for teaching or studying transfer. However, below we isolate several trends consistent with other studies and suggest the need for more systematic investigation. We also describe some of our plans for future research.

Value and self-regulation emerge as critical dispositions. Both dispositions shaped negotiation and thus our participants' engagement with prior knowledge by influencing perceptions of instructor intent and efficacy and by influencing the depth and quality of student engagement with the genres at the center of their writing tasks. As Susan Ambrose and colleagues explain, creating supportive environments is important, but we note that student perception of value was equally powerful for our participants. In addition, value had more co-occurrence with identity negotiation than did any other disposition. This phenomenon suggests that writing researchers who seek to support the role writing can play in developing students' professional identities need to continue exploring how value and self-regulation support or discourage transfer.

Negotiation offers a useful metaphor for understanding diverse types of adaptive transfer. Unlike some narrower metaphors, negotiation can describe a variety of adaptive transfer behaviors and allows researchers to attend to interpersonal dimensions of writing such as identity formation. As disposition research matures, and as scholars learn which dispositions are most influential for writing transfer, we will have the opportunity to explore the interactions of dispositions and negotiation. This work will build on the efforts to describe adaptive transfer we have highlighted here (Blythe; DePalma and Ringer). We are not suggesting that a single metaphor for adaptive transfer is needed, but rather, that it may be possible to develop a theory of adaptive transfer that can help us understand which dispositional influences are most important when student writers consider their prior knowledge.

The disposition and negotiation profiles of participants suggest that attribution and yielding are areas for pedagogical interventions related to first-generation and continuing-generation students. The first-generation students in our study tended to look outside themselves when assigning causality to their educational successes and failures. They also tended to yield in unproductive ways because of the way value shaped their relationship to authority. We thus encourage faculty working with first-generation students to attend to attribution and yielding in particular. Faculty can help first-generation students ask what about themselves is contributing to their success or failure as writers. Faculty need to be more open to the sometimes surprising ways first-generation students negotiate prior writing knowledge, rather than encourage them to ignore or forget that knowledge. Some continuing-generation participants persisted in using disruptive self-regulation strategies, such as pulling all-nighters, even when they acknowledged the value of planning ahead. As a result, they tended to ignore advice from authority, forcing their own prior knowledge in writing situations that suggested adaptation would work better. Rather than assume continuing-generation students will succeed because of their backgrounds, we encourage faculty to learn how writers come to believe in their capabilities.

Definitions of first-generation students may need to consider the academic cultures of community colleges, especially at institutions where a large number of students matriculate with associate's degrees or transfer course credit. As we show above, several of our participants exhibited behaviors that blend typical first- and continuing-generation traits and that appeared to be distinct from the behaviors of our five students whose parents did not earn a degree and our four students who had either one or two parents who did earn a degree. The landscape of higher education is likely to change radically in the next twenty years, as demographic shifts suggest declines in the numbers of students attending college (Bransberger and Michelau 11). How that change will affect community colleges remains to be seen: they may struggle to compete with four-year schools, or locally focused funding models may help them weather enrollment pressures. Either way, more work is needed to determine if students with parents or guardians with associate's degrees are well-served by approaches to supporting first-generation students.

Notes

We are grateful to our participants for the time they shared with us. Our study at WIU was supported by a WIU University Research Council grant, the Conference on College Composition and Communication Research Initiative, and a Council of Writing Program Administrators Targeted Research Grant. Thank you to Angela Bonifas for her help with the statistics we shared and to our research assistants, Susan Reid, Emily Terrell, Nan Norcross, Tim Nicholas, Ruby Kirk Nancy, and Beth Towle.

1. All names in this essay are pseudonyms. Some personal details have been altered to protect participant confidentiality.

2. We refer to skills, experience, and knowledge here. In the remainder of this essay, though we often use just one of these terms, all three are often in play in the writing-transfer experiences of first-generation students.

3. Given space limitations, our literature review is selective. For a more comprehensive review, see Yancey et al. 37–59.

Works Cited

Ambrose, Susan A., et al. *How Learning Works: Seven Research-Based Principles for Smart Teaching*. Jossey-Bass, 2010.

Baird, Neil, and Bradley Dilger. "Dispositions in Natural Science Laboratories: The Roles of Individuals and Contexts in Writing Transfer." *Across the Disciplines*, vol. 15, no. 4, 2018, pp. 21–40.

———. "How Students Perceive Transitions: Dispositions and Transfer in Internships." *College Composition and Communication*, vol. 68, no. 4, 2017, pp. 684–712.

Beach, King. "Consequential Transitions: A Sociocultural Expedition beyond Transfer in Education." *Review of Research in Education*, vol. 24, no. 1, 1999, pp. 101–39.

Beaufort, Anne. *College Writing and Beyond: A New Framework for University Writing Instruction*. Utah State UP, 2007.

Blythe, Stuart. "Attending to the Subject in Writing Transfer and Adaptation." *Critical Transitions: Writing and the Question of Transfer*, edited by Chris M. Anson and Jessie L. Moore, UP of Colorado, 2016, pp. 49–68.

Bransberger, Peace, and Demarée K. Michelau. *Knocking at the College Door: Projections of High School Graduates*. Western Interstate Commission for Higher Education, 2016, knocking.wiche.edu/wp-content/uploads/sites/10/2020/12/Knocking-pdf-for-website.pdf.

Bronfenbrenner, Urie, and Pamela A. Morris. "The Bioecological Model of Human Development." *Handbook of Child Psychology: Theoretical Models of Human Development*, edited by Richard M. Lerner, 6th ed., vol. 1, Wiley, 2006, pp. 793–828.

Cai, Deborah A., and Edward L. Fink. "Conflict Style Differences between Individualists and Collectivists." *Communication Monographs*, vol. 69, no. 1, 2002, pp. 67–87.

de Dreu, Carsten K. W. "Conflict at Work: Basic Principles and Applied Issues." *Maintaining, Expanding, and Contracting the Organization. APA Handbook of Industrial and Organizational Psychology*, edited by Sheldon Zedeck, vol. 3, American Psychological Association, 2011, pp. 461–93.

DePalma, Michael-John, and Jeffrey M. Ringer. "Toward a Theory of Adaptive Transfer: Expanding Disciplinary Discussions of 'Transfer' in Second-Language Writing and Composition Studies." *Journal of Second Language Writing*, vol. 20, no. 2, 2011, pp. 134–47.

Donahue, Christiane. "Student Writing as Negotiation: Textual Movements in French High School Essays." *Writing in Context(s): Textual Practices and Learning Processes in Sociocultural Settings*, edited by Triantafillia Kostouli, vol. 15, Springer, 2005, pp. 137–63.

Downs, Doug, and Mark Schlenz. *Learning Transfer from Metacognition-Enhancing Writing-about-Writing FYC Courses: A Longitudinal Study*. Conference on College Composition and Communication, 2017.

Driscoll, Dana Lynn, and Roger Powell. "Straits, Traits, and Dispositions: The Impact of Emotion on Writing Development and Transfer across College Courses and Beyond." *Composition Forum*, vol. 34, 2016, compositionforum.com/issue/34/states-traits.php.

Driscoll, Dana Lynn, and Jennifer Wells. "Beyond Knowledge and Skills: Writing Transfer and the Role of Student Dispositions." *Composition Forum*, vol. 26, 2012, compositionforum.com/issue/26/beyond-knowledge-skills.php.

Dubow, Eric F., et al. "Long-Term Effects of Parents' Education on Children's Educational and Occupational Success: Mediation by Family Interactions, Child Aggression, and Teenage Aspirations." *Merrill-Palmer Quarterly*, vol. 55, no. 3, 2009, pp. 224–49.

Dyson, Anne Haas. "Transforming Transfer: Unruly Children, Contrary Texts, and the Persistence of the Pedagogical Order." *Review of Research in Education*, vol. 24, no. 1, 1999, pp. 141–72.

Elbow, Peter. *Writing with Power: Techniques for Mastering the Writing Process*. 2nd ed., Oxford UP, 1998.

Ivanič, Roz. *Writing and Identity: The Discoursal Construction of Identity in Academic Writing*. John Benjamins Publishing, 1998.

Moore, Jessie. "Mapping the Questions: The State of Writing-Related Transfer Research." *Composition Forum*, vol. 26, fall 2012, compositionforum.com/issue/26/map-questions-transfer-research.php.

Nowacek, Rebecca S. *Agents of Integration: Understanding Transfer as a Rhetorical Act*. Southern Illinois UP, 2011.

Odell, Lee, et al. "The Discourse-Based Interview: A Procedure for Exploring the Tacit Knowledge of Writers in Nonacademic Settings." *Research on Writing: Principles and Methods*, edited by Peter Mosenthal et al., Longman, 1983, pp. 221–36.

Pruitt, Dean G., and Peter J. Carnevale. *Negotiation in Social Conflict*. Thomson Brooks / Cole Publishing, 1993.

Reiff, Mary Jo, and Anis Bawarshi. "Tracing Discursive Resources: How Students Use Prior Genre Knowledge to Negotiate New Writing Contexts in First-Year Composition." *Written Communication*, vol. 28, no. 3, 2011, pp. 312–37.

Saldaña, Johnny. *The Coding Manual for Qualitative Researchers*. 3rd ed., SAGE, 2016.

Slomp, David H. "Challenges in Assessing the Development of Writing Ability: Theories, Constructs and Methods." *Assessing Writing*, vol. 17, no. 2, 2012, pp. 81–91.

Wardle, Elizabeth. "Creative Repurposing for Expansive Learning: Considering 'Problem-Exploring' and 'Answer-Getting' Dispositions in Individuals and Fields." *Composition Forum*, vol. 26, 2012, compositionforum.com/issue/26/creative-repurposing.php.

———. "Identity, Authority, and Learning to Write in New Workplaces." *Enculturation*, vol. 5, no. 2, 2004, www.enculturation.net/5_2/wardle.html.

Yancey, Kathleen Blake, et al. *Writing across Contexts: Transfer, Composition, and Sites of Writing*. Utah State UP, 2014.

First-Generation College Students' Constructs of Writing in First-Year Writing and Workplace Contexts

Aubrey Schiavone

As a working-class, first-generation college student in the early 2000s, I received funding for my undergraduate education mostly through federal and private student loans, and I always kept jobs throughout the semesters and summers in college. I worked at the university telethon, checking out equipment and registering members at the campus gym, as a resident assistant in my sophomore dorm, as a summer camp counselor, as a waitress, and in retail. As an undergraduate, my earned income would support me in paying bills, buying books, and socializing with friends on and off campus. I was simultaneously resentful of my peers whose parents sent them a monthly allowance for expenses in college, grateful to my roommate who would cover my share of the Chinese food takeout we would sometimes order on Friday nights, and proud of myself for working so hard while maintaining good grades and attendance throughout college.

When I started teaching college students and doing research about them, I recognized those students whose experiences mirrored my own. One student participant, Beth,[1] describes a similar history with work before and during college: "I started working sometime during my junior year [of high school] at a nursing home in the kitchen. . . . During the summers I would babysit. . . . I tutored in high school too. That was sometimes volunteer, sometimes paid. . . . I worked on a research project last year with a professor in the Nursing School, . . . at the University Commons at the information desk, . . . at a restaurant." For first-generation college students, like Beth and me, work is a constant presence in their lives before and during college, and, I argue in this essay, it enriches their learning beyond the limited rhetorical contexts of college classrooms.

Recent survey data confirm that forty-eight percent of students work during college (Eagan et al. 45), and first-gen students are more likely to work during college (Mehta et al.). As such, studying working students helps administrators, faculty, and staff to better understand a wide swathe of the college student population, especially first-gen students. Bringing greater attention to working students also allows us to differentiate between the kinds of work students do during college—divisions that are highly dependent on social class and familial background. Upper- and upper-middle-class students often have family networks and financial support that allow them to work unpaid internships or preprofessional jobs directly related to their majors and intended careers (Armstrong and Hamilton 186). By contrast, first-gen students, who largely hail from lower-middle- and working-class families, tend to work for pay in labor and service settings that may not directly relate to their academic and career trajectories (148). These different types of work entail an array of literacies and communicative practices. Consequently, workplaces of all kinds are influential sites of learning that interact productively with the academic knowledge and skills that students acquire in college, including their writing. However, these workplaces and attendant literacies are often assigned dissimilar, hierarchical value in ways that diminish first-gen students' considerable work experiences.

With these contexts in mind, I present findings from a study of first-gen students' writing across contexts, showing that students explicitly valued the writing they did at work but less so than they valued their academic writing. In first-year writing (FYW) first-gen students developed a construct of writing as persuasive, and in workplaces these students added to their writing constructs an understanding of writing as multimodal and as a way to professionalize in their intended fields.

These findings challenge commonly held assumptions about working in college. Typical portrayals of student workers posit that students are compelled to work out of financial need and that their time at work detracts from time, energy, and attention they might otherwise have devoted to academics (Aguiar; Armstrong and Hamilton; Bollig; Mandery; Pascarella and Terenzini; Renn and Reason; Warner). While these drawbacks to working in college may in some cases hold true, students in my study also describe positive experiences with work and workplace writing. College also constitutes for these students a pathway into middle-class professional jobs and careers that differ from the jobs and careers of their (often) lower-middle- and working-class families. Depending on the kinds of work contexts students participate in, literacy events encountered at work might be similar to those encountered in home communities, as is often the case with the kinds of labor and service jobs that first-gen students populate, where they encounter such literacy events as writing inventory notes or register or drawer counts. Conversely, while working in more professional or white-collar jobs on and off campus during college, first-gen students begin to encounter new literacy events more aligned with middle- and upper-class careers—for example, composing grant proposals or writing formal letters to donors of a particular community organization. In other words, work remains a constant for these students: a through line from their home communities, to their educational present, to their future professional careers. Work does not interrupt these students' college educations; work is a parallel and equally valuable context for learning and writing.

Data Collection and Analysis

I excerpt findings from a broader qualitative study comprising a three-interview sequence with fifteen first-generation college students at the University of Michigan (UM). Semistructured interviews spanned approximately ninety minutes each: the shortest interview lasted fifty-five minutes, and the longest lasted two hours and six minutes. In total, I recorded approximately seventy-eight hours of interview data. My study's guiding research questions include the following: how do first-generation college students describe the literacies they practice in the first-year writing classroom? and how do they describe the literacies they practice outside the classroom?

To best respond to these broad research questions, I designed a sequence of three interviews with the following themes and purposes: an initial interview, in which students describe their first-gen identity and their family, work, and educational backgrounds; a second interview focused on students' recently completed FYW courses, the first portion of which centered on a paper composed by each student in their FYW course, allowing for detailed responses from students; and a third interview that asked students to describe their out-of-school writing and speaking, practiced in their families and homes, workplaces, and extracurricular contexts. Many of the data reported in this essay derive from the second and third interviews. Student interviews were audio recorded, transcribed, and coded. Interview coding occurred in stages, including preliminary analyses to develop a working codebook and then a more comprehensive coding stage in which I applied codes and identified trends or patterns across individual students' three interviews as well as trends or patterns between the study's fifteen student participants.

Participants and Institutional Contexts

Though first-gen students share a common defining characteristic where educational status is concerned, no two first-gen students are identical; to better represent a range of first-generation college student experiences, I recruited a diverse population for participation in this study. Consequently, the income of participants' parents ranged from $15,000 to $75,000 annually; additionally, parents' occupations included a variety of blue and pink collar jobs, from security guard to education paraprofessional to hair stylist to automobile factory worker. These ranges of incomes and occupations are notable in that they influence first-gen students' exposure to varying jobs, careers, and earning potentials—influences that likely direct students' choices of jobs.

In addition to a variety of parents' incomes and occupations (i.e., social class markers), this study includes students who identify in diverse ways across several other demographic categories. Seven students identify as women, and eight identify as men. Students also disclosed a range of racial and ethnic identities: seven students in this study identify as black or African American, one of whom also identifies as Jewish and another of whom also identifies as Mexican. Five students identify as white or Caucasian, one as Haitian, one as Bengali, and one as Middle Eastern / Yemeni. Notably, three students in this study identify as first-generation or generation 1.5 Americans in addition to as first-generation college students. Because my study includes students with a range of gender, racial, ethnic, and national identities, my findings represent both commonalities and varieties of experience among first-generation college students.

UM is a large, four-year, primarily residential public university with very high research activity whose enrollment is "more selective" ("University of Michigan–Ann Arbor"). First-generation college students' experiences of exclusion from campus culture tend to be heightened at elite, more selective institutions like UM (Guerra; Klein; "University of Michigan Student Profile Comparison"; Stephens; Wang). At the time this study was conducted, only thirteen percent of the total first-year undergraduate student population at UM was first-gen, based on institutional survey data for parents' education (University of Michigan Office of Student Life). This low percentage stands in marked contrast to nationwide data in which approximately thirty-seven percent of first-year students at public universities are first-generation (Eagan et al. 32). With these institutional contexts in mind, I designed interview questions and developed codes that account for disparities between on-campus and off-campus experiences—disparities highlighted in the descriptions of FYW and workplace writing analyzed below.

Constructs of Writing

In this section, I analyze first-gen students' constructs of writing by comparing students' definitions of good college writing to good writing in general. These findings are collated from student responses to interview questions about their experiences writing both in FYW classroom contexts and in work, home, and extracurricular settings. Interestingly, participants describe both good college writing and good writing in general as evidence-based argumentation that engages particular audiences and has strong organization. With their descriptions of good college writing and good writing in general, first-gen students demonstrate a rich construct of writing as persuasion. However, because they ascribe this construct of writing to both good college writing and good writing in general, their construct of writing might be considered reductive. Especially given first-gen students' experiences with a wide variety of features and purposes of writing outside academic contexts, this construct of writing as only persuasion seems limited.

The particular contexts of FYW at UM certainly influence these students' definitions of what writing is and is for. At the time this study was conducted there were twelve possible courses that fulfilled the FYW requirement at UM; those courses were located in a variety of departments and programs on campus. Through a directed-self placement process and attendant academic advising, students at UM choose a FYW course that they believe best fits their needs and academic trajectory.

The fifteen students in this study were enrolled in four kinds of required FYW courses. Five students in this study—Luna, Ivy, Henry, Tom, and Armin—completed College Writing; three students—Beth, Ben, and Daquan—completed Writing and Literature; one student, Sarah, completed an honors writing course, Classic Works; and six students—Chris, Jason, Jack, Levi, Dana, and Tina—completed College Writing through the First-Year Connections Program (FYCP), a bridge program designed to support a variety of nontraditional students including first-gen students.[2] UM also offers a few sections of Professional Writing each semester—a course that would presumably connect more directly to students' work experiences than FYW might. However, as first-semester sophomores, none of the study's fifteen participants had enrolled in or completed this course at the time the study was conducted. Participants each shared with me a paper that they had written in their FYW course; they discussed drafting and receiving feedback on these major writing assignments. Overall, the fifteen papers that students shared with me might be categorized in the following ways: seven argumentative research papers, four literary analyses, two comparative analyses, and two personal narratives. Table 1 offers a brief summary of the assignments.

Student responses about good college writing drew heavily from their literacy learning around particular literacy events in FYW like writing the papers described in table 1. Their responses about good writing in general might have included FYW experiences but also drew from their experiences writing in contexts outside the academy, for example writing job applications or designing and delivering presentations in particular workplaces. Table 2 offers an overview and comparison of students' definitions of good college writing and good writing in general. As the table shows, students' descriptions of good college writing and of good writing in general are not distinct from one another and instead focus

Table 1. First-year writing major writing assignments

Student	FYW course	Genre	Summary of paper
Chris	College Writing FYCP	Researched argument	Supports Common Core as an effective education policy
Jack	College Writing FYCP	Researched argument	Uses Roland Barthes's theories to consider the wrestler The Rock
Jason	College Writing FYCP	Researched argument	Supports pro-choice and proabortion stances
Beth	Writing and Literature	Researched argument	Considers first-gen students' challenges in transitioning to college
Levi	College Writing FYCP	Researched argument	Considers the influence of technology on people
Daquan	Writing and Literature	Researched argument	Considers the effects of books on people
Henry	College Writing	Researched argument	Considers the pop-culture importance of The White Stripes
Tom	College Writing	Comparative analysis	Compares the Roman gladiatorial games to contemporary boxing
Luna	College Writing	Comparative analysis	Compares a band's two different albums using music theory as a lens
Dana	College Writing FYCP	Personal narrative	Discusses life before college
Sarah	Classic Works	Personal narrative	Discusses being first-gen and transitioning to college
Tina	College Writing FYCP	Literary analysis	Analyzes racial tensions in the novel *Disgrace*
Armin	College Writing	Literary analysis	Analyzes a character's leadership in the novel *The Mosquito Coast*
Ivy	College Writing	Literary analysis	Analyzes debt and obligation in the novel *Song of Solomon*
Ben	Writing and Literature	Literary analysis	Analyzes the main character in *Dr. Jekyll and Mr. Hyde*

Table 2. Good college writing versus good writing in general

Features of good college writing (number of students naming each feature)	Features of good writing in general (number of students naming each feature)
Evidence-based argument (13)	Audience (11)
Organization (9)	Evidence-based argument (4)
Audience (6)	Organization (3)

on three major features—argument, audience, and organization—to varying degrees.

Good Writing in College

Students offered clear descriptions of common features of good college writing. The most prevalent of these features was evidence-based argument, which thirteen out of the fifteen participants in this study mentioned. Dana offered a clear articulation of the importance of an evidence-based argument in college writing, and her statement is representative of those offered by many other students in the study. "I would say good college writing has a clear thesis. . . . It's something that has a lot of supporting details and uses primary sources you can go to. . . . It also needs to have supporting details. A lot of the stuff that we write about now, we're always supposed to have proof of . . . whatever our topic is. By using quotes or different life examples, just something to explain in detail what it is that we're trying to get across." Dana's description identifies that good college writing should have a clear thesis or point with supporting details. Dana clarified that supporting details might include source material, quotations, or different life examples—so long as those details provide proof of the argument or thesis. However, her comments also demonstrate the way in which students conflate persuasive writing with all other forms of writing. Dana's comments about good college writing "whatever our topic is" show a kind of formula she's developed. Dana's description lacks nuance about purposes or modes of writing. Dana's comments show a trend in the other participants' comments, wherein persuasive writing is ascribed not only to good college writing but also to good writing in general.

In conjunction with evidence-based argument, nine students mentioned organization as a feature of good college writing, and six talked about audience awareness as being important to good college writing. Henry offered a description of both organization and audience awareness, saying that good college writing should be "organized to an extent where, when the person reads it, they don't feel like they're reading it, I guess you could say. It just kind of happens, and that they feel something afterward. Even if they're just thinking about it for a few minutes afterward or something." Henry's description shows a rich construct of persuasive writing wherein major features like structure and audience awareness overlap and interact.

At times, students' construct of persuasive writing included descriptions of audience awareness as being tied closely to evidence-based argument. For example, Sarah described good college writing as having "a clear argument or a message that the reader can walk away with and be able to say what the writing was about. I think within that writing, there should be evidence of or at least support from other sources that also builds upon what they say." These examples show students' understandings of complex and challenging concepts. These students grasped the culminating purpose of persuasive writing—to persuade an audience or reader with a particular message—and recognized the role of evidence and structure in achieving that purpose. Their descriptions of their learning in FYW show a rich construct of writing as persuasive; however, it is problematic that this construct of persuasive writing gets attributed to both college writing and writing in general.

Good Writing in General

Student participants showed less agreement about what good writing in general looks like than they did for good college writing, but the same three features emerged, as table 2 shows. In the case of good writing in general, eleven of the fifteen students described audience awareness or engaging the reader, four mentioned evidence-based argument, and three mentioned organization.

Audience awareness was the most prevalent feature of good writing that students mentioned. For instance, Beth described good writing as writing that is "very clear to understand and that a wide audience could understand. Maybe not everybody, but it could reach a wide audience of people." In a similar vein, Ivy described good writing as "knowing who your audience is." Additionally, students stated that a writer should not only be aware of their audience but also write to engage their audience. Luna said that good writing should "just be able to convey to your reader or your audience what you're trying to do." Similarly, Tina stated that writing is good "if whoever is reading it can understand what you're saying . . . like what idea you're trying to get across." Taken together, these students' responses show that good writing in general should not only reflect the writer's awareness of audience but also the writer's ability to engage and convey meaning to that audience.

Some responses show that for these students, audience awareness is closely connected to argumentation. For example, Jack stated, "As long as you have some sort of thesis, you're [doing] good writing. As long as you can convey this thesis to people and you have it, it's there, beautiful. Awesome. You are great." In Jack's view, engaging audience is closely connected to having a thesis that the writer can convey to readers. Tom connects audience awareness to an additional feature of good writing—organization. Tom says of good writing that "the reader can relate to it. It's not going above their head. It flows . . . . While you're reading it, you're never thinking how does this fit in. It has transitions. . . . Has a good intro that catches the reader's attention. And the conclusion is not a cliff hanger. It summarizes it nicely and closes up." With his descriptions of flow, transitions, an intro, and a conclusion, Tom links engaging the audience to organization in writing, and in total three students in this study named organization as a defining feature of good writing in general. As with good college writing, students' descriptions of good writing in general reveal an acute awareness of persuasive writing, its overarching purpose (to persuade an audience), and the role of organization in pursuing that purpose. Again, these students' construct of persuasive writing is rich and complex. However, they reductively attribute this construct to both college writing and writing in general and thus overlook purposes for writing outside persuasion and the features of such writing.

One student, Daquan, offers a helpful reflection on why there might be parallels between good writing in general and in college. Daquan says the two are "[s]imilar because college writing prepares you to write well. They should go hand in hand." While the acknowledgment of some continuities between college writing and writing in general is admirable, these students' definitions of good writing overlook several valuable features of writing including specific workplace writing practices with which they have considerable experience. For example, in workplace settings, these students value the multimodality that writing for social media allows. I explore this and other features of workplace writing more fully in the sections below.

Students' tendencies to collapse together their definitions of good writing and good writing in college show the force of the socially powerful institution of education on these students' literacy learning, including on their understandings of what writing is and is for. However, writing constructs are not static; they are dynamic and complex. In the case of first-gen students, I argue that their overall construct of writing is informed both by the curricular construct of persuasive writing that they explicitly describe as good writing and by the more capacious construct of writing they encounter in workplaces.

Constructs of Writing in the Workplace

Student participants described thirty-eight different jobs and thirty-two different genres of writing at those jobs. First-gen students' workplace writing adds to their constructs an understanding of writing as multimodal and as a way for them to professionalize in their intended fields or careers. Additionally, writing in these workplaces also confirms features of their writing constructs, including the use of writing to persuade audiences, that they first encountered in academic contexts. In this section, I first focus on features of writing that students value in both workplace and academic writing—namely, persuasion and audience awareness—and then analyze valuable features unique to first-gen students'

Table 3. Features of writing in various contexts (and number of students naming each feature)

Features of good college writing	Features of good writing in general	Features of academic and workplace writing	Features of workplace writing
Evidence-based argument (13)	Audience (11)	Persuasion (3)	Multimodality (3)
Organization (9)	Argumentation (4)	Audience (2)	Professionalization and engaging interests (5)
Audience (6)	Organization (3)		

descriptions of workplace writing, including multimodality and connecting to individuals' professional interests. Table 3 offers a summary of these valuable aspects of workplace writing and a comparison with good college writing and good writing in general.

Students' valuing of consistencies between academic and workplace writing confirms recent survey findings that having "an internship or job that allowed [students] to apply what [they were] learning in the classroom" greatly enriched the learning and working lives of students during and after college (*Great Jobs* 14). I suggest that faculty and administrators might better communicate and emphasize this symbiotic relationship between academic and workplace writing.

Reciprocity between First-Year Writing and Workplace Writing

Students valued workplace writing that allowed them to practice persuasion. For her on-campus desk job at the university ID card office, Luna described writing emails to students and parents as well as interoffice emails—emails she described as "persuasive in a way." Specifically, Luna gave the example that "the medical center . . . printed a bunch of [ID] cards, and they sent them to us for some reason. I had to write an email to all of these nursing students explaining how to find our office. Telling them to come get their cards basically." In comparing this workplace writing task to her essay writing for her college classes, Luna said: "Both of them are very formal. I'm pretty formal in emails that I send to students and parents, that's the same [as essays for class]. The content is different. It's just instructions and very to the point, which my writing for class is concise too. It's just a different tone. Like, 'Please come and pick up your [ID] card. Our hours are 8am to 5pm. We're located at this location behind the union,' as opposed to an essay." In her workplace emails, Luna had to make requests of students, parents, and coworkers—requests that often included a call to action like encouraging readers to come down to the office to pick up their ID cards. In her workplace, Luna confirmed and put into practice persuasive writing techniques—for example, striking a balance between a formal but not too commanding tone and integrating informative and persuasive aspects of writing into her emails—similar to those techniques students also mentioned learning and valuing in their academic writing.

Ben also described his workplace writing as persuasive; Ben wrote letters asking for donations for his internship at a performing arts intensive summer program, where he worked on the development team. "People would fund and give donations, so I'd have to write to sponsors sometimes to sponsor kids to get scholarships because it's a very expensive intensive." With a real-world audience and purpose in mind, Ben had the opportunity to practice persuasive writing and reinforce his classroom learning. Ben went on to say that these letters were "persuasive writing" because this style of writing "definitely gave me that information I needed to ask without asking, kind of informing you to be on my side, hooking you in rather than saying this is why you should give me money. I'm like, 'No see there are these people and they need it, I'm not asking you for it, they just need it. And I know you have it, so, why not?' . . . It taught me how to be more persuasive with the words I use." For Ben, writing letters asking for donations was valuable workplace writing because it allowed him to put into practice persuasive writing techniques similar to those he and other students emphasized as valuable to their academic writing as well.

Workplace contexts added to these students' constructs an understanding of real audiences embedded in particular writing contexts, whereas academic contexts offered an understanding of imagined or invoked audiences (Ede and Lunsford) that often accompanied persuasive writing assignments. As such, the workplace allowed for nuance in these students' writing constructs by providing real audiences and exigencies for persuasive writing and by offering students repeated opportunities to practice and adapt their persuasive writing with each new audience or purpose. With both features of writing—persuasion and audience awareness—first-gen students in the study confirmed and mobilized learning about writing that they had gained in academic contexts. This kind of cross-context learning about writing strengthens students' understandings of what writing is and does in the world and, perhaps most important, apprentices first-gen students into the kinds of writing that will be demanded of them in the white-collar professional careers they aspire to after college. In these ways, the data show that first-gen students' practice of persuasive writing in workplace contexts is a valuable feature of their writing constructs—one that goes overlooked when academic contexts for learning are valued or emphasized to the exclusion of extra-academic contexts for learning.

Students also valued workplace writing genres like *PowerPoint* presentations and social media posts in which they could engage new and different audiences. For example, in his performing arts internship, Ben also described doing a lot of "social media writing" and "social media marketing" on several platforms, including *Facebook*, *Twitter*, *Instagram*, and *Snapchat*. On these platforms, Ben was writing to "participants in the foundation, also to get people who were already in [the foundation] excited, like pump-ups type of stuff. We also did a lot of daily quizzes, trivia type things . . . or we would do [a competition for] who could get the most selfies." While describing these kinds of social media posts, Ben reflected on such aspects of his writing as engaging particular audiences, saying this kind of writing "taught me to point out the important things . . . I wasn't able to describe them as much on social media, but it definitely taught me to put in the writing the things that will catch someone's eye." With his emphasis on catching someone's eye and pointing out important things, Ben highlights the influence of audience on his social media writing for his internship. Ben's version of engaging an audience in his workplace social media writing was likely markedly different from how he engaged an audience in his literary analysis papers in FYW. Ben's recognition of the constrained time and space in which to engage an audience on social media productively complicated and strengthened his understanding of audience awareness as well as his overall construct of writing.

Sarah similarly described working to engage audiences in her workplace writing. In her on-campus job at the Foreign Language Center at UM, Sarah worked the desk, answering phones and checking out materials like books and movies for students. At this job, Sarah says: "There was one time I had to make a *PowerPoint* of Spanish words, because I have some Spanish experience, for a middle school that's visiting, so that was fun; . . . It was bringing me back to my middle school phase, because it's like, 'Okay. If I'm a middle schooler, sitting in a library for a *PowerPoint*, what do I want to see?' I included some pictures of *Frozen* stuff, and I tried to make it fun." In this example, Sarah considers a different audience for her writing and composes her *PowerPoint* presentation in an effort to engage this audience effectively. While audience awareness is often a feature of academic writing, and one that first-gen students report valuing, in the classroom these audiences are often only imagined or invoked, whereas in workplaces these audiences become real.

Workplace Writing and Multimodality

The first-gen students in the study also identified valuable features of writing specific to workplace contexts. In their workplace writing, first-gen students valued the opportunity to integrate multiple modes and media and to connect to their professional and academic interests. In the above example, Sarah's use of images from the movie *Frozen* in her *PowerPoint* presentation for middle schoolers showcases one way in which these students engaged multiple modes and media in their workplace writing. In addition to this *PowerPoint* presentation, Sarah also contributed to the Foreign Language Center's blog. Sarah notes: "over the summer I wrote two passages for it. That was fun. . . . I blogged about the spelling bee, actually, and how knowing a language of origin can tell you a lot about how to spell a word. . . . I added GIFs. It was a fun blog." These findings for Sarah's and other students' multimodal writing in the workplace confirm previous studies that show students value the few opportunities for multimodal writing they encounter in the classroom and that students most often encounter multimodal writing in workplace or extracurricular contexts (Heath 123).

Ben's example of social media writing and marketing also demonstrates the use of multiple modes and media in workplace writing, going beyond what might be typical in academic writing. In his social media writing for his performing arts internship, Ben described how

> *Instagram* was so short, caption-y, hashtag-y, emoji. *Twitter* usually involved photos and links to things. And just like four big words and then maybe a hashtag. *Snapchat* of course had video, and then *Facebook* was usually the longer posts, for which you would write a headline, then you would have to write a little description, maybe attach a photo, and attach a link, so it kind of just had to be like "click here for more information," but put the most important thing. . . . So you had to strategize: what did you want to capture within this little ten second window that people would scroll up and down?

In his description, Ben shows a sophisticated understanding of various social media platforms and their attendant purposes, modes, and media. In this example, Ben again is writing for an addressed—rather than invoked or imagined—audience; the use of real-world audiences and purposes for combining and leveraging different modes and media can rarely be authentically recreated in the classroom, and in this way Ben's workplace writing offered him a useful understanding of writing as multimodal.

Workplace Writing and Professionalization

Some students valued workplace writing that connected to their professional or academic interests, including Sarah's use of multiple languages in a *PowerPoint* presentation and Ben's use of social media writing to market a performing arts intensive. In her description of composing her presentation for middle school students learning Spanish, Sarah said, "It was fun because I hadn't used Spanish in a while and I missed it. I looked for that job, or I was interested in applying for that job, because it got me back into the foreign language areas, which is something that I haven't had time to study in college, but I really miss." Sarah, a neuroscience major who also speaks three languages, leveraged her work-study job as an opportunity to engage an academic interest outside of the coursework for her major. In this workplace context, Sarah also took up a construct of writing as multilingual. In Sarah's work at the Foreign Language Center, writing was used to communicate with many different speakers and learners of different languages—a facet of writing that most college courses likely overlook but that Sarah is deeply interested in.

Sarah also used her individual writing tasks at her job to help her engage topics that interested her. As mentioned above, Sarah wrote a blog post about her personal experiences watching and participating in spelling bees in middle school and "how knowing a language of origin can tell you a lot about how to spell a word." Sarah says of her blog post: "I kept it pretty third-person, but my experience in spelling bees definitely made me aware of how much [knowing another language] helps. Watching the National Spelling Bee is so much of a spectator sport for me." While writing in coursework might usually be limited to the particular themes or content of a single course, workplace writing allows students to pursue academic and professional interests of their choosing. Writing a blog post showed Sarah that writing could help her explore professional interests that were parallel to but often distinct from the interests she explored in strictly academic contexts.

Like Sarah, Ben also chose to pursue a job that related directly to his academic and professional interests in theater and education. Ben described his job application essay as an opportunity to make comparisons and connections between his different theater experiences: "You basically just have to take what you already gained and then say what you have and then what you hope to get. So, you kind of have to make them mix in together, compare and contrast them basically from your past experiences to the experiences you have had and hope to have and are having." Ben leveraged his application essay writing as a chance to take stock of his theater experiences and set goals for the future, and this application writing showed him that writing is useful both for reflection and for connecting to professional and academic interests. Even though some FYW courses at UM allow for narrative and reflective writing similar to that which Ben describes here, Ben's FYW class focused on literary analyses. Moreover, student participants, in their definitions of good writing, emphasized the persuasive, argumentative aspects of their writing in FYW over any reflective or narrative aspects. Writing applications for jobs allows students to synthesize, reflect on, and make meaning from their personal experiences in ways that are less commonly valued in their FYW contexts.

Overall, first-gen students' accounts of writing at work demonstrate their range and depth of expertise in both their work responsibilities and their writing. At work, these students composed in a variety of genres for specific purposes, but in their definitions of good writing, these students overlooked the value of this workplace writing. These findings confirm wider trends wherein working students often discount the value of their considerable workplace experience (Armstrong and Hamilton 200)—a move that can be especially detrimental to first-gen students. Because first-gen students are more likely to work during college (Mehta et al.) and because their parents often lack the expertise or influence to help position workplace experience as valuable (Armstrong and Hamilton 206–08), college administrators and faculty would do well to help these students value and augment their workplace learning and writing.

Implications

The data analyzed in this essay reveal that first-generation college students develop a more nuanced understanding of what writing is by working during college. Whereas writing in academic contexts like FYW affords these students an understanding of writing as persuasive, evidence-based argumentation, writing in workplace contexts not only includes this construct of writing as persuasion but also expands that construct to include such features as multimodality and professionalization in particular fields. By demonstrating the contributions of workplace writing to first-generation college students' constructs of writing, my analysis recovers an often-overlooked site of literacy learning and positions working in college as a strength or opportunity rather than a deficit or burden for these students. The question now is, how can teachers and scholars help students to ascribe value and power to their considerable workplace writing experiences, to augment those aspects of their writing constructs that students themselves seem to overlook? As the analyses in this essay show, better acknowledging the wide variety of settings in which these students write before and during college makes for an expanded construct of writing that is richly complex and nuanced and that better aligns with these students' lived experiences as first-gen.

With these findings in mind, I suggest a constellation of changes in our approach to teaching writing. Ideally, students could enroll in a sequence of writing courses including first-year writing and professional writing. Where professional writing courses are possible, the findings presented here demonstrate the wide variety of genres students might take up in workplaces and might usefully learn about in such courses. My findings suggest that a generic or templated approach to professional writing courses, wherein students compose predetermined genres of writing (like the common résumé, cover letter, memo), are of limited usefulness. Instead, students might investigate their intended fields of work or study, focusing on discourse analysis and rhetorical genre analysis to determine and analyze the most influential genres of writing in their fields. Moreover, a focus on rhetorical genre analysis would support students in developing transferable knowledge and skills they might use to suss out and deploy appropriate genres of writing (and related communicative practices) in the array of workplaces they will likely occupy throughout their professional lives. Additionally, professional writing courses might integrate reflective writing to help students account for the considerable workplace experiences they already have and to draw on and adapt those literacy and writing experiences to the college environment and to current or future workplace environments.

Regardless of whether professional writing courses are offered, first-year writing instructors might adjust their course design. First, instructors might include content, readings, and discussions about work and other class-based experiences that students bring with them to college (Kohn). Additionally, writing assignments like Nancy Mack's multigenre folklore writing assignment ("Ethical Representation") and literacy narratives ("Emotional Labor"), David Seitz's work memoir project, Genesea Carter's discourse community identity profiles, and Donna LeCourt's literacy autobiographies would support new college students in valuing and making meaning from their previous and concurrent work experiences and literacy practices. Such opportunities to reflect on personal experiences and topics like work and literacy that are so intertwined with students' social class backgrounds open up an empathetic space, which Julie Lindquist calls for (195), and ideally would allow students to see their work experiences as valuable even (and especially) in the context of their college educations. Apart from reflective and narrative assignments, a focus on rhetorical analysis, audience engagement, and the variety of ways to interact with an audience outside of persuasion might better empower first-gen students, and all working students, to complicate their ideas of good writing and to see persuasion and argumentation as one kind of writing, not the best or only writing available to them.

Finally, these findings indicate new and important contexts for research. Researchers would do well to conduct more research about first-gen students and about working students, research that takes seriously these students' voices and empowers them to account for their own experiences and expertise rather than speaking for them. As the data presented in this essay demonstrate, allowing for detailed descriptions of first-gen students' experiences reveals previously overlooked strengths, knowledge, and skills. These students are underserved when we focus only on the challenges they may face rather than celebrate their considerable resilience and impressive positive contributions to our classrooms and campuses.

Notes

1. All student names are pseudonyms.
2. All course and program names are pseudonyms.

Works Cited

Aguiar, Christian. "'What Work Is': Writing about Work in First-Year Composition." *Teaching English in the Two-Year College*, vol. 46, no. 2, 2018, pp. 147–52.

Armstrong, Elizabeth A., and Laura T. Hamilton. *Paying for the Party: How College Maintains Inequality*. Harvard UP, 2012.

Bollig, Chase. "'People Like Us': Theorizing First-Generation College as a Marker of Difference." *Literacy in Composition Studies*, vol. 7, no. 1, 2019, pp. 22–43.

Carter, Genesea M. "'Being Part of Something Gave Me Purpose': How Community Membership Impacts First-Year Students' Sense of Self." Carter and Thelin, pp. 282–97.

Carter, Genesea M., and William H. Thelin, editors. *Class in the Composition Classroom: Pedagogy and the Working Class*. Utah State UP, 2017.

Eagan, Kevin, et al. *The American Freshman: National Norms Fall 2014*. Higher Education Research Institute, 2014, www.heri.ucla.edu/monographs/TheAmericanFreshman2014.pdf.

Ede, Lisa, and Andrea Lunsford. "Audience Addressed / Audience Invoked: The Role of Audience in Composition Theory and Pedagogy." *College Composition and Communication*, vol. 35, no. 2, 1984, pp. 155–71.

Great Jobs Great Lives: The 2014 Gallup-Purdue Index Report. Gallup / Purdue U, 2014, www.luminafoundation.org/files/resources/galluppurdueindex-report-2014.pdf.

Guerra, Jennifer. "Coming Out as Poor at an Elite University." *State of Opportunity*, Michigan Radio, 29 Jan. 2015, stateofopportunity.michiganradio.org/post/coming-out-poor-elite-university.

Heath, Shirley Bryce. *Words at Work and Play: Three Decades in Family and Community Life*. Cambridge UP, 2012.

Klein, Jesse. "Relative Wealth." *The Michigan Daily*, 16 Feb. 2015, www.michigandaily.com/opinion/02jesse-klein-relative-wealth16.

Kohn, Liberty. "We're All Middle Class? Students' Interpretation of Childhood Ethnographies to Reflect on Class Difference and Identity." Carter and Thelin, pp. 161–77.

LeCourt, Donna. "Performing Working-Class Identity in Composition: Toward a Pedagogy of Textual Practice." *College English*, vol. 69, no. 1, 2006, pp. 30–51.

Lindquist, Julie. "Class Affects, Classroom Affectations: Working through the Paradoxes of Strategic Empathy." *College English*, vol. 67, no. 2, 2004, pp. 187–209.

Mack, Nancy. "Emotional Labor as Imposters: Working-Class Literacy Narratives and Academic Identities." Carter and Thelin, pp. 140–61.

———. "Ethical Representation of Working-Class Lives: Multiple Genres, Voices, and Identities." *Pedagogy*, vol. 6, no. 1, 2006, pp. 53–78.

Mandery, Evan J. "Teaching Working Students." *The New York Times*, 10 Sept. 2015, www.nytimes.com/2015/09/13/magazine/teaching-working-students.html.

Mehta, Sanjay S., et al. "Why Do First-Generation Students Fail?" *College Student Journal*, vol. 45, no. 1, 2011, pp. 20–35.

Pascarella, Ernest T., and Patrick T. Terenzini. *How College Affects Students: A Third Decade of Research*. 2nd ed., Jossey-Bass, 2005.

Renn, Kristen A., and Robert D. Reason. *College Students in the United States: Characteristics, Experiences, and Outcomes*. Jossey-Bass, 2012.

Seitz, David. "Making Work Visible." *College English*, vol. 67, no. 2, 2004, pp. 210–21.

Stephens, Nicole M. *A Cultural Mismatch: The Experience of First-Generation College Students in Elite Universities*. 2009. Stanford U, PhD dissertation.

"University of Michigan–Ann Arbor." *The Carnegie Classification of Institutions of Higher Education*, 2021, carnegieclassifications.iu.edu/lookup/lookup.php. Accessed Feb. 2015.

University of Michigan Office of Student Life. "Re: Accessing CIRP Data for First-Gen Students." Email to the author, 17 Dec. 2016.

"University of Michigan Student Profile Comparison with Other Highly Selective Public and Very Highly Selective Private Institutions." U of Michigan, Student Affairs Research, Center for Teaching and Learning, 2014, www.crlt.umich.edu/sites/default/files/resource_files/StudentProfileDatafor2013.pdf.

Wang, Jenny. "A Response to 'Relative Wealth.'" *The Michigan Daily*, 17 Feb. 2015, www.michigandaily.com/opinion/jenny-wang-response-relative-wealth.

Warner, Michael. *Publics and Counterpublics*. Zone Books, 2002.

Research-Writing Pedagogy as Sustaining First-Generation College Student Identities in a Bridge Program

Christine Alfano, Megan Formato, Jennifer Johnson, and Ashley Newby

Writing and research in the collegiate setting are often viewed as the work of already established academics. The ideas around what "good" writing looks like, and what "real" research is, permeate our ivory towers and set expectations before our students ever set foot into our classrooms. Too often, those ideas limit what our students believe is possible, alienating them from their own ideas, voices, and research goals. As writing instructors at Stanford University, a private West Coast R1 university, we have endeavored to create spaces that allow first-generation college (FGC) students to see themselves as both writers and researchers in academic settings. According to one such student, JM, "[Writing] the op-ed was, I think, the defining thing, the defining moment that changed my perception of writing . . . knowing that I'm a writer, and I can write and put my ideas down and be confident that my ideas are important because my ideas and my writing are more powerful than I felt it was in high school. And I actually thought [it] came from [the summer bridge program]." JM's reflection speaks to the ways that increased confidence in one's writing and ideas is integral to how our students see not only themselves but also how they position themselves in higher education institutions. Too often our FGC students come to us having been defined by others. This essay tells the stories of our students' relationship to writing and research in their own voices.

Through our narrative inquiry's focus on the FGC students' attitudes and experiences with research and academic writing practices, we add new narratives to current understandings of the transitioning student in writing scholarship, which has seen an overrepresentation of the generic student. A neutral approach to viewing incoming students equally "erases the presence" of underrepresented identities and students of color (Royster and Williams 568; see also Kareem). We describe the research-based writing course in a low-income bridge program for first-generation students focused on creating spaces for them to become researchers and collaborators or to develop a "scholarly habitus" (McCoy and Winkle-Wagner 428). This course is underpinned by a culturally sustaining pedagogy (CSP) that emphasizes students' navigational capital (Paris and Alim; Yosso).

Within their narratives, the students also spoke to the importance of their aspirational capital in both their journeys in college and their development as writers and researchers in the university setting. Our FGC students' shifts in perspectives on writing and research from high school to college are shaped by the bridge program's cultivation of pedagogical opportunities to see research in new ways—not solely as work done in a science laboratory, but rather as multidisciplinary work connected to the communities and experiences that students identify as integral to their FGC identities. The personal narratives shared by FGC students in this study confirm their positionalities as intersectional (Nguyen and Nguyen; Nuñez, "Employing") and as having rich "rhetorical potential" (Bollig 38). Our research suggests that it is necessary to develop pedagogies and practices that open spaces for students to view their FGC identities as resources and motivations in the research-writing process.

Institutional Context of the Summer Bridge Program

In 2017, Stanford University's incoming class was made up of more than eighteen percent first-generation college students—the highest in the university's history ("Report"). This increase, although incremental, reflects the increase in the national average, where one-third of undergraduate college students are first-generation, according to a 2018 report by the National Center for Education Statistics (Cataldi et al. 2). Many of these incoming FGC students applied to the bridge program, a four-week residential program for incoming first-generation and low-income students, which they attend in the summer prior to their first quarter at college. Of the students in the 2018 bridge program cohort, ninety-two percent identified as low-income and seventy-two percent as first-generation; according to their self-reported race or ethnic identity, the cohort was thirty-eight percent Hispanic or Latino, twenty-seven percent African American or Black, sixteen percent Asian, ten percent international, seven percent White, and two percent American Indian or Alaskan (Internal annual report). In comparison, for the institution as a whole, the incoming class self-reported as thirty-three percent White, twenty-three percent Asian, fifteen percent Hispanic or Latino, eleven percent international, seven percent African American or Black, and one percent American Indian or Alaskan.

Originally launched in 2011, the bridge program initially focused on serving STEM students who might feel underprepared for college-level science curricula.

However, because of an increase in first-gen students at our institution and the wide success of the summer program, in 2016 admission to the bridge program was opened to non-STEM majors, including students intending to major in humanities and in social science and undecided students. The program doubled in size, expanding from thirty to sixty students, and a focus on academic writing was integrated into the bridge program course. In the feedback on the bridge program, students in this cohort asked for more opportunities to explore diverse disciplines in their research and writing projects. In response, the 2017 and 2018 bridge program cohorts took a new interdisciplinary summer course, Exploring Research, Writing, and Problem-Solving. The course comprised two parallel tracks: one focused on the development of critical problem-solving in chemistry and a second focused on an introduction to academic writing and college-level research. A third component, a research poster project, represented a collaboration between instructors in the STEM-focused and writing-focused tracks, giving students access to more mentors and research topics across different disciplines.

A Narrative Inquiry Approach

Through the voices and experiences of our students, in this study we seek to better understand how our pedagogy supports FGC students' development as cross-disciplinary student researcher-writers. As women from different academic fields who teach writing and rhetoric to first- and second-year students, we bring our voices and different cultural, linguistic, and educational experiences to our teaching and research. One coauthor felt her own experience as a first-gen low-income student shaped her dialogue with the student interviewees in our study. Another drew from her experiences as a woman of color and as a mother to inform her approach. A third coauthor found that growing up in a bilingual home and her experience as a low-income student underpinned her researcher positionality. While three of us serve as instructors for the bridge program, all four of us were involved in the planning and implementation of the writing-specific portion, and all of us interviewed students for this essay. We take a narrative inquiry approach to understanding the lived experiences, past and present, of FGC students (Clandinin and Huber). A narrative approach "represents knowledge from the bottom up" and opens up the possibility for participants of the communities studied to "participate in knowledge construction" (Canagarajah 327) as both "participants" and "tellers" of their stories (Clandinin and Huber 439; see also Carr).

We conducted semistructured interviews with seventeen students from the bridge program's 2018 cohort, exploring FGC students' relationships to writing and research before the bridge program (i.e., in high school) and after the bridge program (at the close of their first undergraduate year). The majority of students in the program and in our study are students of color, many of whom come from multilingual backgrounds. In the interviews, we used their research poster as an artifact to "represent aspects of lived experiences" (Clandinin and Huber 439) and to unfold stories behind the collaborative research project. Following the individual interviews, we conducted three focus groups of three to four students, with the aim of hearing from a diversity of voices on the lived FGC experience. We transcribed and coded the interviews through a grounded theory approach (Glaser and Strauss). We see the narrative approach as "a collaboration between researcher and participants, over time, in a place or series of places, and in social interaction with milieus" (Clandinin and Connelly 20). Our participation in these spaces plays a role in the way participants shape their stories and in how we interpret them.

Sustaining Cultural Resources in Research-Based Writing Contexts

Our pedagogical approach to the bridge program course reflects a commitment to CSP. A CSP approach recognizes that students' "linguistic and cultural dexterity and plurality" are skills students have had to cultivate throughout their lives (Paris 95). Rather than conforming to an imagined or perceived academic standard, CSP views this lifelong skill set as an access point to educational opportunities. Django Paris encourages us to develop pedagogies that are "more than response or relevant to the cultural experiences" of our students but rather that sustain cultural and linguistic competences—seeing them as resources, while "simultaneously offering access to dominant cultural competence" (95).

In shaping a more interdisciplinary research-based writing pedagogy, we aim to sustain the intersectional identities of FGC students. FGC students are not lacking specific cultural capital to succeed in academic contexts but, rather, are in possession of a fuller range of cultural resources, especially for home or community cultural wealth (Yosso). Anne-Marie Nuñez echoes this perspective in their research, finding a link between culturally and personally relevant content to expanding student opportunities, cultivating a sense of belonging and developing students' confidence ("Counterspaces"). Faculty as mentors in this framework must not only affirm cultural identities (Engle and Tinto) but also facilitate cultural agency in a bidirectional way (Schademan and Thompson). Faculty and students share a mutual agency around college readiness that allows for interpersonal and interactive pedagogical spaces underpinned by "asset-based views of individuals and their communities" (Schademan and Thompson 197).

Alicia Gonzalez Quiroz and Nora Garza's 2018 study examining effective summer bridge programs points to the importance of content as "relevant to motivate, engage, and retain today's student" (109). Similarly, Dorian McCoy and Rachelle Winkle-Wagner discuss how maintaining FGC students' "prior experiences, identities, and backgrounds" is key for cultivating in students a passion for undergraduate research and a "scholarly habitus" (435, 428). While McCoy and Winkle-Wagner examine summer bridge programs to prepare students for graduate school, we propose that this cultivation needs to take place in the transition to undergraduate education and through a broader range of disciplines. We designed the research-writing pedagogy for incoming first-year undergraduates in our bridge program with a focus on research as interdisciplinary and methodologically diverse in order to bridge cultural relevance and research.

The development of students as researcher-writers is the main objective of our summer bridge program course, as implied by the name of the course (Exploring Research, Writing, and Problem-Solving). The research-writing sequence moves students through a series of engagements designed to help them transition to college-level work, scaffolding the development of strategies for finding and evaluating sources, for identifying and entering into a scholarly conversation, and for sharing findings in different modes. In addition to research and problem-solving components offered by the chemistry track, the research-based writing assignments include an annotated bibliography, a research conversation synthesis, a research summary, an op-ed, and a poster project with a public presentation component. The assignments place emphasis on student agency in research, with opportunities for both individual and collaborative writing, and focus on argument delivery in a variety of oral and written genres. Students select preferred topics from several disciplines and are paired with a mentor with expertise or interest in that area. Individually, students develop an annotated bibliography that feeds into the group's research interests. Group topics range from STEM-focused areas (Saving Our Oceans; and Designing and Delivering New Drugs) to social sciences areas (Bias in Tech: Race, Gender, and Silicon Valley; and Music and Identity / Hip-Hop Rhetorics). In the last assignment of the sequence, the op-ed, students circle back to their individual research topic ideas, informed by the work they have done on their collaborative project.

First-Generation Students' Identities

As a first step in understanding how their growth as researcher-writers is connected to their first-gen identity, we invited students to offer their own definitions of what it means to be a first-generation college student. Along with scholars like Thai-Huy Nguyen and Bach Mai Dolly Nguyen who point to the ways that "the [*first-generation student*] term . . . simultaneously seeks and fails to capture the richness and complexity of students' lives" (148), our students define and theorize their first-gen identities along a flexible and dynamic range or "spectrum" (SB, student).

While they express this identity differently, across their conceptions of what it means to be a FGC student there is a shared understanding of a fixed outside definition of FGC students. However, their own lived experiences incorporate both layers and flexibility of meaning to the FGC identity, one that changes and intersects with other identities, particularly when they enter university. Students go beyond the definitions of first-gen students we see in the scholarship to incorporate nuance that both speaks to their levels of innate cultural wealth and acknowledges the ways that they are conceptualized by others (Yosso 75). They identify and expand on forms of aspirational, resistant, and familial capital that they bring to college, and they acknowledge the development of navigational and social capital as a result of their college transition.

Scholarship that relies on fixed definitions of FGC students, such as the US Department of Education's definition—"students who ha[ve] parents with no postsecondary education experience" (Redford and Hoyer 1)—does not acknowledge or incorporate the voices of the students whom the term is meant to describe (Quinn et al.). These fixed definitions emphasize these students' struggles without appreciating their assets and run the risk of "reproducing the very inequality that education researchers wish to mitigate" (Nguyen and Nguyen 148). While our students bring up the effects of not having family members who can explain all of the steps in the college process (Gibbons et al.), they also talk about how they have developed their own navigational capital as a result (Yosso). The student PK reflects on their experience navigating college on their own: "And I think for me, just like any first gen, you're kind of navigating on your own the college experience and doing the right thing that is great for you."

PK's interview highlights the ways that FGC students see their navigational journey as being good for themselves. They build on the navigational capital, or ways of maneuvering through institutional spaces (Yosso 80), that they bring with them to the college experience. One student, AP, acknowledged that while others in her family have attended institutions of higher education, she conceptualized *first-gen* as meaning something different specifically because of her experience attending Stanford or attending an elite private institution in general: "I think both words [*first-gen* and *low-income*] have changed for me ever since I arrived [at the university] in the sense that *first-gen* is no longer just a first in your family to go to college but more first to reach a new height of education level."

AP's concept of first-generation students was centered on the difference in the kind of institution that AP was navigating: "I don't have a backup from home to say 'oh this one [parent or relative] will get this, this one will understand this.'" For our students, navigational capital was frequently tied to feelings or beliefs about the kind of institution they were attending and the difference that the institution itself made in their navigation. The student LL reflected: "I think it's definitely made it harder. Because you're surrounded by your classmates . . . a lot of which are legacy students. So their parents came here or other elite institutions. . . . You feel like you're playing this catchup game of how behind you are in academics compared to your peers, who have already had experience in these higher-level classes." Speaking about the "nuance" used when talking about being a FGC student at Stanford, JL extended the institutional difference even more, noting that a parent's technical school or trade school experience is "a very different experience than living on campus at a four-year university."

While fixed definitions of FGC students don't speak to the navigational capital that our students bring with them to our institution, they also do not acknowledge the different kinds of education contexts that students emphasize and speak to in their own definitions. At the same time that students point to having less cultural capital within a space like our institution, they emphasize the development of their navigational capital through the necessity of maneuvering this space (Yosso 80). The student CS described this process clearly when she talked about an absence of mentorship or guidance from her family and, in the same breath, discussed the labor and time she put into figuring out how to navigate these institutions for herself:

> I feel like for someone to say they are first-gen, what it really means is they didn't have a lot of resources in terms of cultural capital when it comes to approaching higher education and the institutions that are a part of that: networking, office hours, how to time manage in college, how to organize your courses so you aren't overwhelmed. A lot of things that just come with experience, and they're passed down through generations of advice. The lack of that is usually a result of not having close family members or close connections who have gone to college and are able to provide those. . . . My parents are super supportive, but I never ask them questions like "What classes should I take? How does FAFSA work?"

She then pivots from talking about the absence of familial resources to describing how she has developed navigational capital:

> I figure most of it out on my own or with the help of programs that helped me get through them, but whenever I needed help with it, my instinct was never "Let me ask my mom or dad." My instinct was "Let me ask my teacher, let me ask my high school counselor, let me email the university." So kind of like first-gen means the first person you turn to for support in navigating these institutions is not your close family; it's usually sources without, and that extra labor

> that it takes [to] find those people that will help you through it. It's the struggle that I feel really unites a lot of students who are first-gen because it is difficult to navigate.

Several other students echoed CS as they pointed to the skills, confidence, and resilience they formed navigating hardships and institutions unfamiliar to their family and claimed the resilience and navigational capital developed through those experiences as a key part of their first-gen identity. The student YN reflected that *first-gen* means "being responsible for your own . . . utilization of the resources that you have on campus and being able to find a way to make the most of your time here." YN frames first-gen status as an asset: "being first-gen comes along with a lot of hardships growing up, and I feel like that kind of resilience that you build through going through those things is . . . something that puts us above some of our other peers."

In addition to their own navigational capital, students also reflected on the importance of communities that they became a part of on campus. When talking about their sense of belonging on campus, they talked about ethnic-based communities and the personal connections that they were able to make through the spaces that welcomed and supported FGC students explicitly (such as the bridge program and the first-generation office). Their reflections highlight the ways that those spaces have aided in their navigational capital and simultaneously provided them with increased levels of social capital.

As powerful as the student reflections on their own navigational and increasing social capital are, stopping here and privileging a lack of experience in their families with elite institutions of higher education would risk affirming a deficit perspective and devalue the communities and families from which the students come. According to Tara Yosso, "Deficit thinking takes the position that minority students and families are at fault for poor academic performance because: (a) students enter school without normative cultural knowledge and skills; and (b) parents neither value nor support their child's education" (76). While our students did point to gaps in specific kinds of knowledge about higher education in their families, they did not stop there. Through their theorizing on FGC student experiences, they highlighted both their own resilience and skills at navigating new spaces *and* the importance of the other kinds of capital that their families and home communities equipped them with, including values around education. Extending her definition of first-gen students, the student BW offered: "But I think personally it means so much more because it means being grateful for everything that your family has sacrificed in order for you to get this far. And just representing not only yourself but the community where you came from and where you grew up." AP described how the definition "means carrying my community with me as well." As students transitioned to college, they described increasing reliance on their families' values around education. The student SB explained, "[E]ducation has always been very important to my family, and just because my grandparents from either my mom [or] dad's side, they stopped their education when they were in middle school. . . . Especially my grandpa from my mom's side, he was very influential in me persisting in going to school because . . . having an education, a higher education, would lead me to better stability and just a better place in society." For SB, it was the fact that their grandfather didn't have a higher education that led them to pursue it for themselves; he instilled in them an aspirational capital, or "the ability to hold on to hope in the face of structured inequality" (Yosso 77). The student MN also echoed this sentiment: "I guess education has always been stressed by my parents to me as fundamental to doing better than what they did in life." FGC students may not be able to ask specific questions about the college experience of their families, but their families are the ones who instilled the aspirational capital in them that got them to the university in the first place.

These forms of aspirational capital that our students emphasized overlapped with familial forms of capital that they brought with them to college. The students pointed out both the motivation their parents had to achieve and their parents' strength and resilience. Students also brought with them additional kinds of experiences and cultural connections from their families. AP, for example, found campus community and belonging not only in the African student group but also in the campus's Irish community: "[F]or reasons of my family and my mom, having lived [in Ireland] for some time. It's something, well the Irish traits, some Irish traits have passed on in such a manner so it's like I do enjoy being in that community as well." Because of her mother's experiences in Ireland, AP was able to connect with a community that she might not have otherwise interacted with.

For many of our students, motivational, navigational, and aspirational capital and educational values are inseparable from their families and home communities. As students reflected back on their experience as researchers and writers in the bridge program, they described how choosing a topic connected to their FGC student identities allowed them to reconceptualize what they saw as research, feel more freedom in their research choices, and be more intentional about inserting their own voices into academic research projects.

Voice and Agency in the Research-Writing Process

When asked to describe why they chose the research topic intersectionality in the collaborative research process, one student, KL, captured how many students viewed their intersectional first-gen identities as motivating their research:

> All three of us identified really deeply with having intersectional identities. Actually me and another girl [in the group] are both mixed White and Viet[namese], so we automatically clicked, we're like, "Oh my god like you understand my struggle!" And [a third group member was] also a lot of intersectional identities, and we just said that we really explored them together before, and we thought it would be really cool, we were really interested and excited about it.

Students valued being able to select a topic that mattered to them. Such perspectives were often in contrast with their prior experiences. When students reflected back to high school, they described education as "regurgitative" (AP) or as "memorization" of facts or processes (YN). Writing, specifically, was viewed as more linear, structured, formulaic, and prompt-driven, somewhat separate from what was considered research. Students noted that they had to write "to hit all the points on the rubric" (KL) or "for the grade" (JM). Research was overwhelmingly considered by participants to be "STEM-based" or what takes place in "white lab coats." One student, CS, recalled her high school perspective: "I feel like I could ask my high school self, I would have immediately pointed you to STEM. . . . I never thought of research as something that you could do outside of STEM fields until I came to [this university], and I can say that quite definitely."

During and after the bridge program, the perspectives of these transitioning students on writing and research emphasized having more agency in their writerly choices, seeing audience move from "just my professor" to include broader public and academic readers, and having more freedom in conceptions of research and research topics connected to identities and communities that mattered to them. The freedom to explore a research topic and see the research process as removed from grades was noted across many participants and captured by the student RD: "One thing that did stand out to me with the bridge program is more kind of like get a bit more freedom, I think, and it wasn't as if you were writing to get a certain grade . . . so just like here's the broad topic, go with the flow and see what happens, which I definitely enjoyed a lot." Similarly, MN focused on personal interest and investment as important to the process: "I think we're open to doing research now, especially for grad school, because I found that once you find a topic you're actually interested in, it doesn't really feel like work, and it's just like 'I want to learn more' or 'Yes, this is exactly like how I feel it is.' Putting all those pieces together and coming up with this final product is really interesting."

When given a broad range of STEM and social science topics to explore, students began to find the spaces to insert their voices and connect research questions to their own identities and communities. For example, one student in the Language and Culture in Medical Context group, which explored reproductive health care for low-income women, wrote an op-ed for her home newspaper in Montana arguing for the need to support local clinics like Planned Parenthood. When she reflected back to her experience writing for both academic and home audiences, she emphasized the importance of research opportunities that aligned with both her background and her academic future, as she planned to become a gynecologist.

The design of the bridge program's pedagogy and practice aims to bring FGC student identities into the research process. However, this process isn't always linear, and students still face apprehension about inserting their voices when in new academic writing contexts that emphasize a structured approach that aligns with ways they were trained to write academic papers in high school. While developing their voices as researcher-writers increased their confidence, the students we interviewed noted that this agency of "not being set in the mold of academic writing" (PK) came with some tension and could even be "scary" or "overwhelming." The development of this confidence was key to giving students the ability to push back against academic discourses in new spaces. AP, in reflecting on what she learned about research writing in the bridge program, discussed the agency in inserting her voice into a research context, which she also described as "terrifying." The sense of confidence she developed in the bridge program was crucial for AP to sustaining her voice in a first-year college composition classroom: "I can use my creative voice and apply it to my writing because I felt that academic writing is going to be more okay. I'm going to write about statistics and the way in which they do this, but I can still add my own voice . . . even though it's terrifying and I don't like academic writing, but I can still make it my goal. . . . I have grown to understand that there are so many different ways I could approach both research and writing. I'm growing with my writing." AP next discussed her FYC classroom experience: "I survived my [FYC class] happily and did everything. My point was to write it and write it as I want it and not as everybody says it should be but how I wanted my style."

Another student, JM, utilized his navigational capital to seek additional support through the writing center with a former bridge mentor. The confidence he gained through the bridge program and access to different campus resources he learned about in the program allowed him to find a way to negotiate his voice with the academic expectations in a new writing context: "I wanted to put my thing in my writing, but my professor was saying 'No, this is supposed to be an objective paper.' But I still found a way to do it. . . . But I thought it is important to put in a piece of your identity. Your own voice in your paper." Students noted that there were moments in their college classes when their

FGC student identity required them to make extra efforts to demonstrate their research-writing skills and to show that they belonged in the academic conversation. As the student SR pointed out, "[S]ometimes, as an FLI [first-generation and/or low-income] student, I feel I need to use more formal vocabulary in my writing and how I speak in class, especially seminars, to sound as educated as my peers."

Throughout the choices that they made, and their shifts in their understanding of writing and research, students emphasized that their families' values around education were an important resource and motivation. For some students, reflecting on their families' sacrifices and values around education intensified during their transition to college:

> *BW.* I guess education has always been stressed by my parents to me as fundamental to doing better than what they did in life, since they didn't have an opportunity to continue their school. And they had to come to the US to work. So it has always just been really important.
>
> *INTERVIEWER.* Do you still think about that here?
>
> *BW.* Yeah, I actually think about it more now that I'm here, and that I'm actually out of my town, and I'm able to reflect on how far I've come.
>
> *INTERVIEWER.* When does it come to you? Or is it just always on your mind?
>
> *BW.* It's always in the back of my mind. But I think it comes more especially since we have a lot of conversation about where we came from coming here and like just our roots and our identities.

For a student like BW, whose FGS identity encompassed drawing motivation and aspirational capital from her family and representing the low-income, migrant Hispanic farming community she came from, the ability to connect those facets of her FGC identity through her choice of research topic was crucial. When asked about why her group selected its research topic, Why Doesn't My Doctor Understand? The Importance of Cultural Competency in Sexual and Reproductive Healthcare for Women in Low-Income Communities, she emphasized the importance of choosing a research question connected to her community and low-income identity:

> I remember that obviously we were all interested in low-income communities and then our overarching theme . . . had something to do with medicine. And so we remember trying to research it and there was nothing. . . . But there wasn't a lot of research on specifically sexual reproductive health care of women in low-income communities. So we wanted to take that approach since there just wasn't that research yet and see why there wasn't that research and that fact of not having cultural competency for those women.

Other students also spoke directly to how they selected topics and crafted research questions that mattered to their communities. When asked why she chose a research topic on food and crafted a question about agriculture and farming, AP spoke to choosing a topic that was relevant and useful to her home and community:

> I like food. I'd like for everybody to have food. . . . And back home also we are very big on farming in our family. So I was like, well, farming mechanisms: what else is there beyond what we are doing? Are there some things we could implement? Some things we could not? What would it cost? What would countries have to do? Considering the countries that are developing, countries that are developed? So I had a prior interest in it. And it was just a matter of "Oh, there is a foodie-related one. I want to find out about that."

Moving from topic selection to distilling and presenting research, BW described how relevance to their communities continued to inform the choices the members of her group made in designing their research poster. Gesturing at a section of her group's poster highlighted in purple, she explained why it felt important for her group to emphasize solutions: "also the purple is our solution to it. We mean like 'This is a possible solution.' And these are the three steps or three parts of it." For the members of her group, it was important to arrive at solutions and prominently feature them on their poster because of their personal investment in the communities they addressed in their research:

> *BW.* It was like, well "We can't just say there is no research being done." We have to say "OK, this is what needs to happen in order to improve this cultural competency."
>
> *INTERVIEWER.* And you say "have to"; why did you feel like you had to?
>
> *BW.* It was more . . . to represent the women of these communities where many of [us] come from. . . . Because we come from these communities, we couldn't just stop with "Oh well, there is no research being done." None of us would have been comfortable stopping there.

Pedagogical and Programmatic Implications

Programs can support first-generation students as they transition to college by collaborating with mentors from across disciplines (humanities, social sciences, STEM) to develop open-ended research topic choices that frame research as both interesting and applicable to students' lives. In our four-week summer bridge program, students choose from topics within four interdisciplinary research clusters: the impacts of human activity on the environment;

healthcare and medicine; language, identity, and culture; and science, technology, and society. Students work collaboratively in groups of four with a mentor who has expertise in their topic area. Collaborative research and writing offer students a more robust research opportunity over a short time frame while also encouraging students to see research and writing as a social practice. Across the four weeks, students work on two related research genres: the research proposal and the research poster presentation. These genres give students the opportunity to practice both oral and written communication collaboratively, drawing on different strengths in the research process. Their work in these mentor groups is supported by assignments in their writing course that teach them research methods and reading strategies along with how to do rhetorical analysis, write annotated bibliographies, and follow ethical citation practices.

During small group meetings and through feedback on writing, mentors can invite students to connect the practice of research to communities that they care about and identities that they already strongly hold. Students should be encouraged to integrate their voices into their writing and offered models of research and writing that demonstrate that academic writing does not mean writers remove themselves from their writing. Mentors can further facilitate their students' reflections on identity and positionality—how scholars come to research and writing as whole people—by acknowledging and positioning themselves as whole people with families and outside commitments and communities. For this kind of mentorship to work best, it is helpful for mentors to be available in both formal and informal settings, interacting with students in the classroom and also over lunch, on field trips, and in social settings.

As a kind of third space, bridge programs offer ways "students begin to reconceive of who they are and what they might be able to accomplish academically and beyond" (Gutiérrez 148). The pedagogical suggestions in this section ask educators across disciplines to reframe pedagogical practices to cultivate different ways to build on the lived experiences of students in all classroom spaces. Through their narratives, the FGC students in the summer bridge program defined for themselves the different kinds of cultural capital they brought to educational contexts. The students' narratives point to the importance of opening up pedagogical counterspaces or third spaces for sociocritical literacies that recognize FGC students' capital (Nuñez, "Counterspaces"; Gutiérrez).

The bridge program's pedagogical spaces, as culturally sustaining spaces (Paris), or spaces that "support young people in sustaining cultural and linguistic competence of their communities while simultaneously offering access to dominant cultural capital" (95), served to cultivate personal voice and agency in the research and writing process. And it is through these spaces, both in and out of the classroom, that first-generation college students, our students, are redefining research for themselves, focusing on topics that reflect their own communities and inserting their voices into their academic writing.

Works Cited

Bollig, Chase. "'People Like Us': Theorizing First-Generation College as a Marker of Difference." *Literacy in Composition Studies*, vol. 7, no. 1, 2019, pp. 22–43.

Canagarajah, A. Suresh. "From Critical Research Practice to Critical Research Reporting." *TESOL Quarterly*, vol. 30, no. 2, 1996, pp. 321–31, https://doi.org/10.2307/3588146.

Carr, David. *Time, Narrative, and History.* Indiana UP, 1986.

Cataldi, Emily Forrest, et al. *First-Generation Students: College Access, Persistence, and Postbachelor's Outcomes.* US Department of Education, National Center for Education Statistics, 2018, nces.ed.gov/pubs2018/2018421.pdf.

Clandinin, D. Jean., and F. Michael Connelly. *Narrative Inquiry: Experience and Story in Qualitative Research.* Jossey-Bass, 2000.

Clandinin, D. Jean, and J. Huber. "Narrative Inquiry." *International Encyclopedia of Education*, edited by Penelope Peterson et al., 3rd ed., Elsevier, 2010.

Engle, Jennifer, and Vincent Tinto. *Moving beyond Access: College Success for Low-Income, First-Generation Students.* Pell Institute for the Study of Opportunity in Higher Education, 2008.

Gibbons, Melinda M., et al. "How First-Generation College Students Adjust to College." *Journal of College Student Retention*, vol. 20, no. 4, 2019, pp. 488–510.

Glaser, Barney G., and Anselm L. Strauss. *The Discovery of Grounded Theory: Strategies for Qualitative Research.* Routledge, 1967.

Gutiérrez, Kris D. "Developing a Sociocritical Literacy in the Third Space." *Reading Research Quarterly*, vol. 43, no. 2, 2008, pp. 148–64, https://doi.org/10.1598/rrq.43.2.3.

Internal annual report. Stanford University, 2018.

Kareem, Jamila M. "Transitioning Counter-stories: Black Student Accounts of Transitioning to College-Level Writing." *Journal of College Literacy and Learning*, vol. 44, 2018, pp. 15–32.

McCoy, Dorian L., and Rachelle Winkle-Wagner. "Bridging the Divide: Developing a Scholarly Habitus for Aspiring Graduate Students through Summer Bridge Programs Participation." *Journal of College Student Development*, vol. 56, no. 5, 2015, pp. 423–39. *Project MUSE*, https://doi.org/10.1353/csd.2015.0054.

Nguyen, Thai-Huy, and Bach Mai Dolly Nguyen. "Is the 'First-Generation Student' Term Useful for Understanding Inequality? The Role of Intersectionality in Illuminating the Implications of an Accepted—Yet Unchallenged—Term." *Review of Research in Education*, vol. 42, no. 1, 2018, pp. 146–76, https://doi.org/10.3102/0091732X18759280.

Nuñez, Anne-Marie. "Counterspaces and Connections in College Transitions: First-Generation Latino Students' Perspectives on Chicano Studies." *Journal of College Student Development*, vol. 52, no. 6, 2011, pp. 639–55, https://doi.org/10.1353/csd.2011.0077.

———. "Employing Multilevel Intersectionality in Educational Research: Latino Identities, Contexts, and College Access." *Educational Researcher*, vol. 43, no. 2, 2014, pp. 85–92, https://doi.org/10.3102/0013189X14522320.

Paris, Django. "Culturally Sustaining Pedagogy: A Needed Change in Stance, Terminology, and Practice." *Educational Researcher*, vol. 41, no. 3, 2012, pp. 93–97, https://doi.org/10.3102/0013189X12441244.

Paris, Django, and H. Samy Alim, editors. *Culturally Sustaining Pedagogies: Teaching and Learning for Justice in a Changing World*. Teachers College Press, 2017.

Quinn, Dory E. et al., "The Success of First-Generation College Students in a TRIO Student Support Services Program: Application of the Theory of Margin." *Critical Questions in Education*, vol. 10, no. 1, 2019, pp. 44–64.

Quiroz, Alicia Gonzalez, and Nora R. Garza. "Focus on Student Success: Components for Effective Summer Bridge Programs." *Journal of Hispanic Higher Education*, vol. 17, no. 2, 2018, pp. 101–11.

Redford, Jeremy, and Kathleen Mulvaney Hoyer. *First-Generation and Continuing-Generation College Students: A Comparison of High School and Postsecondary Experiences*. US Department of Education, National Center for Education Statistics, 2017, nces.ed.gov/pubs2018/2018009.pdf.

"Report on Stanford's Undergraduate Education." *Stanford Families*, 1 May 2018, parents.stanford.edu/2018/05/01/report-on-stanfords-undergraduate-education/.

Royster, Jacqueline Jones, and Jean C. Williams. "History in the Spaces Left: African American Presence and Narratives of Composition Studies." *College Composition and Communication*, vol. 50, no. 4, 1999, pp. 563–84.

Schademan, Alfred R., and Maris R. Thompson. "Are College Faculty and First-Generation, Low-Income Students Ready for Each Other?" *Journal of College Student Retention*, vol. 18, no. 2, 2016, pp. 194–216, https://doi.org/10.1177/1521025115584748.

Yosso, Tara. "Whose Culture Has Capital? A Critical Race Theory Discussion of Community Cultural Wealth." *Race Ethnicity and Education*, vol. 8, no. 1, 2005, pp. 69–91, https://doi.org/10.1080/1361332052000341006.

Playing the Expectation Game: Negotiating Disciplinary Discourse in Undergraduate Research

Heather M. Falconer

The academic and social challenges first-generation college students face entering higher education are well documented. Feelings of isolation and marginalization can cause students to withdraw (Jehangir), a lack of social and financial support affects self-esteem and school engagement (Mehta et al.; Nuñez; Stuber), and academic competencies and remediation can affect students' academic identities negatively (Rodriguez et al.; Huerta et al.). Added to these challenges is the reality that first-generation college students and students from historically underrepresented groups encounter additional obstacles related to cultural capital (Bourdieu), "codes of power and academic discourse" (White and Lowenthal 301). As a result of these challenges, attrition rates for these students are often high.

In an effort to improve retention and persistence, many institutions have turned to high-impact interventions like undergraduate research with scholarly mentors. Since the National Science Foundation released a report in 1989 advocating for increasing the research experience of students and for providing faculty mentorship (*Annual Report*), apprenticeship through formalized undergraduate research experiences (UREs) have grown in popularity and have been integrated into higher education institutions nationally (Kardash), and there has been a more recent trend of URE programming in nonscience disciplines (see, for example, CCCC). While such growth has been encouraged and supported by organizations such as the Association of American Colleges and Universities and the Council on Undergraduate Research, it is important to note that the positive effects of mentoring through UREs have been widely presumed. There is little empirical evidence to support such claims and little understanding of what factors influence successful experiences (Thiry et al.; Hunter et al.; Seymour et al.). Little is understood about the experiences of students engaging with disciplinary-specific research spaces and discourses and how these experiences affect their retention and persistence in academia generally, and majors specifically.

In this essay, I examine the impact of discourse expectation on first-generation college students in science as a factor that can push students from, or pull them toward, the discipline. Drawing on the experiences of Ruben, a Latino father in his mid-twenties pursuing his bachelor's degree in toxicology, and Chloe, a White woman in her late teens studying epigenetics, I examine how expectations about the reading and writing practices of scientists disrupted their sense of competency as they participated in a college URE.

Ruben's and Chloe's stories are part of a larger, longitudinal case study of the Program for Research in Science and Math (PRISM), a unique undergraduate research program housed at John Jay College of Criminal Justice. John Jay is a senior college within the City University of New York system and has been recognized as the largest Hispanic-serving institution in the Northeast. The program offers STEM students at the college—predominantly those who identify as first-generation and as Black, Latinx, or both—opportunities to conduct real-world research in state-of-the-art laboratories under the guidance of faculty mentors. PRISM has had an important impact on increasing the number of John Jay students graduating and entering graduate programs (particularly PhD, MD, and MPH programs)—an outcome that was virtually unheard of before the program's inception in 2006. As both qualitative and quantitative data from PRISM demonstrate, mentoring in this specific URE has not only had positive effects on the persistence of minority students in the science majors (Carpi et al., "Development") but also positively affected self-efficacy and career ambitions for this same student body (Carpi et al., "Cultivating"). Still unexplored in the undergraduate research literature broadly, however, are the factors that influence the uptake of disciplinary rhetorical practices within such contexts.

Drawing on semistructured interviews that took place over the course of three years, I present the experiences of Ruben and Chloe as they navigated their own expectations and the expectations of faculty mentors and family regarding the reading and writing practices of scientists. These narratives provide insight into the various factors that influence the development of disciplinary writing skills and its impact on scientific identity—factors that may also be applicable to other disciplinary areas and of interest to writing-across-the-curriculum practitioners.

Reading Scientific Literature outside the Classroom

I began working with Ruben and Chloe when they were both entering their junior year at the college. They had each completed the prerequisites for applying to PRISM (maintaining a GPA above 2.5 and successfully completing organic chemistry) and had completed the required research training workshop. However, neither of them had officially begun working with a mentor when they joined this study.

Though both students were part of the same forensic science major, their reported experiences with reading in the major courses varied considerably, largely because Chloe took an honors track, while Ruben pursued the traditional route. Chloe described most of her classes as "requiring a lot of reading and writing." "We read a lot of papers in our classes," she explained. "We read a research paper every week, and then we write a one-page summary on it." These papers were provided by the instructor and were directly applicable to the course content and vocabulary. Though he took many of the same required courses as Chloe, Ruben described the work differently. He explained that his courses did not require reading peer-reviewed scholarly articles from science journals. Rather, they involved self-sourcing information ("If you go to Google and you do a search [for the topic], you get a website") and depended heavily on textbooks and laboratory guides. Many courses did offer extra credit activities that involved reading scholarly texts and writing short summaries, but Ruben did not engage in any of these. Despite these differences, both students felt confident that they could handle the reading requirements of undergraduate research because of their general success in classroom spaces. They had, effectively, passed the instructor expectation threshold in reading and writing for coursework (Sommers and Saltz). Yet, as research has shown (e.g., Middendorf and Pace; Wilder), specific disciplinary ways of thinking and communicating are often assumed by college instructors and not made explicit to students. As such, students moving from coursework to undergraduate research encounter a new threshold they were not prepared for despite disciplinary continuity.

While both students could be described as active, highly proficient readers—Ruben regularly read novels with complex plot lines, and Chloe was an English minor who read a wide variety of fiction and nonfiction texts—neither was actually prepared for the kind of reading their mentors would expect in the undergraduate research experience. Chloe's mentor, who studies the epigenetics of various cancers, welcomed her to the laboratory with a challenge:

> Basically, she said, "I have this topic, now go find some papers." I started out [finding] three papers, and she was like, "Oh, these are the papers I basically used to come up with the project," and I was like, "Wow! Score!" And then every time we met she would ask me another question and would say, "Find out more about this." I think in two weeks I had read twenty published papers and met with her every other day. Every time we met I would go home, look up some more papers. . . . It was a lot of reading.

Though Chloe was collecting many scholarly texts in epigenetics, she was not necessarily engaging efficiently with them. To keep track of the articles, Chloe printed and marked up each one then stored them in a large three-ring binder. Much of her focus in reading was identifying the research question and the rationale for the work, adopting the same practice required of her in her coursework: "I write a little bit of an intro to the paper, with some background info, and then explain why they did each procedural step and what that ended up completing. It's just more big picture." Yet, as she quickly learned, this approach was not particularly helpful in research: "One of my biggest issues when I read papers is that they just put [in] all these words that mean nothing [to me]. A lot of papers, you pick it up and you're like, 'What did I just read?'" The fact that Chloe was lacking significant contextual knowledge and vocabulary made the papers almost indecipherable to her. While getting the gist of the paper was sufficient in coursework, Chloe's mentor expected her to be able to pull out details regarding protocols, as well as to compare multiple texts to identify gaps in research—skills that were beyond Chloe's reach at the start of the experience.

Ruben's experience with reading scientific texts was similar. When Ruben met with his mentor for the first time to discuss conducting research, she tasked him with finding articles related to the toxicology research she was conducting. When she realized that he did not know what the *PubMed* database was, let alone how to search it for scholarly texts, she sent him three articles to get started. Ruben described the challenge he had navigating these texts with a hint of frustration: "The words and the instruments and the techniques, basically all are challenging." Much of Ruben's reading work involved decoding the jargon in the articles at the sentence level, to the point where he could understand the basics of what was being discussed. It was a slow process, though, and because he often got lost in definitions, he relied heavily on his mentor to explain the meaning of the findings and how the articles related to one another. Like Chloe, he struggled to conceptualize what he had read within the context of the field. Where the reading assignments related to course laboratories helped students clearly connect the reading with the experiment and often guided them toward predetermined findings, the open-ended work of inquiry in undergraduate research was far less certain. Ruben explained that, in both reading and laboratory activities, "I usually go by what she tells me to do." In the undergraduate research context, he felt immediately restricted by the reading expectations. This restriction would continue for much of his research experience.

As Elizabeth Moje and colleagues suggest, "[A]ny stretch of language (discourse) is always embedded in a particular way of knowing (Discourse)" (470). The experiences of these students as they initially engaged with the practical reading work of science outside of the classroom reflect the need "to become discursively fluent in a particular set of modes of disciplinary discourse" (Airey and Linder 41) before it's possible to effectively engage with the ways of knowing that are endemic to the field. Vocabulary and jargon posed barriers to access for both students, as did genre and information literacy skills. Though their traditional coursework prepared them for some of the technical, practical aspects of working in a laboratory (e.g., pipetting), they had not sufficiently built the rhetorical or conceptual knowledge needed to engage with the practice of science as novices. There was, as Moje and colleagues similarly found with seventh-grade science students engaged in project-based learning activities, a conflict between the discourses of the URE and that of the curriculum.

As newcomers to their respective fields, Chloe and Ruben experienced and responded to these conflicts differently. Chloe, with a little more experience encountering scholarly articles, was able to recognize the gap between her existing knowledge and skills and those expected by her mentor. Ruben, however, did not have prior direct experience reading scholarly articles, nor any explicit guidance on reading such texts, and as such internalized his challenges with these genres as a deficit in himself. The immediate impact of these experiences was that Chloe saw a steep learning curve ahead of her, but one that was strategically manageable. Ruben saw a large gap between his skills and knowledge base and those of practicing scientists and questioned his own capabilities to the extent that he questioned his future career options.

Writing and Revising for Scientific Research

As part of the undergraduate research experience, students in PRISM are required to work with their mentors to design a research project that they will largely lead. While the writing requirements vary from laboratory to laboratory, all students are required to compose and submit a research proposal to acquire funding from the program. These funds help to offset income that many students lose by devoting time to the laboratory, so the proposal is an important writing activity for them to complete correctly. For Ruben, this was a particularly high-stakes writing activity, as he was the sole provider for a young son and worked thirty hours per week in construction while paying out-of-pocket for school. For Chloe, these funds helped cover the costs associated with commuting two hours by bus each day to attend classes, and they also contributed to her family's income.

To compose a research proposal, students must work with their mentors to identify a research question that can be answered within the time frame of an academic year and that fits within the scope of the work being conducted in the laboratory. A significant part of this process is completed while students are reading—thus, being able to access the reading material cognitively and to make meaning of it is critical. Many mentors, including both Ruben's and Chloe's, use writing as a means of meaning making during this reading stage and expect some version of that writing to make its way into the proposal.

As with their expectations of reading requirements, both Ruben and Chloe entered the PRISM program feeling confident that they could handle the writing requirements. Both wrote regularly for fun—primarily creative writing pieces in short fiction and poetry. Both also had a sense of the differences between these creative forms and the styles expected in scientific texts. Ruben reported being familiar with how to "make a bibliography in the scientific way" and with the organizational structure of laboratory reports; Chloe was prepared to write in a way that was "very formal, very clear and not too jargony." At the same time, both were intimidated. Chloe explained that "writing in such a specific way—it just sounds like such a difficult process." In her coursework, instructors regularly emphasized mechanics as key factors in writing assignments: "no plagiarism; really intense with grammar. They say things like, 'Spelling mistakes will not be tolerated!' And citations—they're really picky with citations." Similarly, Ruben explained how he had received these same messages about writing in classes and was slightly intimidated by writing for his mentor and for funding. The effect of this intimidation, he explained, was that "[the writing is] always confused; I'm not sure what to write." As with reading, the expectations of writing created a restriction—a paralysis invoked by not wanting to get it wrong.

In the early stages, Ruben's mentor required Ruben to build an annotated bibliography of sources so that she could understand how he was reading the texts and what he was taking away from each. These allowed her to check comprehension and understand Ruben's skill level, while also building a body of research to draw on for the proposal. Though such bibliographies are a common form of task-oriented writing in science, helping researchers review literature to identify themes, findings, and gaps, Ruben saw it as busywork. He described this activity as something his mentor assigned so she could "see if I was reading the papers." While he completed this work for her, he did not see it holding the same level of importance as the work of the proposal and was only partially engaged mentally in this task.

Likewise, Chloe's mentor required extensive note-taking as part of the reading process, but rather than use these to check comprehension, Chloe and her mentor used the notes collaboratively to identify useful protocols to replicate and to find gaps in the literature. "We connected, like, five different papers," Chloe explained, "and we asked, 'What hasn't been done?' It made it a little easier to come up with an actual experiment." With her mentor's guidance, Chloe shifted her note-taking from simply summarizing the research questions and findings of articles to identifying methods and protocols used, which would be more useful in identifying a research question and designing her experiments.

Once research questions were identified, both mentors worked with their students in the process of composing the research proposal. Ruben and Chloe each composed first drafts based on a template provided by PRISM, which were subsequently heavily edited by their mentors. Much of this editing involved clarifying processes and making the texts sound more professional. As Chloe explained: "It was really crazy because I like writing and everything. But everything in science—in an actual proposal—has to be super, super specific and in a very specific order. So I had basically written the proposal, and [my mentor] went on *Google Docs* and teared it to pieces. (But not in a mean way.) She was like, 'What did you think—that it'd be perfect on your first time around?' I [laughed]. . . . Clearly it's not!"

Though Ruben's mentor approached Ruben's draft with less vigor, the process likewise involved a significant amount of revision and reworking. Instead of seeing this proposal as one step in a process toward learning to write as a scientist, though, Ruben saw it as evidence that he did not possess the skills expected of him, which caused him to disengage further. "It was challenging because I didn't know," he explained. "In the beginning I wasn't sure what to write, or if it was fine what I was doing, but I [did what I could]." This feeling of uncertainty was exacerbated when, after submitting the proposal to the PRISM coordinator for funding, he was asked to revise the text a third time and received many comments on grammar and mechanics.

Writing studies research has long supported the idea that revision and thoughtful feedback help students become stronger writers (e.g., Sommers; Taylor). Yet there isn't much understanding about the impact of repeated revisions on students who are not expecting such revisions. For Chloe and Ruben, the experience of being asked to rewrite proposals had different effects on their sense of self within the laboratory and discipline of science, despite their mentors' taking a similar approach to presenting those revision needs. Chloe viewed it as a learning opportunity, recognizing that there was more to crafting a request for funding than she originally thought. Ruben saw it as additional labor without clear instructions on how to meet expectations.

Like many students who encounter feedback on writing that includes significant notes on grammar and mechanics, Ruben focused his revisions on line edits that were marked by the PRISM coordinator, rather than revising the text for flow and content. He viewed the revision work as a significant form of labor that was competing with the demands of work and parenting. As with the first-generation Latinx students interviewed in Yolanda Vasquez-Salgado and colleagues' research, Ruben experienced a home-school conflict that was always salient. The time he spent decoding a scientific article or writing a proposal was time that was not being spent with his son or mother or earning money on the construction site. If he spent time working or engaged in family duties, then he was not doing what was needed to succeed in the research. As discussed in the next section, Ruben was constantly having to make decisions about where his time would best be spent.

Because Chloe had already understood that she was on a journey to becoming a scientific writer, she understood that revision requests were to be expected. She identified this labor as a worthwhile part of her development as a scientist and trusted that neither her mentor nor the PRISM coordinator would ask her to spend time on something that was not important. As Nancy Sommers has described in her work with Harvard undergraduates, in revision requests and feedback Chloe saw her mentor's belief in her "as a thinker, someone capable of doing good work, even if . . . [she was] not yet accomplishing it" (255). Because of this perspective, the revision labor was worthwhile. While Ruben's mentor had a similar view of his mentee's capabilities, Ruben did not recognize it as such and saw the revision requests as simply a drain on his available time.

Forming Identities as Scientists and Meeting Expectations

First-generation students commonly find that a lot of extra work is required to navigate academic spaces, and that extra labor affects their uptake of disciplinary discourse. Though undergraduate research could be considered a new contextual space for most incoming first-year students, I argue that the pressures become more salient for first-generation students, for whom the stakes may feel more pronounced. As noted earlier, Ruben was acutely aware of the familial sacrifices he was making to attend college. In addition to having to cut back on his hours at the construction site to attend class and participate in research, he was also spending time away from his family and young son. There was the additional question of what forms of employment he could expect after graduating and whether those positions would offer him a higher income than the foreman's position already waiting for him.

Likewise, Chloe regularly reported feeling anxious because of external factors. She traveled two hours one way by bus to attend classes each day, occasionally staying a night with friends in a dormitory so that she could work in the laboratory. Her father, an automotive mechanic, often questioned her career options, asking, "How are you going to make money?" when she talked about pursuing a graduate degree in marine sciences, and she frequently spoke of taking a gap year after completing her degree to save money and help her parents. Interestingly, the cost of materials in the laboratory also weighed heavily on her.

Though PRISM covered the cost of reagents and other lab materials, Chloe regularly worried about being wasteful: "There's a lot of pressure to do things right when your school isn't well-funded."

Working alongside faculty in research laboratories made the practice of science feel real for both students. Chloe remarked, "It's a real lab. I'm excited, [but] it's a little intimidating because you're working with people with their PhDs, and you're just the little undergrad." However, because the mentors and PRISM as a whole had high expectations, and because both students wanted to perform well and meet those expectations, these interactions influenced the students' conceptions of self as scientists and scientific readers and writers.

PRISM has an explicit expectation that all students will apply to graduate school as they near the end of their undergraduate career. Though this expectation complicates some of the initial rationale for the program, it has nevertheless moved from being an implicit to an explicit expectation over the course of my study. Rather than bringing students who otherwise would not pursue such degrees into research experiences in an effort to show them possibilities, the program now uses the URE space to support students who have already clearly defined such a route for themselves. Other initiatives (such as guest lectures, job shadows, and field trips to laboratories) are being implemented to target those students who would otherwise be "leaked" from the "pipeline."

More recently, expectations about summer activities have also become explicit. Rather than allowing PRISM students to continue research (with funding) during the summer, students are now expected to pursue external research opportunities to become more competitive for graduate programs. The program coordinator is currently pursuing efforts to make external research a formal requirement of PRISM participants, as there is anecdotal evidence that external research experiences increase the likelihood of participants being accepted to graduate school. Yet for students like Chloe and Ruben, such expectations pose significant impediments to their success in the long term and interfere with their progress through the program in the short term.

While Chloe had a strong desire to pursue graduate work in marine sciences, she chose undergraduate research with PRISM as the mode to complete her capstone requirement for her bachelor's degree. The alternative option—an external internship—posed significant challenges in terms of travel, funding, and time. While a PhD was her long-term goal, she felt strongly that finding a local job and engaging in civic activities after graduation would be the immediate path she would follow. Ruben, likewise, chose undergraduate research for this same reason and did not see an external internship during the summer as a viable option. Though he entertained the idea of pursuing a master's degree at John Jay after graduating, the idea of more education literally and figuratively exhausted him. These internship and graduate school expectations were salient presences as the students entered their UREs, as was an additional expectation: that they would attempt to write and submit a research article with their mentor during, or shortly after, their research experience.

Rather than seeing the tasks of reading, writing, and conducting research as disparate elements in the undergraduate research experience, both students experienced these three as an amalgamation. The reading and writing could not be separated from the research because they saw the reading and writing tasks as being specific to the individualized research experience. While the interconnected nature of these tasks is something many educators hope students will recognize over time, there are some important implications for that way of thinking at the early stages of students' academic careers . Most critical was the correlation of reading and writing with labor. To engage with the reading and writing practices as expected by their mentors and PRISM, Chloe and Ruben had to devote more time and energy to these tasks than had been required of them in coursework. To view that labor as worthwhile, each student had to either see pursuing scientific research as a viable career option or recognize that the rhetorical skills being demanded of them would be relevant in their future.

With her sights set on eventually attending graduate school, Chloe viewed these demands as appropriate. Even if she did not work in epigenetics after the URE, the acts of reviewing the literature and composing a proposal would be applicable to other academic research situations. Ruben, however, was questioning his career path. Because of his challenges with the rhetorical tasks of the laboratory, he began to view his future opportunities as being limited to the role of a laboratory technician—a position that would draw heavily on the practical laboratory skills he had already developed and that would require an ability to follow protocols rather than generate new lines of inquiry. However, as his URE continued, he began to research potential incomes in these types of positions and recognized that higher earnings were more likely if he continued in construction. This questioning of his career possibilities began to influence his affinity with science, which subsequently influenced his engagement with the genres used as part of the research experience. He effectively engaged with task-oriented genres, such as laboratory notebooks and other reports on what was completed, because they were tangible products that would be consumed by his mentor in her overall research project. Genres more common to research scientists, such as funding proposals, conference posters, and scientific papers, were less enticing—they seemed to be useless things that would not be taken up by others (e.g., he did not believe that he would actually write and publish a scientific paper based on his research).

Coupled with this conflict were microaggressions from nonschool friends and coworkers who questioned Ruben's motives for earning a degree in science and challenged his allegiances. Though Ruben had been doing the work required, his mentor noticed that his motivation and engagement had been on a steady decline. His presence in the laboratory was not frequent or long enough to really achieve the results needed, and they had had some conversations about the value of the degree he was earning. If he could already earn a strong income on the construction site, what was the point of the degree?

Though Chloe's progress could not be seen as anything other than excellent, this extra labor spent reading and writing did affect her. Reflecting on the URE at graduation, she commented: "I didn't expect it to take such a toll on me emotionally." She had been successful in her research and had begun composing a research article with her mentor, but she was clear that she needed a break before considering applying to PhD programs. The physical and emotional labor of learning in the URE had seemingly used more energy than that of some of her peers in the program, and she needed some time to catch up with herself—to reconcile who she had been at the start of her undergraduate education with who she was at the end.

Implications for Teaching

In examining the impact of reading and writing expectations on first-generation college students in science, I have found that personal, familial, and collegial expectations are all clear factors that can push students from, or pull them toward, the discipline. As I have written elsewhere (Falconer), Ruben's is a complicated story. As a student juggling the demands of work, family, and school, Ruben was in a constant state of flux that pulled his attention in a multitude of directions. Without a clear understanding of why he needed to do the reading and writing labor being asked of him, he experienced a conflict with school-work-life balance that disrupted his skill development in scientific discourse. After recognizing how these various factors were affecting Ruben's success, his mentor adopted an approach of explicitly teaching the rhetorical moves and genres of science in a way that helped Ruben see the discourse as something that could be learned over time (and that was within his grasp), and his mentor showed him how practicing the process of critical inquiry in undergraduate research would benefit him in all facets of his life.

Though no less labor-intensive, Chloe's experience involved a different type of personal conflict. Though Chloe recognized the work she needed to do to succeed in the reading and writing practices of undergraduate research and occasionally was self-deprecating about the amount of work she needed to do, she was able to see a clear path forward with the help of her mentor. As Laura Wilder found in her study of faculty and students in introductory literature courses, making explicit the rhetorical conventions, genres, and purposes of disciplinary writing can help underprepared students access the rhetorical practices that lead to success within disciplinary contexts. Ruben and Chloe's stories help us see how this pedagogical approach can also alleviate some of the anxiety and paralysis students might experience when encountering disciplinary texts early in their academic and professional careers.

Among the lessons learned from Ruben and Chloe's experiences are that coursework—advanced or traditional—does not always adequately prepare students for the realities of practicing a discipline. Students are not typically taught how to do this discursive work in courses or given tools to navigate new rhetorical contexts, and as a result they encounter another threshold later in their academic careers—whether in undergraduate research or graduate work. For students who are already experiencing the extra labor of being a first-generation college student, this extra work can feel defeating. If these differences between coursework and levels of disciplinary practice are not made explicit, students will internalize their struggle to adjust as a personal deficit.

Similarly, a heavy emphasis on grammar and mechanics can cause paralysis for students and slow down their willingness to take risks when it comes to writing in new genres and discourses. The fear of getting things wrong can disrupt students' sense of competency, and revision requests without explicit direction and context can cause a home-school conflict whereby students perceive the request as unnecessary labor interfering with their other commitments. Connected to this is that career identity and personal identity play critical roles in whether students will fully engage with new discourses and genres—particularly when there is significant labor involved. Program expectations that do not easily reconcile with the challenges that many first-generation students encounter can disrupt the paths that they see as viable, and unless the reading and writing work requested has a useful application to their immediate or future academic lives, students questioning their place in the discipline may disengage with learning the discourse.

As educators and mentors, we must be conscious of these things in our teaching and in undergraduate research experiences. Explicit teaching of decoding practices (i.e., how to read disciplinary texts), disciplinary discourse (i.e., specific vocabulary and discourse conventions), and writing processes should be integrated into instruction to aid students in that transition into so-called real disciplinary practice. As Chloe's experience shows, simply telling students that they will not get it perfect the first time and that revisions should be expected can go a long way toward helping students understand that everyone must learn particular ways of communicating in new contexts. Likewise, being careful to explain the ways in which different reading and writing tasks relate to other work—showing the practical application of an annotated bibliography, for example—is important in helping students understand the larger picture of learning and research. It is critical that instructors working with first-generation students keep in mind that students are not simply learning the conventions of participating in a disciplinary space; they are simultaneously learning the conventions and expectations of academia generally. Thus, educators should be thoughtful about the expectations they have about students' ability to navigate academic spaces, the ways this extra labor can affect students' sense of belonging in school and in a major, and the outside commitments students may be juggling with schoolwork.

Works Cited

Airey, John, and Cedric Linder. "A Disciplinary Discourse Perspective on University Science Learning: Achieving Fluency in a Critical Constellation of Modes." *Journal of Research in Science Teaching*, vol. 46, no. 1, 2009, pp. 27–49, https://doi.org/10.1002/tea.20265.

Annual Report 1989. National Science Foundation, 1989, www.nsf.gov/pubs/1989/1989-NSF-Annual-Report.pdf.

Bourdieu, Pierre. "The Forms of Capital." *Handbook of Theory and Research for the Sociology of Education*, edited by J. G. Richardson, Greenwood Press, 1986, pp. 241–58.

Carpi, Anthony, et al. "Cultivating Minority Scientists: Undergraduate Research Increases Self-Efficacy and Career Ambitions for Underrepresented Students in STEM." *Journal of Research in Science Teaching*, vol. 54, no. 2, 2017, pp. 169–94, https://doi.org/10.1002/tea.21341.

Carpi, Anthony, et al. "Development and Implementation of Targeted STEM Retention Strategies at a Hispanic-Serving Institution." *Journal of Hispanic Higher Education*, vol. 12, no. 3, 2013, pp. 280–99, https://doi.org/10.1177/1538192713486279.

Conference on College Composition and Communication (CCCC). "CCCC Position Statement on Undergraduate Research in Writing: Principles and Best Practices." *Conference on College Composition and Communication*, National Council of Teachers of English, Mar. 2017, cccc.ncte.org/cccc/resources/positions/undergraduate-research.

Falconer, Heather M. "Mentored Writing at a Hispanic-Serving Institution: Improving Student Facility with Scientific Discourse." *Bordered Writers: Latinx Identities and Literacy Practices at Hispanic-Serving Institutions*, edited by Isabel Baca et al., State U of New York P, 2019, pp. 213–30.

Huerta, Jeffery, et al. "An Examination of AVID Graduates' College Preparation and Postsecondary Progress: Community College versus Four-Year University Students." *Journal of Hispanic Higher Education*, vol. 12, no. 1, 2013, pp. 86–101.

Hunter, Anne-Barrie, et al. "Becoming a Scientist: The Role of Undergraduate Research in Students' Cognitive, Personal, and Professional Development." *Science Education*, vol. 91, no. 1, 2007, pp. 36–74, https://doi.org/10.1002/sce.20173.

Jehangir, Rashné R. "Cultivating Voice: First-Generation Students Seek Full Academic Citizenship in Multicultural Learning Communities." *Innovative Higher Education*, vol. 34, no. 1, 2009, pp. 33–49.

Kardash, CarolAnne M. "Evaluation of an Undergraduate Research Experience: Perceptions of Undergraduate Interns and Their Faculty Mentors." *Journal of Educational Psychology*, vol. 92, no. 1, 2000, pp. 191–201, https://doi.org/10.1037/0022-0663.92.1.191.

Mehta, Sanjay S., et al. "Why Do First-Generation Students Fail?" *College Student Journal*, vol. 45, no. 1, 2011, pp. 20–35.

Middendorf, Joan, and David Pace. "Decoding the Disciplines: A Model for Helping Students Learn Disciplinary Ways of Thinking." *New Directions for Teaching and Learning*, vol. 98, 2004, pp. 1–12.

Moje, Elizabeth B., et al. "'Maestro, What Is "Quality"?': Language, Literacy, and Discourse in Project-Based Science." *Journal of Research in Science Teaching*, vol. 38, no. 4, 2001, pp. 469–98, https://doi.org/10.1002/tea.1014.

Nuñez, Anne-Marie. "Latino Students' Transitions to College: A Social and Intercultural Capital Perspective." *Harvard Educational Review*, vol. 79, no. 1, 2009, pp. 22–48.

Rodriguez, James L., et al. "Promoting Academic Achievement and Identity Development among Diverse High School Students." *The High School Journal*, vol. 87, no. 3, 2004, pp. 44–53.

Seymour, Elaine, et al. "Establishing the Benefits of Research Experiences for Undergraduates in the Sciences: First Findings from a Three-Year Study." *Science Education*, vol. 88, no. 4, 2004, pp. 493–534, https://doi.org/10.1002/sce.10131.

Sommers, Nancy. "Across the Drafts." *College Composition and Communication*, vol. 58, no. 2, 2006, pp. 248–57.

Sommers, Nancy, and Laura Saltz. "The Novice as Expert: Writing the Freshman Year." *College Composition and Communication*, vol. 56, no. 1, 2004, pp. 124–49.

Stuber, Jenny Marie. "Integrated, Marginal, and Resilient: Race, Class, and the Diverse Experiences of White First-Generation College Students." *International Journal of Qualitative Studies in Education*, vol. 24, no. 1, 2011, pp. 117–36.

Taylor, Susan M. "Students as (Re)visionaries; or, Revision, Revision, Revision." *Touro Law Review*, vol. 21, no. 2, 2005, pp. 265–96.

Thiry, Heather, et al. "What Experiences Help Students Become Scientists? A Comparative Study of Research and Other Sources of Personal and Professional Gains for STEM Undergraduates." *The Journal of Higher Education*, vol. 82, no. 4, 2011, pp. 357–88, https://doi.org/10.1353/jhe.2011.0023.

Vasquez-Salgado, Yolanda, et al. "Exploring Home-School Value Conflicts: Implications for Academic Achievement and Well-Being among Latino First-Generation College Students." *Journal of Adolescent Research*, vol. 30, no. 3, 2015, pp. 271–305.

White, John Wesley, and Patrick R. Lowenthal. "Minority College Students and Tacit 'Codes of Power': Developing Academic Discourses and Identities." *The Review of Higher Education*, vol. 34, no. 2, 2011, pp. 283–318.

Wilder, Laura. *Rhetorical Strategies and Genre Conventions in Literary Studies: Teaching and Writing in the Disciplines*. Southern Illinois UP, 2012.

From Literacy Narrative to Identity-Conflict Memoir: Agency in Representation

Nancy Mack

Although recently retired, I have no trouble recalling moments when I felt like an unwelcome outsider in the elite academic universe. I taught for twenty-eight years at Wright State University, located in the working-class town where I grew up. When introducing myself to students on the first day of class, I would always declare my status as a former first-generation college student. Many students who shared my feelings of otherness often revealed their fears during advising or writing conferences. Confused feelings of anger and shame would bubble to the surface while they were discussing other matters. These students worried that their individual differences from some mythical traditional student marked them as unacceptable. Institutions of higher learning marginalize students who have not lived a life of entitlement. Marginalization inscribes and enlarges difference so that identity becomes an inescapable issue for these students' survival.

Experiences like these fueled my interest in identity formation and the intersection between the academic and emotional needs of students. In this essay I explain how I focused my pedagogy on analyzing the discomfort of marginalization by gradually changing a literacy narrative assignment into a group of assignments for developing an identity-conflict memoir in the courses I taught for undergraduate education majors. This change in methodology privileges the learning experience of a series of scaffolded activities rather than advocating for one writing assignment as an automatic panacea. Linked class activities guide the metacognitive reflections of students about difference and emotional labor when selecting an experience from the past, representing a complex identity in a present draft, and taking agency in academic identity formation in the future.

From Literacy Narrative to Identity-Conflict Memoir

This essay would be more dramatic if I had suddenly become unhappy with the literacy narrative and replaced it with a new and improved memoir assignment.

Instead, my plodding pedagogical evolution began with smaller attempts to develop methods for incorporating critical analysis into an existing assignment and eventually led to reconceptualizing the whole assignment. I assigned the literacy narrative at the beginning of the term. Most students enjoyed writing about a memorable teacher or book. I encouraged students to expand their definitions of literacy by writing about experiences outside of school. I incorporated revision activities to help them develop description, dialogue, action, and inner thoughts in their drafts. After I became confident with teaching the literacy narrative, I began to add class activities that changed the focus of the assignment.

A few remarkable students' essays and new literacy scholarship influenced my desire to emphasize critical analysis. One student narrated how arguing with his father as they traveled to Disney World resulted in his being dumped at his grandparents' trailer, where he discovered a stack of Louis L'Amour novels. While reading the westerns out of sheer boredom, this gay teen realized that he identified more with the misunderstood Native American characters than with the dominating cowboys. Treasured essays like this one drew significant connections between literacy and life conflicts.

In addition to reading other remarkable student papers, I was reading scholarship that influenced my hopes for the assignment. Mary Soliday portrays the literacy narrative assignment as an opportunity for writers from diverse cultures to examine experience not as simply factual but as subject to interpretation, thus expanding their agency through the representation of difference (511–12). Soliday encourages students to analyze the complex conflicts that result from "crossing the social and affective borders of language worlds" (517). During this time, I read two powerful narratives that analyzed the influence of literacy on the process of identity formation. In "Writing on the Bias," Linda Brodkey interprets her early literacy experiences as evidence of gendered and class-based differences. Brodkey's memoir demonstrates how writers can select, narrate, and interpret life experiences to construct an academic analysis. Reading *This Fine Place So Far from Home*, a volume devoted to the experiences of working-class academics, had a profound effect on my developing academic identity. In particular, the essay by Laurel Johnson Black portrays several experiences from her life that represent conflicts related to literacy and language. My students loved Black's memoir, and the majority of them identified with some aspect of her essay. The aforementioned texts gave me direction for fostering critical analysis in narrative writing as well as a growing interest in memoir. If culture provides scripts for our lives, then memoir offers one way to reinterpret life experiences that normalize limitations. I renamed the assignment a literacy memoir for a few semesters until critiques of the literacy narrative persuaded me to consider how writing assignments limit the identities that students can assume.

Critiques of the literacy narrative assignment by Bronwyn Williams and others problematize the identities represented in students' essays (Alexander; Bryson; Chandler; Carpenter and Falbo; Hall and Minnix). Williams classifies these stereotypical identities as "heroes, rebels, and victims." I had to admit that the weakest papers I received from students often fell into these categories and lacked depth and complexity. Kara Poe Alexander's research characterizes these representations as evidence of a larger cultural narrative of success that romanticizes the power of education and promotes "the upward mobility literacy myth" (610). Alexander suggests that the assignment itself might unwittingly provoke success narratives by asking students to relate a progress narrative (624). Both Williams and Alexander advocate that teachers direct students to interrogate their assumptions in their narratives "to arrive at complex and nuanced understandings of how literacy works in their lives" (Alexander 625). The critical analysis activities that Williams and Alexander each describe are well conceived but are designed to take place after the literacy narrative is completed—to work against the narratives that the original assignment provokes.

If students' representations are problematic, then why not begin by asking students to examine a past conflict involving a cultural identity? Conflicts arise when a person cannot comfortably assume the expected traits and behaviors of an identity. Critically analyzing a past identity conflict may help first-generation students to interrogate the identity conflicts that lie ahead during their time at the university. My students' fears were connected to cultural labels assigned to their differences: ADHD, Black, ESL, factory worker, military, older, transgender, single parent, and so on. Identity differences are something that first-generation students have in common, and I suggest that they will benefit from subjecting those differences to critical examination.

Switching the focus from literacy to identity also prevents limiting critical analysis to only one cultural myth. Most first-generation students probably believed in some type of success narrative at one time, as I did. Believing in a success narrative may be what motivated these students to pursue a bachelor's degree to begin with. Chase Bollig contends that the label *first-generation* may be more amenable than other marginalizing identifiers because it implies mobility, adaptation, or assimilation (31). Success narratives have complex functions for first-generation students and may be a part of their critical agency for social justice in representing their family and community at college rather than solely a desire for individual upward mobility (Bean). Starting from an identity conflict increases the likelihood that students will select experiences fraught with cultural contradictions. We experience identity conflicts at different times in our lives and are open to analyzing some conflicts more than others—especially when factoring in a new environment where that analysis will be given a grade.

Reconceptualizing the literacy narrative as an identity-conflict memoir expands the possibilities for critical analysis without excluding issues related to literacy and language differences. For some students, analyzing any type of conflict may be uncomfortable, but that discomfort may indicate their need to understand emotional labor. All writing involves rhetorical decisions about what type of identity to represent that affect choices in content, stance, and language. Not only is identity representation foundational to teaching writing; discomfort about identity differences can be a major factor in first-generation students' decisions to leave the university. Hiding our discomfort about identity differences will not make them go away.

Identity Conflicts and Emotional Labor

In a quantitative study of over 1,700 first-year students, Ann Penrose found significant contrasts between first-generation and continuing-generation students. In particular, first-generation students have lower perceptions of their academic language skills (437). Penrose documents that first-generation students do not come to college doubting their literacy skills, but rather their perceptions of their abilities are undermined during college—even despite their academic performance (457). This large-scale project and other smaller studies indicate that first-generation students may feel isolated, alienated, or excluded because of their negative perceptions about their language habits (Adair; Dunstan and Jaeger; Eliason and Turalba; White and Lowenthal). In addition to the attitudes of their teachers, first-generation students fear judgment from their peers. John White and Patrick Lowenthal's qualitative study of minority students describes how students withhold their participation in class because of their peers' use of academic discourse. In the study, one Native American student explains that he remained silent in a course about race and oppression—a topic that he knew a great deal about—because he feared that his language would disclose that he was there on a scholarship (298). This student believed that his scholarship was a detriment, rather than an accolade highlighting his academic ability, because it revealed his social class.

Contributing to the emotional labor that first-generation students must endure in the university context are the larger culture narratives about inappropriate language use, in which one slip results in humiliation or total rejection. This binary of elite versus substandard language is likely present in students' home cultures, where academic language may be labeled as showing off, acting like a big shot, or even worse, as a betrayal of family, community, or ethnic identity (Law 3; Hurst, *College* 113; Svoboda 169–73). There is no indication that these language conflicts lessen or dissipate for first-generation students as they continue their education. Instead, some studies suggest that the feeling of being an impostor increases for graduate students (Michell; Svoboda; Zorn) and for professors and administrators (Khadka et al.; Law; Hutchins; Parkman; Muzzatti and Samarco).

Given that first-generation students are likely to suffer discomfort about their language differences, the question might change, from how can these students be made to feel comfortable, to how can this discomfort be examined in a productive manner? Interest in a pedagogy of discomfort has steadily grown since Megan Boler's early work in 1999. Boler and Michalinos Zembylas forward a pedagogy of discomfort that exposes cultural binaries of identity difference: "Our aim is to question some of our contemporary certainties about the kinds of identities that we take for granted and the common normativity that is often at work in all diverse practices of individuals" (112). Boler and Zembylas link a process of critical examination to both cognitive and emotional labor that can lead to the construction of "new narratives that erode the biases we so often ascribe to others, and to ourselves not least" (129). A pedagogy of discomfort exposes the relationship among cultural, individual, and collective narratives of identity.

Writing teachers may be reluctant to risk a pedagogy of discomfort because of the emotional labor that they already experience while working with first-generation students. Teachers may be equally inspired by their first-generation students' heroic efforts and depressed by the many barriers to students' success. Just getting to class, accessing course materials, and completing assignments on time can be extremely difficult for first-generation students as their personal relationships and finances become destabilized. Teachers have an ethical obligation to help marginalized students rethink limiting cultural narratives for both their home and school lives (Gee 127). My position is that memoir writing provides one potential means for examining issues of difference and the emotional labor that directly jeopardizes the success of first-generation students. However, one writing assignment by itself cannot accomplish all these feats. Rather, a more effective approach is a series of linked activities that target specific instructional goals. In the next two sections I detail several writing and reflection activities to assist students in selecting an identity conflict and developing a complex representation of that identity that culminates in an identity-conflict memoir.

Selecting an Identity Conflict

Writers need to read multiple models, experiment with ideas, evaluate choices, and receive supportive feedback before committing to a topic. This process takes time and is fraught with emotional labor for both teachers and students. This section includes strategies that are familiar to most teachers; however, the trick is not to shortchange the effectiveness of these strategies by giving in to the pressure to move on to other writing assignments. Students gain a clearer idea of the assignment from reading essays written by both students and published authors. I selected a range of former students' papers that I had permission to share. In addition, students read Black's memoir "Stupid Rich Bastards," chosen for the similarity of Black's life to their lives and for the memoir's inclusion of critical analysis. When introducing the models, I displayed my genuine love for these essays and noted the risks that the authors took. In *Teaching with Emotion: A Postmodern Enactment*, Zembylas advocates that teachers take agency in their emotional labor by seeking the parts of teaching that feed their enthusiasm and express joy. I wanted students to know that I value writing that represents their complex lives and that they have experiences that deserve to be explored in writing.

Another useful type of modeling happens when teachers demonstrate an activity that students will next attempt. To introduce the multiplicity and fluidity of identity, I drew on the board several of my overlapping identity circles, such as being a woman, member of the working class, student, teacher, divorcee, mother, caregiver, and so on. As I labeled these circles, I described how my identities conflicted and changed through various life experiences. My brief disclosures gave permission for students to risk considering their own identity development. Students then selected two or more identities and listed experiences that provoked conflict and change. To generate more possible topics, students filled out a brainstorming sheet about language conflict experiences: when words that were spoken or written caused them to feel like an insider or outsider, be upset or angry, become a peacemaker, change an opinion, and choose silence as the only option.

The point of multiple brainstorming activities was to develop a pool of life experiences from which students could choose. I agree with Roz Ivanič that a better beginning cognitive approach to understanding identity comes from narratives of embodied experiences rather than an abstract academic lecture (330). Nikolas Rose refers to these life experiences as the "little territories of the everyday" that may provoke a small space for action (280). Hackneyed topics like car wrecks or winning awards are often cast aside during this early period of writing. Students need time to explore several different topics before committing fully to one topic. I insisted that all writers declare a plan B topic in case the first idea didn't work out.

Sharing at every stage of incubation encouraged reflection and analysis. Students liked starting with a quick, paired sharing activity, in which listeners would ask for more details, and I enjoyed hearing the classroom buzz with engagement. Later students posted on the course website a summary of their two possible topics, so I could respond to each student individually. To reduce feelings of anxiety, first-generation students may avoid emailing or visiting a professor's office to discuss an idea. One indication of this insecurity in my classes was that first-generation students sometimes deferred to my authority by requesting that I choose the better of two potential topics. Generally, I responded by describing the assets of both topics, leaving the writer to make the decision. Students were guided to assess their emotional response to their topics rather than to just decide which seemed easiest to do. I always cautioned that a topic might be too personal to be graded or shared. Experience has taught me when to recognize my own biases and when to assert the infrequent no to a topic choice. After all the brainstorming, talking, and reflecting, students did a timed freewrite for one topic and followed this with more sharing in pairs and with the whole class. Example topics that students have chosen include the following: realizing dialect differences with one's peers while playing basketball, filling a diary with hateful entries about an abusive stepfather, being labeled as shy and rejected for a leadership position, and learning about a relative's stigma as an unwed pregnant high school girl.

Feedback indicated that about a third of students in each class did not end up writing about their first idea for a topic. Good topics tend to emerge and develop from several incubation activities. First-generation students were not used to asking for permission to change their topics, and they often apologized and worried that they would be penalized. Students gained courage to pursue difficult topics by listening to the topics of peers. Occasionally, a student would suddenly change topics to an overlooked life hurdle such as a medical or relationship crisis. My motive for giving more time for selecting a viable topic was to reduce the number of major problems during revision.

Including multiple moments for students to reflect metacognitively about their topic increased their awareness of the many factors related to development and audience that writers must consider. Reading their freewrites or drafts was less productive for my purposes than just listening to students' reflections about their emotional responses to their topics and early drafts. I gained useful information about individuals' stress levels and misconceptions about the assignment. I often told students that feeling confused or uncertain about what they were writing was normal and that part of the reason to write was to make sense of complicated situations.

Representing a Complex Identity

My goal for this assignment was for students to produce complex texts that narrate significant experiences related to their identity development. This assignment differed from those students might have learned to follow in high school to produce functional texts for testing purposes, such as assignments that use the five-paragraph structure or that require formulaic arguments. I wanted students to experiment with including critical analysis in a text that at first may have been a simple chronicle of an event. Writing offers an elaborated method for debriefing experience through which the writer can discover patterns, explore connections, and consider alternative points of view—all of which are essential to academic writing in any discipline. Soliday describes the interpretation of experience as "narrative agency" (511). For far too many first-generation students, their narrative agency has been narrowed to reproducing prevailing cultural stereotypes. First-generation students have a keen sense of critical analysis, including how they evaluate their home, school, and work experiences. I viewed my task as building on students' existing critical awareness of daily life by sharing strategies for incorporating more analysis into their writing. I began this process by focusing their attention on emotion.

Students ranked positively a series of activities related to developing multiple, changing emotional responses to an experience. This sequence began with my reading aloud a model monologue in which the narrator expresses a range of emotions. I stopped several times and had students name the type and degree of emotion that was being portrayed, the point being that a person often experiences conflicting emotions in response to a significant experience prior to arriving at one or more dominant reactions. After selecting a powerful moment in their narratives, students completed three freewrites: their thoughts and feelings prior to that moment, worries and fears during the actual event, and reactions and interpretations after considerable time had passed. Many students incorporated these responses into their drafts. This sequence demonstrated for them that the interpretation of an event changes over time. The next series of freewrites were my favorite; they pushed students to widen their analysis to consider cultural and historical influences on interpretation. Using Ira Shor's time and space heuristic as a guide (164–66), I gave students a series of prompts that had them consider social, political, economic, and historical factors. I generated a page of these prompts for critical analysis and permitted students to choose three or four for their freewrites. I emphasized critical analysis in part because university courses frequently require social, political, economic, or historical analysis in writing assignments. The space prompts related to students' local community, area of the country, and global region by requiring students to identify how social expectations and pressures affect the interpretation of an event. I have used prompts like the following:

> Connect this experience to other regional and national events, especially American cultural preferences.
>
> Tell who might benefit from your reaction to this experience, either monetarily or through increased social status.

Explain the connections between this experience and your ethnicity or race.
Imagine how living in a totally different community or global location would have changed this experience.

The prompts related to time asked students to consider past, current, and future differences in interpretation:

Describe the responses of people from other generations who would disagree with your reaction or might misinterpret the event.
Explain the connections between this experience and your values or your friends at the time.
Imagine how reactions of the current generation might differ if there were changes in politics and economics.
Describe how this experience relates to the type of person you want to become.

Although I asked students to reconsider their interpretation of an event, students had the right to interpret life experiences according to their own beliefs and values. A. Abby Knoblauch cautions that teachers should avoid a liberatory agenda of persuasion and instead use an invitational pedagogy that is willing to privilege critically listening to difference (127). As I have argued elsewhere, complex narratives should represent dynamic identities that develop and change in awareness (Mack, "Being"). This could be a forming identity from the past, an identity revised in the present, or an identity to be inhabited in the future. Representation of past identities may matter the most because narratives give the writer agency over the past (Smith and Watson 59). This may be why it is so meaningful for people to reinterpret past traumatic events as catalysts for positive change. Rather than ignoring the traumatic events that many first-generation students have suffered, teachers should emphasize the positive role that writing can have in analyzing troubling experiences so that students take agency in deciding how best to move forward.

Lest my teacher narrative become overly heroic, I must reveal that these activities had uneven results when it came to students' final version of their memoirs. Although they generated layers of critical analysis, many students had difficulty inserting their insights into their drafts. I used a color-marking system to help students visualize how analysis can be combined with narration (Mack, "Colorful Revision"). I had the class revisit Black's memoir and mark the commentary lines surrounding her conference with a writing teacher (22–23). Next, groups took different pages of the essay and color-marked more of the author's critical analysis. All the pages were posted on the board to demonstrate how critical analysis created a theme throughout a text. Then students experimented with inserting commentary into their current drafts. Volunteers shared before and after versions of a section from their drafts. Students were assigned to continue adding commentary to the current draft or to create a new draft that integrated an analytic theme. When I read their last drafts on the website, I digitally highlighted places with critical analysis in green and indicated places for more possible inclusions in pink. I used yellow for minor problems. This system focused my feedback and reduced the time spent commenting on drafts. Students responded positively to this system and explained that teacher comments were often confusing, overwhelming, and negative, whereas color marking was clear and easier to understand.

Reflection, Emotion, and Agency in Academic Identity Formation

As hopeless as it sounds, requiring students to use multiple writing strategies during the term does not mean that they will ever choose to utilize any of those strategies again. Metacognitive reflection can play a significant role in learning about writing (Yancey). However, asking students to reflect about what they learned during a writing experience is too vague. Metacognitive prompts should ask for specific information about the learning experience, as in the following examples:

Select three effective strategies from the list provided and describe your use of each strategy.
Explain how you felt about trying each strategy.
Detail the reasons why each strategy was helpful.
Compare each strategy to your previous methods.
Imagine how each strategy might be useful for another writing task.

Sometimes, students wrote their reflections individually, and at other times they compiled them in small groups and shared them with the class. I often gave examples of how past students' insights and preferences led to changes in my teaching. I also emphasized that reflection was a form of research that helps students become more aware of effective writing strategies. Writers need to understand that knowledge of multiple writing strategies can be helpful for future assignments (Wardle 82). In addition to this cognitive knowledge about the work of academic writing, first-generation students need to gain knowledge about the emotional labor of writing from a cultural position of marginalization.

Even successful first-generation students may feel like outsiders or impostors (Hurst, *Burden*). For many first-generation students, cultural categories stereotype their identities and limit their learning experiences because of how assignments are structured and their perceptions of teachers' expectations.

Scholarship in rhetoric and composition is replete with theories of a self that is fluid, multiply conflicted, embodied in experience, and socially interpreted; yet most writing assignments require students to perform a static, singular, subject bound by societal norms. Ivanič's qualitative study reveals the limitations that academic assignments impose on nontraditional students' identities: "Writers construct a 'discoursal self' not out of an infinite range of possibilities, but out of the possibilities for self-hood which are supported by the socio-cultural and institutional context in which they are writing" (28). Although Ivanič's research is about adult returning students, the analysis applies to many other diverse subgroups of first-generation students who struggle to write themselves as acceptable to the academy. Those positioned outside the privileged student identity are most likely to suffer "stereotype threat." The psychologist Claude M. Steele explains how stereotype threat subtly affects the success of female and African American students. Steele asserts that these students are affected by societal stereotypes even if they do not identify with the stereotyped group or believe a stereotype applies to them: "This is a threat that in the short run can depress their intellectual performance and, over the long run, undermine the identity itself, a predicament of serious consequence. But it is a predicament—something in the interaction between the group's social identity and its social psychological context, rather than something essential to the group itself" (627). Because these larger cultural biases also influence students' assessments of themselves and others, many first-generation students believe that continuing-generation students have superior language skills that first-generation students cannot acquire. Basil Bernstein fears that marginalized students will leave school having only learned their place within the larger social classification system (17). Where there is unequal distribution of power, there is a great deal of emotional labor for those who do not possess it.

To help first-generation writers, a distinction needs to be made between general self-confidence and self-efficacy. Self-confidence can be misguided. First-generation students may believe that hard work alone should pay off with a high grade. Misconceptions about the effectiveness of a particular writing strategy may explain the appeal of rigid formats and overly generalized sentence structure rules. Self-efficacy in writing is defined by psychologists as a belief that one has the skill and resources to complete a specific writing task (Pajares). Beliefs about competence and resourcefulness can calm the stress of facing problems when completing a rigorous academic writing task.

Composing a piece of high-stakes academic writing involves a great deal of emotional labor (Schmertz 279). The emotional labor related to the writing process tends to be disregarded in the curriculum as a dysfunction or weakness of the individual writer (Ivanič 339). All writers benefit from recognizing the ups and downs of composing: being disappointed in a draft, feeling disorganized, discovering connections, abandoning a whole section, elaborating on a difficult idea, and so on. Metacognitive questions about fears, disappointments, and satisfactions during the writing process can help first-generation students be aware of emotions as entities that can be recognized, analyzed, and controlled (Ballenger and Myers). Being able to respond to the emotional labor of writing as a problem-solving process may motivate first-generation students to value writing strategies as a means to take agency over their emotions.

To emphasize their emotional agency at the end of the writing assignment, I had students name one writing problem or fear that they experienced and explain which activity or strategy helped them cope with or resolve that problem. Students enjoyed telling about discovering a good idea, dealing with a disappointing draft, and receiving suggestions from peers. As students shared their problem-solving experiences, they were identifying themselves as resourceful academic writers, and others were hearing testimonies about effective strategies such as reading a paper aloud to catch errors and visiting the writing center. I also had students imagine solutions to writing problems that might occur in other classes, for instance professors who might not explain the assignment clearly or share example papers (see Mack, "Emotional Labor" 151). First-generation students can learn to take agency to find support. A qualitative study by Billy Wong and Yuan-Li Tiffany Chiu explains that even high-achieving nontraditional students may not readily seek support because of fear of exposure or pride in self-sufficiency (878). Psychological studies indicate that marginalized students can benefit from writing about feelings related to difference and strategies for transitioning to college (Stephens et al.; Walton and Cohen; Yeager et al.). In these studies first-year marginalized students also learned about the experiences of culturally similar upper-division students who solved problems by seeking various types of support. Writing-task knowledge that includes emotional self-regulation and problem-solving strategies can increase the self-efficacy of first-generation students. High self-efficacy for writing is essential for the development of an identity as an academic writer.

Reflective writing assignments taking place over an entire term provide narrative research about learning to write. I became disappointed with having students write a paper at the end of the term about their learning experience because the papers were too general and seemed more like thank-you notes. Had I asked students to use their metacognitive reflections from the whole term as data, their final paper could have cited their reflections as evidence. Julie Lindquist and Bump Halbritter describe "a pedagogical approach that moves from *teaching narratives* to *learning via narrativizing*" (439). Lindquist and Halbritter privilege the total integrated learning experience of students rather than each isolated paper: "we treat narratives, insofar as they participate in a program of *narrativizing*, both as a practice that enables learning as a change in one's orientation to the affordances of one's experience, as well as a move that works in conjunction with opportunities for deliberately scaffolded informed reflection" (416). This approach is unlike the model designs for most introductory writing courses, which usually offer what appear to students as a series of unrelated reading and writing assignments. As shown in another of their works, Halbritter and Lindquist value reflective activities that promote inclusive learning through writing about experience (52). Perhaps the discipline is moving away from earlier course designs that privilege the evaluation of individual papers and is beginning to emphasize what students learn about writing from a series of scaffolded learning activities and reflective writing. The papers that students write are ephemeral in comparison to what remains as their knowledge and beliefs about themselves as writers.

The academic identity that first-generation students have as writers will need to be revised as they progress through their coursework. They need to work through the cultural myths that they have about successful writers and how those writers deal with problems. In an extensive study of identity formation and the transition to college, Michael Berzonsky and Linda Kuk categorized successful students as willing to seek information to revise aspects of their identities, being self-reflective, coping with problems, and accepting complexity (83). The problem for first-generation students is that the cultural model for a successful academic identity excludes people like them. This is painfully apparent when first-generation students deny their own academic success. I was most frustrated by the students who dropped out late in the term after successfully completing most of the coursework. Usually, I never got the chance to communicate with these students about their emotional distress; however, I learned about some of their feelings when one student unexpectedly blew up in a capstone course with only weeks before graduation. This student was having problems securing childcare, so she brought her toddler to class. Before class several of us were remarking positively about her daughter sitting at one of the big desks. Embarrassed about having a child, the student blurted out that no one would hire her as a teacher because she was an unwed mother who had been rejected by her parents. The other students empathized with her fears by sharing their own stories about being older, almost failing a class, having to retake a test several times to get into a program, and so on.

The emotional distress that the whole class shared bothered me, so I made a one-page handout for students to examine their negative feelings about themselves. I titled it "Dr. Mack's All-Purpose Crap Detector"—in homage to a chapter in Neil Postman and Charles Weingartner's *Teaching as a Subversive Activity*. The first column asked students to list reasons why they believed they weren't as good as other students, including bad choices they had made, things they were ashamed of, or things that they felt guilty about. The second column instructed students to rewrite those negatives as positives by praising themselves for not giving up, and so on. The third column required students to identify five advantages that wealthy students had but that they did not have. On the bottom of the handout I listed several myths that lead to self-hate as well as questions about how schools define students' experiences and home cultures as a deficit. Volunteers shared their responses and discussed their assets, resourcefulness, and perseverance. This activity may have helped me feel better, but I have no way of knowing if it helped any of the students. The good news is that the young woman who was the first to reveal her fears returned ten years later with her daughter. She wanted her daughter to visit a college campus to start thinking about college. My former student shared that she was a successful high school teacher and had accepted a position in her hometown to be nearer to family.

First-generation students must continually renegotiate their many identities in relation to their developing academic identity. Min-Zhan Lu believes that students should not invalidate their experiences, histories, and languages to learn academic discourse. Lu envisions a classroom that "would replace the myth of writers necessarily writing either comfortably inside or powerlessly outside the academy with a vision of writers writing at sites of conflict, at borders which divide academic and other discourses but which are contested and constructed anew each time one writes" (20). First-generation students have linguistic assets and critical insights that can be used to negotiate the emotional labor of participating in an institutional context that creates difference as a deficit and perpetuates inequality. Donna LeCourt describes the need for marginalized students to recognize the exclusionary practices of academic discourse so they can enact a hybrid academic identity (202). LeCourt's description suggests that first-generation students can take agency to form an identity that is not a poor imitation of the identities of elite students but rather that recognizes the problems of marginalization and has strategies for negotiating them. Expecting first-generation students to disrupt the entire social structure of the academy to change stereotypes about difference may be overly optimistic.

The narratives of first-generation students are complex and diverse and must be examined and represented in their learning experiences. Many advocates for educational change draw from Bernstein's sociology of pedagogy to analyze how learner identities are constructed and their voices are silenced within schools (Bourne; Kress et al.; Arnot and Reay; Power). Madeleine Arnot and Diane Reay refer to the marginalized students as having a type of pre-agency in which they recognize the influence of oppressive power relations within the pedagogical context that precedes the yet-to-be-realized category of being heard. This model of educational reform does not privilege upward mobility as the transformation of first-generation students; instead, it values the diverse knowledge that first-generation students bring as well as the unrealized new knowledge that they can create. University administrators may realize that the retention of first-generation students is an economic necessity, but they have not proved that they value and can learn from the meaningful life experiences of these students.

Works Cited

Adair, Vivyan C. "Poverty and the (Broken) Promise of Higher Education." *Harvard Educational Review*, vol. 71, no. 2, 2001, pp. 217–39.

Alexander, Kara Poe. "Successes, Victims, and Prodigies: 'Master' and 'Little' Cultural Narratives in the Literacy Narrative Genre." *College Composition and Communication*, vol. 62, no. 4, 2011, pp. 608–33.

Arnot, Madeleine, and Diane Reay. "Power, Pedagogic Voices and Pupil Talk: The Implications for Pupil Consultation as Transformative Practice." Moore et al., pp. 75–93.

Ballenger, Bruce, and Kelly Myers. "The Emotional Work of Revision." *College Composition and Communication*, vol. 70, no. 4, 2019, pp. 590–614.

Bean, Janet. "Manufacturing Emotions: Tactical Resistance in the Narratives of Working-Class Students." *A Way to Move: Rhetorics of Emotion and Composition Studies*, edited by Dale Jacobs and Laura R. Micciche, Heinemann, 2003, pp. 101–12.

Bernstein, Basil B. *Pedagogy, Symbolic Control, and Identity: Theory, Research, Critique*. Vol. 5, Rowman and Littlefield, 2000.

Berzonsky, Michael D., and Linda S. Kuk. "Identity Status, Identity Processing Style, and the Transition to University." *Journal of Adolescent Research*, vol. 15, no. 1, 2000, pp. 81–98.

Black, Laurel Johnson. "Stupid Rich Bastards." Dews and Law, pp. 13–25.

Boler, Megan. *Feeling Power: Emotions and Education*. Routledge, 1999.

Boler, Megan, and Michalinos Zembylas. "Discomforting Truths: The Emotional Terrain of Understanding Difference." *Pedagogies of Difference: Rethinking Education for Social Justice*, edited by Peter Pericles Trifonas, Routledge, 2003, pp. 110–36.

Bollig, Chase. "'People Like Us': Theorizing First-Generation College as a Marker of Difference." *Literacy in Composition Studies*, vol. 7, no. 1, 2019, pp. 22–43.

Bourne, Jill. "Vertical Discourse: The Role of the Teacher in the Transmission and Acquisition of Decontextualised Language." *European Educational Research Journal*, vol. 2, no. 4, 2003, pp. 496–521.

Brodkey, Linda. "Writing on the Bias." *College English*, vol. 56, no. 5, 1994, pp. 527–47.

Bryson, Krista. "The Literacy Myth in the Digital Archive of Literacy Narratives." *Computers and Composition*, vol. 29, no. 3, 2012, pp. 254–68.

Carpenter, William, and Bianca Falbo. "Literacy, Identity, and the 'Successful' Student Writer." *Identity Papers: Literacy and Power in Higher Education*, edited by Bronwyn T. Williams, Utah State UP, 2006, pp. 92–108.

Chandler, Sally W. *New Literacy Narratives from an Urban University: Analyzing Stories about Reading, Writing and Changing Technologies*. Hampton Press, 2013.

Dews, C. L. Barney, and Carolyn Leste Law, editors. *This Fine Place So Far from Home: Voices of Academics from the Working Class*. Temple UP, 2010.

Dunstan, Stephany Brett, and Audrey J. Jaeger. "Dialect and Influences on the Academic Experiences of College Students." *The Journal of Higher Education*, vol. 86, no. 5, 2015, pp. 777–803.

Eliason, Michele J., and Ruby Turalba. "Recognizing Oppression: College Students' Perceptions of Identity and its Impact on Class Participation." *The Review of Higher Education*, vol. 42, no. 3, 2019, pp. 1257–81.

Gee, James. *Social Linguistics and Literacies: Ideology in Discourses*. 5th ed., Routledge, 2015.

Halbritter, Bump, and Julie Lindquist. "Collecting and Coding Synecdochic Selves: Identifying Learning across Life-Writing Texts." *How Stories Teach Us: Composition, Life Writing, and Blended Scholarship*, edited by Amy E. Robillard and D. Shane Combs, Peter Lang, 2019, pp. 47–75.

Hall, Anne-Marie, and Christopher Minnix. "Beyond the Bridge Metaphor: Rethinking the Place of the Literacy Narrative in the Basic Writing Curriculum." *Journal of Basic Writing*, vol. 31, no. 2, 2012, pp. 57–82.

Hurst, Allison L. *The Burden of Academic Success: Loyalists, Renegades, and Double Agents*. Lexington Books, 2010.

———. *College and the Working Class: What It Takes to Make It*. Sense Publishers, 2012.

Hutchins, Holly M. "Outing the Imposter: A Study Exploring Imposter Phenomenon among Higher Education Faculty." *New Horizons in Adult Education and Human Resource Development*, vol. 27, no. 2, 2015, pp. 3–12.

Ivanič, Roz. *Writing and Identity: The Discoursal Construction of Identity in Academic Writing*. John Benjamins, 1998.

Khadka, Santosh, et al., editors. *Narratives of Marginalized Identities in Higher Education: Inside and outside the Academy*. Routledge, 2019.

Knoblauch, A. Abby. "Disrupting Disruption: Invitational Pedagogy as a Response to Student Resistance." *Disrupting Pedagogies in the Knowledge Society: Countering Conservative Norms with Creative Approaches*, edited by Julie Faulkner, IGI Global, 2012, pp. 122–34.

Kress, Gunther, et al. "Knowledge, Identity, Pedagogy: Pedagogic Discourse and the Representational Environments of Education in Late Modernity." *Linguistics and Education*, vol. 11, no. 1, 2000, pp. 7–30.

Law, Carolyn Leste. Introduction. Dews and Law, pp. 1–12.

LeCourt, Donna. *Identity Matters: Schooling the Student Body in Academic Discourse*. State U of New York P, 2004.

Lindquist, Julie, and Bump Halbritter. "Documenting and Discovering Learning: Reimagining the Work of the Literacy Narrative." *College Composition and Communication*, vol. 70, no. 3, 2019, pp. 413–45.

Lu, Min-Zhan. "Writing as Repositioning." *Journal of Education*, vol. 172, no. 1, 1990, pp. 18–21.

Mack, Nancy. "Being the Namer or the Named: Working-Class Discourse Conflicts." *JAC*, vol. 27, nos. 1–2, 2007, pp. 329–50.

———. "Colorful Revision: Color-Coded Comments Connected to Instruction." *Teaching English in the Two-Year College*, vol. 40, no. 3, 2013, pp. 248–56.

———. "Emotional Labor as Imposters: Working-Class Literacy Narratives and Academic Identities." *Class in the Composition Classroom: Pedagogy and the Working Class*, edited by Genesea M. Carter and William H. Thelin, Utah State UP, 2017, pp. 140–60.

Michell, Dee. "Academia as Therapy." *Women Activating Agency in Academia: Metaphors, Manifesto, and Memoir*, edited by Alison L. Black and Susanne Garvis, Routledge, 2018, pp. 89–99.

Moore, Rob, et al., editors. *Knowledge, Power and Educational Reform: Applying the Sociology of Basil Bernstein*. Routledge, 2006.

Muzzatti, Stephen L., and C. Vincent Samarco, editors. *Reflections from the Wrong Side of the Tracks: Class, Identity, and the Working Class Experience in Academe*. Rowman and Littlefield, 2006.

Pajares, Frank. "Self-Efficacy Beliefs, Motivation, and Achievement in Writing: A Review of the Literature." *Reading and Writing Quarterly*, vol. 19, no. 2, 2003, pp. 139–58.

Parkman, Anna. "The Imposter Phenomenon in Higher Education: Incidence and Impact." *Journal of Higher Education Theory and Practice*, vol. 16, no. 1, 2016, pp. 51–60.

Penrose, Ann M. "Academic Literacy Perceptions and Performance: Comparing First-Generation and Continuing-Generation College Students." *Research in the Teaching of English*, vol. 36, no. 4, 2002, pp. 437–61.

Power, Sally. "Disembedded Middle-Class Pedagogic Identities." Moore et al., pp. 94–108.

Rose, Nikolas. *Powers of Freedom: Reframing Political Thought*. Cambridge UP, 1999.

Schmertz, Johanna. "Writing Our Academic Selves: The Literacy Autobiography as Performance." *Pedagogy*, vol. 18, no. 2, 2018, pp. 279–93.

Shor, Ira. *Critical Teaching and Everyday Life*. South End Press, 1980.

Smith, Sidonie, and Julia Watson. *Reading Autobiography: A Guide for Interpreting Life Narratives*. U of Minnesota P, 2010.

Soliday, Mary. "Translating Self and Difference through Literacy Narratives." *College English*, vol. 56, no. 5, 1994, pp. 511–26.

Steele, Claude M. "A Threat in the Air: How Stereotypes Shape Intellectual Identity and Performance." *American Psychologist*, vol. 52, no. 6, 1997, pp. 613–29.

Stephens, Nicole M., et al. "Closing the Social-Class Achievement Gap: A Difference-Education Intervention Improves First-Generation Students' Academic Performance and All Students' College Transition." *Psychological Science*, vol. 25, no. 4, 2014, pp. 943–53.

Svoboda, Victoria. *Constructing Class: Exploring the Lived Experience of White Female Student Affairs Professionals from Working Class Families*. 2012. U of St. Thomas, Minnesota, PhD dissertation.

Walton, Gregory M., and Geoffrey L. Cohen. "A Brief Social-Belonging Intervention Improves Academic and Health Outcomes of Minority Students." *Science*, vol. 331, no. 6023, 2011, pp. 1447–51.

Wardle, Elizabeth. "Understanding 'Transfer' from FYC: Preliminary Results of a Longitudinal Study." *Writing Program Administration*, vol. 31, nos. 1–2, 2007, pp. 65–85.

White, John Wesley, and Patrick R. Lowenthal. "Minority College Students and Tacit 'Codes of Power': Developing Academic Discourses and Identities." *The Review of Higher Education*, vol. 34, no. 2, 2011, pp. 283–318.

Williams, Bronwyn T. "Heroes, Rebels, and Victims: Student Identities in Literacy Narratives." *Journal of Adolescent and Adult Literacy*, vol. 47, no. 4, 2003, pp. 342–45.

Wong, Billy, and Yuan-Li Tiffany Chiu. "'Swallow Your Pride and Fear': The Educational Strategies of High-Achieving Non-traditional University Students." *British Journal of Sociology of Education*, vol. 40, no. 7, 2019, pp. 868–82.

Yancey, Kathleen B. *Reflection in the Writing Classroom*. Utah State UP, 1998.

Yeager, David S., et al. "Teaching a Lay Theory before College Narrows Achievement Gaps at Scale." *Proceedings of the National Academy of Sciences of the United States of America*, vol. 113, no. 24, 2016, pp. 3341–48.

Zembylas, Michalinos. *Teaching with Emotion: A Postmodern Enactment*. Information Age, 2005.

Zorn, Diana M. *Enactive Education: Dynamic Co-emergence, Complexity, Experience, and the Embodied Mind*. 2011. University of Toronto, PhD dissertation.

First-Generation Writing Program Administrators as Literacy Sponsors for First-Generation College Students

Courtney Adams Wooten and Jacob Babb

The recent scholarly recognition of first-generation students and the lack of sociocultural capital they bring with them to college is complicated by common narratives in circulation about today's students. These include narratives about how privileged today's students are (Nilson) and how much hand-holding they need (Bradley-Geist and Olson-Buchanan), narratives often in direct conflict with first-generation students' experiences. One way to read this disconnect is through the words of one of our study's interviewees, a first-generation student turned writing center director: "privilege goes to privilege." Although some students are privileged in their understanding of college and how to navigate higher education by virtue of their parents' college experiences, first-generation students do not typically have this privilege, and they also often have intersectional identities that overlap with the identities of other underprivileged student populations in terms of race or ethnicity, class, and so on. As a result, many kinds of information that continuing-generation students have access to are unavailable to them.

This essay examines the educational histories and work of a particular subset of first-generation students who became writing program administrators (WPAs). WPAs are at an interesting intersection of privilege; their backgrounds as first-generation students mark their experiences in the past, and often in the present, as underprivileged in many ways. However, their current positions are positions of privilege in which they are often viewed as literacy sponsors (to borrow Deborah Brandt's term; 18–21) who, through their work as administrators, either approve or disapprove of students' literacy practices. Some of the most scathing critiques of WPAs' roles have come from Marc Bousquet and Donna Strickland, the former questioning the managerial apparatus around which he claims WPA work is built, and the latter viewing writing programs as "sites of class struggle" (15) through a historical examination of the rise of managerialism in writing studies. Although the managerial function of WPA work doesn't always equate to institutional power, as some of our interviewees point out, WPAs make programmatic decisions that affect the college literacy experiences of many students, a form of privilege that enables them to shape how literacy is viewed on their campuses. First-generation WPAs—that is, WPAs who were first-generation students—must navigate this insider status in their institutions while operating from identities that were partly shaped by their underprivileged backgrounds. They are well-positioned to understand how first-generation students receive conflicting messages about the support they should expect from institutions of higher education, including literacy support through writing programs and writing centers.

Although no firm data are available about how many first-generation students go into the field of rhetoric and composition, and writing program administration specifically, some data about first-generation students' chosen majors suggest that WPA work could be particularly appealing to those students. Sam Trejo's study of nine thousand youth in the National Longitudinal Study of Youth 1997 Cohort (which included students who began college by the year 2010) found that first-generation undergraduates prefer majors that "have low unemployment, high average wages, and a high occupational concentration": that is, a clear career path after graduation. While first-generation undergraduates enter humanities fields at a lower rate than continuing-generation students (Chen 16), the perceived pragmatic value of writing studies could affect their choice of major. As Carrie Leverenz's work has shown, the number of job ads for academic positions in writing studies that include WPA work is quite high (in 2014–15, around forty-seven percent). Thus, writing program administration may be more attractive to first-generation students who view such work as being more practical and as offering a clearer career path than other types of academic fields. However, this conclusion is based on a patchwork of research that does not directly ask if first-generation students constitute a higher percentage of professionals in writing studies as compared to other fields; research that asks the question would be valuable but remains to be undertaken.

Regardless of why first-generation students become WPAs, they provide unique insights into the needs of first-generation students and how writing programs can address those needs through literacy education. Although research has explored various WPA subjectivities—including pre- and untenured WPAs (Charlton et al.), Black WPAs (Perryman-Clark and Craig), feminist WPAs (Ratcliffe and Rickly), and veteran WPAs (Sternberg and Minter), we have yet to understand what WPAs who were themselves first-generation students bring to their institutions and programs. To better understand who first-generation WPAs are and how their backgrounds influence their work in writing programs, in this essay we analyze the results of a survey of first-generation WPAs and interviews with survey respondents, discussing patterns in the ways they talk about their backgrounds, how their backgrounds have influenced their writing program work, and how they draw on their educational experiences to shape programs that are responsive to first-generation students. We conclude with a discussion of how intersectionality is often elided in discussions of first-generation students and how these WPAs call for more attention to these issues in writing programs writ large.

Survey and Interview Methodology

To gather information about first-generation WPAs, we sent a survey through multiple disciplinary Listservs (WAC-L, WPA-L, WCenter) and social media websites (*Facebook* and *Twitter*), inviting WPAs who identified as former first-generation students to complete the survey and then conducted interviews with a sample of survey respondents. The forty-two-question survey was designed to solicit information about respondents' demographics, family backgrounds, experiences as first-generation students, and WPA work experiences and how respondents' programs serve first-generation students. We built a question into the survey asking whether respondents had been first-generation students; if they responded no, their survey concluded. Discounting three respondents who were not first-generation WPAs, we received fifty-four complete survey responses.

At the end of the survey, we solicited names and contact information for participants willing to be interviewed. Forty individuals (almost seventy-five percent of all respondents) submitted contact information. We contacted twelve of those individuals for interviews, interviewing nine of those invited. We sought a range of interviewees by selecting participants from different types of institutions and age ranges as well as participants who held different kinds of WPA roles, such as directors of first-year writing, writing center directors, and writing-across-the-curriculum directors. Interviews were twenty to forty-five minutes, recorded through video conferencing software. Because some interviewees requested anonymity, we have opted to identify all participants with a generic number label (table 1). After the interviews, we transcribed the recordings and devised a coding schema by identifying common themes and collapsing these into three categories that include ten individual codes. These codes are not exhaustive, but they provide readers with considerations about how the backgrounds of these respondents as first-generation students affect their work as WPAs. The survey and interview data provide insights into how first-generation-students-turned-WPAs view connections between their own experiences as first-gen students and their administrative work (table 2).

Table 1. Interview participant demographics

Interviewee	Type of institution	Most recent administrative role
1	Public research university	Writing center director
2	Private research university	First-year writing director
3	Public research university	Writing center director
4	Private research university	Writing center director
5	Two-year college	First-year writing director and writing-across-the-curriculum director
6	Public comprehensive university	First-year writing director
7	Public research university	Writing center director
8	Public research university	Dean (former first-year writing director)
9	Public research university	First-year writing director

Table 2. Interview coding schema

What WPAs experienced as first-gen students	How background has influenced the work of WPAs	How WPAs can be responsive to first-gen students
Privilege and class differences	Went into writing studies because they were first-gen	WPAs can be advocates
Impostor syndrome	Make assumptions about first-gen students	Serving first-gen students means serving all students
Faculty advocates	Serve first-gen students	Writing programs could do more
	Ensure levels of institutional support for first-gen students	

First-Generation Writing Program Administrators' Backgrounds

To learn more about how the backgrounds of WPAs as first-generation students shape their work, we posed several survey questions about family and educational experiences, expanding on those questions in interviews. Here, we first discuss definitions of first-generation students and how these are used by interviewees. We then highlight the ways that first-generation WPAs experienced the intersections of their often underprivileged status during their college careers to foreground the ways these experiences feed into their WPA work, which we discuss later in the essay. Many interviewees referred to things that they weren't aware they didn't know as students but that certainly affected their college experiences. These things included not having family members, especially parents, or other sponsors who could help them navigate college; a lack of cultural capital that can create barriers to college entry in particular, according to Susan A. Dumais and Aaryn Ward; the long-term financial ramifications of lack of financial support and dependence on student loans; the constraints put on the students by their holding down one or more jobs while in college; the socioeconomic markers that often distanced them from other students and academia in general; and perhaps exacerbated impostor syndrome.

A crucial yet difficult question whenever talking about first-generation students is how to define them. Although our survey depended on the US Department of Education's definition, which is that no parent or guardian of the student completed a postsecondary degree, the term *first-generation student* remains definitionally fluid, as reflected in the fact that a couple of our survey participants initially answered no to the question of whether they had been first-generation students and then asked to retake the survey using their own definition of the term. Other definitions in scholarship of first-gen students specify that parents did not obtain a four-year degree and that parents obtained no education after high school (see Sharpe for an overview of different definitions). Historically, the term also has been used in a variety of ways to a variety of effects (see Kelly Ritter's introduction to this collection).

In the interviews, we asked participants how they defined first-generation students, and their answers, perhaps not surprisingly, reflected the definitional fluidity. For example, interviewee 8 held perhaps one of the strictest definitions of first-generation students: "My understanding of first-gen is that no one in your immediate family has gone to college before you. So your parents have not gone to college and if you have older siblings they have not gone to college." Other interviewees offered more flexible interpretations of the term. For instance, interviewee 5 based her definition on whether students have access to particular kinds of cultural capital: "My definition of first-generation student is kind of colloquial—people who may not be familiar with the college culture. People who don't have the connections or the previous experience to know that they can ask for certain things and to give them the confidence to know that they can ask for a certain thing." These statements speak to the different ways that first-generation students are defined, whether in scholarship about this population, in government agencies and higher education institutions, or by first-generation students themselves.

We asked several survey questions about family background to ascertain what types of financial stability and support first-generation-students-turned-WPAs experienced. Almost forty percent of respondents said that their primary caregiver or caregivers worked jobs that required manual labor or paid an hourly wage, and forty-one percent identified their group household income as $35,000 or lower, even as eighty percent answered that their families owned their homes when they were growing up. While a limited set of questions, these illustrate the range of financial situations that these first-generation students experienced and show that many had the stability of a family home but did not have the stability of a high family income. We further recognize the challenges of making broad claims about the financial backgrounds of our survey respondents because the ages represented in our respondent pool ranged from twenty-five to seventy-four. We asked participants to identify their ages across a range of a decade, with the highest number of respondents, thirty-two percent, in the thirty-five to forty-four range. The other age ranges, in descending order from highest to lowest number of respondents, are forty-five to fifty-four (twenty-seven percent), twenty-five to thirty-four (eighteen percent), fifty-five to sixty-four (fourteen percent), and sixty-five to seventy-four (nine percent). Given a pool of respondents born between 1945 and 1994, making generalizations surrounding income and student debt are difficult to make because of inflation and higher costs for higher education in recent decades.

The impact of these family situations becomes clearer in survey questions about respondents' undergraduate and postgraduate experiences. In terms of what motivated them to attend college, thirty-one percent of respondents cited family encouragement, twenty-four percent cited encouragement from a mentor, and twenty-two percent cited financial gain or advancement. During their undergraduate experience, forty percent of respondents lived off campus, thirty-seven percent lived on campus, and twenty-three percent lived in both of these situations at different times. Only one respondent said that they did not work either full-time or part-time while obtaining their undergraduate degree, and sixty-four percent responded that they worked a part-time job of thirty-two hours or fewer. Seventy-four percent of respondents took out student loans while in their undergraduate programs, and twenty-six percent of these respondents acquired debt of $10,001–$20,000; twenty-nine percent acquired debt of ten thousand dollars or less; and forty-five percent acquired debt of $20,001 or more. This high amount of student loan debt coupled with the hours worked by respondents point to the financial struggles they faced in obtaining an undergraduate degree.

Some of these trends are mirrored in respondents' postgraduate experiences. Only two respondents did not work either full-time or part-time while earning advanced degrees, and again, the majority (fifty-five percent) worked part-time jobs of thirty-two hours or fewer; forty-six percent of respondents worked both on and off campus. Speaking to increased financial support at this level, however, thirty-three percent of respondents reported that they did not have to take out student loans while obtaining their postgraduate degree or degrees. On the other hand, fifteen percent of respondents had to take out student loans of $100,000 or more while obtaining their postgraduate degree or degrees.

Many interviewees noted that such precarity and lack of cultural capital, in addition to financial constraints and the jobs worked during their education, influenced their educational experiences in both positive and negative ways. Interviewee 8 spoke about his background growing up on a farm and how this created a strong work ethic that he carried forward with him: "Every term I took two, three courses, I taught three courses, I worked as a computer consultant on the side. I was the custodian in the apartment building in which we lived and I was also the maintenance person for the apartment where we lived. And I sold blood plasma twice a week to make ends meet." His pride in his work ethic is evident, but also clear are the pressures he faced to support himself and his family by working multiple jobs.

Interviewee 7 said that financial considerations limited her choices for undergraduate and graduate education. She said that while her family urged her to attend college and her mother romanticized the concept of college, she was restrained by finances and still feels burdened by student debt that she has accrued. She repeatedly said, "You don't know what you don't know," capturing in one sentence the difficulties and complexities often experienced by first-generation students. As Dumais and Ward find, first-generation students who don't have access to "parents who are experienced in selecting colleges, applying to them, choosing classes once enrolled, and so forth" (246) are missing crucial forms of socialization that can negatively affect whether they attend college. They also found that financial constraints were "an obstacle to first-generation college enrollment" (263), echoing many of the concerns of our survey respondents and interviewees.

Recognizing the disconnect that her financial and cultural capital constraints caused, interviewee 3 stated, "I paid for school myself, so I didn't have anyone in my family paying for my education. I think I felt more of a difference between me and classmates when it came to issues of money and just how they were able to go out for meals." Interviewee 1 similarly spoke to the disconnect between her and her fellow graduate students, although she recognized the attitudes and cultural capital that created this gap. Her experiences in Ivy League schools left her with the recognition that "privilege goes to privilege," or that systems of sponsorship are often inaccessible or invisible to first-generation students. Initially, she thought she could get into any graduate program and failed to understand how difficult it is to get into what she calls "very privileged schools." Her interactions with graduate students at Harvard only further distanced her from them: "I'd sit down and I'd listen to them talk and some of them were very down to earth, kind people but others were just like 'I don't watch TV, I've never heard of *Lost*, oh I only watch TV to watch the Olympics' or . . . 'Oh, I love Proust, I only read Proust in the original French.'" Given her experiences, interviewee 1 concluded, "[I]n the eight years after I finished my undergraduate work, I learned the very hard reality of how class and background affect your outcomes and how you get a kind of benefit of the doubt with where you come from that you're expected to do great things well, whereas I had to continuously prove that I could do great things." Her experiences speak to the privileges she saw that did not adhere to her as a first-generation student and to the noticeable differences she felt in the way the education system rewards those who are from different backgrounds.

Commenting on a social marker that makes her particularly mindful of her background, interviewee 9 explained, "I don't drink wine. I've never developed a taste for it. And I still after how many years now being in academia, I feel this nervousness any time I go to an event, wondering what are we going to be drinking? What am I going to eat? Do I need to eat before I go? It's this weird marker of cultural capital and class. And I still don't have those markers." She went on to state that she performs the role of colleague and mentor differently because of her background.

Perhaps not surprisingly, first-generation WPAs often experienced impostor syndrome as students. Interviewee 4 noted that she struggled as an undergraduate, going on academic probation twice in the first two years, and she struggled again in graduate school, eventually opting to leave one doctoral program in favor of another. "I felt that I had an inability to participate in the way that I was expected to." She also postulated that part of why she felt drawn to writing studies was a sense that the field interacted more with student populations like first-generation students, so while she experienced difficulties in college that she attributed to her first-gen status, she also felt drawn to work with students with similar experiences.

Interviewee 8 talked about how he thought college wasn't for farm kids like him: "For the longest time I thought that college was only for city kids, I didn't think that farm kids could go to college and so when I got there I had a huge case of impostor syndrome. Here I am, this country kid at college, how presumptuous of me. It took a long time for me to get past that." Later, he also guessed that perhaps first-generation students have impostor syndrome more frequently than other students, an impression shared by several other interviewees. Interviewee 5 complicated this idea of impostor syndrome by recounting how attending college can make first-generation students feel as if they belong neither at school nor at home: "I still struggle with my identity because when I come home and I start using big words, I have a Richard Rodriguez-esque experience at home with my father, who's like, 'You're home now. You don't have to bullshit anymore.'" Similarly, interviewee 7 described college as "almost a dividing mechanism. My parents don't really understand who I am now." This feeling of belonging nowhere is a common one that bell hooks describes in relation to working-class students (177–90), and it feeds into the disconnect that first-generation WPAs can feel about their backgrounds.

Speaking about the support he received in terms of his strong grades and faculty mentors, interviewee 8 said,

> My first semester [my GPA] was around a 2.5, and I thought, "Well, I was right. I'm not cut out for this," but then I started to gain a little more success. And then by the time I was a junior I made the dean's list every semester. And there were a few faculty along the way who encouraged me, and actually in high school there were some faculty who encouraged me, and I sort of believed them. I got to college, and some of those faculty encouraged me. That was helpful.

Here, this student felt motivated in part because he had faculty both in high school and college who encouraged him to pursue postsecondary education. Interviewee 5 discussed how central similar relationships were to her experiences: "So I declared [my major]. That's when [my faculty mentor] came into my life, and the rest is history. I should also mention that [another faculty mentor] was the first person to say 'I think you have a future in this.' If [these mentors] hadn't reached out, I don't know where I would be today." In part because of the lack of a familial support system, these first-generation WPAs clearly valued the positive feedback and support they received from faculty in their role as students.

Thinking about these respondents' experiences both at home and in school helps foreground the framework they use when considering the first-generation students in their programs and how to serve these students. The next section discusses how the backgrounds of the respondents have influenced the work that they do in their own writing programs and institutions while also exploring some of the complexities of working with a population as difficult to define as first-generation students.

Responsiveness to First-Generation Students in Writing Programs

Our survey respondents worked in a variety of types of writing programs: thirty-eight percent worked in first-year writing programs, twenty-one percent in writing centers, eighteen percent in writing-across-the-curriculum or writing-in-the-disciplines programs, and the remaining twenty-three percent in basic writing programs, graduate or undergraduate writing programs, and other types of administrative roles that aligned with writing programs. These WPAs had a variety of duties in their positions, including assessment, mentoring, faculty development, hiring and evaluating faculty or tutors, and curriculum design, among others. Thus, they approached the survey from a variety of perspectives, lending more diversity to the lenses through which they invited us to view their jobs as first-generation-students-turned-WPAs.

In thinking about first-generation students in their own institutions, seventy-two percent of respondents said their institution served a large population of first-generation students, while seventeen percent said their institution did not, and eleven percent were unsure. When asked if programs existed in their institutions to serve first-generation students, sixty-nine percent said yes, fifteen percent said no, and seventeen percent were unsure. These numbers indicate a high percentage of institutions in which first-generation students are acknowledged and served through programs such as TRIO, PUERTA, and Connect and other resources and initiatives such as mentoring, counseling, bridge programs, and learning communities. When asked how well their institutions serve first-generation students, WPAs largely recognized the need for more support to be provided: fifty-two percent said their institution served first-generation students moderately well, nineteen percent said very well, and only two percent said extremely well. On the flip side, twenty-percent said their institution served first-generation students only slightly well, and seven percent said not well at all. Generally, then, most surveyed WPAs thought their population of first-generation students was served moderately well through such programming. One of our interviewees took time to discuss his institution's nationally recognized program, which involves success coaches for first-generation students and the recognition of first-generation students at graduation among other things. So there are some institutions that focus on this population intensely while others do not. Given that some institutions have a higher percentage of first-generation students, such discrepancies should be expected as institutions make efforts to attend to the specific needs of their student populations.

In the interviews, however, the issue of how to identify first-generation students came up with many interviewees when they were asked about how often they worked with first-generation students. Interviewees 4 and 7, both writing center directors, pointed out that because they routinely gather data on students who come to their centers, they could ask whether students are first-gen when they come to the center, although they don't necessarily do so yet. The writing center run by interviewee 7 does not ask if students are first-gen; the interviewee was "interested in collecting this data on intake, but at the moment, this is an ignored demographic." The writing center run by interviewee 4 does collect information about first-gen students, and the interviewee noted an encouraging finding in her institutional research—a higher percentage of first-generation students use the writing center than expected—but she said she needs to do more to support first-gen students. Likewise, interviewee 2 stated, "I don't think I do enough"—a common sentiment among interviewees—even as she noted several efforts on her and her institution's part to identify and assist first-generation students. The questions we asked in these interviews appeared to inspire some participants to think more about working with first-gen students at the programmatic level in the future.

Remarking on the difficulty of identifying whether WPAs are working with first-generation students, interviewee 8 stated, "I'm guessing that I interact with first-gen students every day. And I also do a lot of work with student groups, like student government groups, for example. And I know that a fair number of those students are first-gen, so I'm interacting with them daily. There might be a few exceptions, but I'm guessing daily." The emphasis on "guessing" here, echoed in other interviews, is revealing. Although WPAs at schools with high populations of first-generation students can guess that they interact with them, whether they are actually interacting with them isn't always clear.

Further, some participants were concerned about the biases that may play a role in our well-intentioned efforts to help specific student populations. Interviewee 5 explored what it means to make assumptions about students and their first-gen status: "This is kind of like how often do I interact with second language writing students and in what capacity, right? How do you actually identify them? What biases are you using to identify these students? Because of my training in second language writing, I just kind of treat everyone as if they had all of these culturally significant markers and try to give them the same kinds of understanding." Because first-generation students are a heterogeneous group, identifying them often means making assumptions about who they are based on limited interactions with them.

However, some first-generation students are open about their status. Interviewee 6 mentioned that she has had students openly talk to her about being first-generation: "I can't always tell when they're first-gen students. But sometimes you can because they just own it. They're like, 'I don't know what I'm doing. I need your help.'" Interviewee 2 called being a first-generation student a "badge of honor," adding that she talks about her first-gen status with students because "it's important that these folks know that you don't have to come from a home that has a long legacy of college to be able to succeed in college." Even these WPAs, though, recognize that first-generation students are effectively invisible unless they self-disclose.

When asked how often they consider first-generation students' needs when they make administrative decisions, only nine percent of survey respondents said never or a little; thirty-one percent said some, forty-one percent said a lot, and nineteen percent said always. When respondents were asked which types of decisions were most affected through their consideration of first-generation students, the top four answers were faculty development, connecting with others on campus about writing, mentoring, and curriculum design, and their comments recognized the links respondents saw between their own educational experiences and the ways they approach their programs. However, what became clear is that, because of the relative invisibility of first-generation students, WPAs do not necessarily think about working with this population from a programmatic perspective.

Interviewees focused a lot on how individual faculty members or tutors—rather than programs—are expected to serve or do serve these students, and this focus aligns with Brett Griffiths and Christie Toth's finding that "individual [faculty members'] discretion" provides more support for students experiencing poverty than do "larger programmatic or institutional initiatives" (248). This isn't to say that programs do not undertake wider measures; the survey respondents thought that they do. Instead, the survey results shows that WPAs may make individual rather than programmatic interventions when working with first-generation students, perhaps because it is in these interactions that they feel a real difference can be made, especially in reflecting on their own academic mentoring relationships that were so formative for some of them as first-generation students. For instance, interviewee 6 recognized the work her faculty, which she calls "magic faculty," does to serve these particular students: "I have good humans in my program, and they look at their students as whole people, and they think about how can we help those whole people." Several interviewees felt that first-year writing often functions as an important site for inviting and folding students into the academic and social aspects of college life.

Other WPAs see mixed or no responsiveness from programs and faculty toward first-generation students. As a writing center director, interviewee 4 sees herself as peripheral to a department that does not think about this student population: "I don't think my department is doing anything about first-gen students at all, in the same way that I don't think our department is thinking about teaching writing. I don't think we're doing anything to think about how the teaching of writing is affecting specific populations or having an impact on them." Interviewee 5 also noted that she does not feel her faculty serves first-generation students well: "I was expecting at a community college [that] the culture of students [would be] prioritized because our primary job is to teach, and I was unpleasantly surprised at the lack of enthusiasm for professional development. I honestly don't think that [first-gen students] are served very well, but one of my missions here is to make sure that they get treated better."

These interviewees reveal the ambivalence some faculty members feel toward initiatives to help different student populations, ambivalence lacking simple explanations or remedies. Their comments also show the difficulty WPAs have in wielding their limited programmatic power to make significant changes in how faculty members work with students. Ultimately, we can conclude from these findings that WPAs need to conduct more institutional research on first-generation students—following the research possibilities presented in this volume—to refine how their programs address this population.

Writing Program Administrators as Sponsors for First-Generation Students

While WPAs may lack concrete strategies for helping first-generation students at a programmatic level, they often interact with first-generation students as individuals. Individual interventions are the more typical engagements with first-generation students found in this study. Those interventions are best framed as sponsorship, making WPAs "agents, local or distant, concrete or abstract, who enable, support, teach, and model" sociocultural literacy for first-generation students (Brandt 19). As sponsors, WPAs function as local, concrete support for first-generation students, modeling how to navigate academic environments. First-generation WPAs in our study often viewed themselves as advocates for first-generation students, but because of the difficulty of recognizing who first-generation students are, WPAs conflated this advocacy work with advocacy for other vulnerable student populations. We do not see this as a problem, since many underrepresented students need advocates.

Many interviewees mentioned thinking of themselves as advocates, both in how they interacted with students and how they encouraged faculty and tutors to advocate for first-generation students. Interviewee 1 said, "I recognize that I am not in a state with a lot of unions and that I have to be the advocate for my workers because I don't want them to be taken advantage of. So I offer things like flexible work policies, the ability to bank time so that you can make up time later." Because this writing center director has many first-generation students who work as tutors, she views worker advocacy as one way to advocate for this student population. Interviewee 5 talked about keeping students' best interests in mind in her work: "I'll just try to make sure that everything I do is student-centered. Is this in the best interests of the student? It's like, what is best for the student and how can I be an advocate for the student?" Interviewee 3 also talked about trying to keep faculty and tutors focused on how to support first-generation students: "I think it makes me a more explicit advocate for students to remind people what students might not know. I think just reminding faculty and tutors that sometimes students need coaching about how to behave in college and what to do when they're sick, what to do when they can't make it to class, where to turn things in online when that's not always obvious, what to do when something is late." Most of our interviewees explored the concept of helping others to understand the gaps in first-generation students' knowledge about college, demonstrating that their advocacy was one of the most important results of their own backgrounds as first-generation students.

Some interviewees also thought of themselves as campus-wide representatives for first-generation students and their needs. Interviewee 3 spoke about her role in this work: "We need to remain inquisitive and keep trying to figure out new ways to reach those students. One thing I'm trying to do on my campus is I have the ear of some administrators and I just keep mentioning that our students need childcare. I try to use my position to make changes on campus that might help those students, and then I try to make my center as accessible to those students as possible." Interviewee 8 also mentioned being a voice for first-generation students around campus: "Whenever I have the opportunity to talk about being a first-gen student, I do that. I think we have a responsibility to talk about those experiences so that others feel, 'Hey, if he can do that, I can do it, too.'" As first-generation WPAs, these interviewees identified their jobs as offering a unique platform from which they could speak with some authority in their institutions and with personal knowledge of this student population's experiences.

In this advocacy work, several interviewees recognized that serving first-generation students really serves all students by increasing the transparency of the support that institutions offer to multiple groups of students. When asked about how first-generation students struggle on her campus, interviewee 5 said, "We have a lot of food-insecure students, we have a lot of technology-insecure students, we have a lot of financially insecure students, and they work really hard to come up with the money to come to school. And so I want them to get everything that they can in the shortest time possible." Students increasingly face such challenges, whether they are first-generation or not, and such advocacy is becoming vital.

Several participants who work with graduate students noted that their advocacy for first-generation students took on a more pronounced form because they had more sustained interaction with their first-generation graduate students. First describing her own relationship with her graduate mentor, interviewee 9 noted, "You know, the impostor syndrome stuff never goes away." She said that as a mentor to graduate students, she finds it imperative to make transparent to them how academia works and that many of the feelings they experience are issues they will still contend with once they finish their degrees. Interviewee 9 modeled a form of honesty and emotional vulnerability that demonstrate an important strategy for working with first-year students, whether they are undergraduate or graduate students: students can benefit from learning about their instructors' educational histories, particularly when those instructors come from underrepresented groups, different classes, or a first-generation background.

We can make two intertwined conclusions about writing programs and first-generation students. First, most writing programs do not explicitly focus on first-generation students, and second, programs aim to implement strategies that help students from multiple backgrounds that may present challenges for those students. If we conceive of first-generation WPAs as sponsors of first-generation students, we find that such WPAs are powerful sponsors on an individual level, but we do not yet find significant evidence that sponsorship reaches the programmatic level unless we see such sponsorship in a broader framework of support for vulnerable undergraduate populations. As we discuss below, the intersectional identities of first-generation students often mean that advocating for these students also necessitates advocating for other underrepresented student populations on campus.

Sponsoring the Literacies of First-Generation Students

Given our conclusions that WPAs are not necessarily focusing on first-generation students at a programmatic level, we offer here suggestions about how we can build writing programs that are more beneficial sponsors of first-generation students' literacy practices. *First-generation* is the kind of identity marker that can serve as an effective lens for examining the impact of intersectional identities within student populations on campuses. While the first-generation WPAs who responded to our research call were overwhelmingly white (almost ninety-five percent of survey respondents), many came from working-class or poor families, which suggests that *first-generation* as a marker is, in reality, marking working-class or poor students who otherwise may not be recognized. Because *working class* "is a contested term" (Thelin and Carter 4), using the term *first-generation* may serve as a more transparent way to mark those who do not have the typical markers of class privilege and who identify with other underrepresented groups in terms of race, religious background, and geographical region. Thus, failing to pay attention to first-generation students means that we are also failing to pay attention to some intersectional identities, including, perhaps most prominently, the identities of lower-class and poor students. In other words, any attention WPAs pay to first-generation students will only prove beneficial to other students who may not typically receive support as well.

Building on their own backgrounds and experiences, first-generation WPAs recognize the multifaceted struggles that first-generation students face as they navigate unfamiliar educational contexts. Given the often intersectional identities of first-generation students, both survey respondents and interviewees recognized that their programs and institutions could do much more to serve these students. WPA scholars need to conduct more research on both first-generation students and first-generation-students-turned-WPAs, not only in scholarship but at the institutional level. WPAs need to learn more about who their first-generation students are through engagement with other offices and initiatives on campuses that are already focused on first-generation students. One concrete first step is for WPAs to find out what offices on their campuses track this data or create programming to support first-generation students. Such engagement is necessary for getting an accurate sense of what their institutions are already doing to help first-generation students and how their writing programs can connect with this ongoing work or begin new initiatives if none exist.

Additionally, we assert that continuing to study who first-generation students are and who they become after college provides opportunities to learn more about how to serve students from underprivileged backgrounds who can struggle to acclimate to institutions and writing programs. In this work, it is important to recognize and integrate the experiences of WPAs who were themselves first-generation students while listening to student voices to acknowledge an ever-changing landscape of what it means to engage in literacy practices as a first-generation student.

Works Cited

Bousquet, Marc. "Composition as Management Science: Toward a University without a WPA." *JAC*, vol. 22, no. 3, 2002, pp. 493–526.

Bradley-Geist, Jill C., and Julie B. Olson-Buchanan. "Helicopter Parents: An Examination of the Correlates of Over-parenting of College Students." *Education and Training*, vol. 56, no. 4, 2014, pp. 314–328.

Brandt, Deborah. *Literacy in American Lives*. Cambridge UP, 2001.

Carter, Genesea M., and William H. Thelin, editors. *Class in the Composition Classroom*. Utah State UP, 2017.

Charlton, Colin, et al. *GenAdmin: Theorizing WPA Identities in the Twenty-First Century*. Parlor Press, 2011.

Chen, Xianglei. *First-Generation Students in Postsecondary Education: A Look at Their College Transcripts*. US Department of Education, National Center for Education Statistics, July 2005, nces.ed.gov/pubs2005/2005171.pdf.

Dumais, Susan A., and Aaryn Ward. "Cultural Capital and First-Generation College Success." *Poetics*, vol. 38, no. 3, 2010, pp. 245–65.

Griffiths, Brett, and Christie Toth. "Rethinking Class: Poverty, Pedagogy, and Two-Year College Writing Programs." Carter and Thelin, pp. 231–57.

hooks, bell. *Teaching to Transgress: Education as the Practice of Freedom*, Routledge, 1994.

Leverenz, Carrie. "Finding a Fit: The Rhet/Comp Job Search, 2014–2015." Conference on College Composition and Communication, 8 Apr. 2016, Hilton Hotel, Houston, Texas.

Nilson, Linda B. *Teaching at Its Best: A Research-Based Resource for College Instructors.* 4th ed., Jossey-Bass, 2016.

Perryman-Clark, Staci M., and Collin Lamont Craig, editors. *Black Perspectives in Writing Program Administration: From the Margins to the Center.* National Council of Teachers of English, 2019.

Ratcliffe, Krista, and Rebecca Rickly, editors. *Performing Feminism and Administration in Rhetoric and Composition Studies.* Hampton Press, 2010.

Sharpe, Rochelle. "Are You First Gen? Depends on Who's Asking." *The New York Times*, 3 Nov. 2017, www.nytimes.com/2017/11/03/education/edlife/first-generation-college-admissions.html.

Sternberg, Shari J., and Deborah Minter. "'Always Up Against': A Study of Veteran WPAs and Social Resilience." *College Composition and Communication*, vol. 69, no. 4, 2018, pp. 642–68.

Strickland, Donna. *The Managerial Unconscious in the History of Composition Studies.* Southern Illinois UP, 2011.

Thelin, William H., and Genesea M. Carter. Introduction. Carter and Thelin, pp. 3–16.

Trejo, Sam. "An Econometric Analysis of the Major Choice of First-Generation College Students." *The Developing Economist*, vol. 3, no. 1, 2016. *Inquiries Journal*, www.inquiriesjournal.com/a?id=1407.

Afterword: The New Student Majority Deserves Fundamental Reform in Higher Education

Elaine P. Maimon

Higher education is at a pivotal moment, and the English profession must rise to the occasion. Articles with titles like "The University Is a Ticking Time Bomb" should be recognized not as superficially alarmist but as factual (Hanlon). My decades of experience as a university president confirm the urgency for change. US higher education is now populated by a majority of students who deserve and require more explicit guidance through the higher education universe. Traditional students who acquired knowledge of academic vocabulary and practices around the family dinner table would also benefit from greater academic transparency, but for first-generation students, it is a necessity.

The essays in this book present the reality of higher education today. While the stated emphasis in these essays is on first-generation students, we should also be concerned about those students whose parents may have attended college but who nonetheless lack the social capital to benefit optimally from that experience. US higher education has a new majority made up of overlapping groups: first-generation students, students of color, adults, and military veterans. Yet we continue to depend on structures and practices that were developed a hundred years ago to prepare an elite leadership group then in the majority, while narrowly opening the doors for what was then an underserved minority. The result is an increasingly stratified society and a disappearing middle class. According to the National Center for Education Statistics, the lowest-achieving, highest-income students are more likely to complete a university degree than the highest-achieving, lowest-income students (Gould). Every year at commencement ceremonies, when graduates turn their tassels from right to left, I say ritually, "Welcome into the company of educated women and men." In a democracy, family income should not be the deciding factor on whether a student is welcomed into that company.

Our democracy depends on educating the new student majority to become engaged citizens, prepared for employment and for life. We cannot continue to allow a student's zip code to be the most powerful predictor of success. While continuing to educate students of traditional age and comfortable circumstances, we must at the same time transform universities to address the needs of new majority students (St. Amour). These needs are not all (or even mostly) cognitive. New majority students often listen to demeaning and unhelpful internal voices that tell them they are not fit for college because they are too old, too poor, too different. We must shift the emphasis from what's wrong with students to what's not right with our institutions.

As president of Governors State University (GSU) for thirteen years, and as chief executive officer at two other regional public universities with new majority populations, I witnessed every day the courage of first-generation students as they navigated the university. The physical structure of GSU is intimidating. The buildings are internally connected to allow comfortable movement from place to place during Chicago's harsh winters, but the result is labyrinthine. Investing in clear and effective signage as a student support system may not be obvious to all university constituencies. But as a university president, I know that such investment—and it is expensive—is essential. No one likes being lost. But first-generation students are already hearing those negative voices in their heads telling them that they don't belong. Being lost is an objective correlative for estrangement. We must help students find their way geographically as well as academically.

In Illinois, state leaders lament the loss of top-achieving high school students to other states. Certainly, the fact that students go elsewhere highlights problems in public support for higher education. But I am more worried about students who go nowhere. At GSU, "nowhere" is our biggest competitor. Each year about thirty-four percent of GSU's admitted freshmen do not go out of state, nor do they stay in state to attend another public university, a private liberal arts college, or a community college. They simply do not go to college at all, even though their admission to GSU testifies that they are qualified for college work. Students go nowhere mainly because of financial fears and a lack of bureaucratic savvy to acquire information about available federal and state grants. Outreach to these students is costly, requiring time, effort, and cooperation between high schools and higher education institutions. Recent state statutes in Louisiana, Texas, and Illinois recognize the need for this cooperation by requiring high school seniors to fill out the FAFSA, the basic document necessary for most student aid (need- as well as merit-based).

In Illinois, Governor J. B. Pritzker in his first meeting (April 2019) with public university presidents brought up the possibility of passing a statute making FAFSA mandatory—by requiring students to opt out instead of opt in. It would always have to be possible for students and their families to opt out, but making that more difficult by requiring written reasons would encourage those who are reluctant, for example, to share IRS information to better understand privacy protections and to ultimately opt in. Undocumented students would legally have to opt out, but schools could then assist them in finding scholarships specially designed for DACA students.

At a meeting of US governors, Governor Pritzker had heard from the governor of Louisiana about that state's success in increasing FAFSA applications by twenty-five percent in the first year of requiring students to opt out (Kreighbaum). As soon as Governor Pritzker mentioned the idea to the assembled Illinois public university presidents, we embraced the concept and offered our own ideas to support local high schools in fulfilling this new mandate. We suggested media marketing efforts to promote state-wide FAFSA days, on which university and community college staff volunteers, armed with laptops, could assemble at high schools to support students and their families in filling out these forms and in general improving their understanding of higher education funding. Many families of first-generation students associate financial aid exclusively with loans. They are not aware of federal grants (Pell Grants) and state grants (in Illinois, through the Monetary Award Program) that provide money that does not have to be paid back—a just and worthy entitlement.

Other erroneous assumptions prevail among the families of first-generation students. Some assume that students would benefit from declaring themselves independent of their parents, so that only the students' income would be considered for financial aid assessment. These families are not aware that stringent federal verification processes make it almost impossible for students younger than twenty-four to qualify for aid independent of their parents' income. It's ironic that this federal verification process did not uncover the scam perpetrated by Illinois upper-middle-class parents who, before their children enrolled in college, transferred guardianship of their children to friends of lesser income. Those of us who are presidents of universities serving large numbers of first-generation students have observed that the lengthy and intrusive verification process is applied widely to our students. The new FAFSA statute will allow our financial aid counselors to advise parents on several points: for example, that declarations of independence by traditional-age students won't work, and—an important tip—that using the technology to import family IRS information to FAFSA usually results in not being flagged for second-stage verification. The delay in aid necessitated through verification has driven away many first-generation students, even when the university keeps the student enrolled in anticipation of financial aid. Involving the colleges in advising high school students will help prevent these losses.

The new FAFSA statute will also assist in addressing up front another financial aid challenge facing first-generation students. Financial aid officers are obligated by federal statute to inform students of the maximum amounts available to them in loans. Some families opt for the largest loans possible—and use the money for noneducational purposes, paying off the family mortgage, for example. Required counseling will enable university advisers to explain the shortsightedness of this approach, which results in a mountain of debt that will eventually have to be repaid.[1]

Making FAFSA mandatory in high school will also allow universities to dispel another financial aid myth. Some families of first-generation college students are reluctant to apply for any federal loans at all. They think that they will be better off owing money directly to their friendly, neighborhood public university. Every year GSU must face the consequences of this assumption. If students neglect to pay their university bills, the university is obligated by state law to hold their transcripts and to take other measures that are not student-friendly. Learning from Georgia State University, GSU has instituted a special merit-based scholarship for college seniors with excellent grade-point averages who are on track to graduate in May but who owe money to the university. These scholarships will cover a portion of their indebtedness to the university and will encourage them, we in the administration hope, to apply for student loans to cover the rest. Not all students will be eligible for this help, so it is essential that families understand up front the importance of applying for reasonable loans for college expenses.

Illinois public university presidents also support another state strategy for making college affordable—a merit scholarship program called Aim High. When the Aim High legislation was pending, some argued that the new allotment of merit-based grants would compete with need-based awards and that any additional funds should go into the state Monetary Award Program grants. At GSU we welcomed Aim High because it was another way to get the attention of first-generation students and their families. We decided to define merit to include talent, allowing us to recruit students skilled in the visual and performing arts and to jump-start our new debate team. Many GSU recipients of Aim High funds are also receiving need-based financial aid. Other talented first-generation students who just miss qualifying for need-based aid are supported and encouraged to apply for Aim High scholarships.

Radical change in the demographics of the student majority obligates us to illuminate application procedures and other bureaucratic practices, but few universities have taken on this work. We still operate too much under the assumption that the right people will figure it out. Elitism of this sort no longer has a place in the academy. First-generation students need professors as well as administrators committed to helping them navigate universities and build social capital.

The need for fundamental reform in our assumptions, including the integration of scholarly and administrative roles, is underlined by the revolution in epistemology. In the nineteenth century, Charles Dickens warned educators not to view students as empty vessels to be filled with facts. More than a century and a half later, some educators continue to miss the message. As we proceed through the third decade of the twenty-first century, it is essential that professors everywhere and in every discipline recognize that education can no longer be about the simple exchange of information. Facts are available with the click of a key. Our challenge as educators is to teach students to evaluate these facts, since some are not facts at all but lies. Students must learn how to parse the phrase *alternative facts* and understand how misinformation and disinformation distort perception. Then we must help students to connect the dots—to see patterns that lead toward knowledge creation. And finally, we must teach how to transfer knowledge gained in one setting to areas that look dramatically different. First-generation students need special guidance in understanding the new epistemology. Many see universities as authoritarian and transactional. They assume that if they obey the rules (if they can figure them out), they will then gain information sufficient for higher levels of employment. These assumptions work at cross-purposes to what university education is really about, and universities have a special obligation to dispel false assumptions about accumulated information as the coin of the realm.

Thought leaders in the humanities and particularly in English have a special responsibility to bring about these fundamental reforms. And yet we continue for the most part to ignore our responsibilities for initiating new members of our profession into these realities. We grow our own problems. We perpetuate reward systems and hierarchies that undermine our abilities to serve students, especially first-generation college students, and to keep democracy alive.

The Maimon hierarchical fallacy goes like this: If I teach graduate students, and you teach freshmen, I must be smarter than you. If I teach at a flagship university, and you teach at a comprehensive public or community college, I must be smarter than you. If my research is esoteric, read and understood by the smallest number of readers, and you are a public scholar, I must be smarter than you. If I'm a tenured professor, and you are an adjunct, I must be smarter than you.[2] I'm sure you can supply your own additional examples.

This hierarchical fallacy leads to what Kevin Birmingham calls "The Great Shame of Our Profession." Most English departments depend on underpaid and overworked adjuncts to teach first-year courses, while the departments continue to support tenured graduate professors who teach their specialties (in other words, whatever they like) each year to a large contingent of graduate students. Most of these students will not find tenure-track positions and will join the growing population of adjuncts or, if they are lucky, will leave the academy for jobs in business, government, and not-for-profit organizations. I would argue that most of those jobs would have been available to them years before, if they had been counseled properly, when they were articulate holders of an English bachelor's degree. The subtitle of Birmingham's article (originally a talk) is "How the Humanities Survive on Exploitation." This afterword calls for fundamental reform in PhD preparation in English and outlines principles informing revolutionized programs.

Principle 1: Prepare PhD candidates to teach and research foundation-level study, especially in composition.

The first step is to recognize the responsibility of English PhD programs to prepare graduate students to teach first-year courses and to do so with skill and with joy. If we are to have real reform in American higher education, first-year courses must be recognized not as requirements to be checked off but as true foundations for higher-order thinking and learning. Even well-intentioned reformers call only for improved pedagogy rather than for recognizing foundational education as worthy of serious research as well as expert teaching (Bowen and McPherson). PhD programs should prepare future faculty members to be outstanding teachers and first-rate researchers on questions inherent in foundational study. While seriousness about first-year courses would help all students, first-generation college students would benefit the most. Retention of first-generation students is a big challenge, and the first year of their college careers is crucial.

I like to imagine English PhD candidates preparing for the excitement of teaching first-year courses by discovering what Linda Adler-Kassner and Elizabeth Wardle call "threshold concepts"—transformative ideas that open up new pathways of thought and fundamentally change prior conceptions. Adler-Kassner and Wardle use the phrase "naming what we know" to define these threshold concepts. And there are many things we as educators do know, evident only if we provide time and space for novices to access fundamental ideas. We also know a great deal about another essential idea in Wardle's work—teaching students to transfer what they learn in one setting to another setting that looks very different (Wardle).

But there is also so much we don't know. For example, faculty members at GSU have begun research on the national problem of students' reading—or lack thereof—in first-year courses. Why do students avoid reading assigned texts? How do students manage without reading them? What can we do to promote the productive practices in students that in earlier times we might have (erroneously) taken for granted? Ultimately, how and what do students read, and in what format? We also know very little about remediation. Every year tens of thousands of students across the nation are assigned to remedial or developmental courses based on a range of evaluative tools. Underlying student placements into such courses are assumptions of cognitive deficiency or serious gaps in K–12 preparation. Yet we have discovered lately that we are teaching students who are traumatized by food and housing insecurity (Smith; Laterman; Goldrick-Rab). How might such traumas relate to remediation? If we address the food and housing insecurities, will students be better prepared to compensate for gaps in their academic preparation? And what about the application of neuroscience to learning in general and to remediation in particular? James E. Zull's books, *The Art of Changing the Brain* and *From Brain to Mind*, summarize brain research and possible implications for education at all levels. Zull highlights the idea that learning is change and that "the brain is a natural transformation machine" (*From Brain* 16).

English PhD programs should motivate students to work with PhD candidates in other disciplines to address significant questions. The encouragement of research teams of graduate students would undoubtedly carry over to doing problem-solving research once the PhD was achieved and the tenure-track position attained. Organizational change networks are already improving STEM undergraduate education, so why should they not improve education in English and the humanities (Rundell Singer et al.)?

Preparing PhD candidates for actual needs at liberal arts colleges, comprehensive public colleges, and community colleges would be a much better plan than helping graduate students find jobs outside the academy (*Report*). Entering a PhD program is a strong indication of wanting a professional life at a college or university. Rather than overproducing PhDs for the jobs that exist, our profession should be stimulating the principled transformation of higher education on the national level. The first step is to change English PhD programs to prepare faculty interested in the teaching and research of first-year courses, thereby encouraging the hiring of full-time, tenure-track faculty members to teach those courses.

Regional universities, liberal arts colleges, and community colleges must do their part by creating full-time, tenure-track positions for faculty aspirants with the appropriate graduate school preparation and experience. Through budget reallocation—for example, by eliminating unfilled positions in underenrolled programs—GSU has developed a framework of courses in our first-year curriculum taught exclusively by full-time faculty members. Our hiring practices require that any tenure-track faculty member who is hired must demonstrate a commitment to undergraduate education. Even faculty hires with specialized expertise at the master's and doctoral levels must be willing to embrace the mission of the university to serve first-generation undergraduates. Faculty members from a range of disciplines volunteer to teach Mastering College—GSU's overview of the intellectual and cultural venue of a university education. While all students benefit from the engagement of full-time faculty members, first-generation college students profit the most. Those unaccustomed to forming relationships with professors have a better chance of building this cultural capital with instructors who are not juggling two or three part-time jobs in different geographic locations.

For reasons of coherence and commitment, GSU requires freshmen to take a full-time course load (thirty credits per year, including summer) in GSU's version of Complete College America's Fifteen to Finish campaign. Underpaid and overworked part-time faculty should not be the ones to undertake the enormous challenges of successfully teaching these first-year courses. The first-year program is structured around learning communities, in which students take at least three courses with the same group of students. Faculty members are expected to work together to emphasize connective elements. This is not a job for adjuncts—even those who are excellently prepared.

Despite assumptions to the contrary, dependence on adjuncts to teach first-year courses is not ultimately cost-effective. Most general education courses are within the expertise of liberal arts faculty members, whose upper-division and master's degree courses are often underenrolled. A strategic look at all course assignments can yield faculty workloads that balance lower-division and upper-division needs. Dispelling the Maimon hierarchical fallacy is key. If faculty members embrace the importance and excitement of encouraging potential student growth in the freshman year, they will stop lamenting the loss of their seriously underpopulated master's courses. Truth be told, adjunct positions should be used in upper-level courses to expand students' education through exposure to full-time professionals in a variety of fields, not to cobble together a first-year program. Creating full-time, tenure-track positions, many of which could be filled by dedicated, exhausted, and financially struggling contingent employees, would lead to greater rates of student retention and graduation—and that is the decisive return on investment both ethically and financially.

Principle 2: Encourage interdisciplinary electives and essential required courses in English PhD study.

Anyone planning to teach in higher education today should have some background in leadership, particularly in change management. Rather than bemoaning the corporatization of the academy, we should acculturate the best minds to understand leadership, whether eventually as faculty leaders or as deans, provosts, or presidents. Such elective courses would help break down the firewall that we academics create between faculty and administration. If we think that universities should be run by those who believe in the core values of the academy, then we must stop instilling an us-them attitude in graduate students. Faculty members who believe that accepting administrative positions means going over "to the dark side" will create a vacuum, opening up spaces for nonacademics to assume leadership roles. To protect the core values of the academy, we should prepare scholars to be leaders.

Leadership in the twenty-first century means motivating and dealing with change. It would be beneficial to encourage English PhD candidates to scan the graduate catalogue for courses that include books like John P. Kotter's *Leading Change*. This classic text on change articulates an eight-stage process, the first being establishing a sense of urgency. For today's English PhD candidates, we might paraphrase that principle to recognizing and articulating "the ticking time bomb" in higher education (Hanlon). If higher education is to survive and ultimately prevail, the academy needs leaders in every field—visionaries who can look beyond surviving the status quo. As William Bridges and Susan Bridges write in *Managing Transitions: Making the Most of Change*, "Changes of any sort . . . finally succeed or fail based on whether the people affected do things differently" (6). English PhD candidates must learn about leadership in educating new majority students within the context of a transformed epistemology. Elective courses in organizational behavior, cognitive psychology, and neuroscience would also be useful. Dissertation research on remediation could benefit from such formal study and would prepare future faculty members for the team approach to problem-solving research discussed above. In addition to these suggested electives, English PhD candidates should be required to think seriously about teaching. Systematic mentorship is essential, preferably combined with coursework exemplifying the integration of teaching and research.

Another required course should involve PhD candidates in the romance of US higher education and its relationship to democracy. The legacy of Thomas Jefferson and the Morrill Land Grant Acts is increasingly under attack in the United States. This history is complicated by the fact that some of the lands reserved for universities were obtained by the US government from indigenous tribes. Nonetheless, the commitment to expanding higher education to new populations is worth contemplating and examining. Yet we omit the story of the act from PhD preparation. Instead we prepare PhD candidates to think of themselves as independent contractors more affiliated with their disciplines than with their universities and colleges. Orienting newcomers to join and strengthen the narrative of our nation's higher education history would safeguard the academy from its enemies, while at the same time encouraging newcomers to join in a revolutionary cause. David Thiele writes: "Every doctoral student who plans to work in the academy should be required to take a course in higher education." A respondent to Thiele's article, Tracy Mitrano, goes even further: "I agree but for reasons even greater than preparing the candidate professionally. As a historian of higher education, I learned that the history of higher education is the history of the United States at its finest. To read that history is to know something about ourselves, our ideals and our disappointments. And most importantly: why it matters." Preparing future faculty in this manner would create campus environments equipped for transformational change, ready to invite the new majority to learn within the new epistemology.

Principle 3: Prepare specialists who are also generalists.

Comprehensive colleges and universities, liberal arts colleges, and community colleges cannot afford to hire full-time faculty members who teach only specialized courses. The problem of an adjunct or contingent underclass can be solved only if full-time, tenure-track faculty members are prepared to teach a broad range of courses and to develop new courses as curriculum revisions demand. The current national model is unsustainable. PhD programs prepare specialists for the handful of jobs available at R1 universities. Institutions outside that elite group can hire these specialists for limited tenure-track appointments and then fill other positions with underpaid, overworked adjuncts. On many campuses centers for teaching and scholarship address the problem by reeducating full-time faculty members to teach a broader range of courses.

How different the higher education landscape would be if the universities and colleges that teach the vast majority of students and especially the new majority could hire faculty members with the intellectual flexibility to teach happily and productively outside their specialty. We must also examine what specialization means in the twenty-first century. One thing it does not mean is the vast accumulation of information. Instead, it should signify the expertise to create new knowledge in all forms of language and literature. That shift leads to changing our perception of the generalist as someone who has a watered-down understanding of many things. Instead, scholars who are both specialists and generalists are capable of making new connections across traditional and nontraditional fields.

The terms *flexible* and *generalist* have a negative history in the field of English, as Annie S. Mendenhall outlines in "The Composition Specialist as Flexible Expert." As English PhD programs began offering specialization in rhetoric and composition, universities wrote job advertisements seeking flexible generalists who could teach a wide range of writing courses and administer first-year composition or writing across the curriculum. Ads for Shakespeare scholars, although diminishing in number, did not call for this kind of administrative accommodation. Mendenhall implies that the problem is with the unique call for flexibility in composition specialists, while other scholars were allowed to be more narrow and rigid. I would argue that today flexibility is a virtue required of most scholar-teachers seeking jobs in English departments. The composition and rhetoric specialists who see the teaching of composition as beneath them—and such individuals do exist—are just as useless in the twenty-first-century university as the Shakespeare specialist who refuses to teach undergraduates. If we are to provide first-rate educations for first-generation students—and for all students—we must restore positive connotations to the words *flexible* and *generalist*.

Principle 4: Make PhD study more efficient and shorten the time to degree attainment.

We cannot continue to allow English departments—and humanities departments in general—to survive on exploitation. Nothing justifies PhD programs that require more than four or five years to complete. Delaying the completion of a dissertation beyond four or five years leads to a latter-day form of indentured servitude. A dissertation is apprentice work and should be treated as such. Long-term apprentice appointments become even more questionable when after many years the completers find only adjunct positions available on the job market. We have better models. We simply must use them.

My own PhD preparation at the University of Pennsylvania was supported by the Ford Foundation and the National Defense Education Act at a time when it was considered in the national interest to prepare English professors. Perhaps, if we reform English PhD programs, that national interest will again be recognized. Back then, the University of Pennsylvania English Department designed a four-year PhD program. The first year was heavy with coursework, but the proseminar provided an opportunity to explore possible dissertation topics—yes, in our first year. The idea was to connect our studies with our future professional lives. As coursework continued into the second year, each graduate student was assigned a tenured faculty mentor to assist and learn from. My mentor, Malcolm Laws, took the mentorship seriously. My job was to assist him in one of his classes, but he saw that assistance as a learning opportunity for me—actually for both of us. He never used me simply as a paper grader to relieve him of that duty. Instead, we would each grade the same set of papers and then talk about our agreements and disagreements. During the third year, graduate students taught their own sections of freshman composition. At the end of that year we took comprehensive exams in three areas, ensuring broad general knowledge. The fourth year was dedicated to writing the dissertation, and it was understood that the coursework of the preceding three years would provide some basis for this large-scale research. Adhering to this plan, I completed my PhD in four and a half years, accommodating time for marriage and the birth of my first child.

Because of this structured PhD program, at the age of twenty-five, I could begin my academic career in earnest.

In addition to the structure and the clear expectations mapped out for each year, another important principle allowed for an efficient PhD program at the University of Pennsylvania. Because of the wisdom of my dissertation supervisor, Robert Lucid, I understood that my dissertation was apprentice work. Too many PhD candidates try to write the dissertation and their first book simultaneously, dragging the process out. The dissertation is its own genre and is written to satisfy the requirements of a faculty committee. The book must and should come later, when the author has achieved a greater degree of intellectual independence. My dissertation, *The Autobiographical Myth of F. Scott Fitzgerald*, yielded just one scholarly article. And as my professional career progressed, my interests moved to writing across the curriculum. I may be the only one who sees the connection between my literary dissertation and my later work in rhetoric and composition. But I would argue that the questions that motivated my exploration of Fitzgerald's writing were connected to the questions that fascinated me about student writing. English PhD programs should inspire students to make these broad connections. If that were to happen, PhD candidates would be more employable, and full-time, tenure-track faculty members would be more open to new ideas—and more responsive and helpful to first-generation college students.

Later I had the privilege of advising the University of Pennsylvania English Department on writing across the curriculum and developing Writing across the University. As a by-product of that consultancy, Penn developed a team approach to teaching freshman composition—a model for reform at other R1 universities. A senior faculty member taught his own section of freshman composition and met with graduate students who were teaching their own sections. No one expects flagship and Ivy League universities to staff freshman composition courses exclusively with full-time faculty members. It's the job of these universities to prepare graduate students to value the teaching of first-year courses. If other suggestions in this afterword are accepted, these teaching experiences will not stretch out over the years but will prepare future faculty members for full-time, tenure-track appointments at comprehensive public colleges, liberal arts colleges, and community colleges.

Peter Conn was the leader of the University of Pennsylvania model in the 1980s. He developed a graduate course at the university, setting up a system for teams of graduate students to work with senior professors; they all taught composition and met to discuss and assess their work. Conn, himself a distinguished scholar in American literature, led a team and encouraged other Penn professors to join him in this project. Here is what Conn wrote about the project in 1982: "The design of each course depends on three acts of premeditated connection: between graduate study and freshman teaching, between the study of composition and the study of literature, between the faculty and graduate students" (4). Conn's idea was for the graduate professor and graduate students to become a genuine "teaching company." "What we did," he wrote, "is easily replicable in almost any university setting" (6). One of the graduate student participants reflected on the experience: "English 886 introduced second-year graduate students to the profession of teaching English. Each element of the course contributed to the graduate students' process of discovering an institution" (6).

Unfortunately, this course does not exist today, but it could and should. Its approach introduces PhD candidates to the excitement of teaching and scholarship and the connection between the two. It breaks down hierarchies and moves the English profession away from the bankrupt notion held by professors that only those hired at universities like their own are successful. More important, this kind of PhD preparation defuses the ticking time bomb. Graduate students are acculturated into a profession that values teaching and learning. That acculturation will benefit all students, but it is essential to teaching the new majority of students.

The title of this volume, *Beyond Fitting In*, suggests that new majority students must not be expected to fit into the procrustean bed of an outdated university context. We must transform colleges and universities into settings that will promote transformational change in the lives of students and prepare them for the twenty-first and twenty-second centuries. To do that, we must rethink the way we acculturate newcomers into the profession. Right now, we admit candidates to PhD programs and expect them to fit out-of-date assumptions about what defines an English professor. If new majority undergraduates are to go beyond fitting in, we must stop requiring that PhD aspirants fit into an obsolete model.

Notes

1. Many university presidents and financial aid officers have urged the federal government to modify the statute that obligates universities to present to students the maximum loan obligations available to them.

2. Only about seventeen percent of college instructors are tenured faculty members: see Birmingham.

Works Cited

Adler-Kassner, Linda, and Elizabeth Wardle, editors. *Naming What We Know: Threshold Concepts of Writing Studies*. Classroom ed., UP of Colorado, 2016.

Birmingham, Kevin. "The Great Shame of Our Profession." *The Chronicle of Higher Education*, 12 Feb. 2017, www.chronicle.com/article/The-Great-Shame-of-Our-Profession.

Bowen, William G., and Michael S. McPherson. *Lesson Plan: An Agenda for Change in American Higher Education*. Princeton UP, 2016.

Bridges, William, and Susan Bridges. *Managing Transitions: Making the Most of Change*. Kindle ed., De Capo Press / Perseus Books, 2016.

Conn, Peter. "Combining Literature and Composition: English 886." *ADE Bulletin*, vol. 72, summer 1982, pp. 4–6.

Dickens, Charles. *Hard Times: For These Times*. Bradbury and Evans, 1854.

Goldrick-Rab, Sara, et al. *Still Hungry and Homeless in College*. Wisconsin Hope Lab, Apr. 2018, hope4college.com/wp-content/uploads/2018/09/Wisconsin-HOPE-Lab-Still-Hungry-and-Homeless.pdf.

Gould, Elise. "High-Scoring, Low-Income Students No More Likely to Complete College Than Low-Scoring, Rich Students." *Working Economics Blog. Economic Policy Institute*, 9 Mar. 2012, www.epi.org/blog/college-graduation-scores-income-levels/.

Hanlon, Aaron. "The University Is a Ticking Time Bomb." *The Chronicle of Higher Education*, 16 Apr. 2019, www.chronicle.com/article/The-University-Is-a-Ticking-Time-Bomb.

Kotter, John P. *Leading Change*. Harvard Business Review Press, 2012.

Kreighbaum, Andrew. "Making the FAFSA Mandatory." *Inside Higher Ed*, 10 July 2019, www.insidehighered.com/news/2019/07/10/texas-becomes-second-state-require-fafsa-completion.

Laterman, Kaya. "Tuition or Dinner? Nearly Half of College Students Surveyed in a New Report Are Going Hungry." *The New York Times*, 2 May 2019, www.nytimes.com/2019/05/02/nyregion/hunger-college-food-insecurity.html.

Mendenhall, Annie S. "The Composition Specialist as Flexible Expert: Identity and Labor in the History of Composition." *College English*, vol. 77, no. 1, 2014, pp. 11–31.

Mitrano, Tracy. Comment on "The Citizenship We're Not Talking About." *Inside Higher Ed*, 2006, www.insidehighered.com/advice/2016/06/21/every-doctoral-student-should-take-course-higher-education-essay. Accessed 5 Jan. 2020.

Report of the MLA Task Force on Doctoral Study in Modern Language and Literature. Modern Language Association of America, 2014.

Rundell Singer, Susan, et al. "Improving Quality and Inclusion in STEM Undergraduate Education through Organizational Change Networks." *AERA Online Paper Repository*, Apr. 2019, www.aera.net/Publications/Online-Paper-Repository/AERA-Online-Paper-Repository/Owner/936357.

Smith, Ashley A. "Federal Report Agrees Some Low-Income Students Are Going Hungry." *Inside Higher Ed*, 10 Jan. 2019, www.insidehighered.com/news/2019/01/10/gao-report-reviews-studies-student-hunger.

St. Amour, Madeline. "ZIP Codes and Equity Gaps." *Inside Higher Education*, 9 July 2020, www.insidehighered.com/news/2020/07/09/report-finds-racial-equity-gaps-college-attendance-debt-and-defaults-based-zip-codes.

Thiele, David. "The Citizenship We're Not Talking About." *Inside Higher Ed*, 21 June 2016, www.insidehighered.com/advice/2016/06/21/every-doctoral-student-should-take-course-higher-education-essay.

Wardle, Elizabeth. "Creative Repurposing for Expansive Learning: Considering 'Problem-Exploring' and 'Answer-Getting' Dispositions in Individuals and Fields." *Composition Forum*, vol. 26, fall 2012.

Zull, James E. *The Art of Changing the Brain: Enriching the Practice of Teaching by Exploring the Biology of Learning*. Stylus Publishing, 2002.

———. *From Brain to Mind: Using Neuroscience to Guide Change in Education*. Stylus Publishing, 2011.

Notes on Contributors

Christine Alfano is associate director of the Program in Writing and Rhetoric at Stanford University and has been a lecturer in the program since 1998. She also teaches a writing course for the Stanford SOAR program, an online bridge program for incoming first-year students, and consults on the development of the writing and research curriculum for the on-campus bridge program. With Alyssa O'Brien, she is the coauthor of the Envision textbook series, the most recent editions being *Envision: Writing and Researching Arguments*, fifth edition; and *Envision In Depth*, fourth edition. She has published on topics related to cross-cultural rhetorics and multimodal invention practices and has participated in grant-supported research related to transnational rhetorics, active-learning in online environments, and developing curricula to support multilingual writers. Her current research interests include online writing instruction, digital rhetorics, and writing program administration.

Jacob Babb is associate professor of English at Appalachian State University. He is a former coeditor of *WPA: Writing Program Administration*. He publishes on composition theory and pedagogy, writing program administration, and rhetoric. He has published articles in *Composition Forum*, *Composition Studies*, *Harlot*, and *WPA: Writing Program Administration* and chapters in several edited collections. He is the coeditor of *WPAs in Transition: Navigating Educational Leadership Positions* (2018) and *The Things We Carry: Strategies for Recognizing and Negotiating Emotional Labor in Writing Program Administration* (2020).

Neil Baird is associate professor of English and director of the University Writing Program at Bowling Green State University. Baird previously worked at Western Illinois University as University Writing Center director. While at Western Illinois, he and Bradley Dilger started the transfer research shared in this volume. They have published their findings in *College Composition and Communication*, *Across the Disciplines*, and *WPA: Writing Program Administration*. Baird is team lead for Project Chameleon, a study of writing transfer at work. He is collaborating with scholars in the United States, Czech Republic, and Kenya to learn how alumni adapt prior writing knowledge in workplace settings. Preliminary results will appear in a collection titled "Writing Beyond the University: Implications for Fostering Writers' Lifelong Learning and Agency."

William DeGenaro is professor of composition and rhetoric at the University of Michigan, Dearborn, where he teaches composition and creative writing. His work on service learning, basic writing pedagogy, and working-class studies has been published in journals including *Rhetoric Review, WPA: Writing Program Administration*, and *The Journal of Basic Writing.* He is a recipient of two Fulbright Fellowships, in Lebanon (2010–11) and Jordan (2019–20).

Bradley Dilger is professor of English at Purdue University, where he was recently director of Introductory Composition. Dilger previously worked at Western Illinois University, where he and Neil Baird started the transfer research shared in this volume. Baird and Dilger have shared findings on writing transfer in *College Composition and Communication, Across the Disciplines*, and *WPA: Writing Program Administration.* Dilger is a leader of Crow, the Corpus and Repository of Writing, an interdisciplinary team building a learner corpus articulated with a repository of pedagogical materials. Dilger has published with other Crow researchers in the *Journal of Business and Technical Communication.* Dilger has also contributed extensively to the Transculturation project, a teaching and research team using linked courses to improve the intercultural competence of domestic and international college students.

Heather M. Falconer is assistant professor of professional and technical writing in the University of Maine's English Department. In addition to this role, Falconer is a coeditor for the Perspectives on Writing book series, cochair of the Research and Publications Committee of the Association for Writing across the Curriculum, and serves on multiple editorial and regional boards. As a writing studies scholar, her research focuses on the intersections of culture, discipline, and pedagogy, with a special emphasis on creating inclusive educational spaces. Falconer's research has appeared in journals such as *Written Communication, The WAC Journal*, and *The Journal of Hispanic Higher Education*, as well as in multiple edited collections.

Megan Formato is a lecturer in the Program in Writing and Rhetoric at Stanford University, where she also teaches research, writing, and argument for the Leland Scholars Program, a program for first-generation and low-income students transitioning to college. As a historian of modern science and technology, she brings methods from book history, the history of science, and writing studies to bear on questions about scientific communication and culture. Her research and teaching focus on how women's writing and administrative labor shape the production of scientific knowledge.

Clint Gardner is program manager of the College Writing and Reading Centers at Salt Lake Community College in Salt Lake City, Utah.

Anne Ruggles Gere is Arthur F. Thurnau Professor of English and Gertrude Buck Professor of Education at the University of Michigan, where she chairs the Joint PhD in English and Education. A former chair of the Conference on College Composition and Communication and a former president of the National Council of Teachers of English, she was the 2018 president of the Modern Language Association. Her most recent work is *Developing Writers in Higher Education: A Longitudinal Study*, and she is currently working on a book titled *Agents of Survivance: Indigenous Women Teachers in Boarding Schools*.

Kathryn Henderson studies anthropology, history, and writing and rhetoric at the University of Utah. She worked in the mortgage industry for twenty years. She is interested in human history and ecology and how research in these areas might be leveraged to facilitate responsible and ethical interactions among humans and between humans and the planet. After graduating, she hopes to use her education and work experience to contribute to a more sustainable and humane human experience through research, public outreach, conservation, and social activism.

Jennifer Johnson is lecturer in the Program in Writing and Rhetoric at Stanford University and teaches first- and second-year research-based writing and oral communication courses. She also teaches in the Leland Scholars Program, a summer bridge program supporting first-generation and low-income students. Her research focuses on applied linguistics, writing pedagogy, and multimodal communication. She has published articles in the *L2 Journal* and *Applied Linguistics*, was guest coeditor on a recent special issue of *Composition Forum* titled *Promoting Social Justice for Multilingual Writers on College Campuses*, and is coeditor of the collection "Linguistic Justice on Campus: Pedagogy and Advocacy for Multilingual Writers."

Caitlin Larracey is the Mellon Postdoctoral Fellow of Program Design and Student Mentoring in the Office of Undergraduate Research, Scholarly, and Creative Activity at Johns Hopkins University. She received her PhD at the University of Delaware, where she taught first-year writing to two- and four-year students. Her dissertation focuses on student experiences and identities in hybrid institutional spaces, particularly branch campuses' first-year writing classrooms. A first-generation student herself, she completed her bachelor's degree at Bridgewater State University. There she frequently worked with first-gen and otherwise structurally disadvantaged students through the university's writing center, university-specific support initiatives for first-year writing, and Upward Bound. She is past associate editor of *College English* (2018–19) and past editorial fellow of *Teaching English in the Two-Year College* (2019–20).

Eric S. Lee is the former division chair for communications and director of the Creative Writing School at Arizona Western College, a Hispanic-serving institution in southwestern Arizona. His poetry and fiction has appeared in numerous literary journals and won the Page Davidson Clayton Prize.

Jose Loeri grew up in Utah and in 2021 graduated from the University of Utah, where he majored in writing and rhetoric studies, minored in linguistics, and earned a TESOL certificate. He is a writing tutor at Salt Lake Community College.

Michael T. MacDonald was a first-generation college student who is now associate professor of composition and rhetoric at the University of Michigan, Dearborn, where he teaches courses on transnational rhetorics, global cultures, and the writing studio model. His work has appeared in *College English*, *Reflections*, *The Journal of Basic Writing*, *Community Literacy Journal*, *The Journal of Curriculum Theorizing*, and *Prompt*. His research interests include literacy theory, forced displacement, and the role of governance in the international community.

Nancy Mack is professor emeritus of English at Wright State University and the author of *Engaging Writers with Multigenre Research Projects* and two volumes about teaching grammar with poetry. She edited a special issue of the *English Journal* about bullying and has published several articles and chapters on memoir, emotional labor, the working class, and teaching writing. She has won several state and university teaching awards. Her community service projects include partnerships with the National Endowment for the Arts, the Ohio Arts Council, Dayton Public Television, and the Ohio Department of Education.

Elaine P. Maimon is a Founding Distinguished Fellow of the Association for Writing across the Curriculum. Her cowritten text, *Writing in the Arts and Sciences*, has been designated a landmark book by the Writing across the Curriculum Clearing House at Colorado State University. She is proud to be recognized as a founder of the writing-across-the-curriculum movement, which has outlived the century in which it was named. For twenty-four years, in the top administrative positions at Arizona State University West; University of Alaska, Anchorage; and Governors State University, she presided over transformative change. Her book *Leading Academic Change: Vision, Strategy, Transformation* (Stylus, 2018) is a road map for accelerating reform in higher education. A founding executive board member of the Council of Writing Program Administrators, she has directed national institutes to disseminate writing-across-the-curriculum principles. As an adviser at the American Council on Education, she contributes to policy reform on the national level.

Shurli Makmillen teaches at Claflin University in South Carolina. Her research primarily uses rhetorical genre theory to understand legal, paralegal, literary, and academic genres—especially in settings involving the participation and frameworks of minority or underserved populations. Her articles have appeared in *College Composition and Communication*, *Rhetor*, *Text and Talk: An Interdisciplinary Journal of Language, Discourse and Communication Studies*, and *Canadian Journal for Studies in Discourse and Writing/Rédactologie*. She also has written a chapter in *The Pragmatic Turn in Law: Inference and Interpretation* (2017) and cowritten a chapter in the *Naylor Report on Undergraduate Research in Writing Studies* (2020).

Casie Moreland is director of dual credit at the University of Idaho. Her research interests include dual enrollment, multilingual writing, critical race theory and whiteness studies, assessment, and dual enrollment policy. She is a member of the Conference on College Composition and Communication Executive Committee and cochair of the conference's standing group Dual Enrollment Collective. She has contributed chapters to Tammie Kennedy and colleague's *Rhetorics of Whiteness: Postracial Hauntings in Popular Culture, Social Media, and Education* and to Mya Poe and colleague's *Writing Assessment, Social Justice, and the Advancement of Opportunity*. She is also coeditor of *The Dual Enrollment Kaleidoscope: Reconfiguring Perceptions of First-Year Writing and Composition Studies*. Moreland is in the process of completing her monograph, *The Impossible Plan: A History of Dual Enrollment in an Era of White Complacency* (State U of New York P).

Joseph Andrew Moss is a transfer student from Salt Lake Community College who is studying writing and rhetoric, journalism, and creative writing at the University of Utah. He writes for the student paper, *The Utah Daily Chronicle*, and works with the student radio station K-UTE.

Ashley Newby is director of undergraduate studies for the African American Studies department at the University of Maryland, College Park. Newby taught for three years in the Program in Writing and Rhetoric at Stanford University, working with both the Leland Scholars and Pre-collegiate Studies Programs. Her research interests lie at the intersection of hip-hop culture and educational spaces, particularly critical literacy and culturally sustaining pedagogies. Her publications include the chapters "The Rhetoric of the Womb," in *The Lauryn Hill Reader* (2018), and "Hip-Hop Is Not a Metaphor," in *In This Together: Blackness, Indigeneity, and Hip-Hop* (2019).

Cristina Guerrero Perez earned her associate's degree at Salt Lake Community College and completed her bachelor's degree at the University of Utah, where she majored in writing and rhetoric studies and minored in linguistics. She was a first-generation and DACA student. She is interested in working professionally with students and in using her voice to represent not only herself but also her community. She hopes future generations in her family will follow in her journey and pursue their aspirations.

Jenny Rice is professor of writing, rhetoric, and digital studies at the University of Kentucky. Her work dips into public rhetoric, affect, argument, space and place, and many modes of weirdness. Her most recent book, *Awful Archives: Conspiracy Theory, Rhetoric, and Acts of Evidence* (2020), examines the strange and the fringe in order to explore the lifeworld of what we call evidence. She has published essays in *Philosophy and Rhetoric*, *Rhetoric Society Quarterly*, *College English*, and *Quarterly Journal of Speech*, among others.

Kelly Ritter is professor and chair of the School of Literature, Media, and Communication at the Georgia Institute of Technology. She received her PhD in English from the University of Illinois, Chicago, her MFA in creative writing from the Iowa

Writers' Workshop, and her BA in English and communication studies from the University of Iowa. Previously at the University of Illinois, Urbana-Champaign, she served as associate dean of liberal arts and sciences and director of the Center for Writing Studies, and interim head of the Department of Philosophy. She also served for seventeen years as faculty director of the first-year writing programs at the University of Illinois, Urbana-Champaign; the University of North Carolina, Greensboro; and Southern Connecticut State University. Ritter's scholarship focuses on archival histories of US writing programs and pedagogies and on cultural-historical conceptions of social class and literacy education. Her books are *Before Shaughnessy: Basic Writing at Yale and Harvard, 1920–1960* (2009); *Who Owns School? Authority, Students, and Online Discourse* (2010); *To Know Her Own History: Writing at the Woman's College, 1943–1963* (2012); and *Reframing the Subject: Postwar Instructional Film and Class-Conscious Literacies* (2015). She is also the author of numerous articles and chapters and editor or coeditor of four collections. From 2012 to 2017, Ritter served as editor of *College English*, a journal of the National Council of Teachers of English.

Todd Ruecker is associate professor of rhetoric and writing and director of Core Writing at the University of Nevada, Reno. His research is primarily focused on investigating issues surrounding the increasing linguistic and cultural diversity of education worldwide and on working to transform educational institutions and writing classrooms into more welcoming spaces for all students. He has published articles in journals such as *College Composition and Communication*, *Composition Studies*, *Computers and Composition*, *Critical Inquiry in Language Studies*, *TESOL Quarterly*, and *Writing Program Administration*. He has published four edited collections on topics ranging from the high-school-to-college transitions of multilingual writers residing in the United States to the politics of second language writing assessment. He published a monograph, *Transiciones: The Pathways of Latinas and Latinos Writing in High School and College*, in 2015.

Christina Saidy is associate professor of English at Arizona State University. Her research focuses on writing and writing transitions with secondary students, teachers in professional development groups, and students entering college. Her cowritten book is *Creating Literacy Communities as Pathways for Student Success: Equity and Access for Latina Girls* (2018). She is the author of many articles published in journals such as *English Journal*, *College Composition and Communication*, *WPA: Writing Program Administration*, *Journal of Adolescent and Adult Literacy*, *Teaching/Writing: The Journal of Writing Teacher Education*, and *Teaching English in the Two-Year College*.

Aubrey Schiavone is teaching assistant professor in the writing program at the University of Denver, where she teaches first-year and upper-level writing courses with a variety of themes. Her research focuses on two distinct topics: first-generation college students' literacy experiences in college and pedagogical approaches to multimodal composition, blogging, and digital media. She was a first-generation college student and embraces every opportunity to mentor fellow first-gen students on their pathways to and through higher education.

Sarah Elizabeth Snyder is writing program administrator and non-tenure-track professor of English at Arizona Western College in Yuma, Arizona. Her research and administrative work revolve around the administration of two-year college writing programs, multilingual writing, composition workload issues, and pedagogical exploration for equity, access, and inclusion of traditionally and currently underserved populations. Her scholarly work takes the form of book chapters as well as articles appearing in *Kairos* and *WPA: Writing Program Administration*, including "Preparing to Become a Two-Year College Writing Program Administrator" (2020), "Sustainable Becomings: Women's Career Trajectories in Writing Program Administration" (2019), and "Assessing the Field of WPA with Edward M. White: An Interview with an Influential Scholar in WPA" (2019). She is also coeditor of the collection *Professionalizing Second Language Writing* (2017).

Jacque Thetsombandith is an undergraduate student at the University of Utah and majors in writing and rhetoric and chemistry. He is a member of the Asian American Student Association and Rotaract. Prior to attending the university, he attended Salt Lake Community College, where he completed his general education. He volunteers in his free time.

Adilene Tolentino graduated from the University of Utah with a major in writing and rhetoric studies in 2019.

Christie Toth is associate professor in the Department of Writing and Rhetoric Studies at the University of Utah, where she coordinates the department's transfer and graduate partnerships with Salt Lake Community College. Her 2022 book, *Transfer in an Urban Writing Ecology: Reimagining Community College–University Relations in Composition Studies*, was published in the Conference on College Composition and Communication's series Studies in Writing and Rhetoric.

Beth A. Towle is assistant professor of English and associate director of the University Writing Center at Salisbury University in Maryland. She received her PhD in rhetoric and composition from Purdue University in 2019, with a focus on writing center studies. Her scholarly interests include institutional research methodologies, writing center labor issues, and writing support for first-generation and working-class students. Her work has been published in or is forthcoming from *The Writing Center Journal*, *WLN*, *The Peer Review*, and the edited collection *Out in the Center.*

Courtney Adams Wooten is director of composition and assistant professor at George Mason University. Previously, she served as the director of the writing program at Stephen F. Austin State University. Her scholarship focuses on feminist rhetorics, writing program administration, affect theory, and emotional labor. She is currently working on a book project about the affectual and discursive circulations of reproductive doxa in childfree women's rhetorics. She is a coeditor of *WPAs in Transition: Navigating Educational Leadership Positions* (2018) and *The Things We Carry: Strategies for Recognizing and Negotiating Emotional Labor in Writing Program Administration* (2020). Her work has also appeared in *College English*, *WPA: Writing Program Administration*, *Composition Studies*, *Academic Labor: Research and Artistry*, *Peitho*, and *Harlot* as well as several edited collections.